Christoph Marcinkowski (Ed.)

The Islamic World and the West

Freiburger Sozialanthropologische Studien
Freiburg Studies in Social Anthropology
Etudes d'Anthropologie Sociale de l'Université de Fribourg

herausgegeben von/edited by/edité par

Christian Giordano (Universität Fribourg, Schweiz)

in Verbindung mit/in cooperation with/avec la collaboration de

Edouard Conte (Universität Bern),
Dobrinka Kostova (Bulgarische Akademie der Wissenschaften, Sofia),
Véronique Pache Huber (Universität Fribourg, Schweiz),
Klaus Roth (Universität München),
François Rüegg (Universität Fribourg, Schweiz)

Band 24

LIT
and
The Asia-Europe Institute (AEI),
University of Malaya, Kuala Lumpur

The Islamic World and the West

Managing Religious and Cultural Identities in the Age of Globalisation

edited by

Christoph Marcinkowski

LIT
and
The Asia-Europe Institute (AEI),
University of Malaya, Kuala Lumpur

Veröffentlicht mit der Unterstützung des Hochschulrates der Universität Fribourg

Layout: Tomislav Helebrant

Gedruckt auf alterungsbeständigem Werkdruckpapier entsprechend
ANSI Z3948 DIN ISO 9706

Bibliographic information published by the Deutsche Nationalbibliothek
The Deutsche Nationalbibliothek lists this publication in the Deutsche Nationalbibliografie; detailed bibliographic data are available in the Internet at http://dnb.d-nb.de.

ISBN 978-3-643-80001-5

A catalogue record for this book is available from the British Library

Dufourstr. 31
CH-8008 Zürich
Tel. +41 (0) 44-251 75 05
Fax +41 (0) 44-251 75 06
e-Mail: zuerich@lit-verlag.ch
http://www.lit-verlag.ch

LIT VERLAG Dr. W. Hopf
Berlin 2009
Fresnostr. 2
D-48159 Münster
Tel. +49 (0) 2 51-620 32 22
Fax +49 (0) 2 51-922 60 99
e-Mail: lit@lit-verlag.de
http://www.lit-verlag.de

Distribution:

In Germany: LIT Verlag Fresnostr. 2, D-48159 Münster
Tel. +49 (0) 2 51-620 32 22, Fax +49 (0) 2 51-922 60 99, e-Mail: vertrieb@lit-verlag.de

In Austria: Medienlogistik Pichler-ÖBZ GmbH & Co KG
IZ-NÖ, Süd, Straße 1, Objekt 34, A-2355 Wiener Neudorf
Tel. +43 (0) 22 36-63 53 52 90, Fax +43 (0) 22 36-63 53 52 43, e-Mail: mlo@medien-logistik.at

In Switzerland: B + M Buch- und Medienvertriebs AG
Hochstr. 357, CH-8200 Schaffhausen
Tel. +41 (0) 52-643 54 85, Fax +41 (0) 52-643 54 35, e-Mail: order@buch-medien.ch

Distributed in the UK by: Global Book Marketing, 99B Wallis Rd, London, E9 5LN
Phone: +44 (0) 20 8533 5800 – Fax: +44 (0) 1600 775 663
http://www.centralbooks.co.uk/html

Distributed in North America by:

Transaction Publishers
New Brunswick (U.S.A.) and London (U.K.)

Transaction Publishers
Rutgers University
35 Berrue Circle
Piscataway, NJ 08854

Phone: +1 (732) 445 - 2280
Fax: + 1 (732) 445 - 3138
for orders (U. S. only):
toll free (888) 999 - 6778
e-mail: orders@transactionpub.com

"To avoid any form of intolerance from developing and to prevent violence, we must encourage sincere dialogue based on ever truer mutual knowledge [...]. Such dialogue requires us to train competent people to help know and understand the religious values we have in common and to faithfully respect our differences".

(Pope Benedict XVI on 20 September 2007, addressing visiting bishops from Benin)

"Politics, rather than religion, is at the root of polarisation between Muslim and Western societies. The idea that we are witnessing some kind of 'clash of civilisations' is a grave misunderstanding. [...] Faiths, in themselves, do not generate hatred or violence."

(Kofi Annan, former seventh Secretary-General of the United Nations, Newsweek, 20 July 2007)

"The West should treat Islam the way it wants Islam to treat the West and *vice versa*. They should accept one another as equals".

(Datuk Seri Abdullah Ahmad Badawi, Prime Minister of Malaysia, in a keynote address at the international conference "Who Speaks for Islam? Who Speaks for the West", Kuala Lumpur, 10 February 2006)

Contents

Preface

The Islamic World and the West: Managing Religious and Cultural Identities in the Age of Globalisation is the first project within the framework of the recently signed *Memorandum of Understanding* between Switzerland's University of Fribourg and the Asia-Europe Institute (AEI) in Kuala Lumpur's University of Malaya, Malaysia's oldest university, which celebrated only recently its 100th anniversary.

This volume brings together contributions by distinguished Muslim and Western scholars. The articles contained in this book try to preserve a balance between academic fact-presentation and accessibility to the wider public. This timely volume is intended to present a somewhat more positive outlook in the relations between the Islamic World and the Western world by drawing on shared values and possibilities of cooperation in various fields, such as reflected in worldview, education, economics, multiculturalism, religious dialogue, politics, as well as security issues, and it also contain a historical revaluations of some of those contacts. If we look back to history, we notice that the contacts between the Ottomans and Europe, for instance, were not always marked by violence and war, to wit the mutual cultural cross-fertilisation in particular from the eighteenth century onwards. As has been argued by several scholars in this volume, in particular the Ottoman experience is also of special interest for this dialogue enterprise as its legacy is still present in the multi-cultural and multi-religious setting of a European country like Bosnia-Herzegovina, for instance.

The distinguished contributors to this volume have been carefully selected, bearing in mind the idea of presenting a rather broad picture of how Muslim academics of today see the current state of relations with the West. Contributions by some leading non-Muslim scholars have been included in order to demonstrate that the need for looking ahead is also seen by the Western academia. However, in particular the selection of the contributions by our Muslim colleagues is intended to reflect a wide range of interpretations, depending on the way they see and position themselves and the role of their religion, Islam, in the contemporary world. Some of them would define themselves as more 'liberal', whereas others could perhaps be described as more 'traditional-minded'. Together, however, they present a holistic picture of contemporary scholarship, a picture that should be considered more carefully – in particular by our colleagues in the West – when trying to overcome stereotypes of a supposedly 'monolithic' and 'static' Islamic world. The 'red thread' running through all of the articles contained in this book is to look into the future by also considering relevant aspects of the past in the relations between both civilisations.

The articles contained in this volume have been arranged in three parts: The first introductory part features *"Between 'Turkish Delights' and 'Eurabia': The Islamic World and Europe at the Crossroads"*, a paper by the present writer. It argues that among the prerequisites for a meaningful dialogue between contemporary Europe and the Islamic World would be a more comprehensive understanding of each other's *weltanschauung,* a truly 'civilisational' dialogue that goes beyond the reference to mere religious issues. Unfortunately, approaches of the past often missed its direction as the place of religion in largely secular Western societies differs diametrically from that which it enjoys in the Muslim mind. In this paper, the author has chosen as exemplary cases the issues surrounding Turkey's desire to become a member of the European Union and the polemical 'Eurabia' debate in order to make out deficits that need to be overcome in order make the dialogue between the Muslim world and the West a meaningful one.

The second part, *"Muslim-Western Encounters – Past and Present"*, consists of six contributions that address historical as well as present aspects of the multi-faceted interactions between Europe and the world of Islam.

The paper *"Interdependent Diversities: Self-Representations, Historical Regions and Global Challenges in Europe"*, has been contributed by Professor Christian Giordano of Fribourg University, one of the world's leading social anthropologists. It argues that the notion of Europe is linked to the "mirror-like construction of its opposite" and cannot be regarded as a socially and culturally monolithic, homogeneous, and consistent unit, but rather as a system of historical regions, which are structurally interdependent and therefore different from each other.

The next paper, *"Islamic Roots of Knowledge in Europe: A Historical Essay"* by the German scholar Professor Hans Daiber – one of the world's foremost experts on the historical transmission process of the Ancient Greek intellectual heritage to the West via the Muslims – delineates the many facets of the impact of Arab-Islamic sciences and thought on Europe, an impact that was not only reflected in a mere exchange of material goods, agricultural products, and technical skills, but also in the transfer of ideas. This process became ultimately the backbone for the subsequent intellectual and scientific revival of Europe on its way from the Middle Ages onward.

"Muslim Communities of the European North-Eastern Frontiers: Islam in the Former Polish-Lithuanian Commonwealth", by Professor Kopanski, a Malaysia-based American Muslim historian of Polish origin, presents another very fascinating facet of Islam in Europe that is often forgotten in the contemporary discourse: the presence of Muslims in Eastern Europe. While much has been (and continues to be) written about the Muslims in former Yugoslavia – Bosnia-Herzegovina and Kosovo in particular – knowledge among the wider public of the centuries-old presence of Muslims in what in now Poland, Belarus and Ukraine – one of the continent's oldest Islamic communities – has to be considered insufficient. As Kopanski argues, the Muslims of Eastern Europe – mostly of Tatar extraction – "can look back proudly to a long history of multifaceted interactions with other Europeans, a

history that was not always marked by conflict and bloodshed, a history should be remembered as it is a constituent part of the European heritage".

"Multiculturalism and EU Enlargement: The Case of Turkey and Bosnia-Herzegovina", an essay by Dr Muhidin Mulalić, a scholar from Sarajevo, a truly multicultural city situated on the crossroads between Europe and the Muslim world, discusses the question as to whether and how an EU admission of Turkey and Bosnia-Herzegovina could enrich and strengthen Europe's multicultural diversity in order to provide other policymakers with some ideas in terms of addressing contemporary challenges of multiculturalism. This might also be of strategic relevance in terms of maintaining security and political stability on the Old Continent.

"Between the Muslim World and Europe? A Brief Note on the Balkan Muslims" – a short contribution by Dr Mesut Idriz, a Kuala Lumpur-based Macedonian Ottomanist and scholar of Islamic cultural history – provides nevertheless insightful views as to how many Southeast European Muslims might see themselves and their own cultural and historical traditions within contemporary Europe. It offers also a concise overview on some current trends among them.

The last paper of the book's second part is entitled *"Muslim Intellectual Responses to Modern Western Science and Technology: Between Ottoman Westernisation and Post-Colonial Islamisation"*. The Malaysian scholar Professor Dato' Osman Bakar – one of the world's premier authorities on Islam and science – identifies some of the reasons behind the failure of the reforms of the later period of the Ottoman Empire and other Muslim responses of the past to modern Western-dominated science and technology with the view of deriving useful lessons. As he argues, a proper analysis of those failures of the past "will have a great significance not only for the revival of the Islamic intellectual tradition but also for the future development of modern science itself".

The third part of this volume appears under the headline *"Contesting Worldviews, Contesting Civilisations?"*. It consists of papers that discuss various contemporary aspects pertaining to different as well as shared values between both civilisations.

"Islamism, Women, and Political Participation: Comparative Perspectives" by Professor Narli, a prominent scholar from Turkey specialising in research on the position of women in the Muslim world, takes a look at the political participation of Islamic women within the context of Turkey, Egypt, and Tunisia, three countries that can be considered secular countries – although to a varying degree. In all three of them, Islamism, feminism, and what Professor Narli refers to as 'Islamic feminism' have become factors shaping the political and religious attitudes of women – factors that led to new demands by Islamic women in many countries of the Muslim world for stronger representation in the political arena.

In her *"Islam as Social Capital: Reinventions of Nationhood in an Age of Economic Globalisation"*, the Malaysian scholar Professor Dato' Wazir Jahan Karim, an eminent economic anthropologist, argues that the current Malaysian discourse on 'Islam Hadhari' or 'Civilisational Islam' seems to offer a development perspective to the theory of practical religion by reinventing nationhood in a developing economy to face the challenges of economic globalisation, offering an alternative to economic liberalism. Muslims are encouraged to accommodate to cultural diversity and multiculturalism without losing perspective of their commitment to productive welfarism. Muslims in particular are currently facing a growing global divide between fundamentalism and modernity. Within this scenario, the discourse on 'civility' in the implementation of the tenets of faith provides a neutral ground for those Muslims who are concerned with the advancement of productive life in an increasingly global domain.

"Islamic Economics: An Approach to Development in Muslim Societies" by Professor Amer Al-Roubaie, a prominent Canadian economist of Iraqi descent based in Bahrain, highlights the importance of socio-economic development in Islam by reflecting on the current challenges facing Muslim societies including poverty, globalisation, environmental degradation, knowledge, and human development. He argues that Western models and theories have proven to be inadequate to formulate planning strategies and construct policies capable of promoting change and sustaining development in the developing countries. As Professor Al-Roubaie sees it, Islamic economics emphasises the importance of the Islamic fundamentals of justice, freedom and equity in societal change, as sustainable development in Islam comprises the sharing of resources to ensure equity and fair distribution of income and wealth.

The following paper, *"Building a Knowledge Society in the Arab World"*, which Professor Al-Roubaie wrote in collaboration with his colleague Dr. Rasha Shaker Abdul-Wahab, a computer scientist, sheds light on the role played by modern information technologies in the Arab world and outlines some of the efforts that should be taken in order to close the gaps in this important field of knowledge that seems to widen between the West and Muslim nations.

"Law, Commerce and Ethics: A Comparison Between Sharī'ah and Common Law", by Professor Mohammad Hashim Kamali, one of the world's foremost authorities on contemporary and comparative Islamic law, argues that both legal systems appear to pursue similar goals and that the ethical contents of their respective rules governing trade and commerce bear harmony despite their other differences. He expresses his hope that the resources of the *sharī'ah* and its guidelines on commerce will in the future attract sufficient interest to stimulate cross-fertilisation of ideas between the two legal traditions.

Professor Kazemi-Moussavi, born in Iran, is a Canadian scholar based in the United States. His paper, *"Modern Approaches to Islamic Law"*, deals with the various approached of Muslim scholars to the role and practise of Islamic law in the contemporary world, an extremely significant subject which touches upon core issues. As a matter of fact, most scholars of past and present would agree that the *sharī'ah* is not a static entity, as it was often reshaped and represented in form of *fiqh* (lit. 'jurisprudence'), echoing the requirements and fashions of each particular period in history. Some contemporary Muslim scholars seek to reform both Islamic law and its legal methodology not only by using traditional principles recognised in the *sharī'ah*, but by borrowing methods, such as empiricism and hermeneutics. Kazemi-Moussavi's paper provides a handy overview of current Muslim reformist legal thought.

The concluding essay *"Muslims and Resources for Peace in Islam"*, by the American Muslim scholar of Lebanese descent, Professor Karim Douglas Crow, argues that "examples for Islam's vital emphasis on various levels of active struggle, the commitment in Islam to social equity and political justice, and Islam's specific ideals and practices for active reconciliation between individuals and groups, were set by the Prophet of Islam himself as the primary precedents for using peaceful action during his mission". Based on Islamic traditional thought, Crow tries to make out *alternative* peace-building approaches to the concept of 'Islamic Action' *(jihād)*, "as there is a widespread perception that contemporary Muslims have lagged behind in pondering the nature and causes of violence, blood-shed and war, while the religion of Islam is commonly seen by many non-Muslims to possess an inherent disposition or bias facilitating violence".

* * *

I wish to thank a number of individuals – not all of them had been connected to the work on this volume, but all of them had been supportive friends. Space allows mention of only some of them.

The first is my dear Italian friend Dr Eva Rossi of AEI, because of her friendship sincere collegiality. I will always treasure the memories of our mutual 'coaching-cum-coffee sessions' that took for the most part place in my AEI office. Sharing a common humorous approach when trying to master problems and adversities, Eva (and also her husband Marco) continue to be wonderful companions.

During my compilation of this volume, I also got to know Professor Christian Giordano, with whom I entered into a very fruitful exchange of ideas on the issues of European identity and multiculturalism and who invited me to give a lecture in September 2008 at his university in Fribourg, Switzerland. For decades, Christian has been a frequent visitor to Malaysia, a country which is particularly dear to him (I guess he will make Penang his home some day …). Aside for his being such a great friend and mentor, I would like to thank him for accepting this volume as a part of the *Freiburger Sozialanthopologische Studien*, of which he is the General Editor. In this regard, many thanks are also due to the patient colleagues at LIT Verlag, the publisher of this excellent series.

Moreover, for more than a decade now, I have been enjoying the friendship of Drs Mesut Idriz and Syed Ali Tawfik Al-Attas, the Director General of IKIM, the Institute of Islamic Understanding Malaysia. It was Syed Ali in the first place who introduced me to AEI, where I had been doing research between May 2007 and August 2008 as a Senior Research Fellow.

At AEI I was, among other things, also involved in the developing and subsequent teaching of the postgraduate course "Multiculturalism in Asia and Europe". I should like to thank my students at AEI, as I received from them a lot of fresh ideas from the realm of real life that have helped me to understand better the opportunities and challenges for a more meaningful and mutually enriching togetherness.

As already mentioned at the beginning, the current volume is the first project within the framework of the recently signed *Memorandum of Understanding* between Fribourg University and AEI. In our globalised world of today, the importance of institutions, such as AEI, is growing. AEI is positioning itself in the world of scholarship as a leading regional centre of civilisational and multicultural dialogue between the Islamic world and the West, a dialogue that emphasises common and shared values, but also a dialogue that does not shun away from pointing out differences of view and perception.

In closing, then, I should like to express my sincere hope that this volume will have a significant impact on redefining (and hopefully reshaping) in a *constructive* fashion the relations between Muslims and the West – Europe and the European Union in particular – by looking into the future.

Dr Christoph Marcinkowski
Principal Research Fellow and Chairman of the Publications Committee,
International Institute of Advanced Islamic Studies (IAIS),
and Adjunct Professor,
Asia-Europe Institute (AEI) in the University of Malaya,
Kuala Lumpur, 10 October 2008

Part I

Introduction

1

Between 'Turkish Delights' and 'Eurabia': The Islamic World and Europe at the Crossroads

Christoph Marcinkowski

Abstract

Without any doubt, the relations between the West and the Muslim world used to be better. The hotly disputed issue of Turkey's bid for full membership in the European Union (EU) shall be discussed in the first part of this essay as one of the key indicators of the present state of affairs of European-Muslim relations. Not only the United States, but post-9/11-Europe as well appear to see themselves increasingly under 'threat' by the Muslim world of which Europe is a direct neighbour. In the course of the all too often emotional debate of the Turkish EU membership issue it is often forgotten that Turkey has tried hard to adjust to what is considered EU standard in terms of its economy and – more significantly – its constitutional and legal framework. As a matter of fact, playing on the fear of unlimited 'floods' of – mostly Muslim – immigrants to Europe appears to be a major characteristic of the current discourse. Consequently, the second example in this article for the current rather sorry state of affairs shall be the apparent increase of sentiments amounting to 'Islamophobia' – not only among the wider European public, but also among the academia. This is exemplified by the publications of Bat Ye'or who constructs in most of her writings what she refers to as 'Eurabia', the notion of a Europe that is dominated by an 'alien culture' – Islam. The paper argues that Europe would be in a better position than other major Western nations to enter into a meaningful dialogue with Islam, due to its contacts with the Muslim world and its indebtedness to Muslim learning in the past. In the view of the author, such a dialogue should not be based on religious considerations (Christian Europe – Muslim 'Orient') which are largely obsolete – contemporary Europe being largely secular – and should not shun from pointing out differences in worldview and civilisation.

Introduction

Perhaps no other topic is currently so often present in the headlines of the international media than 'Islam and the West'. The discussion of this issue – currently still characterised by a tsunami of hasty and emotional conclusions and irrational evaluations on both sides of the fence – should rather be addressed based on knowledge and mutual respect which could help rationalising international relations. Afghan-born scholar Amin Saikal, Professor of Political Science and Director of the Centre for Arab and Islamic Studies at the Australian National University (ANU) in Canberra, to a certain extent, rightly observed that

> [w]hilst relations between the West and the world of Islam are today complex and multidimensional, with elements of both conflict and cooperation, in general they are very tensed. This tension has its roots not so much in religious but in political and politically motivated perceptual differences, the intensity of which has fluctuated according to the political utility of the issues that have occasioned the two sides to expose their differences. Since the horrific attacks on the United States on 11 September 2001 the tension has sharply escalated. On the whole, two opposing views have come to dominate the Western and Islamic approaches for dealing with each other. One is a Western contention, which has resonated more strongly in Washington than in any other Western capital, that the forces of political Islam which have defied American control or influence constitute a brand of Islamic fundamentalism that threatens Western interests and must be combated. Another is a view, which is widespread among not only the political forces of Islam but also moderate Islamists and ordinary Muslims, that the U.S. 'cold-warrior' realists have deliberately fabricated the notion of an 'Islamic threat' for one important purpose – to maintain a Western sense of superiority and hegemony over the Muslim world (Saikal 2004: 19).

To the mind of the present contributor, however, post-World War II Europe on the other hand has often been able to maintain a somewhat more sober and fact-oriented attitude when dealing with the Islamic world, than certain other leading Western powers. In this essay, a somewhat more holistic outlook with regard to the relations between the Islamic world and Europe shall be presented, by emphasising shared values while at the same time pointing out divergences in approaches to current issues. It goes without saying that among the prerequisites for a successful dialogue between those two partners are truthfulness and honesty – admittedly often purely philosophical rather than political values during our present times. Equally important is a comprehensive understanding of each other's *weltanschauung* or worldview. The Islamic world, for instance, would need to come to terms with the deeper meaning and experience of secularism (without necessarily being coerced to ascribe to it), which characterises the European societies of today. European partners, on the other hand, should recognise the multifaceted trait of

Islamic history, thought and civilisation, rather than considering it a 'threatening' monolithic block.

When discussing *practical* aspects of mutual respect and tolerance, there are certain key issues at stake between Europe and the Muslim world that shall be addressed synoptically by this essay, focusing in particular on the question surrounding Turkey's full membership in the European Union and the fears and phobias dominating European public opinion of a 'hijacking' of that continent by 'hordes' of Muslim immigrants, transforming it into what had been referred to as 'Eurabia'. Both issues could be considered key indicators for the currently prevailing climate of distrust between both civilisations – the Islamic world and the West.

The return of the Turk: Ankara and the EU membership issue

The 'Turkish case' seems to be emblematic when considering the current state of the relations between the Muslim world and the West, Europe in particular. In the more prosperous EU member states, in Germany in particular, large numbers of Turks have been present since decades as what was earlier known as *Gastarbeiter*, literally 'guest workers'. Since the first arrivals in the 1950s, their number has reached several millions but many of them are still not integrated into German society – although many of them are economically active with their own small and medium-scale businesses catering for the needs of their compatriots. Apparently, their marginal status in German society at large is in striking contrast to that of other post-WW II migrants, such as those who came from Italy or Greece, countries with a more or less Christian-dominated cultural background.

In spite of this visible Turkish presence in Europe, it does not add to the credit of the general level of knowledge of 'ordinary' Europeans that not much is known among them about modern Turkey. Turkey, being the left-over of what was once known as the mighty Ottoman Empire – for centuries present as a major power in Europe and until the early 1920s the seat of the universal Sunnite caliphate – is all too often lumped together with other rather more conservative and economically often backward members of the family of Muslim countries. Most of the latter are mere successor states of the former Ottoman world empire, artificial creations that came into existence on the drawing boards of Whitehall or the Elysée Palace as a result of European post-World War I colonial adventurism in the Middle East. Seven decades after the demise of Ataturk his republican and strictly laicist anti-clerical reforms – tolerance, based on the absence of a state religion and the separation of State and 'Church' following French models – are largely unknown among ordinary Europeans, although millions of them use to travel to Turkey every year as tourists, enjoying her pristine beaches without having to adhere to any kind of particularly 'religious' dress code.

As a matter of fact, in terms of her constitutional framework, Turkey is now still perhaps one of the most rigorously secular countries on our planet, more secular even than most western European countries themselves, among them again being Germany whose relations with the Vatican are still subject to the *Reichskonkordat*. The *Reichskonkordat*, a treaty made by Nazi Germany with Pope Pius XI, is still in force and enshrines – and even perpetuates – the influence of the Roman Catholic Church in Germany to the extent that the German state collects from the 'flock' religious taxes on behalf of Rome, non-payment of which would be punishable under German law. Similar treatises exist with Germany's Protestant communities, and clerics of both Christian denominations are often 'officiating' even at the opening of public buildings. All the while, in the West, churches are often empty as European society is, religiously speaking, rather 'non-committal' to say the least. There is thus a dichotomy between the continued presence and influence of the churches on European politics and society and the fact that Western societies are in practice secular with only a veneer of Christian culture left that is merely evoked on specific occasions, such as Christmas. Thus, when considering supposed or actual threats proceeding from an increasingly self-conscious Muslim world, Europe – Germany in particular – would do well to start with looking at the role and influence of the churches in social life and politics within its *own* domains.

Turkey, on the other hand, had initially – since the foundation of the republican regime in the early 1920s – been an example of a movement into the opposite direction towards limiting religion to the private sphere. Although Atatürk's laicist reforms have not resulted in (and, as a matter of fact, never aimed at) uprooting religious practice and sentiments from larger segments of society, Turkey has tried hard to adjust large parts of its entire legal corpus to what is considered EU standard. Among the most dramatic changes had been the abolition, in August 2002, of the death penalty, the ultimate prerequisite for being considered for admission in the EU. In line with this, Ankara commuted to life-long aggravated imprisonment the death sentence of Abdullah Öcalan, the eccentric turned 'prophet' founding leader of the militant Kurdistan Workers Party (PKK). The PKK, referred to as a 'terrorist organisation by several Western countries, is considered responsible for the deaths of tens of thousands of people, ethnic Turks as well as Kurds, most of them civilians. Although Turkish is the country's national language, Ankara has also lifted the ban on the public use of the Kurdish language which is spoken by millions of its citizens, in particular in the eastern and south-eastern parts of the country.

Moreover, in recent years, the country's chronically high inflation has been brought under control and this has led to the launching of a new currency to cement the acquisition of the economic reforms and erase the vestiges of an unstable economy. On 1 January 2005, the Turkish Lira was replaced by the New Turkish Lira (Turkish: *Yeni Türk Lirası*, abbr. YTL) by dropping off six zeroes (1 YTL= 1,000,000 TL). As a result of continuing economic reforms, the inflation has dropped to 8.2 percent in 2005, and the unemployment rate to 10.3 percent. With a per capita GDP (nominal) of US$ 5,062, Turkey ranked sixty-seventh in the world in the same year. The GDP growth rate for 2005 was 7.4 percent, thus making Turkey one of the fastest growing economies, ranking seventeenth by

GDP in the world. In addition, Turkey is a member of the G20 grouping which brings together the twenty largest economies among what used to be known as the 'developing world'. Turkey's economy is no longer dominated by traditional agricultural activities in the rural areas, but more so by a highly dynamic industrial complex in the major cities, mostly concentrated in the western provinces of the country, along with a developed services sector. The agricultural sector accounts for 11.9 percent of GDP, whereas industrial and service sectors make up 23.7 percent and 64.5 percent, respectively. The tourism sector has experienced rapid growth in the last twenty years, and constitutes an important part of the economy. In 2005, there were more than 24 million visitors to the country, who contributed $US 18.2 billion to Turkey's revenues. Other currently booming key sectors of the Turkish economy are construction, automotive industry, electronics and textiles (The economic data given above are based on the Wikipedia online-article, "Turkey", where further references are to be found).

On the political front, Turkey joined NATO as early as 1952. Located at the strategic 'south-eastern flank' of Europe, Turkey has played a crucial role during the Cold War in the defence of Europe against the likelihood of an attack on the West by what was then the Soviet Union. Today, the Turkish Armed Forces are still the second largest standing military force within NATO, immediately after those of the United States. On 14 April 1987, Ankara made its formal application to join the European Community, the predecessor of the European Union. Before that, Turkey had already been an Associate Member since 1964. Subsequently, on 12 December 1999 at the Helsinki summit of the European Council, the country was officially recognised as a candidate for full membership. Negotiations began in earnest on 3 October 2005 and the process is likely to take at least a decade to complete.

It is remarkable, however, that in spite of Turkey's impressive record in terms of moving towards regional integration the issue of the country's future EU accession constitutes to date the central controversy of the ongoing enlargement of the European Union. Among the Turkish public as well as in the present Turkish government (both of which had been rather enthusiastically supportive of the bid for EU membership in the past) significant changes of 'mood' in this regard are noticeable. The ruling Justice and Development Party (Turkish: *Adalet ve Kalkınma Partisi* or AKP, or *AK Parti*) is a right-wing, conservative political organisation, emulating Christian Democrat parties in Western Europe. In the West, with the post 9/11 scenario of distrust of anything smacking of 'Muslim revivalism', the AKP is often perceived as 'moderately Islamist' and thus as a danger and detriment for Turkey's EU membership, regardless of the fact that it had been the AKP government itself which has carried out most of the above-mentioned dramatic institutional and economic reforms.

Turkey's recent 22 July 2007 snap parliamentary elections – the country's 16th general elections –resulted in a resounding victory for the AKP. They were fought mostly on the debate over the future role of secularism and the controversial presidential election held earlier that year. The July 2007 elections are expected to set the course of Turkish internal politics well into the next decade. The instability in neighbouring Iraq and security issues related to the Kurdish question, as well as secular and religious concerns, the intervention of the military in politics, relations with the EU, the United States, and the rest of the Muslim world were the main issues. While the AKP gained almost 47% of the votes – more than compared with the 2002 elections – the resurgence of the right-wing Nationalist Movement Party (*Milliyetçi Hareket Partisi*, MHP) resulted in a slight net loss of 23 parliamentary seats for the ruling AKP party. Still, with 61.8 percent of the seats, the AKP maintains a large outright majority in the new Parliament. The resurgence of the MHP gives them 71 seats making them the third-strongest party. Their resurgence proved far more costly for the staunchly secular social democrat Republican People's Party (*Cumhuriyet Halk Partisi*, CHP), which lost 66 seats but maintained their position as the second-strongest party. One should remember that the CHP is the oldest Turkish political party which established the Republican regime in Turkey and which traces its origins directly back to Ataturk (Detailed treatment of the Turkish 2007 polls on which the figures in the text are based: Wikipedia, "Turkish General Election, 2007"; see also Narlı 2007, also forthcoming in print in *The Asia-Europe Forum* 1, no. 1, a new journal that is going to be launched by the Asia-Europe Institute (AEI) of the University of Malaya towards end of 2007/early 2008.).

The outcome of this election, which brought also the Turkish and Kurdish ethnic/nationalist parties – MHP and DTP, respectively – into the parliament, will also affect Turkey's bid for European Union membership, as Turkish perceptions of the current process (or lack thereof) have clearly influenced the results and will also cast a shadow on policymaking in the coming years. In the view of many Turks, criticism from the part of European politicians and organisations of the Turkish army interference into politics appears to amount to pure hypocrisy. With still fresh memories of the civil war-like situation of the late 1970s which was brought to an end by the 1980 military intervention, the majority of the Turks used to agree on the role of the army as the ultimate guarantor of the inner stability and survival of the Republic of Turkey. In spite of the recent AKP victory, which does not say much about the actual resurgence of religious practice among the wider strata of the Turkish population, the respect for the Armed Forces is still high. One has to admit that any abrupt departure from this overall setting could result in just that what is feared in the West (and among politically aware secular Turks, for that matter), namely a takeover by religious or nationalist extremists. Brussels appears also not to be too happy with the AKP government which is considered by its enemies as a covert 'hearth of extremism' or a 'wolf in the lambskin'. Thus all three scenarios, i.e. the current 'mildly Islamist' AKP government in Ankara, the continued presence of the staunchly secular army in Turkish politics and its opposite, a country prone to fall into the hands of fanatics, are not acceptable to Europe. One wonders what would?

According to the Turkish daily *Hürriyet* (2006) and based on what it views as merely lukewarm support for its accession to the EU and alleged double standards in its negotiations, the Turkish public has become increasingly 'euroskeptic' in recent times. A mid-2006 survey revealed that only 43 percent of Turkish citizens view the EU positively; just 35 percent trust the EU; 45 percent support enlargement and just 29 percent support an EU constitution. The earliest date that Turkey could enter the EU is 2013, which is the year when the next six-year EU budget (2013–2019) will come into force. Ankara is currently aiming to comply with EU legislation by this date, but Brussels has refused to back 2013 as a deadline. It is believed that the accession process will take at least fifteen years, if not longer.

Certainly, these developments cannot be considered helpful when trying to overcome mutual distrust. The Turks for their part appear to become increasingly frustrated. It appears to be a common perception among the wider public in Turkey, that whatever the country is doing to comply with EU standards and regulations, it would never be accepted as a full member, due to the fact that it is a Muslim nation. German chancellor Merkel's talk of an 'alternative privileged partnership' – whatever that would mean in practice – or France's President Sarkozy's 'Mediterranean Union' – based on what had already been envisaged by De Gaulle in the middle of the last century when post-World War II France was desperately struggling to maintain her disintegrating colonial empire – have been perceived in Turkey as means to keep the country out of Europe – and thus as grave offence.

To the mind of this writer then, one has not necessarily to ascribe to 'conspiracy theories' of whatever shape and colour in order to more or less share those Turkish sentiments. There seems to be a strange common perception – strange because it is shared by secular as well as observant Muslim Turks on the one side and Europeans on the other – of Europe and the EU as an essentially 'Christian club'. As I have argued elsewhere (Marcinkowski 2006a: 18), the controversial 'Regensburg speech' of Pope Benedict XVI was perceived by wider strata in the Muslim world at large as an affront of Islam, and even his choice of pontifical name – that of St. Benedict of Nursia, the sixth-century patron saint of Europe – appears to reflect his programme, i. e. what can be termed the re-Christianisation of largely neo-pagan Europe vis-à-vis the resurgence of and increasingly self-assertive Muslim world. Although I am aware of the hysteria that let to the gruesome murder of a Catholic nun in Somalia by Muslim mob, the unfortunate timing of the Pope's speech might cause grave concern among those who are interested in maintaining peace and understanding between the West and the world of Islam.

Especially among the wider European public, again in Germany in particular, irrational fears of *Überfremdung* or 'foreign infiltration' appear to dominate over more reasonable approaches and arguments. As a matter of fact, Turkey would indeed become a rather influential new member, as its almost 70 million inhabitants would send the second largest number of representatives into the European Parliament, right after Germany. With the current rate of Turkey's population increase some fear it might even surpass Germany by the time of accession, thus drastically altering the make up of the European Parliament and of the EU at large.

As the secular-dominated EU could not possibly refuse entry to Turkey based on the fact that it happened to be a country of Muslim culture and heritage, other 'reasons' must serve to achieve that goal. In line with this, Turks perceive the persistent reference from the part of European politicians and organisations to the World War I killings of the Armenians in the Ottoman Empire as 'genocide' as gross interference into their interior affairs and as one-sided condemnation, which disregards the *actual* causes, among them being the cooperation of larger segments of the Armenian population in World War I (and even before that) with the invading Russian enemy. As this admittedly grave issue is not anymore part of *recent* history, many Turks today doubt the overall sincerity and credibility of Europe and they are thus suspicious of the real motives behind the constant bringing up of the 'Armenian question'.

There are, however, also other issues which do affect negatively the present situation and which are – to my mind rightly so – perceived as obstacles for which Ankara alone is to be blamed. Among them is Turkey's refusal to recognise the EU membership of the Republic of Cyprus by at the same time maintaining support for its own creature on that island, the 'Turkish Republic of Northern Cyprus', which is only acknowledged by Ankara. Ankara perceived the EU stand on that issue again as biased. However, to my mind it is not necessarily impossible to find a workable solution as the issue does not concern Turkey's territorial integrity. More serious, however, is the constant harping on the 'Kurdish issue' from the part of Europe – NGOs, national governments and political parties, as well as the EU as a whole – in spite of the above referred to improvements, whereas it would be the West itself which actually would never agree to a Kurdish state as this would lead to alter the balance of power between the regimes in the Middle East, most of which happen to be pro-Western. The Washington-sponsored and maintained 'Kurdistan region' of northern Iraq, for instance, is still not an independent state, and, to the judgment of this writer, will never be one as long as Iraq and Turkey continue to exist.

All these issues leave even the most dispassionate political observer in doubt in terms of the sincerity of the EU's intentions vis-à-vis Turkey, as well as towards the Muslim world at large. Although it is true that Turkey, too, has to ensure that reforms are actually implemented, the EU's stance could be considered illogical at least as it would only be insincere to always raise the stake and to make new demands once Turkey has fulfilled earlier requirements. Perhaps no other Muslim country one can think of has gone such a long way towards entering into a practical dialogue with the West. It would be about time to create clarity: Is Turkey still welcome in Europe or not? The answer to this question will have far-reaching consequences for the relations between the Islamic world and the West, as Turkey would look for other partners further east should the answer be negative.

Islamophobia: tales from 'Eurabia'

To the judgment of this writer then, the uneasiness with Turkey's bid for EU full membership appears to be part of a larger picture. One does not have to refer to the 'Danish cartoon issue' of recent fame – the defamation of the founder of Islam, one of the world's main religions – in order to arrive at the conclusion that tolerance and mutual respect are all too often a one-sided affair.

On the cover of its 24–30 June 2006 edition, for instance, *The Economist* magazine (2006) produced a picture of the Eiffel Tower in Paris, crowned by a crescent, a symbol of Islam. The background constitutes a sunset scenario, which is apparently thought to echo the meaning of the word 'occident', derived from Latin *occidens*, 'the land where the sun sets' – thus 'the West'. The German language has preserved this particular meaning of 'occident' (which is largely lost among native English-speakers) by expressing the underlying concept somewhat more poetically (and holistically) as *Abendland* (lit.: 'the land of the evening', and usually together with the qualifier *christlich*, 'Christian'). More relevantly and apart from the artistic qualities of the *Economist* cover page which shall be left to the judgment of the readers of that magazine, the cover design featured also the expression 'Eurabia', certainly a reference to some sort of new continent consisting of Europe and the Arab world, a hybrid continent that is thought to be dominated by the later.

The coining of the term 'Eurabia', its dissemination in Europe, and the creation of phobias in the minds of somewhat less thorough-minded people in the West is closely connected to the activities of Bat Ye'or, a naturalised British but Egypt-born (thus non-European) Jewish writer. Ye'or specialises in the history of non-Muslims in the Middle East, and in particular the history of Christians and Jews living under Islamic rule where there were considered in the past in Arabic as *dhimmīs. Dhimmī* is an originally qur'anic term referring to a protected non-Muslim monotheist, a member of the 'People of the Book' (Arab.: *ahl al-kitāb*). In her publications (See, for instance, Ye'or 1985, 1996, 2001, and 2005, all of which follow the pattern set by Ye'or 1971), the academic value of which continues to be a matter of heated debate among scholars, Bat Ye'or often focused on the rapid transformation of formerly majority-Eastern Christian lands, such as the Levant, into Muslim-ruled territories, concluding that corruption and division among Christians supposedly contributed and may even have afforded Islam certain models of legal control of subjugated populations. In her view, what had been until recently known as Yugoslavia could well be considered an example of the long-term 'scars' of what she and other like-minded writers use to call 'dhimmitude', a supposed semi-slave, second-class status of Christians and Jews living under Islam.

In his review of one of Ye'or's works, *The Decline of Eastern Christianity under Islam: From Jihad to Dhimmitude, Seventh-Twentieth Century,* Sidney H. Griffith, Professor in the Department of Semitic and Egyptian Languages and Literatures at the Catholic University of America, writes that:

> They [the documents used as sources] are presented out of context with no analysis or explanation. The trouble with The Decline of Eastern Christianity is that in spite of the gathering of an enormous amount of historical

> material, and although she has raised an issue that well deserves study, Bat Ye'or has written a polemical tract, not responsible historical analysis (Griffith 1998).

In spite of the doubtful academic value of her output, Ye'or has become increasingly popular among those who are looking for justifications for their prejudices. Her writings (and underlying motives) are highly controversial and have not only been condemned by Muslims of any political persuasion and degree of religious practice, but also by non-Muslim academics who are still interested in peaceful coexistence between the world's two largest faiths and civilisation. When talking about mutual tolerance and respect, Ye'or's works need to be brought to the attention of the wider public, for they could well be considered highly seditious, and in part even dangerous, as they could inflame further the currently rather strained relations between Muslims and the West.

In her most recent book, *Eurabia: The Euro-Arab Axis* (Ye'or 2005), which, like the above-referred to *Economist* issue, features a cover that is an expression of the currently prevailing Islamophobia, Ye'or interprets the history of the relationship from the 1970s onwards between what was then still the European Economic Community (EEC) and the Arab countries, tracing in her particular abstruse way what she sees as connections between 'radical Arabs and Muslims', on the one hand, and extreme nationalists, fascists, neo-Nazis, and socialists, on the other hand, in the origins and growing influence, as she sees it, of Islam over European culture and politics.

Already the appearance of the word 'axis' in the work's subtitle is highly malicious, as it evokes – at least to her English-speaking readers – associations with the infamous 'Berlin-Rome Axis', the World War II alliance between Nazi Germany and Fascist Italy. One cannot help but wonder what brought her to those outbursts of hatred and what makes people in the West, in particular in the United States, where she enjoys particular popularity, listen to her?

In her view, the transformation of Europe into 'Eurabia' is the result of a deliberate strategy that was set in motion by French Gaullists who wanted to create a European-Arab counterweight to the United States. The European Union of our time is seen by her as continuing this policy, which aims to create a united Mediterranean continent based on a symbiosis between the Northern and the Southern shores of the Mediterranean Sea. In her 'Eurabia' book she developed her view on how this strategy has been implemented during the past 35 years and how the promotion of Muslim immigration to Europe constitutes part of this plan. Summarising Ye'or's line of thought, she wants to make her readers believe that Eurabia's 'destiny' was 'sealed' when it decided, willingly, to become a covert partner of what she considers to be an Arab global jihad against America and Israel, the latter country being supposedly sacrosanct and beyond any criticism of its human rights record, due to the Jewish holocaust experience. The 'tragic' development of Eurabia is thus seen by her as of special interest to Americans and with profound implications for them. They would do well to consider the 'despair' and 'confusion' of many Europeans, prisoners of a 'Eurabian totalitarianism' that foments a culture of deadly lies about Western civilisation. Americans should thus know that this 'self-destructive calamity' did not just happen out of the blue, rather it was the result of deliberate policies, executed and monitored by ostensibly responsible people. Finally, Americans should 'understand' that Eurabia's supposed contemporary anti-Zionism and anti-Americanism are the 'spiritual heirs' of 1930s Nazism and anti-Semitism, which is perhaps her most outrageous 'theory'. Anyone criticising Israeli human rights violations would thus automatically be an anti-Semite. Similarly, she equals Islam with Nazism just as plain and simple.

On the other hand, one might note that similar comparisons of Israel's wars against its Arab neighbours and the treatments of the Palestinians living under its occupation regime would be considered 'anti-Semitism' which is punishable by law in a country such as Germany, for instance. Ye'or, in turn, has still not been indicted and her seditious books continue to be bestsellers in many Western countries. To my mind, nothing could demonstrate better double standards when it comes to Western attitudes toward the world of Islam. One also wonders whether it would have been possible to write something like that in the *pre*-9/11-period, which was to a lesser degree characterised by fanatical Islamophia as our present times. As a matter of fact, Ye'or started to enjoy her popularity beyond hardcore pro-Israel circles only after the terrorist attacks on the World Trade Center in New York City on 11 September 2001.

Ye'or's constant invocation of what she considers to be the 'Judeo-Christian Western heritage' against the 'flood' of Muslim immigration into (and ultimately dominance over) Europe is quite surprising, to say the least. As already stated earlier, Ye'or was born in Egypt into a local Jewish family which was expelled and deprived of their Egyptian citizenship by Nasser in the aftermath of the 1956 aggression of France, Britain, and Israel against the land on the Nile. Considering that she herself is an 'Oriental' immigrant who had been welcomed at some point of time by *us Europeans* – I can't help expressing myself here in this way – her hate tirades against anything Arab or Muslim and her constant efforts towards creating animosities and frictions in the transatlantic relations between Europe and the United States, can thus only be explained as some sort of not yet worked up psychological damage due to her traumatic childhood experiences.

Ye'or's main points when referring to a 'Eurabian axis' are for the most part focusing on an overall perceived threat to Israel (apparently still her spiritual home), which appears to be her main concern. In her view, one of the most important corner-stones of Arab-European relations has been the latter's recognition of the Palestinians as a distinct people, whereas until 1973 they had merely been referred to merely as 'Arab refugees'. This is actually in line with official Israeli policy towards the Palestinians which could be acerbically summarised by the rhetorical question "why do you want to have a separate state, you got already so many!". Closely linked to this is her criticism of the European recognition of the Palestinian Liberation Organisation (PLO) and its late leader Yasser Arafat as the sole representatives of the Palestinians, the obligation for Israel to negotiate exclusively with Arafat when he was still around, the European insistence on comprehensive rather than separate peace agreements of Israel with its neighbours, including the Palestinians, and on Israel's retreat to the 1949 armistice lines. Other points that run like a red thread through her work as supposed 'key positions' of European policy in the Arab-Israeli conflict, are the European support for the restoration of Muslim sovereignty over Jerusalem, European 'pressure' on the United States to side with their Arab policy, the 'demonisation' of Israel as a threat to world peace, and the moralisation of Palestinian 'terrorism' as a just war against the injustice of Israel's existence.

Palestinians, however, who are not receiving supplies and funds due to EU embargos, might see European Middle East policy towards them less rosily than Ye'or – although a leadership in the Gaza strip other than the extremist Hamas would indeed have been preferable to many Palestinians themselves. It could even be said that to a certain extent it had been Israel itself which has created the Hamas-Fatah frictions, based on the ancient Roman scheme *divide et impera*, 'divide and rule' – to the extend that we have now in practice *two* Palestinian states that are at each others throats, a dream-come-true for Israel and its allies.

A European foreign policy vis-à-vis the Muslim world?

The reason for having dealt above with Ye'or's Eurabia-fantasies to such a large extent is the circumstance that Europe would indeed have to play an important role in the relations between the West and the Islamic world – a more *positive* role, however, that would differ significantly from what Ye'or wants to make her readers to believe.

There can be no doubt that the existence of Israel as a state is a fact that is one of the results of the horrors of World War II. The existence of Israel within fixed international borders (let's say within the pre-1967 setting and an international arrangement for Jerusalem, a city which is sacred to *all* three major monotheistic traditions, including Christianity) – alongside a *viable* Palestinian state – should be made the subject of a *comprehensive* peace agreement. However, and this is also a point that should be emphasised here again, Jerusalem's Christian facet and the fate of Arab and other Christians living within the confines of the Jewish state should also be made the subject of any future peace package. As any other member of the United Nations, Israel, too, has to abide by international law. It is this past and present disregard for UN resolutions and basic humanitarian considerations that continues to enrage politically aware observers of Middle Eastern affairs, Muslims and non-Muslims alike.

Here, it can only be mentioned in passing that what is usually referred to as the 'Israeli-Palestinian conflict' has also several *Christian* perspectives – admittedly, perspectives that are becoming increasingly lost among contemporary, largely 'de-christianised', Europeans. A considerable percentage of the Palestinian Arabs, for instance, are Christians and it is imaginable that they, too, would like to see a more active involvement of the Europeans when facing the Israelis in peace negotiations. Above all, however, Europe – although largely secularised – has still a moral and historical obligation toward what was once known as the Holy Land – the birthplace of Christianity and thus of a large part of the European heritage that is so often invoked during festive speeches. Unfortunately, the incidences of at times rather strong wording proceeding from the Holy See in times of human rights violations from the part of Israel have so far remained rather unnoticed among the Muslim public opinion, which tends to see itself victimised by the 'West' without any further distinction (For details on the sometimes not easy Vatican-Israeli relationship see Breger 2004). Moreover, as this writer has argued elsewhere (Marcinkowski 2006a), the present pope's controversial 'Regensburg lecture' could and perhaps should also be interpreted as a sincere attempt to enter into a more *meaningful* dialogue with the world of Islam on ethics and moral values, although others might come to other conclusions and interpret his speech differently (on some facets of the thought of the present pope on dialogue and European identity see Benedict XVI 2004 and 2005).

The Middle East would thus be a good testing ground for the sincerity and workability of concerted EU peace efforts (independently from the answer to the question whether former British prime Minister Tony Blair – a staunch supporter of the latest US-led Iraq War – would be the right choice as the official Envoy of the Quartet on the Middle East on behalf of the United Nations, the European Union, the United States and Russia). The EU would have to develop its *own* strategies, strategies that would hopefully differ from what we have seen in the past coming out of Washington. Realistically speaking, it has so far not become clear to the public what 'EU foreign policy' does actually mean – considering the often diametrically opposed geopolitical interests of major member states, such as France, Germany, and Britain. However, already the fact of the presence of millions of migrants and citizens with a Muslim background residing in those countries should determine them to seek for peaceful coexistence with the world of Islam. Although, to the mind of this writer, it would be difficult to talk of the existence of any kind of *concerted* 'EU foreign policy' at the moment, Europe would have several advantages in its future dealings with the Muslim world.

Among those advantages is the circumstance that several of the major EU member states have had deep historical experiences with the Muslim world. Since the fifteenth century, Germany, for instance, in the shape of the Holy Roman Empire and the therein dominating Habsburg Empire, had been practically a neighbour of the Ottomans on the Balkans and similar can be said about Poland. The new EU members Bulgaria and Romania had even been provinces of the Sultan's empire. During those days, those contacts had not always been violent and there are still several remnants of Ottoman Muslim culture left on the Balkans and even in Poland. Moreover, France – during the sixteenth century even an ally of the Porte against the fellow Christian Habsburgs – was one of the first Western countries that were allowed to entertain permanent diplomatic representations in what was then known as Constantinople – aside from the fact that Paris also had been the colonial power in the Maghreb as well as in Syria and Lebanon. Similar could be said about Italy, the Netherlands, and, of course, Spain and Portugal, two countries that were even ruled for centuries by the Muslims.

For better or worse, all those countries are thus in the unique position of having at their disposal a repository of experiences with the Muslim world that could be drawn upon when addressing current issues. Of all those countries just mentioned, Germany had been until quite recently seen by many Muslims if not as a 'friend' but then at least not as an 'enemy' of the Muslims. As I have tried to develop elsewhere (Marcinkowski 2006b), this is mainly due to the fact that Germany did not appear as a colonial power in the Middle East (as a matter of fact Germany and the Ottomans had been close allies throughout World War I). The historical experiences of those European countries with the world of Islam as well as the presence of millions of Muslims among them should be considered assets rather than obstacles when trying to bridge the current gab of misunderstandings between the Muslim world and the West. Aside from that, Western Europe received from the medieval Arab-Muslim world – mainly through Spain and Sicily – major parts of the Hellenic scientific and philosophical heritage that would have been otherwise lost.

This compares rather encouragingly positive with the lack of constructive involvement from the part of other leading Western powers, among them the United States whose closest encounters with Muslims – aside from those of recent Iraq and Afghanistan ill-fame, as well as the involvement in Iran under the last Shah – date merely back to the Barbary Wars of the beginning of the nineteenth century and their confrontation with Tripolis.

Constructive approaches

In spite of the differences in worldview between Islam and the West in terms of the role of religion in contemporary society, Muslims, too, can do their part to make better relations between those two major players of our world a reality.

What is all too often forgotten when discussing the attitude of the religion of Islam in general with regard to conflict-solution is that there does in fact exist a variety of approaches that are directed towards peaceful conflict solution. For instance, it is true that the often misinterpreted concept of *jihād* can at times also possess a rather militant aspect. In this context, it should be noted that the Arabic word *jihād*, originally one of the cornerstones of Islamic *spirituality* rather than warfare and literally meaning 'struggle', 'effort', or 'spiritual struggle with oneself' (i.e. with one's Self), is often misinterpreted in the media, and even by scholars, as 'Holy War', originally a concept of medieval Christianity. Moreover, it goes without saying that the contemporary Roman Catholic Church, too, accepts the concept of 'just war'.

There can also be no doubt, that any kind of approach towards conflict-solution should as long as possible remain peaceful. Most people will be surprised to hear that Islamic approaches in this regard vary, as had been demonstrated by the American Muslim Professor Karim Douglas Crow. According to this scholar,

> Islam provides a set of powerful teachings and practises with universal relevance for humanity. These have the potential to make a great contribution for peaceful change and just societies. Islam clearly possesses a comprehensive methodology and set of values for 'Peaceful-Action'/al-Jihad al-Silmi. The challenge for Muslims now is to present Islamic Values in authentic terms for the 21st century. Thinking Muslims must search for ways to realize and make these values real and effective in our world today (Crow 2000–2001: 11; cp. also Crow 2000).

Practical and workable conflict-solutions are needed in order to avoid further radicalisation. What is needed is a '*true jihād*', i. e. a universal *effort* against poverty and ignorance. Such a *progressive* understanding of *jihād* from the part of Muslims could also involve a proper reflection on how to support the fight against poverty, lack of education and disease, and the HIV and AIDS drama, which doesn't stop at the borders of the *Dār al-Islām* or the Lands of the Muslims, as well as how to avoid a demonisation of its victims, the latter showing a frightening lack of compassion in sharp contrast to the true teachings of Islam and by any of the other major religious systems, for that matter (For some rather bizarre views on the AIDS drama see Schönig 1990; clearly into the category of demonisation falls Badri 1997).

In the light of what has just been pointed out, Islam *per se* should thus not be considered an obstacle. The central question, however, even from the Islamic point of view, is how to define the correct place of religion in dealing with the present issues at stake, without necessarily following secular systems that are perceived as alien. The real confrontation is thus not 'Islam versus the West', but rather populism, ignorance (on both sides of the fence) and, at times, 'collective paranoia' (revealing in that context is Pipes 1996) and 'conspiracy theories versus knowledge and practical help'. There is an urgent need of knowledgeable people on the pulpit, as well as of spirituality and knowledge of the original tenets of religion.

In spite of the undeniable fact that Muslims throughout the world did (and still do) suffer grave injustices that are often not addressed with the same vigour as those perpetrated by Muslims, those injustices appear to be perpetuated in the Muslim mind as conspiracy theories. In the view of Professor Ahmad Ashraf, Managing Editor of Columbia University's *Encyclopedia Iranica* (and a friend and former colleague there of the present writer), and within the context of the Iranian experience, Muslim conspiracy theories are mainly the result of a misinterpretation of the surrounding world perceived as 'hostile'. He clarifies this by stating that those theories

> [...] are a complex set of beliefs attributing the course of Persian history and politics to the machinations of hostile foreign powers and secret organizations. In contemporary social psychology such theories are defined

> as elaborate and internally consistent systems of "collective delusions," often tenaciously held and extremely difficult to refute. Many conspiracy theories are based on a simple dualism in which the world is viewed as divided between good and evil forces with the latter determining the course of history. Various failures and disasters, for example, defeats in war, revolutions, and general backwardness can thus be blamed on powerful enemies. Conspiracy theories often serve an important social function, helping to assuage certain kinds of anxiety among group members but also often limiting or hindering their capacity to respond effectively to external and internal social and political challenges. Particularly since the beginning of the 20th century, Persians from all walks of life and all ideological orientations have relied on conspiracy theories as a basic mode of understanding politics and history. The fact that the great powers have in fact intervened covertly in Persian affairs has led ordinary people, political leaders, even the rulers themselves to interpret their history in terms of elaborate and devious conspiracies. The acceptance of such theories has in itself influenced the course of modern Persian history, for it has engendered a sense of helplessness in dealing with the rumored activities of foreign conspirators. Conspiracy theories in modern Persia can generally be divided into two categories: those focused on supposed plots by Western colonial powers and those focused on satanic forces believed to have been active against Persia from antiquity to the present (Ashraf 2000a; for an earlier, more detailed version see Ashraf 2000b [with extensive bibliographical material]).

According to Ashraf, Iranian conspiracy theories focused mainly on colonial powers, plots from the part of the 'cunning' British and the CIA, conspiracy between the country's Shi'ite clerics and world powers, by the Freemasons, Baha'is and 'Zionists', as well as what he terms 'satanic theories of conspiracy' – all depending on the particular *weltanschauung* and 'mindset' of the beholder. As Ashraf also clarifies,

> [t]he popularity of conspiracy theories among Persians arises from a combination of political, social, psychological, and cultural factors: frequent foreign interference during the period of semicolonialism in the early 20th century and great-power politics in the 1940s–80s; the legacy of deeply rooted pre-Islamic and Shi'ite cultural beliefs about satanic forces; and the effectiveness of such theories as a collective defense mechanism, particularly during periods of powerlessness, defeat, and political turmoil. Certain deep-rooted aspects of the Persian cultural heritage, which seem to have no parallel in other Muslim societies, may also have contributed to the popularity of conspiracy theories. They include a dualistic world view, probably derived from pre-Islamic religious beliefs, in which good and evil powers were considered to be in conflict, with the latter directing the course of history. The mythological character of traditional Persian historiography, which may reflect a particular receptivity to the mythological mode

> of thought; a propensity to poetic exaggeration *(eghrāq-e shā'erāneh)* among the Persians at all social levels; and a long tradition of attributing miraculous deeds to the twelve Shi'ite Imams are other probable contributing factors. Although blaming others can help assuage anxiety about failures, ready acceptance of conspiracy theories has also proved to be highly dysfunctional; in modern Persia it has contributed to political malaise that has sometimes precluded rational responses to internal and external crises (Ashraf 2000a).

Thus a rational understanding of the mechanisms that underlie history, including that of the Muslims – any history, for that matter – would be essential for arriving at appropriate 'diagnoses' of problems and shortcomings and thus for the finding of solutions that are pertaining to the future of the Muslim community. Several years back, although within the context of education, I was trying to clarify this point further by saying that

> [t]he effort of trying to know each other better, without necessarily giving up prerogatives and belief, should prevail against the falling into stereotypizations, such as ethnic and religious prejudice, which can only be considered as a sign of fear and insecurity with regard to the tenets of one's own religion. This predicament applies, of course to any historical period and religious or social system (Marcinkowski 2002).

Constructive criticism and reflective, analytical thinking, appears to be a good tradition from the classical Islamic period that needs to be revived, since it

> [...] intends to keep the message of Islam 'pure' by pointing the finger on the wounds in order to heal them rather than keeping silence and thus causing the 'death' of the entire 'organism' or the *ummah*, so to speak. [...] This procedure is far from being an attempt to 'secularize' history, or from separating the 'principle of political leadership' from the purely religious tenets. But rather the opposite is the case: Instead of a 'never mind, they still had been Muslims'-attitude [...], I personally would propose an attitude of clear disassociation and ethically motivated criticism, based on the Islamic sources, as well as on the general requirements for any scholarly investigation (Marcinkowski 2000 and 2001).

Finally, this reflective approach is in line with the ideas expressed by some of the greatest thinkers of Islam themselves, among them Sir Muhammad Iqbal (d. 1938), the spiritual 'father of Pakistan', who stated that

> [t]he possibility of a scientific treatment of history means a wider experience, a greater maturity of practical reason, and finally a fuller realization of certain basic ideas regarding the nature of life and time (Iqbal 1999: 140).

Perspectives

Living in an increasingly globalised world of diverse cultures and civilisations, it becomes more and more imperative to rediscover and live the values of tolerance and forbearance. Nevertheless, there are thus also limits to mutual tolerance which need to be demarcated in order to make this dialogue a meaningful one. Therefore, what is needed is a truly 'civilisational dialogue' instead of the myriads of the purely religious approaches of the past which would miss their direction as the place of religion in largely secular Western societies differs diametrically from that which it enjoys in the Muslim mind. Thus, slightly differing from Saikal's earlier quoted statement, I would like to argue that at the core of the problem are not always *political* differences – such as those of Palestine, Iraq, or Afghanistan, for instance – but rather fundamentally *different worldviews* with regard to the 'proper' place of religion and faith in human life. The exemplary case of Turkey's bid for EU membership had been discussed in some detail earlier in order to demonstrate that contemporary Muslim countries are trying to find and keep their identity in an increasingly globalised world. Having said this, from the perspective of many Muslims today, 'proper place' would refer to respect for at least the basic tenets of Islamic civilisation and lifestyle, rather than a theocracy *à la iranienne*. At a conference sponsored by the Phoenix Chamber of Commerce, Dato' Abdul Majid Mohamed, Malaysia's former Ambassador to the United States, brought this issue to the point by stating:

> The difference between your country and mine is that in the United States the power elite is very modern, but has no use for religion. In my country we want to combine modernity and Islam. We understand that life is more than a natural process, it is a gift from God (Woodward 2002: 111).

More concretely, in the words of Professor Syed Muhammad Naquib Al-Attas, the Founder-Director of the renowned International Institute of Islamic Thought and Civilization (ISTAC) in Kuala Lumpur and perhaps one of the most well-known philosophers in the contemporary world of Islam,

> Modern Western civilization needs to resume the dialogue that it used to have with Islam, because only Islamic civilization can be a true and useful mirror for the West, that it may have an insight into its errors, and perhaps climb out of the quicksand of tragedy, meaninglessness, and utter unhappiness (Paraphrased in Wan Mohd. Nor Wan Daud 1998: 21).

In sum, Islam and (culturally-speaking) still Christian-dominated but politically rather secular Europe might differ on the higher levels of metaphysics, so to speak. Nevertheless, more down to earth – and certainly more significantly in practice, in terms of maintaining a climate of mutual respect – they often share common values in the ethical sphere that need to be rediscovered and put to work. True tolerance, however, demands also that each partner of such a dialogue is allowed to draw from his own religious experience and cultural background. At the same time, there can be no doubt that an *active* living of tolerance should first start within one's own community.

References

Printed sources:

Badri, Malik 1997: The Aids Crisis: An Islamic Socio-Political Perspective. Kuala Lumpur: ISTAC.

Benedict XVI [Joseph Ratzinger] 2004: Truth and Tolerance. Christian Belief and World Religions. San Francisco: Ignatius Press.

Benedict XVI [Joseph Ratzinger] 2005: Europe. Today and Tomorrow. San Francisco: Ignatius Press, 2nd ed.

Breger, Marshall J. (ed.) 2004: The Vatican-Israel Accords: Political, Legal, and Theological Contexts. Notre Dame IN: University of Notre Dame Press.

Crow, Karim D. 2000: Nurturing an Islamic Peace Discourse. In: American Journal of Islamic Social Sciences 17, no. 3, 54–69.

Crow, Karim D. 2000–2001: Islamic Peaceful-Action: Nonviolent Approach to Justice and Peace in Islamic Societies. In: Capitol Journal on Culture and Society [Cagayan de Oro City, Philippines] 12, no. 2, 11.

Griffith, Sidney H. 1998: Review of Bat Ye'or, The Decline of Eastern Christianity under Islam: From Jihad to Dhimmitude, Seventh-Twentieth Century. In: International Journal of Middle East Studies 30, no. 4., 619–21.

Iqbal, Sir Muhammad 1999: The Reconstruction of Religious Thought in Islam. Lahore: Sh. Muhammad Ashraf, repr.

Marcinkowski, Christoph 2000: Some Reflections on Predispositions in the Writing and Perception of the History and Civilization of the Muslims. Part One: The Case of Muslim Scholarship. In: Iqbal Review 41, no. 4, 43–59.

Marcinkowski, Christoph 2001: Some Reflections on Predispositions in the Writing and Perception of the History and Civilization of the Muslims. Part Two: The Case of Non-Muslim Scholarship. In: Iqbal Review 42, no. 2, 97–113.

Marcinkowski, Christoph 2002: Challenges and Perspectives for the Perception and Teaching of Islamic History. In: Islamic Culture 76, no. 3, 63–82.

Marcinkowski, Christoph 2006a: The Basis of Pope's Reasoning. In: Straits Times [Singapore], September 18, p. 18.

Marcinkowski, Christoph 2006b: "The Germans to the Front!" Where Should Germany Stand? In: Straits Times [Singapore], 21 August, p. 15.

Pipes, Daniel 1996: The Hidden Hand. Middle East Fears of Conspiracy. Houndsmills, London: Macmillan Press Ltd.

Saikal, Amin 2004: Islam and the West: Challenges and Opportunities. In: Virginia Hooker, Amin Saikal (ed.), Islamic Perspectives for the New Millennium. Singapore: ISEAS, 19–31.

Schönig, Hannelore 1990: Aids als das Tier *(Dabba)* der islamischen Eschatologie. Zur Argumentation einer türkischen Schrift. In: Die Welt des Islams 30, 211–218.

Wan Mohd. Nor Wan Daud 1998: The Educational Philosophy and Practice of Syed Muhammad Naquib al-Attas: An Exposition of the Original Concept of Islamization. Kuala Lumpur: ISTAC.

Woodward, Mark R. 2002: Modernity and the Disenchantment of Life: A Muslim-Christian Contrast. In: Johan Meuleman (ed.), Islam in the Era of Globalization: Modern Attitudes Towards Modernity and Identity. London. New York: RoutledgeCurzon, 111–142.

Ye'or, Bat 1971: Les Juifs en Egypte. Geneva: Editions de l'Avenir.

Ye'or, Bat (with David Maisel, Paul Fenton, and David Littman) 1985: The Dhimmi: Jews and Christians Under Islam. Madison NJ: Fairleigh Dickinson University Press.

Ye'or, Bat 1996: The Decline of Eastern Christianity: From Jihad to Dhimmitude, Seventh-Twentieth Century. Madison NJ: Fairleigh Dickinson University Press.

Ye'or, Bat (with David Littman, tr. Miriam Kochan) 2001: Islam and Dhimmitude: Where Civilizations Collide. Madison NJ: Fairleigh Dickinson University Press.

Ye'or, Bat, 2005. Eurabia: The Euro-Arab Axis. Madison NJ: Fairleigh Dickinson University Press.

Internet resources:

Ashraf, Ahmad 2007a: Conspiracy Theories and the Persian Mind. In: Encyclopaedia Iranica. New York, Columbia University. URL: http://www.iranian.com/May96/Opinion/Conspiracy.html (accessed on 30 January 2007).

Ashraf, Ahmad 2007b: Conspiracy Theories in Persia. In: Encyclopaedia Iranica, New York, Columbia University. URL: http://www.iranica.com/newsite/articles/v6f2/v6f2a012.html (accessed on 30 January 2007).

Hürriyet (English online edition) 2006: New Eurobarometer Poll Results Show a Drop in Turkish Support for the EU. URL: http://www.hurriyet.com.tr/english/4713737.asp?gid=74 (accessed on 18 August 2007).

Narlı, Nilüfer 2007: Turkey's Elections: AK Party Wins Through Broad Appeal. URL: http://www.diplomatictraffic.com/about_us.asp (accessed on 20 August 2007).

The Economist (North America Edition) 2006: 24 June 2006. URL: http://economist.com/printedition/displayCover.cfm?url=/images/20060624/20060624issuecovUS400.jpg&CFID=86288785&CFTOKEN=17bd413-ea9331a9-d95e-440b-a2ee-1b86e4b24730 (accessed on 1 June 2007).

Turkish General Election, 2007. In: Wikipedia. URL: http://en.wikipedia.org/wiki/Turkish_election (accessed on 20 August 2007).

Turkey. In: Wikipedia. URL: http://en.wikipedia.org/wiki/Turkey (accessed on 20 August 2007).

Part II

Muslim-Western Encounters – Past and Present

2

Interdependent Diversities: Self-Representations, Historical Regions, and Global Challenges in Europe

Christian Giordano

Abstract

Most concepts of Europe as a coherent imagined community or as a unitary 'community of destiny' (Schicksalsgemeinschaft) are characterised by a bipolar scheme in which the notion of Europe appears together with contrastive representations of an 'Anti-Europe' (Arab-Muslim culture, Asia, the Orient, Africa etc.). There is a mirrored relationship by which the former's basic traits are identified through a presumed diametrical opposition with the latter's. However, it is misleading to think of Europe as a 'united civilisation', or worse, as a sum of 'cultural areas'. As suggested by Hungarian historian Jenö Szücs, by French historian Fernand Braudel, and by American sociologist Immanuel Wallerstein, Europe must be considered as a system of strictly (inter)dependent yet structurally diverse 'historical regions'. The rise of the capitalist 'world-system' and the emergence of a new international division of labor transformed those regions into core, peripheries, and marginal external areas. The first part of the article illustrates how Europe to this day consists of one core, located mainly in the continent's northwest, four peripheries (Mediterranean Europe, Central-Eastern Europe, Eastern Europe, and Southeast Europe), and some marginal external areas (for example, the Caucasus, especially Georgia). The second part of the article deals with the social, political, and economic transformations in Europe within the framework of the present globalisation processes. Transnational migrations from the Old World peripheries, minority claims for recognition, integration into the European Union, and the emergence of other global governance bodies have eroded to some extent the sovereignty of the nation-state which since the eighteenth century was the dominant institution in the 'Old Continent's' political order. This part of the article illustrates how Europe actually experiences the difficult, extremely tense, and contradictory transition from a Europe founded on 'national imagined communities' to a 'post-national Europe'.

The term 'Europe'

The present concept of Europe has several discordant meanings when the geographic, historical, socio-cultural, anthropological, or political aspects are taken into consideration. History delves into the past searching for the matrix of actual or supposed common traits of today's European societies. While sociology and politics emphasise Europe's spiritual and ideological unity as a cognitive basis for a European *Schicksalsgemeinschaft* (community of destiny), the anthropological view has a tendency to consider Europe a much diversified 'culture area'. These manifold approaches and perspectives emphasise that Europe is an extremely unsettled concept. Therefore, a univocal and clear definition would be deceptive, as this contribution will illustrate.

The masculine Greek descriptive adjective *europos*, which literally means 'he who sees afar', can be found in Homer's Iliad and Odyssey (eighth century BCE) who used it as an attribute of Zeus. The Greek poet Hesiod of Ascra, almost during the same period, mentions the feminine proper noun *Europa* for the first time in his *Theogony*. For him Europa was a divine character: one of the three-thousand nymphs who, he wrote, "along with Apollo and the rivers nourish the youth of men".

The famous myth of Europa, daughter of Agenor (the Phoenician king of Tyre), with whom Zeus will fall in love charmed by her beauty, arose some centuries later. Zeus, in the form of a bull, carried her away to Crete where she became queen and founder of the dynasty to which also Minos, king of Knossos, belonged. Europa's rape has inspired countless poets, painters (amongst them Veronese and Titian), and sculptors from ancient times to our days (for example the bas-relief in Geneva's railway station).

These examples show that in ancient Greece the term Europe evoked legendary or divine characters from the mythological universe rather than a geographic site.

Although Anaximander (610–547 BCE), Hippocrates (460–377 BCE), and even Aristotle (384–322 BCE) used the appellative 'Europe' to define an area distinct from Asia, the indeterminate use of the term concurs with Strabo (58 BCE – 25 CE) who upheld that in ancient Greece it was still a nameless continent. Nonetheless, this Greek geographer who lived under the Roman emperors Augustus and Tiberius gave the first detailed description of the favorable climatic and natural conditions in which European populations lived. Strabo contended that these populations were intellectually superior to those of other continents. The Roman Empire, however, was never particularly Eurocentric. In those days, it was seen as a tri-continental entity, socially and culturally composite, whose hub was the Mediterranean, which, by no coincidence, the Latins knew as *Mare Nostrum*, 'Our Sea'.

The term 'Europe' took on a less geographical and more political and socio-cultural connotation, after the fall of the Roman Empire, during the Carolingian period (seventh-eighth century). In fact, according to an anonymous medieval chronicle, the soldiers led by Charles Martel, who fought victoriously against the

Arabs at Poitiers (732 CE), were 'European'. Some decades later, 'Rex Carolus, pater Europae' (King Charles, father of Europe) and 'Europa vel regnum Caroli' (Europe or the kingdom of Charles) are common rhetorical phrases of the time, which stress the fact that Charlemagne was regarded as founder and sovereign of a political subject bearing the name 'Europa'. These sources record mainly two aspects: that the notion of Europe was assimilated with the Frankish Kingdom and that the idea of Europe as a political-spiritual entity developed along with the expansion of Arab-Muslim settlements north of the Strait of Gibraltar. One of the main recurrent themes of various subsequent concepts on Europe as an 'imagined community' (Anderson 1983) can be noticed *in statu nascendi* from the latter observation.

By examining the following intellectual constructions, it is evident that they are characterised almost without exception by a scheme in which the notion of Europe appears together with another term of comparison. In most cases, it is a contraposition, a dichotomy or bipolarity, rather than a comparison between what Europe is reckoned to be and what is, supposedly, its opposite.

This 'European self-awareness', as Denis de Rougemont (1990) calls it, becomes even more tangible at the time of the geographical discoveries and the first colonial conquests. From an historical point of view, representations of the 'European peculiarity' become clearer in parallel to the 'overseas' expansion (fifteenth-sixteenth century) as well as with the simultaneous failure of the Habsburg King of Spain and Holy Roman Emperor Charles V (1500–1558) and his successors to fulfill the dream of a 'planetary empire'.

From an anthropological point of view, Europe discovers itself by discovering and conquering the rest of the world. Between 'Europe' and 'Anti-Europe', which from time to time could be the Arab-Muslim culture, Asia, the Orient, or to a much lesser extent Africa etc., there is a mirror-like relationship whose upshot is to make the former identify its basic traits through a presumed diametrical difference with the latter. The outcome of the discovery of one's self via the 'other' will make Balthazar Gracian (1601–1658) coin the famous phrase 'Europe is the admirable face of the world'. Following the same train of thought, the *Grand Dictionnaire historique de Louis de Moreri* (published in 1674) illustrates the European traits that have allowed them to overpower the people of other continents. It is quite surprising to read statements in this publication that seem to forebode the stereotypes of German *Völkerpsychologie* (Wilhelm Wundt), as well as American studies on *modal personality* and *national character* (Ruth Benedict).

Carl von Linné (1707–1778) expressed similar arguments more succinctly. The renowned Swedish naturalist describes the 'Homo Europaeus' as 'subtle' and 'creative' while Asians are 'melancholic' and 'miserly' and Africans are 'sly' and 'lazy'. Von Linné is exemplary of his epoch. It is not surprising therefore that a more conspicuous European 'self-awareness' ensues from the Age of Enlightenment. During the 'ère des philosophes' almost all the great eighteenth-century thinkers as Montesquieu (1689–1755), Voltaire (1694–1778), Jean-Jacques Rousseau (1712–1778), Ferdinando Galiani (1727–1787), Melchior-Gaspar de

Jovellanos (1744–1811), Antoine de Condorcet (1743–1794), Edward Gibbon (1737–1794), Edmund Burke (1729–1797) and several others, pondered over the 'European peculiarity' more and more often and from different perspectives. Even these dissertations share a common denominator: a scheme, usually bipolar, in which at least one other term of comparison appears besides Europe and refers mainly to Asia. In other words, the main question for most of the above-mentioned authors is: how come European nations are the only ones that for better or for worse have reached such levels of civilisation, while the 'other' societies are still savage, primitive or barbarian? Leaving aside the tentative answers, almost all eighteenth-century texts on Europe, although not constantly overemphasizing presumed 'endowments', 'qualities' and 'glories' of the Old Continent, draw either implicit or, more often, explicit parallels and hierarchies between 'we' and 'they'. Again, there is the same contraposition between 'Europe' and 'Anti-Europe'.

During the nineteenth century, the notion of Europe within this dichotomy had an increasingly hegemonic connotation. The nineteenth century, which beyond any strictly mathematical chronology ends after World War I, was characterised by a bold optimism that turned out to be an awful self-deception, as German political scientist Carl Schmitt (1888–1985) aptly proved. In historical terms, European 'élites' had surprisingly underestimated, if not disregarded altogether, the considerable changes that had been going on beyond their continent. For example, they had overlooked that there had been dynamic and intensive socioeconomic and cultural relations involving various Asian societies on the Indian Ocean's rim well before the arrival of European colonial empires, the formation of pre-Columbian empires in Mexico and Peru, the Japanese development model spurred by the emperor Mutsuhito, better known as Meiji Tenno (1852–1912), who had opened his country to foreign commerce, and even the American 'Great Transformation'. All along this century as well as the next one, Europeans would have obstinately emphasised their superiority, as Eric Wolf has aptly highlighted, by stubbornly disowning the history of 'others' (Wolf 1982).

It is no surprise that the term Europe was being increasingly used as a synonym of 'civilisation' and 'progress' (Schmitt 1974). From a European point of view, the Old Continent is the only one that could establish a 'civilizing movement' to 'break through the darkness that enfolds entire populations' as Leopold II (1835–1909) King of the Belgians stated in a solemn speech in 1876. For this typical representative of his times, European colonial expansion in the heart of 'Anti-Europe' is 'a crusade worthy of this century of progress'.

Nineteenth-century certainties were radically curtailed by World War I, which the German philosopher Karl Löwith (1897–1973) keenly called 'the first European civil war' (Löwith 1990), by the critical analysis of the nationalistic and totalitarian frenzy between the two World Wars, by World War II traumas, and finally by the melancholic awareness of relentlessly crumbling colonial empires. Europe as a notion would become less trioumphalist and much more defensive.

After 1945, Europe was perceived as suffering from a chronic economic, cultural and above all political and military fragility. This intrinsic deficiency could be checked only by a strong synergy between all the continent's components sharing the same fate. In this respect, French sociologist Edgar Morin (1987) has fittingly spoken about Europe as a *Schicksalsgemeinschaft*, a well-known term first used by Austro-Marxist theorist Otto Bauer (1881–1938).

From a sociological point of view, the 'European fragility' concept implies a 'menace' coming from external hostile forces. Each community, especially if it is a *Schicksalsgemeinschaft,* as Edgar Morin stresses, is strengthened or crystallised if under pressure from an actual or presumed enemy. The part of Europe that after World War II was not under Soviet control always reverted to the 'Anti-Europe' theme to emphasise what was the 'menace'. From 1945 up to 1989, while Europe was establishing its first joint institutions such as the European Coal and Steel Community (E.C.S.C.), the European Common Market (E.C.M.), the European Economic Community (EEC), and finally the European Community (EC), the leading 'Anti-Europe' 'menace' was Soviet communism, often defined as a new form of 'Oriental despotism' and thus regarded as an 'Asian' phenomenon. At that time, 'Anti-Europe' was mainly seen as an intrinsically ideological entity.

The fall of the Berlin Wall in 1989 and the subsequent disintegration of the opposing blocs coincided with the birth of a new European institution – the European Union (EU) – which ratified the Schengen, Amsterdam, Dublin and Nice treaties. A 'fragile' and 'menaced' Europe is still a common perception in the Old Continent despite this new, highly specialised, and official legal apparatus. Behind this defensive attitude some authoritative, though overly severe, 'Euro-skeptic' critics detect the danger of the creation of a 'European fortress' closed within itself that wishes only to defend an acquired economic standing threatened by supposed external 'menaces'. At the beginning of the twenty-first century, the bipolarity between 'Europe' and 'Anti-Europe' still exists although its shape has changed radically. Now 'Anti-Europe' is mainly the planet's boundless south: its migratory waves towards the Old Continent (especially those from Islamic countries of the Middle-East and North Africa), the socioeconomic potentiality of its emerging countries, its high demographic rates, and, last but not least, the new political-religious terrorism masterminded by fundamentalist and integralist groups, which, rightly or not, are regarded as 'enemies' of 'European civilisation'. Two essential conclusions can be drawn from the above discussion:

- The term Europe is certainly very old and Denis de Rougemont (1990) is right about Europe's twenty-eight centuries. The contemporary notion of Europe as an economic, political and spiritual community instead, is quite recent.
- This concept of Europe stems from the comparison with what is deemed its opposite. There would be no 'Europe' without an 'Anti-Europe'.

What Europe is not: some misleading and dangerous ideas

During the entire twentieth century and the beginning of the current one, notions of Europe with powerful ideological implications have occasionally been spread;

yet, they can hardly endure an historical, sociological and anthropological analysis. The idea of 'European civilisation' as a homogeneous and 'monolithic' entity was most popular and politically relevant. However, the term 'Occident' (in the sense of *'Abendland'*, a German term being the opposite of *'Morgenland'* or Orient) was often used as a synonym of 'European civilisation'. More or less explicitly, these concepts call to mind presumed unifying values stemming from a Christian heritage. Therefore, 'European civilisation' was seen as the center and bulwark of Christianity. Historically and socio-anthropologically misleading, this concept of Europe was an ideological backbone, albeit not the only one, of blatantly antidemocratic and totalitarian political movements. Although under many aspects admittedly in conflict with Christian doctrine and ecclesiastic institutions, German Nazism and Italian Fascism envisioned themselves as the sole upholders of 'European civilisation' and strenuous paladins of 'Christianity' particularly against Soviet Bolshevism, which, due to historical mystifications, was stigmatised as 'Asian', hence 'alien' to Europe. Other régimes with similar ideological backgrounds, such as authoritarian and dictatorial governments and movements in Central and East European countries (i. e. Józef Piłsudski in Poland and Miklos Horthy in Hungary, Antanas Smetona in Lithuania, Karlis Ulmanis in Latvia etc.) as well as Francoism in Spain and Salazarism in Portugal, resorted to analogous ideas with a nationalistic bias, usually for anti-Bolshevik purposes.

The most relevant intellectual expression of 'European civilisation' as centre and bulwark of the 'Christian Occident' was the 'Europe congress' significantly held in Rome in 1932 (14–20 November), organised by the 'Fondazione Volta', patronised by Prime Minister and Chief of Cabinet Benito Mussolini. Distinguished scientists attended the most meaningful congress on Europe at that time: among others, Guglielmo Marconi – physicist, Alfred Weber, Werner Sombart and Roberto Michels – sociologists, Claudio Sanchez Albornoz – medievalist, Jerôme Carcopino and Nicolae Jorga – historians, Giuseppe Tucci – orientalist, and Willy Hellpach – psychologist. This line-up of prominent researchers included not only well-known writers such as Stefan Zweig but also two politicians who became ill-famed soon after: German Reichstag President Hermann Göring and Alfred Rosenberg. Europe as a 'united civilisation' was the congress' main point (Dainelli 1933). The lectures reveal that this interpretation of Europe coincides with the idea of 'Christian Occident' from which Russia (as an 'Asian' society), however, must be ruled out, as Alfred Weber and others emblematically underscored in their contributions (Fondazione Volta 1933).

Europe as a 'united civilisation' embodied in the 'Christian Occident' is not a bygone idea since it can still be traced in several political subjects of present European extreme rightists, such as the French *Front National* and neo-Nazi and neo-Fascist fringes in Germany, Austria and Italy. These active although still marginal movements resort to similar concepts to assert their violent hostility towards immigration especially from Islamic and/or non-European countries.

Still, the notion of Europe's 'Christian origins' and 'Christian identity' is not an ideological leitmotif used solely by the radical right, since heated debates about defining the Old Continent in the fruitless European Constitution project not only brought these specters to the fore again but actually strengthened them and made them nearly acceptable.

The 'united civilisation' or 'Christian Occident' vision of Europe is a dangerous idea since it implies the pursuit of cultural, denominational, and maybe even ethnic homogeneity based upon the 'exclusion strategy' and the 'purity myth', which have caused so many of Europe's tragedies during the past century.

This vision of Europe is misleading since it is far from being the continent's past as well as present social structure. Considering only the denominational aspect, a far more differentiated, less compact and congruent setting is due to the millenary or centuries-old presence in Europe of significant non-Christian communities, as Jewish or Muslim, and historical events such as the Great Schism (1054), the Reformation (sixteenth century) and subsequent nefarious wars of religion.

Europe: a system of 'historical regions'

German philosopher Ernst Bloch (1885–1977) advises not to turn a highly differentiated social entity as Europe into a mere sum of 'cultural areas' because this would turn "History [...] into a circus [with] three or more [separate] rings" (Bloch 1985). Europe must be considered a system of strictly (inter)dependent yet structurally diverse 'historical regions' revealing differences and gaps. Hungarian historian Jenö Szücs (1983, 1990) was the first one to apply a strictly scientific method to the problem of Europe's internal frontiers, therefore the question of its historical divisions, and consequently of Europe's socio-structural differences.

Szücs stresses that from the early Middle Ages Europe began to differentiate socio-economically, giving rise to two different poles: *Europa occidentalis* and *Europa orientalis*. The border between the two poles would be an ideal line running from the Elbe River (the socio-economic boundary line between western and eastern Germany) to the Leitha River (for many centuries a pervious frontier between Austria and Hungary). A second economic and socio-structural division, which includes all societies involved in the Great Schism (1054), occurred between the eleventh and fourteenth centuries. Thus, there are three 'historical regions' with very diverse socioeconomic, political, and cultural characteristics. The first one includes the territory from the Atlantic to the above-mentioned Elbe-Leitha ideal line: more or less the Carolingian Europe, which today is believed to be the quintessence of Western Europe. The central 'historical region', east of the Elbe-Leitha line but west of the eastern and southern borders of the original kingdoms of Hungary and Poland (the Grand Duchy of Lithuania included), approximately overlaps what is known today as Central-Eastern Europe also known in German as *Mitteleuropa*, a moot term. Everything east of the Baltic-Black Sea line or south of the Carpathians is East Europe proper.

Szücs' arguments are relevant for social sciences because they reveal how processes dating back to a remote past have created economic, socio-structural, and cultural differences in Europe that still hold true. However, his hypothesis of at least three 'historical regions' must be broadened and specified. On this subject, it is useful to add Immanuel Wallerstein's analysis of Europe incorporated in the 'world-system' yet divided into 'core', 'semi-peripheries' and 'peripheries' (Wallerstein 1974). However, in this article we will not consider the notion of semi-periphery since it appears to be nonessential as well as misleading.

It is currently taken for granted that a new system to organise and manage economy rose and spread from the Old Continent between 1450 and 1640. Max Weber labeled this new system rational capitalism. According to Wallerstein (1974), as well as to French historian Fernand Braudel (1979), among others, expansionist movements are inherent to this new model of economic and social behavior. Capitalist economy's worldwide expansion implies a new setup of relationships between economic partners, i. e. societies, states, regions, towns, etc. These new relationships based on a stronger (inter)dependence also imply a new international division of labor that will permeate social structures and cultural models of all societies involved in the process of capitalist 'world-system' formation. In fact, as Fernand Braudel (1979) points out, economic factors from then on became much more significant not only in defining roles and positions but also inequalities and identities.

However, the international division of labour within the 'world-system' is also based on a systematic separation between core, peripheries and external zones. Europe at first and then the whole world will be divided into a definite number of regions. Some of these underwent an historical acceleration, quickly modernizing most of their socioeconomic structure, while others suffered centuries of socioeconomic stagnation processes if not growing impoverishment. The 'world-system', along with its intrinsic (inter)dependence relationships, has had a tremendous impact on Europe's socioeconomic and cultural setup. In fact, it not only heightened pre-existent divisions but also created new 'historical regions' such as Mediterranean Europe extending from the Atlantic Ocean to the Adriatic Sea. Therefore, from the fifteenth century onward, Europe became more diversified under all aspects due to the differences between its core and its various peripheries.

The following classification highlights roles and tasks of Europe's 'historical regions' within the new international division of labour.

Northwestern Europe

Due to their specific socioeconomic and cultural dynamics, this region's societies are the primordial core of the new 'world-system' which began in Europe. In fact, the feudal system's final and relatively early breakdown, along with the appearance and growth of closely interconnected yet politically and economically autonomous cities, enabled the advent of a fledgling bourgeois strata, which, thanks to their specific outlook, made possible an outstanding economic growth as well as a primitive accumulation of capital, the likes of which did not occur at the time in other parts of the Old Continent or elsewhere. This economic and socio-cultural process went hand in hand with the invention of major technological tools especially in a then leading sector such as textiles. These innovations not only boosted the conjuncture but also expanded the industrialisation and marketing processes of manufactured goods. Such a development model must be regarded as the first appearance of a far more widespread phenomenon known as the 'industrial revolution'.

The consolidation and increase of the accumulation of capital at the core of the rising *"world-system"* of course could not have occurred without other sociologically significant concurrent processes. We need only mention the formation of strong territorial states, (Brunner 1968, 96–99; Wallerstein 1974, 225–294), the colonial expansion of the core countries (Bendix 1980/2, 21–28), and the conversion into bourgeois of aristocratic classes in several regions of England and Holland, which, using Saint-Simon's terminology, from *classes paresseuses* became *classes travailleuses* with their own specific entrepreneurial spirit. From the onset, this core included southern England, north eastern France, Flanders, Holland, and the westernmost part of Germany. Northern Spain and northern Italy, other areas of Germany and most of Switzerland, Austria, Bohemia, and Scandinavia would join in different subsequent periods.

Mediterranean Europe

This 'historical region', for centuries the Old Continent's socioeconomic and cultural hub, was turned into a vast periphery by the new international division of labor inherent in the creation of the 'world-system'. It provided the core with foodstuffs and raw materials for the growing textile industry. From a socioeconomic point of view, the area comprising Portugal (principally Alentejo), Spain (in particular Andalusia, La Mancha, and Estremadura), and Italy (especially the 'Mezzogiorno' south of Rome and the islands) was ruled by a system of latifundistic wheat monoculture and/or stock-farming belonging to an absentee aristocracy. In fact, ever since the seventeenth century this class had deserted its latifundia and, in accordance with its ideal of urban life, had moved to large cities such as Palermo, Naples, Rome, Seville, Madrid, Lisbon etc. where it basically devoted itself to an *otium cum dignitate* disowning the *negotium*, i. e. looking after one's own economic interests. Their vast properties were administrated by large tenants who were subletting to smaller ones, who in turn would sublease to the smallest peasants. This long renting-chain led to a devastating fragmentation. Too many people without a productive activity lived exclusively off the land and backs of those who actually tilled it.

Even though the banking system, rational capitalism's pillar, was developed in Renaissance Italy and the two Iberian States (Spain and Portugal) were the first ones to rely on imperial colonies, Mediterranean Europe's structure was rooted in the above-mentioned agrarian societies and economies from the sixteenth century up to most of the twentieth century. In fact, Fernand Braudel (1982) has fittingly stated that the Mediterranean periphery is where the 'bourgeoisie treason' occurred in Europe. In other words, during the establishment of the capitalist 'world-system', the rising bourgeoisie of this 'historical region' did not play a specific role nor did it have its own specific economic behavior. Its ideal was to imitate the aristocracy as a reference group. This matches the economic and social behavior of large and smaller tenants such as *señoritos* in Andalusia, La Mancha and Estremadura, or *gabelloti* and *galantuomini* in Sicily and southern Italy. Roughly to this day, they have led a typically *Rentenkapitalisten* passive existence based on the principle of 'dignified idleness'. Therefore, the absentee aristocracy's behavior is their model while they hope to rise to nobility through marriage strategies.

Central-Eastern Europe

This 'historical region', with few exceptions, lies between the two ideal boundaries traced by Jenö Szücs. It is Europe's second vast periphery and one of the core's major suppliers of foodstuffs (cereals, potatoes, etc.) and raw materials (pelts, wax, lumber etc.). The typical socio-economic scenery of Europe's second periphery is in western and eastern Prussia, Lithuania, the other two Baltic countries (Estonia and Latvia), the Hungarian plain (Nagy-Magyar Alföldi), and the Rumanian Danube plain (Moldavia and Wallachia), besides Poland's so-called eastern territories (most of which it lost after World War II). In these boundless areas lay the vast landed estates of Central-Eastern Europe's aristocracy: major Polish and Hungarian noble families, Baltic overlords of Germanic ancestry descendants of Teutonic Knights, Rumanian *boyars*, etc. Contrary to the core regions, in which feudal relations had been replaced by waged work in all sectors of economy, the institution of serfdom was the rule in these vast estates nearly up to the end of the nineteenth century. Clearly, as the Romanian example shows, in this historical region there were also free peasant communities, which, despite their ancestral tradition of autonomy, led a socially marginal existence and were characterised by a subsistence economy (Stahl 1980).

The most characteristic social phenomenon of this European periphery after the appearance of the 'world-system' was that serfdom relationships were neither abated nor uprooted. Instead, they were revived in a phenomenon that historians unanimously call *'second serfdom'* (Marx 1988, vol. 23, 249–258; Bloch 1937, 606–610; Sée, Rebillon, Preclin 1950; Stahl 1980, 1–11; Wallerstein 1974, 95–103, 113).

However, 'renewal of serfdom' does not imply a mere reproduction or persistence. Actually, great landowners introduced new farming methods in order to increase crops, mainly cereals, bringing down harsher labor and life conditions on peasants. Products from the great properties became commodities, increasingly traded on the international market, rather than means of subsistence. Central-east European 'second serfdom' was also accompanied by the formation of new groups of great landowners with a strong 'corporate spirit' and staunch political and socio-economic ambitions, such as Prussian *Junker*, Polish *szlachta*, and Hungarian gentry.

Therefore, while the Mediterranean periphery faced the 'bourgeoisie treason' during the 'world-system' formation process, the Central-east Europe periphery underwent the 'manorial reaction' whose significant influence is still rife in the region's social and economic structure (Dobb 1946; Wallerstein 1974, 95–103, 113).

Southeastern Europe

This 'historical region' includes mainly the Balkans (except Romania). It is a peculiar case since Europe's southeast was first marked by a late establishment (only in the eleventh century) of a specific form of feudalism introduced by the Byzantines and was then dominated by the Ottoman Empire for almost five hundred years (Kaser 2002, 102).

The Ottoman Empire became a part of the 'world-system' much later, during the eighteenth century; i. e., during its manifest decadence when it was already known as the 'sick man on the Bosporus'. However, even under Ottoman domination the Balkans was a poor periphery. It was on the precarious border between the Ottoman and Austro-Hungarian empires which had been confronting each other along the so-called *Militärgrenze* for centuries. Therefore, the circumstances of this 'historical region' should not be compared to other more flourishing socio-economic areas of the Ottoman Empire such as the Mesopotamian plain or the Nile valley.

To make matters worse, in the Balkans there was a degeneration of the patrimonial system based on land grants (at first non-hereditary) by the sultan to his soldiers and administrators in exchange for tax-collecting and soldier recruitment from the local populations. This distortion caused a widespread occurrence of a form of hereditary and parasitic latifundism based on the *çiftlik* regime, a type of ownership similar to allodial property that would be abolished only thanks to reforms in the nineteenth century *(tanzimat)* (Adanir 1979, 31). Indeed, in the last European ramparts of the Ottoman Empire, such as Albania and Macedonia *çiftlik* was abolished only in the 1920s.

Autonomous peasants, i. e. not subject to the *çiftlik* regime, as the case of Bulgaria ideal-typically shows, lived nearly exclusively in the mountainous regions and had to cultivate small, scarcely productive plots of land which yielded only a meagre subsistence.

The Balkans' destiny within the 'world-system' was thus to become a 'periphery of the periphery' after being a marginal part of what Wallerstein calls an 'external area': a situation whose consequences endure to this day.

Eastern Europe

This European periphery roughly corresponds to the third 'historical region' described by Szücs, not including however the vast area south of the Carpathian. Therefore, it is the territory that belonged to the defunct Russian Empire west of the Ural Mountains, which then spread south of the Caucasus with the incorporation of marginal external areas, such as Georgia and Armenia, between 1801 and 1878.

During its first centuries this enormous country was an 'external area' as regards to the 'world-system', as Fernand Braudel underlines, with a distinctive socioeconomic system (Braudel 1986, 492–520). A communitarian land property regime *(mir, obščina)* and a peculiar land patrimonialism by which an imperial 'official' 'arrogated' property administrated on behalf of the tsar were the socioeconomic structure's cornerstone.

On the one hand, the peasant communities' agricultural activities were characterised by an extremely low productivity, by the endurance of obsolete farming methods and an archaic technology (Riasanovsky 1984, 429–434; Gerschenkron 1965). It is not surprising that in the late nineteenth and early twentieth century some enlightened reformists, such as prime minister Stolypin, tried, nearly always in vain, to replace communitarian ownership with an individual one (Riasanovsky 1984, 415–417). On the other hand though, the patrimonial ownership system was characterised by a marked absenteeism of the beneficiaries and by an obsolete and parasitic latifundistic production.

Due to these two reasons, historians compared the situation engendered by such a structural peculiarity, which lasted up to the Russian Revolution (1917), to a 'bog of misery' (Riasanovsky 1984, 415). However, East Europe's gradual integration in the 'world-system' beginning in the eighteenth century, would always be wanting. From then on, Russia continued to be a European 'external area' and never became an actual periphery or a core-state as other 'historical regions' already described.

Peripheries in the core and cores in peripheries

The new international division of labour and the establishment of the 'world-system' have not rigidly and concisely differentiated the European continent. There are significant asymmetries within each 'historical region'. In other words, there are peripheries in the core, such as Scotland, Ireland and some mountainous or isolated regions in the Alps or the Pyrenees for example, and 'micro-cores' in peripheries, such as some commercial ports on the eastern part of the Baltic (Königsberg, Danzig/Gdansk, Riga and other Hanseatic cities etc.), on the Adriatic (Ragusa/Dubrovnik), on the Aegean (Thessalonica, Smyrna/Izmir), and on the Black Sea (Odessa).

'Historical regions' and present socioeconomic gaps

If reference is made to historical processes that established and afterwards characterised the social organisation and economic structure of the 'world-system', particularly of Europe's 'historical regions', this is due first of all to a socio-anthropological concern regarding the present relevance of the course of history. Indeed, the establishment of the 'world-system' and the growth of a new international division of labor, which molded the European core and peripheries, are the primary components of an epochal historical change whose socioeconomic and cultural consequences are still visible and acting to this day.

The gaps that appeared between Europe's 'historical regions' during the establishment of the 'world-system' are still plain to see. The north-south gap within the Old Continent mirrors past historical socio-structural and economic differences between the core and the Mediterranean periphery. To date, even the integration of these two 'historical regions' within the European Union has not eliminated the gap. The so-called 'enlargement towards the East' of the European Union is a problematic issue, due specifically to west-east discrepancies (and not only to fifty years of Socialism) that embody old boundaries between the European core and the central-east periphery. The Balkan situation, which is characterised by a feeble industrialisation and an incomplete modernisation from a socio-cultural and economic viewpoint, is due to the fact that for centuries this area was a *periphery of the periphery*. Finally, present-day Russia with its distinct 'development model' torn between capitalistic models and (pre)Socialist communitarian revivals, is adhering to its typical 'tradition' of lingering on the borders of the 'world-system'. The core-periphery gaps are detectable not only inter-regionally but also within the states. In fact, states that straddle 'historical regions' have strongly 'dualistic' societies, economies, and cultures. For example, Italy is divided into north and south; Spain has discrepancies between Catalonia and the Spanish Basque Country on one side, and the rest of the country on the other; in former Czechoslovakia there were differences between Bohemia and Slovakia; in former Yugoslavia, Slovenia and Croatia were more connected to the core, while Serbia, Bosnia and Macedonia belonged to the southeast periphery.

Perceived gaps: core and peripheral identities

Core-periphery gaps go beyond structural data. They are also 'lived', therefore 'perceived' and 'constructed' realities that shape each specific European identity.

In fact, in the core there is a feeling of belonging dominated by the concept of 'techno-economic and social progress', of 'human perfectibility' and based on the values of enlightened rationalism, of 'secularised and individualised societies', of the 'spirit of capitalism', etc. Max Weber would have described such identities as 'disenchanted' ones. Maybe the most fitting description of this type of identity is precisely the one supplied by Max Weber in his model on 'Occidental uniqueness'

(Weber 1978), which, despite what Max Weber intended to prove, was used to validate European superiority and the core's hegemonic aims on the peripheries.

In European peripheries instead, especially among the intellectual élites, there is an awareness of the 'marginality' if not the 'backwardness' of one's country or its 'historical region'. However, there is also a strong belief that one's 'nation' or 'people' have outstanding 'excellence' and 'virtues'. 'Peripheral élites' have been coping with the discrepancy between their nation's perceived socioeconomic 'inferiority' and its presumed spiritual and moral 'superiority' even on the brink of forming their respective nation-states. European peripheries' ruling classes' interpretation of this apparent contradiction has been remarkably ambivalent as regards to relationships with the core as a socioeconomic and cultural complex. Quoting Reinhard Bendix's terminology, the core is looked upon as a 'reference society' with whom there is both an 'identification' and a 'distinction' relationship (Bendix 1978). An emulation of the core is encouraged while dissociation is maintained as well. Over the past one hundred fifty years, almost every European periphery underwent major modernisation processes, emulating the core, which included all aspects of society. However, these processes were accompanied by 'archaistic' counter-trends (agrarian populist movements, nationalisms, etc.), which instead glorified what was deemed as the 'past', 'tradition', 'culture', and ' primordial identity' of one's group. Therefore, a modernisation drive, which also spawned several world-renowned avant-garde movements (especially in the arts, formal logic, mathematics and humanities), and a nativistic revival are both at work.

A modernisation drive basically means 'Europeanisation' particularly of politics (establishment of parliamentary institutions and legal systems molded on the core's ones), economy (industrialisation), culture (more theaters, art museums, avant-garde arts, etc.), and even everyday life (new habits, conventions and/or ephemeral fads from the capitals of 'reference societies', such as Paris, Vienna or Berlin). Nativistic revival means stressing one's 'difference' to be distinguished from the core, revitalizing 'imagined' social institutions - guardians and bearers of 'primordial virtues' – such as the village (Romania, Hungary, Poland, Portugal), rural community (Serbia, Bulgaria, Albania), medieval municipality (Italy), guilds (Italy, Spain, Portugal) etc.

The Europe of political separations and ethno-cultural cultural homogenisations: The 'new' order of nation-states

Since the nineteenth century, capitalist economy expansion in 'world-system' Europe has been accompanied by a proliferation of nation-states. They were established in the Old Continent (except maybe the United Kingdom) through a combination or a separate use of two main models that were first conceived in France and Germany (Brubaker 1992). Notwithstanding some differences, both concepts are based on the *Staatsnation* (nation-state) doctrine, a German term of French origin *(Etat-nation)*, by which each 'nation' is entitled to its own territorial State and each State must include only one 'nation'.

A mono-ethnic territory within specific boundaries is therefore an essential goal that each nation-state must absolutely strive to achieve. Because of this ideal, the last two centuries have been marked by repeated efforts to make single national territories more and more ethnically and culturally homogeneous. Considering an extended long-term outlook, from the twelfth to the seventeenth century Western Europe was overrun by several homogenisation waves in the shape of religious conflicts and persecutions that were essential to the establishment of future 'Staatsnationen' in this area of the Old Continent. However, even in the more culturally homogeneous nation-states of Western Europe such as France, assimilation processes actually continued up to the end of the nineteenth century (Weber 1976). In Central and East Europe instead, where the 'Staatsnation' doctrine was applied only after the downfall of the multicultural empires *(Vielvölkerstaaten)*, the processes of 'ethno-cultural recomposition' aimed at nation-states' 'ethnic purity' were implemented only during the nineteenth and twentieth century through an impressive and ongoing series of boundary revisions, forced assimilations, expulsions, aimed and planned immigrations, deportations, purifications and ethnic wars, genocides, etc.

Four main periods can be identified in the various processes of 'ethnic separation' that over the last two centuries concerned the European nation-states especially in the central and eastern part of the Old Continent. Their virulence was laden with consequences for Europe's entire setup.

The first period was predominantly in the Balkans immediately after the creation of the first nation-states in the nineteenth century. Vast sections of population of Turkish origin or just of Muslim faith were forced to leave the region. As administrators and civil servants of the Ottoman Empire, they did indeed represent the hated occupiers, but members of social strata that had nothing or little in common with the ruling class were involved in the expulsion process as well. During the great 'Crisis in the Orient', which led to the bloody Russian-Turkish War, from 1875 to 1878 alone a million and a half people were repatriated. At that time and for the area involved, it was an exceptional movement of people.

The second virulent phase took place between 1913 and 1925. It was characterised by the forced transfer of entire ethnic minorities, yet it was internationally recognised and guaranteed. In the diplomatic language of those days, it was euphemistically termed 'population exchange'. Some examples illustrate the 'homogenisation' strategies through 'ethnic separation'. Substantial groups of Albanians from Kosovo and western Macedonia were transferred to Turkey after the Balkan Wars (1913) mainly because of their religion. Particularly after the creation of the Kingdom of the Serbs, Croatians, and Slovenians (renamed Kingdom of Yugoslavia after 1929), Muslim populations were substituted by Serbs, Montenegrins, Croatians, and Slovenians with the intention of 're-Slavizing' the region. The alleged 'population exchange' between Greece and Turkey was even more dramatic. It was decreed by the Treaty of Lausanne in 1923, which ratified a series of reciprocal expulsions and hasty repatriations caused by the Greek military catastrophe during the reckless campaign in Asia Minor. After the tremendous defeat, Greece was overrun by refugees from the coasts of western Anatolia plus the Greeks from the Black Sea area and the Caucasus who since 1917 had been fleeing the new Bolshevik régime's repressions. A country with a population of 4.5 million faced the arrival of 1.3 million refugees. At the same time, the 'population exchange' provided for the departure of the 'inhabitants of Muslim faith', mostly Turks, but also Albanians.

The third phase of 'ethnic homogenisation' includes the decade between 1940 and 1950 that was marked by the Nazi policy of annihilation, transfer, and expulsion of entire ethnic groups, and by Stalinist deportations and purges. Along with the holocaust of the so-called 'transnational minorities', i. e. Jews and Roma, there were massive population movements in all of central and eastern Europe, which considerably changed the ethnic map of this part of the continent. Eleven and a half million Germans were expelled from the 'Ostgebiete' (eastern territories) while three million Poles, two million of which from the regions that became part of the Soviet Union after World War II, were re-settled in Silesia and in the southern portion of East Prussia. In this way Poland became an almost mono-ethnic country, quite consistent with the 'Staatsnation' ideal.

Even the treaties between Czechoslovakia and Hungary and between the latter and Yugoslavia, which provided for reciprocal 'population exchanges' as well, date back to the same period immediately after World War II. Finally, Stalin consolidated his conquests in the western part of the Soviet Union through a policy of 'planned', and often imposed 'mobility'. On the one hand, this involved the deportation of populations considered 'accomplices of the enemy', therefore 'traitors of the Great Patriotic War' (Latvians, Lithuanians, Estonians, etc.), to Siberia or Central Asia. On the other hand, it involved substituting them with more 'reliable' immigrants mainly of Slavic origin, such as Russians, Belorussians, and Ukrainians.

The fourth virulent phase of 'ethnic homogenisation' is the wave of 'ethnic separations' that has devastated Central and Eastern Europe over the past fifteen years. It can be traced back to Socialist Bulgaria with its alleged solution of minority problems. At that time, in the second half of the 1980s, the solution was to expel and/or forcibly assimilate 'ethnic Turks'. The phase continued with the disintegration of the three countries that had been born after World War I via a multiethnic and multinational 'logic', namely Yugoslavia, the Soviet Union, and Czechoslovakia. New and old states, originated from this last process, are also all based on the 'Staatsnation' principle.

This latest wave of 'separations', which aims at the homogenisation of territories with highly differentiated ethnic structures and claimed by one or more 'nations', is still in progress as the circumstances in Kosovo and Bosnia prove. Therefore, similar 'ethnic homogenisation' and 'recomposition' processes can be expected to continue in the near future in Europe, particularly in the Balkans and former Soviet Europe.

Globalisation and migrations: 'post-national' Europe in the making?

Over the last fifty years of the twentieth century and the beginning of the current one, there have been relevant population movements in Europe, the most outstanding characteristic of this period. These migrations for economic (job seekers) or political, i.e. humanitarian (asylum seekers) reasons, have currently affected Western Europe rather than Central-East Europe. Up to 1989, Soviet hegemony in this area allowed only a limited and often planned mobility, although immigrant laborers are not totally lacking (Vietnamese in Bulgaria, former Czechoslovakia, the German Democratic Republic, and the USSR as well). Within the EU and its former community institutions (E.C.S.C., E.C.M., EEC, EC), a gradual albeit slow frontier abatement amongst member states has eased transnational mobility. Since the late 1950s, unprecedented numbers of labourers from the Mediterranean and Southeast peripheries (Italy, Spain, Portugal, Greece, and former Yugoslavia) have reached the core (France, Germany, Austria, Switzerland, Benelux, United Kingdom, and Scandinavia). Here they found jobs in industry (heavy industry, construction industry, etc.) and in fields that are not sought after by the 'autochthonous' population because they are considered low status activities. From the 1970s onwards, these immigrants were joined by an increasing number of labourers from the Mediterranean area bordering on the Old Continent (Turkey and the Maghreb). Although to date some countries, as Germany and Switzerland, challenge this denomination, northwestern European countries became 'immigration societies' in this period, notwithstanding strict measures introduced in the early 1970s regulating the permanent entry of foreigners.

The circumstances in Euro-Mediterranean former 'emigration societies' (Italy, Spain, Portugal, Greece), which in the meantime have become 'immigration countries' instead, are slightly different from Northwestern Europe's situation. Migration is mainly from so-called Third World countries (Sub-Saharan Africa, Southeast Asia, China, the Indian subcontinent, Latin America, etc.), and from the Old Continent's most underdeveloped areas (Albania). From the end of the 1980s, however, what became known as 'mass unemployment' worsened in all Western Europe. Therefore, recruitment of foreign workers fell drastically while political and humanitarian immigration increased.

At the same time, large numbers of migrants reached the core from non-European regions and former Socialist bloc countries after the fall of the Berlin Wall (1989) and the subsequent opening of frontiers. Facing a difficult socio-political transformation and an unstable economy, Central-East Europe is not the preferred destination for these migrants who regard it only as a stopover on their way to Western Europe. Therefore, former 'Real Socialism' countries become a 'buffer zone' for the time being.

A transnational characteristic is specific to migrations in Europe from the second half of the twentieth century on. In the first place, from a socio-cultural as well as an economic viewpoint, this implies that the 'new' globalisation-era migrants do not totally break off from their original societies nor become completely assimilated by their societies of residence. Thanks to extensive networks of social relations, modern means of communication, media, etc., they maintain strong relations with their communities of origin. On the other hand, the second and third generations especially, though maintaining these ties, have taken on many social models of the European societies in which they were born and reared. However, transnational migration has increased what may be called the 'social production of difference'.

The above-mentioned migratory circumstances therefore have deeply changed present-day Europe's setup, calling in question the socio-cultural order created by nation-states that is based on the ideal of a mono-ethnic territory. The growing presence of diasporas, transnational groups, creolised communities, and deterritorialised collectivities in Europe's social and cultural setting, plus minorities' emphatic claims and demands (linguistic, religious, and ethnic), have fired discussions on nation-state adequacy and the need for 'postnational' organisations with new types of 'transnational' or 'multiple' citizenships, as Jean-Marc Ferry (1992), Stéphane Pierré-Caps (1995) or Heinz Kleger (1997) foresee.

However, such projects will be for the later part of the twenty-first century since for the time being the nation-state is the political and socio-cultural guideline in Europe both internationally (UN, NATO, OSCE, EU, etc.) and regionally from which different types of autonomism, Euro-regionalism, federalism, 'devolution', and separatism (Catalonia, Galicia, Spanish Basque Country, Corsica, Flanders, Walloon Provinces, Wales, Scotland, 'Padania', etc.) continue to draw inspiration when they pursue an organisational form for their intent.

European nation-states, as distinguished globalisation experts rightly uphold (Castells 1997), have ceded portions of sovereignty to 'global governance' institutions (especially the European Union, NATO and World Trade Organization), as well as to local entities that were born of the various demands for decentralisation and the implementation of the subsidiarity principle. We cannot deny, however, that despite the globalisation process the nation-state and its identity constructions are still the predominant model of the current political-social and cultural structure both in Europe and elsewhere.

Conclusions

The notion of Europe is linked to the mirror-like construction of its opposite, i. e. to what may be very broadly described – given its modifications through the various epochs – as 'Anti-Europe'. Compared to other continents, Asia played a major role in the production of an 'Anti-Europe' carried out by the inhabitants of the Old Continent and even more so by its political and cultural elites. In these inventions of Asia as 'Anti-Europe', we come across representations of a mysterious, dangerous, unruly, cruel, feared, 'orientalised' Asia, yet more or less openly admired for its cultural diversity. Maybe the reason of these visions lies in the fact that Europe's eastern boundary is undetermined and undeterminable. In other words, as French writer Paul Valéry stated, maybe the Old Continent is merely a small peninsula of the Asian continent (Valéry 1934, 23). To sum up,

- Europe cannot be regarded as a socially and culturally monolithic, homogeneous, and consistent unit, but rather as a system of historical regions, which are structurally (inter)dependent and therefore different from each other. This diversity is the outcome of complex *longue durée* historical processes and of ongoing interactions and interrelations.
- The idea of European unity, thus also of United Europe or European Union, must be regarded as the upshots of a social construction by means of which a community of destiny is imagined.
- Internal borders running between historical regions should be regarded as being neither static nor permanent. Borders are continuously redefined and revised by way of the socio-economic dynamics that unfold in history.
- Europe should not even be regarded as a closed system of historical regions. Fixing the Old Continent's external borders would be pointless and would clash with all the foregoing, given the obvious (inter)dependence with the world's other areas.
- However, to envision a generalised transnationalism for Europe now, by which an inevitable elimination of internal and external boundaries is under way, would be tantamount to creating a futurological-like illusion.

References

Adanir, F. 1979: Die makedonische Frage. Ihre Entstehung und Entwicklung. Wiesbaden: Harassowitz.

Anderson, B. 1983: Imagined Communities: Reflections on the Origin and Spread of Nationalism. London: Verso Editions and NLB.

Bendix, R. 1978: Kings or People. Power and the Mandate to Rule. Berkeley CA, Los Angeles, London: University of California Press.

Bloch, E. 1985: Tübinger Einleitung in die Philosophie. Frankfurt am Main: Suhrkamp.

Bloch, M. 1937: Les deux Allemagnes rurales. In: Annales d'histoire économique et sociale 9, no.6, 606–610.

Braudel, F. 1979: Civilisation matérielle, économie et capitalisme, XVe–XVIIIe siècle. Le temps du monde. 3 vols. Paris: Librairie Armand Colin.

Braudel, F. 1982: La Méditerranée et le monde méditerranéen a l'époque de Philippe II. 2 vols. Paris: Librairie Armand Colin.

Braudel, F. 1986: Sozialgeschichte des 15.–18. Jahrhunderts. Aufbruch zur Weltwirtschaft. München: Beck Verlag.

Brubaker, R. 1992: Citizenship and Nationhood in France and Germany. Cambridge MA, London: Harvard University Press.

Brunner, O. 1968: Neue Wege der Verfassungs- und Sozialgeschichte. Göttingen: Vandenhoek & Rupprecht.

Castells, M. 1997: The Power of Identity. Cambridge: Polity Press.
Dainelli, G. 1933: Le ragioni geografiche di una civiltà europea unitaria. In: Fondazione Alessandro Volta (ed.), L'Europa. Convegno di scienze morali e storiche della Fondazione Alessandro Volta, 14–20 Novembre 1932, Rome: Regia Accademia d'Italia, 47–69.
Dobb, M. 1946: Studies in the Development of Capitalism. London: George Routledge & Sons Ltd.
Ferry, J. M. 1992: Pertinence du postnational. In: J. Lenoble, N. Dewandre (eds.), L'Europe au soir du siècle. Identité et démocratie (Paris: Editions Esprit), 39–57.
Fondazione Alessandro Volta (ed.) 1933: L'Europa. Convegno di scienze morali e storiche della Fondazione Alessandro Volta, 14–20 Novembre 1932. Rome: Regia Accademia d'Italia.
Gerschenkron, A. 1965: Economic Backwardness in Historical Perspective. In: The Cambridge Economic History of Europe. Cambridge: Cambridge University Press, vol. vi, pt. 2, 706–767.
Kaser, K. 2002: Südosteuropäische Geschichte und Geschichtswissenschaft. Wien: Böhlau Verlag.
Kleger, H. (ed.) 1997: Transnationale Staatsbürgerschaft. Frankfurt am Main: Campus.
Löwith, K. 1990: Der Mensch inmitten der Geschichte. Philosophische Bilanz des 20. Jahrhunderts. Stuttgart: Verlag J. B. Metzler.
Marx, K. 1988: Das Kapital. In: Marx-Engels Werke (MEW), vol. 23. Berlin [Ost]: Dietz Verlag.
Morin, E. 1987: Penser l'Europe. Paris: Gallimard.
Pierré-Caps, S. 1995: La multination. L'avenir des minorités en Europe centrale et orientale. Paris: Editions Odile Jacob.
Riasanovsky, N. V. 1984: A History of Russia. Oxford: Oxford University Press.
Rougemont, D. de 1990: Vingt-huit siècles d'Europe. La conscience européenne à travers les textes d'Hésiode à nos jours. Paris: Bartillat.
Schmitt, C. 1974: Der Nomos der Erde im Völkerrecht des Jus Publicum Europaeum. Berlin: Duncker & Humblot.
Sée, H.; Rebillon, A.; Preclin, E. 1950: Le XVIe siècle. Paris: PUF-Paru.
Stahl, H. H. 1980: Traditional Romanian Village Communities: The Transition from the Communal to the Capitalist Mode of Production in the Danube Region. Cambridge: Cambridge University Press.
Szücs, J. 1983: Vázlat Európa három történeti régiójáról [The three historical regions of Europe). Budapest: Magvetö Könyvkiadó.
Szücs, J. 1990: Die drei historischen Regionen Europas. Frankfurt am Main: Verlag Neue Kritik.
Valéry, P. 1934: La crise de l'esprit. In: Oevres, Variétés I. Paris: Editions de la N.R.F.

Wallerstein, I. 1974: The Modern World-System. Capitalist Agriculture and the Origins of the European World-Economy in the Sixteenth Century. New York, San Francisco, London: Academic Press.
Weber, E. 1976: Peasants into Frenchmen: The Modernization of Rural France, 1800–1914. Stanford CA: Stanford University Press.
Weber, M. 1978: Gesammelte Aufsätze zur Religionssoziologie, 3 vols. Tübingen: J. C. B. Mohr & Paul Siebeck.
Wolf, E. 1982: Europe and the People Without History. Berkeley and Los Angeles: University of California Press.

3

Islamic Roots of Knowledge in Europe

Hans Daiber

Abstract

'Knowledge' (Arab. 'ilm) in Islam means 'religious knowledge' – based on Qur'ān and Sunnah, the Traditions of the Prophet. Scientific knowledge, therefore, was thus often in the service of religion and the philosophical education of man. Scientific and philosophical knowledge became inspired in an increasing manner by the 'foreign sciences', mainly of the Greeks, whose works were translated into Arabic between the eighth and tenth centuries – sometimes through Syriac versions – and stimulated the Arabs to new conclusions and insights, especially in the fields of astronomy, mathematics and medicine. The Arabs transmitted and commented upon Greek works in the fields of philosophy and sciences, because they found them useful for their qur'ānic concept of God as a transcendent being and creator of the world, and for this reason motivated their interest in Aristotelian and Neo-Platonic philosophy. They considered Greek astronomy and mathematics important for their religious architecture or the orientation towards Mecca during their prayers, which required trigonometric knowledge. This mathematical knowledge became the basis for e.g. the development of cartography in the service of the seafarers and led to a critical revision of the Ptolemaic worldview among the Arabs and – under their influence – in Copernicus during the Renaissance in Europe. The mentioned examples of Arab contributions to new scientific and philosophical insights stimulated the rise of sciences in Europe since the tenth century. The occupation of Spain and southern Italy by Muslims from North-Africa, as well as the contacts between merchants from European and Muslim countries led also to cultural exchange between Orient and Occident. From the beginning of its contacts with the Orient, Europe became interested in Arab astronomy, mathematics, medicine and philosophy. Christian translators – mainly in Toledo (Spain) and Italy translated Arabic versions of Greek scientific and philosophical texts and of works by Islamic scholars. These translations became the starting point for new reflections in the field of medieval Christian philosophy and theology, as well as in theoretical and applied sciences, including mathematics, astronomy, alchemy, optics, and medicine. Moreover, the contacts between the Islamic Orient and Europe resulted in the exchange of material goods, agricultural

products, technical skills, and – perhaps most importantly – of ideas, which became decisive for a prosperous Europe on its way from the Middle Ages to Modernity. The impact of Arab-Islamic sciences and thought is mirrored in many of the European languages, which took over a large number of Arabic words, mainly in the fields of trade and science. The most remarkable echo of those contacts are the so-called 'Arabic numerals', replacing the complicated system of Roman numerals.

Introduction

In view of the religious, political and economic role of Islam in past and present we should not forget, that Islam, in addition, describes a rich culture which had a crucial function in the dialogue of civilisation, and which can continue to do so. 'Dialogue' means also '*encounter* of civilisations', followed by the reception, assimilation, and transformation of knowledge, including religious knowledge. We are told that the Prophet Muḥammad restored the divine message of the prophets in the Old Testament that had been considered distorted by Jews and Christians. His revelation, the Qur'ān, became the foundation of a world religion, which in its concept of belief as a combination of knowing and doing, knowledge *(ʿilm)* and practice *(ʿamal)*, intended to combine religiosity and scientific knowledge (Daiber 1991, slightly revised in Daiber 2008, chap.1; Daiber 1993).

Religion could inspire to the acquisition of knowledge, which as part of universal knowledge for the benefit of mankind appears to be transmitted to other cultures. An example is the history of Islam, which as culture could profit from the cultural heritage of those countries which became part of an Islamic empire reaching in the Middle Ages from Spain in the West until India in the East. In the eighth and ninth centuries, Muslims became acquainted with Greek scientific and philosophical works (Gutas 1998; Daiber 2008, chap. 3). The Abbasid caliph al-Ma'mūn (r. 813–833) organised translations from Greek into Arabic in the library and intellectual meeting-place called *Bayt al-Ḥikmah,* 'house of wisdom'. Christians – among them the famous Ḥunayn b. Isḥāq (d. 873) and his school – translated for the caliphs Greek medical works by Hippocrates and Galen, sometimes from a Syriac version. Apart from the field of the political astrology in the service of the caliphs astronomical works, together with mathematical books on trigonometry were translated, because their practical use met the demands of religion, like the correct orientation at Mecca and timekeeping in the performance of prayer or the orientation of religious architecture (King 1999, 2005). Scientific works by Aristotle were translated, as they offered – in the service of qur'ānic cosmology and ethics – an encyclopaedic knowledge of earth, heaven and physics, of animals, as well as of psychology and the ethics of man. Moreover, Aristotle's logical works provided Muslim scholars with a useful tool for argumentation in the field of theology. Theologians developed a basically qur'ānic concept of God and His attributes by stressing the transcendence of God. This instigated the Muʿtazilites to their thesis of the createdness of the visible Qur'ān and favoured – in the person of the philosopher al-Kindī (d. c. 866) – the early interest in Neo-Platonic works on the transcendence and undescribability of God, combining them with Aristotle's thought, as outlined in his *Metaphysics*. Lesser known was Plato, whose works apparently were available to the Arabs merely in the shape of paraphrases and inspired the philosopher al-Fārābī (d. 950) to his ideal of a society whose different classes cooperate in a harmonious manner and under the rule of a God-inspired leader with the qualities of a philosopher and prophet.

The sketched reception of Greek culture and its amalgamation with Islam appears as a model of the dialogue of cultures, which has had a remarkable continuation in medieval Europe. Greek philosophy and science and their development into new conclusions and insights within an Islamic worldview became the basis for the genesis of a particularly European culture in the Middle Ages, especially of science and philosophy.

The role of Muslim Spain and Sicily as transmitters of knowledge to Christian Europe

Prerequisites for the transfer of Greek knowledge and their transformation within Islamic civilisation were manifold: the expansion of the Islamic empire to Europe – to Spain and Sicily in particular – was the main raison for the increasing influence of Islamic civilisation on that continent. This expansion appears as a continuation of the old tradition of the nomadic *razzia* with the aim to acquire booty. *Jihād* is primarily not the (armed) struggle against the 'infidel'. The submission of non-Muslims was not primarily motivated by the aim to convert them to Islam, but also by the political-economic aim to fill the public treasury non-Muslim monotheists, like Jews and Christians, were allowed to keep to their religion and received the status of 'protected persons' *(ahl al-dhimmah)*. This status was conditioned on the payment of poll-tax which became an extra increase of the budget.

Since the year 710, Muslims from North Africa invaded Spain and, in 732, a raiding expedition reached Tours and Poitiers in central France, where the expansion of the Arabs to the North was stopped by the Frankish *majordomo*, Charles Martel. Since then, the Arabs concentrated their raids on Spain. In 756, the emir ʿAbd al-Raḥmān I became the first ruler of the Umayyad dynasty of Cordova. Islamic Spain reached its height of power during the reign of ʿAbd al-Raḥmān III (r. 912–961), whose son, al-Ḥakam al-Mustanṣir (al-Ḥakam II), was a highly educated man who aspired to combine the knowledge of the literary Islamic heritage with the study of the history of Spain as part of the history of Islam – within the context of peaceful coexistence of Christians and Muslims (Fierro 2005, Wasserstein 1990–91). This is shown by his interest in the genre of Christian universal history, including the history of the Iberian peninsula that was written by the Iberian priest Orosius in the fifth century, translated from Latin into Arabic by the Goth Ḥafṣ b. Albar at the beginning of the tenth century, and used in the middle of that century by the Andalusian historian Aḥmad al-Rāzī in his *Akhbār mulūk al-Andalus* (Daiber 2007).

The changing relations between Muslims and Christians and the declining fortunes of the former in Spain, which finally led to the withdrawal of the Almohads *(al-Muwaḥḥidūn)* from Spain after 1223, to the fall of Cordova in 1236, Seville in 1248 and Granada in 1492, did not exclude intensive cultural contacts between Muslims and Christians and the transfer of knowledge to Europe in the field of theoretical and practical sciences, as well as philosophy. The disintegration of the Umayyad state of Islamic Spain in the eleventh century did not exclude the flourishing of art and letters in the following period of rivalling local rulers, known in Spanish history as the 'party kings' *(reyes de taifas)*. Their dissensions favoured the advance of the Christians, who in 1085 recaptured Toledo, which subsequently became a centre of learning where the Church patronised Latin translations of Arabic philosophical and scientific works. A similar picture we get from the invasion of the Arabs in Sicily, which after first raids already in 652 was occupied by the North African Aghlabids in the ninth century. They were followed, in the tenth century, by the Fatimids, under whose rule the Islamic culture spread in Sicily and left a deep impact on that country. Although the Arab occupation did not last as long as in Spain and although, since the first half of the eleventh century, Sicily was recaptured by the Normans, it remained nevertheless a part of Islamic civilisation for quite some time, to the extend that the Norman king of Sicily, Roger II (r. 1130–1154), and his grandson, the Holy Roman emperor Frederick II of Hohenstaufen (r. 1215–1250), have even been called 'the two baptised sultans of Sicily'.

The increasing expansion of the Islamic dominions in Spain and Sicily gave the Christians in medieval Europe an idea of the power of Islam. Already the Frankish king and subsequent Roman emperor Charlemagne (r. 768–814) found it opportune to have diplomatic relations with the Abbasid caliph Hārūn al-Rashīd and with his enemy in the West, the Umayyad emir in Spain. Such diplomatic relations, in addition to the mercantile contacts and the Christian pilgrimages from Northern Spain and Italy to the shrine of Santiago de Compostela – according to a legend, the resting place of the mortal remains of the apostle St. James which, in 997, was attacked and plundered by Al-Ḥājib al-Manṣūr, the de facto ruler of Muslim Spain in the late tenth to early eleventh centuries, who is known in Spanish history as 'Almanzor' – and finally the obligation of the Pope (since around 880) to save Rome from attacks by Muslims by annual tribute payment to them, shaped the picture of Islam, which was perceived as a 'danger' to Christendom, and prepared the ground for the Christian Crusades and the Reconquista in Spain since the eleventh century.

The contacts between Muslims and Christians in Spain and Sicily since the eighth century and the presence of Europeans in the Middle East during the Crusades led to cultural contacts between Islam and Europe which explain the adaptation of many Islamic elements in European medieval civilisation. This process was strengthened through mercantile contacts between Europe and the followers of Islam, which is often referred to as a 'religion of traders' in the tradition of the merchants of early Mecca – although there was never a correlation between Islamic religion and trade. European countries under Muslim rule, like Spain and Sicily, imported cultural goods and material luxuries which enabled them to continue their lifestyle. Non-Muslim neighbours became impressed by this and by the self-confidence of Muslims. Intermarriage gave rise to new Muslim communities in occupied areas, and this accelerated the assimilation of Islamic civilisation. The trade with non-Muslims in occupied areas became a first bridge of the transfer of goods for the daily life, of new technologies and new ideas (details: Lombard 2005).

From the ninth century onwards, the Arabs dominated with their fleets, and even through pirates, most of the Mediterranean, with the exception of the Byzantine Adriatic and Aegean. Since the second half of the tenth century, the transport of goods from Tunisia, Egypt and Syria was increasingly in the hands of Italian merchants, who operated from Amalfi, Venice, and later from Pisa and Genoa. In exchange for wood, iron, copper, cinnabar, and perhaps also gold, silver, tin, lead and precious or semi-precious stones, the Muslims exported consumer goods (see below), and – for the European textile industry – alum.

As the main vehicle for the exchange of goods was the ship, the Europeans living around the Mediterranean basin profited from techniques of seafaring used by the Arabs, which, subsequently, were further developed by European shipbuilders. I should like to mention here the lateen caravel, which could beat against the wind, the mariner's compass which was known to the Arabs in the thirteenth century (or perhaps earlier) (Needham 1962, 245 ff.; Al-Hassan, Hill 1986, 129), and the nautical charts based on Islamic cartography (Islamic cartography: Harley and Woodward 1992; its reception in Europe: Sezgin 2000, Part 1 and 2). Quite a lot of Arabic terms from the field of seafaring were adopted in European languages, e. g. 'admiral', 'cable', 'shallop' or 'sloop', 'barque'/'bark' or 'monsoon'. The Arabs as seafarers, as travelling merchants, and as conquerors had already early a great interest in cartography. In the middle of the twelfth century, King Roger II of Sicily and his son William I asked the Arab geographer al-Idrīsī (1100–1166) to compose a complete description of the earth, as far as it was known.

The Muslim conquerors in Europe introduced their traditions of agriculture and raised the level of agriculture by using a refined technique of irrigation and by introducing new plants, like apricots, artichokes, aubergines, cotton, lemons, oranges, rice and sugar-cane – all these names have their origin in Arabic. Some newly introduced plants were used for flavouring and colouring, like carthamus or bastard saffron, coriander, henna, madder, saffron and woad. In areas with mulberry trees, silk industry was developed. It is not astonishing that the prerequisite for the introduction of new plants and a refined method of irrigation left its impact on terminology in the Spanish language up to the present day, such as in *acequia* (irrigation ditch), *aljibe* (cistern), or *noria* (irrigation wheel or draw well) (Corriente 1999).

The products of mining and agriculture should guarantee the Arabs in the conquered lands a high standard of living. Muslim Spain produced, also for export to other Islamic and non-Islamic countries, woolen, linen and silk textiles, as well as ceramics. The painting of tiles was introduced to Spain from the East. The manufacturing of crystal was discovered in Cordova in the second half of the ninth century. In this city – the capital of the Umayyad state – we find in the tenth century many craftsmen skilled in the production of fine metal work. They produced vessels or shapes of animals in brass or bronze with silver or gold inlaid work. Others produced jewellery, carvings in wood or ivory, as well as decorative leatherwork, including book-binding.

Perhaps the most impressive impact of the Arabs in Spain is the Islamic architecture, developed to the 'Moorish' style, of which is typical the horseshoe arch, a distinctive feature taken over from Christian Visigothic buildings. However, perhaps the most explicit reflection of the deep impact of Islamic architecture is the Spanish language, in which even terms like *alarife,* 'architect', and *albanil*, 'mason', are remnants of their Arabic origin. It is not astonishing, that in Spanish – aside from architecture – also the fields of administration, commerce and daily life betray the deep influence of Arabic. Here, the so-called Mozarabs (Arab. *al-musta'ribūn*), the Christian 'assimilators of Arabic culture', who during the period of Muslim rule spoke Arabic and in daily life a Romance dialect saturated with many Arabic words, contributed to the 'Arabisation' of Spanish even after the Reconquista, the reoccupation of Muslim Spain by the Christians. As a particular example for the thoroughness of this process, I should like to mention as the today quite common Spanish female first name 'Almudena', which originally is an epithet of the Virgin Mary, the patron saint of Madrid whose statue according to legend was protected in hiding from the Muslims during their rule over the Iberian Peninsula. The name 'Almudena' is probably derived from Arabic *al-mutadayyinah*, 'the pious', 'the godly', and might have been introduced the Spanish by Mozarab circles.

Even under Muslim rule, many Christians of Spain kept to the Islamic or Hispano-Arabic culture, even in the field of poetry, which had an impact on Provençal poetry and the troubadours. The climax of an elevated lifestyle of the Arabs in Europe we find in the field of music. The Arabs invented or developed different kinds of musical instruments. The terms 'lute', 'guitar', 'rebec', and 'naker' betray their Arabic origin. Even books on the theory of music became known to the Europeans through their translation into Latin or Hebrew. The spread and possession of books in Europe became possible through mediation of the Arabs, who already in the middle of the eighth century had learned from some Chinese prisoners of war the fabrication of paper, which replaced the expensive papyrus. Paper was imported to Europe via Spain and Sicily. Rather late – in the fourteenth century – Europeans in Germany and Italy built paper-mills. The existence and spread of paper was vital to the dissemination of Arabic-Islamic literature and sciences in Europe and gave also a fresh impetus to the courts. Frederick II in particular was fond of Arabic-Islamic culture and kept contact with Islamic scholars who partly – in exchange of letters –satisfied his thirst for knowledge in the fields of science and philosophy (Akasoy 2006, Schramm 2001). The emperor even compiled a book on falconry *(De arte venandi cum avibus)* on the basis of Arabic texts and asked Michael Scot to translate for him Arabic scientific books into Latin, among them Aristotle's and Ibn Sina's books on animals (Haskins 1924, esp. pp. 245 ff.).

His interest in Arabic-Islamic sciences and philosophy is a first climax of scientific contacts between Europe and Islamic culture in the twelfth/thirteenth century. They show the respect of Europeans for the Arabic-Islamic achievements and make us aware that Europeans were not only dominated by fear from Islam and on the contrary incorporated Arabic-Islamic sciences into their university curriculum (Rashdall 1987a; Huff 1993, esp. pp. ff., "Western universities and the place of science"). Through their presence in Spain and Sicily, Arabs stimulated the study and Latin translations of Arabic works from the tenth century onwards. The first significant European scholar who was acquainted with Islamic science was Gerbert of Aurillac, known as Pope Sylvester II (pontif. 999–1003). He studied mathematics (and perhaps also astronomy) in Catalonia from 967 to 970 and constructed a new form of abacus by using for the first time Arabic numerals. Possibly, he could use the library of the Catalonian monastery of Ripoll, which owned translations from Arabic works, including treatises on the astrolabe.

In contrast to Spain as a source for the spread of Arabic works on mathematics and astronomy, we find Salerno in southern Italy as a centre for the study of Arabic medicine: in the tenth century we come across the Jew Shabbetai Donnolo writing medical treatises in Hebrew, possibly (since not yet fully investigated) on the basis of Arabic medicine. Above all, in the eleventh century, Constantinus Africanus contributed to a solid knowledge of Arab medicine through his Latin translations of Arabic medical works, among them ʿAlī b. al-ʿAbbās al-Majūsī (fl. tenth century), *Kāmil al-sināʿah* or *al-Kunnāsh al-malikī* (*Liber regius,* also called *Liber pandegni*, a compendium of medicine, using and criticizing Galen and Hippocrates) (Schipperges 1964, esp. pp. 34 ff.; on al- Majūsī see Sezgin 1970: 320 ff.).

Transfer of knowledge, East to West – from the Muslims to medieval Christian Europe

The period between the eleventh and the thirteenth centuries was the great time of translations from Arabic. A centre of translations was Toledo in Spain (López Alvarez and Palomero 1996; Vegas Gonzalez 1998), which was recaptured by the Christians already in 1085, but remained a city of Muslims and Arabic-speaking Jews. Raimundo, archbishop in Toledo from 1125 to 1151, took the chance to make Toledo a centre of scholarship. The translators worked together with Arabic-speaking collaborators, like Ibn Daud, a Jew converted to Christianity, and John of Seville, who worked for Dominicus Gundissalinus (c. 1110–1190). The second great translator in Toledo was Gerard of Cremona (d. 1187), who collaborated with many translators and with a Mozarab called Ghālib or Galippus. Other translators, not belonging to the 'school' of Toledo, were Hugh of Santalla (Hugo Sanctallensis), who translated in the twelfth century Pseudo-Ptolemy's astrological treatise *al-Thamarah (Centiloquium)* into Latin for the bishop of Tarazona. At the same time and in the same region, Hermann the Dalmatian, also known as Hermann of Carinthia (Burnett 1988, 386–404), and the Englishman Robert of Ketton (Chester), later archdeacon of Pamplona, translated works on astronomy and astrology. Moreover, in Barcelona the Italian Plato of Tivoli translated, together with Abraham Bar Ḥiyya (d. after 1136), works on geometry and astronomy from Hebrew and Arabic. Abraham Bar Ḥiyya is an important exponent of Jewish scholarship in Spain, which begins with Hasday b. Shaprut, the court physician of the caliph ʿAbd al-Raḥmān III, and to which also belong Ibn Gabirol (Avicebron, d. 1058), Ibn Ezra (d. 1167), or Maimonides (d. 1204). Jewish scholars who wrote in Arabic and Hebrew, were acquainted with Arabic-Islamic sciences and philosophy, and translated works from Arabic into Hebrew or from Hebrew into Latin. In the thirteeth century, King Alfonso X the Wise (r. 1252–1284) of Castile, who founded institutions of higher education (Rashdall 1987b: 76 ff.), ordered the translation of scientific works into Latin or Castilian (the latter being elevated by him to the status of official language in his realm). Alfonso and his time contributed in an essential manner to the development of astronomy in Europe (Vernet 1983).

The Spanish centres of translations stimulated translators in other countries: Stephen of Pisa in Italy (also known as 'Stephen of Antioch' or 'Stephen the Philosopher') translated for a second time al-Majūsī's already mentioned *Liber regius*. The most influential scientist with a thorough knowledge of the Arabic-Islamic sciences was Adelard of Bath (d. c. 1152), who also translated the astronomical tables of al-Khwārazmī (ninth century) and the *Elements* of Euclid; finally Michael Scot (d. 1232?), who at the court of Frederick II in Sicily translated philosophical and scientific works of Aristotle, the commentaries by Ibn Rushd (Averroes), and Ibn Sīnā's (Avicenna's) book on animals (see above). The given survey of translators has already indicated the main fields of translations, namely mathematics and astronomy, medicine and philosophy. In the following we shall specify these fields and the motives of translations in these fields.

The already mentioned Pope Sylvester II (999–1003), i. e. Gerbert of Aurillac, had no disciples who succeeded him in his dissemination of the use of the more practical Arabic numerals. These numerals were in fact taken over by the Arabs from the Indians in order to replace the clumsy Roman numerals. However, it took more than two centuries until Leonardo Fibonacci (d. c. 1250) from Pisa, who had studied mathematics in Bougie (Algeria), published his *Liber abaci* which facilitated arithmetical operations. This led to the ultimate replacement of the Roman numerals in Europe. The impact of the Arabic numerals is mirrored even in European languages, which, moreover, reveal a remarkable echo of Arabic terminology also in other fields (Aside from earlier referred to relevant literature, see also Al-Sayed 1973; Cannon 1994; Kaye 2005, 223–234; Osman 1992; Sguaitamatti-Bassi 1974; Benhamouda 1996; Lanteri 1991). Arabic *ṣifr*, 'empty', appears as English *cipher,* French *chiffre*, German *Ziffer*, moreover as French and English *zero*. The Arabic word *ṣifr* stands for the sign which indicates that a particular position (unit, ten, hundred etc.) was empty and does not belong to the real ciphers: for this reason it was *nulla figura* (German *Null*, French and English *zero*). Nevertheless, the word standing for *zero* in some European languages became applied to all ten figures (Kunitzsch 2005, esp. pp. 20 ff.).

The mathematician al-Khwārazmī (d. c. 840) from the province Khwarazm in Central Asia (Khiva, Uzbekistan), whose astronomical work we already mentioned, lives forth in the term 'Algorithm'. He is also the author of a work on Algebra *(Al-Jabr wa-l-muqābalah)*, which was translated into Latin by Gerard of Cremona and, again, by Robert of Chester. Besides this translation, the already mentioned Leonardo Fibonacci contributed to the knowledge of Arabic mathematics in Europe (Allard 1996). Here, we should mention one field of applied mathematics, of geometry, in the field of optics: Ibn al-Haytham (965–1041), known in medieval Europe as 'Alhazen', shaped medieval discussions about theories of light until the arrival of Kepler in the seventeenth century. He also worked on the burning mirror and for the first time carried out experiments with the *camera obscura* (Schramm 1963, esp. pp. 211 ff. and 277; Beshara 1977, 149; Lindberg 1976; Lindberg 1996, 716–729). Of similar practical importance in the West became Arabic-Islamic astronomy (Hugonnard-Roche 1996). Apparently, it influenced already in the Carolingian period (eighth/ninth century) the discussions on the calendar among Christians. The Spanish Jew Pedro Alfonso, who in 1106 converted to Christianity, was an expert in Arabic-Islamic astronomy and had a great impact on European astronomers. The astronomical work of the Andalusian scholar al-Zarqalī (d. 1100), especially his astronomical tables, known through its Latin version as 'Toledan Tables', were influential in the Middle Ages (Millás Vallicrosa 1943–1950, esp. chapter 6 ff.). Al-Zarqalī is also the author of a work on the astrolabe, an instrument helpful for travellers and mariners and developed by the Arabs on the basis of Greek mathematical astronomy, apparently already in the eighth/ninth century by al-Fazarī (Sezgin 1978, 124). This might have contributed considerably to the already mentioned development of cartography.

An authority in the field of astronomy until the Renaissance was al-Farghānī (ninth century), whose astronomical work was translated into Latin by Johannes Hispalensis and Gerard of Cremona, who used it in his *Theoria planetarum,* together with al-Battānī (Albatagius), whose work was also available in Latin translations by Plato of Tivoli and Robert of Chester since the early twelfth century. Arab astronomers in some cases offered critical innovations and differed from the Ptolemaic worldview. One of them was Nūr al-Dīn al-Biṭrūjī, a friend of Ibn Ṭufayl. His ideas became known to Albertus Magnus (Albert the Great, d. 1280) through Michael Scot's Latin translation of Biṭrūjī's *Kitāb al-Hay'ah*, which still was influential in the fifteenth century, at the time of the German astronomer Regiomontanus (d. 1476). We get an idea of the strong impact of Arabic-Islamic astronomy on European astronomy from the numerous Arabic terms and names of stars which entered European languages (Kunitzsch 1959, 1983). Recently, it has been shown that Copernicus's (1473–1543) mathematical astronomy in his deviation from Ptolemy follows the planetary theories of Naṣīr al-Dīn al-Ṭūsī from the thirteenth century, which became known to him perhaps through some Arabic manuscripts from the 'school' of al-Ṭūsī already available in European libraries at that time (Saliba 2007, esp. pp.193 ff.).

As in Islamic civilisation, in medieval Europe, too, astronomy often appeared somewhat linked to astrology: knowledge of the influence of the stars and their constellations was of practical importance for the casting of horoscopes. The already mentioned Alfonso the Wise did not only order the translation of astronomical works, but also the Castilian translation of Ibn Abī 'l-Rijāl's (fl. eleventh century) *Kitāb al-Bāri' fī ahkām al-nujūm*. This work was also translated into Latin, which, in turn, became the basis for Hebrew, Portuguese, French and English versions. Together with Abu Maʿshar al-Balkhī's (d. 886) *al-Madkhal al-kabīr* ('The great introduction', i. e. into astrology; see al-Balkhī, ed. Richard Lemay, 1995–1996), translated in 1130 by Johannes Hispalensis, it shaped the cosmological discussions of the twelfth and thirteenth century (Lemay 1962).

The most extensive influence of the Arabs in Europe was in the field of medicine (for more details see the survey and list of major translations of Arabic medical works into Latin in Jacquart 1996). Arabic translations from Hippocrates and Galen (see above) were expanded by practical experience. The medical encyclopaedia *al-Ḥāwī fī 'l-tibb* by Abū Bakr al-Rāzī (d. 925) was translated into Latin *(Liber Continens)* in 1279 by the Jew Faraj b. Sālim in Agrigento, Sicily, and became a reference book of which the 9th part was commented upon in the fifteenth century by Ferrari da Grado in Pavia. Moreover, al- Rāzī's treatise on small pox was translated into Latin and Greek and became one of the most-read medical works in Europe. It was republished many times until the nineteenth century (Sezgin 1970, 283). The most influential medical work, which particularly impressed Western physicians (Borzsák 1981) and which was used as textbook until the seventeenth century, however, was the *Canon* by Ibn Sīnā (d. 1037), who became known in the West as Avicenna. His *al-Qānūn fī 'l-ṭibb* was translated in the twelfth century by Gerard of Cremona and again by Andreas Alpagus (d. 1520). Other eminent medical works by the Arabs that were translated into Latin are the already mentioned compendium *Liber regius* by Haly Abbas (ʿAlī b. al-ʿAbbās al-Majūsī), the *Colliget* by Averroes (d. 1198), medical texts by Ḥunayn (ninth century), Isaac Israeli (d. 932), the ophthalmologic work by ʿAlī b. ʿĪsā (tenth/eleventh century) and ʿAmmār al-Mawṣilī (tenth/eleventh century). Well-known, too, was the chirurgical work by the physician al-Zahrāwī (d. 1013) from Cordova, translated by Gerard of Cremona.

Medical knowledge of the Arabs was spread through the centres Salerno in southern Italy (eleventh century) and Montpellier in southern France (twelfth-thirteenth century), and it is quite imaginable that the first European hospitals since 1200 received inspirations from already existing institutions in the Orient, like those in Baghdad and Damascus. Already in the school of Salerno, the Arabic version of Dioscurides' *Materia medica* played an essential role. Latin versions of selected parts – mostly produced in Toledo in the twelfth century – made the text known to Europeans. Finally, pharmacology received inspirations from the Arabs and used methods of distillation that were developed in alchemy (Needham 1980, 389 ff; on the Latin transmission see Halleux 1996).

Arab alchemy became known in Europe since the twelfth century through Latin translations by scholars like Adelard of Bath, Gerard of Cremona, and Robert of Chester. The influence of what was referred to by the Arabs as *al-kīmīyā'* (further references: Josef Mayerhöfer, ed., 1961), a forerunner of 'chemistry', appears in terms like benzo- (*lubān jāwī*, Javanese or Sumatran benzoin; in benzo the first part lu is omitted, apparently because the first letter was misunderstood as the Arabic determination *al-*; Ullmann, Mojtowytsch-Wielandt 1983, 173a), alcohol or alkali. In the Middle Ages, the term and practice of *al-kīmīyā'* appeared often also in connection with rather doubtful practices, such as the attempt to produce gold by the transformation of metals into their 'primary substance'. It became thus is today referred to as 'alchemy'.

Islamic philosophical thought and medieval Europe

In the following, we shall have a glance at the impact of Islamic philosophical thought on medieval Europe. Islamic philosophy spread in medieval Europe partly in the tow-rope of the Arab scientific works and the Latin translations of Arab astronomical, mathematical and medical books (details: Daiber 1994, slightly revised in Daiber 2008, chapter 6).

Here, too, the central Spanish city of Toledo played an important role. During the twelfth century, it became a centre for Latin translations of Greek-Arabic versions and redactions of works by Aristotle, his commentator Alexander of Aphrodisias (fl. second/third century), and the Neo-platonic philosopher Proclus (410–485) (details: Daiber 1990; slightly revised in Daiber 2008, chapter 5). Besides these translations of Greek authors, who because of the lack of Greek manuscripts became only available in Latin translations of Arabic versions, scholars in Spain concentrated on the translation of Arabic books and treatises that were composed by Muslim philosophers and dealing with actual problems discussed by scholastics. Most of those works dealt with the philosophical problems of the 'unity of the intellect', the 'eternity of the world' and the issue of 'double truth', i. e. the idea held by certain masters at Paris University and condemned by the Church in 1277 as heresy that something might be true according to philosophy but *not* according to the Catholic faith – assuming the possibility of *two* contrary truths in contradiction to the 'truth' of Christian Scripture, making principally possible the existence of 'truth' in the doctrines of other religions, such as Islam.

In their study of *philosophia* – also called *humana scientia* by Dominicus Gundissalinus in his treatise *De divisione philosophiae* (about 1150) and distinguished from the *divina scientia*, i. e. 'revealed knowledge as contained in the Scriptures – the scholars in Toledo, Paris, Naples, and Oxford selected and took over from the Islamic heritage not only what appeared to be useful for the rational interpretation of Scripture, but also that what was perceived as valuable for the development of philosophy and its specific topics. Philosophy, especially dialectics, became thus a tool for the study of the superior aspects of Christian 'revealed truth', i. e. for theology. In medieval Europe, the study of philosophy – and thus also theology – was, in a varying manner, dominated mainly by Aristotle. The selection of the translated texts and their interpretation sometimes betrays the one-sided view of scholastics on Islamic philosophy. A decisive influence on the development of medieval philosophy was carried out by the writings of Ibn Sīnā (Avicenna) and Ibn Rushd (Averroes), whose ideas were partly modified by some writings of the first Islamic philosopher, al-Kindī (Kindius, d. 866), who is often referred to as 'philosopher of the Arabs' *(faylāsūf al-'arab)*. Some treatises by al-Kindī, written in the tradition of Aristotelianism and Neo-Platonism, became known to the West through Latin translations – among them Kindī's treatise on the intellect, which was translated by Gerhard of Cremona and, for a second time, perhaps by Johannes Hispalensis.

Among the philosophical doctrines of Islam, undoubtedly the theory of the intellect was extremely impressive on the scholastics of the Middle Ages. Here, the discussion of this issue by the second great Islamic philosopher, al-Fārābī (d. 950), Ibn Sīnā's adaptation of al-Fārābī's doctrines, and Ibn Rushd's commentary on Aristotle's *On the Soul* were echoed in the writings of Dominicus Gundissalinus (d. after 1181), and in the thirteenth century, in those of Roger Bacon, Bonaventura, Albertus Magnus, and Thomas Aquinas, to name only a few. According this line of philosophical thought, the 'agent intellect' has the task, to lead the human intellect from its potentiality to actuality, to liberate the human intellect from the body and, thus, to pave for it the way to immortality and happiness. This happiness increases through the alliance of the good souls – i. e. the rational souls – in a life full of spiritual contemplation and in an ideal community, without loosing their individuality.

Scholastic philosophers have used, in addition, an Arabic adaptation of Proclus' *Institutio theologica* under the title *Kitāb al-Khayr al-maḥḍ*, which was translated into Latin in the twelfth century by Gerhard of Cremona. His version, entitled *Liber de causis*, in turn, was revised by Dominicus Gundissalinus with the help of the Jew Avendauth. This work was the main source for the transmission of Arab Neo-Platonism in the Middle Ages. It was often quoted and commented upon in the thirteenth century, among others, by Thomas Aquinas and Aegidius Romanus. Albertus Magnus, the teacher of Thomas Aquinas, considered it the culmination of Aristotelian metaphysics. The Neo-platonic heritage of the *Liber de causis* shaped the commentators of Aristotle, above all, in their commentaries on and supplements to Aristotle's treatise *On the Soul*. Here, as well as in other cases, the focus on Aristotle remained the starting-point and determined the selection of texts, which were translated, commented upon and studied by scholars in the Middle Ages. They translated, among others, al-Farabi's commentaries on Aristotle's logic, on Aristotle's book on hermeneutics and rhetoric, as well as two treatises on sciences and their division, entitled *On the Origin of Sciences* and *On the Sciences*.

This particular interest in logic, in the art of definition and in the division of sciences, arose of a practical interest in the art of disputation and argumentation, which included philosophy and natural sciences in an equal manner. It corresponds to an increasing interest in rational-scientific thinking since the eleventh century, which increasingly preferred reason to purely theological authority. This, in turn, motivated an encyclopaedic interest in *all* branches of sciences. Al-Fārābī's encyclopaedic interest was taken over by Ibn Sīnā, who was, besides Ibn Rushd, perhaps the most important Muslim philosopher. Ibn Sīnā became known in the Middle Ages mainly through Latin translations of his encyclopaedia *al-Shifā'* ('The Healing') and of his already mentioned *Canon*. Ibn Sīnā's encyclopaedia – an adaptation of Aristotelian sciences that was integrating al-Fārābī's doctrine of prophecy and adding to it a mystical component – was often quoted by scholastics of the thirteenth century in Oxford and Paris as an explanation of Aristotle.

According to Ibn Sīnā's essentially Neo-platonic view, the soul is something spiritual, which can perceive itself, without requiring an instrument, the body. For this reason, the act of thinking in man, his rational cognition, does not require – contrary to Aristotle – sense-perception. Accordingly, the body is not the essence of man, but the ego of man, which becomes 'the centre of human individuality'. This new accentuation in Ibn Sīnā is echoed in Albertus Magnus' doctrine of the soul as the shaping principle of the body – a doctrine which his pupil Thomas Aquinas modified further. This new accentuation became meaningful for the problem of immortality, which was discussed often in the Middle Ages. Because, according to Ibn Sīnā, the activity of the soul is not primarily dependent upon the body, the soul continues to exist after the death. This point view of Ibn Sīnā, which modifies Aristotelian psychology, was taken over in the Middle Ages.

In particular, Ibn Sīnā developed the principle of individuation through matter, which, too, was discussed frequently in the Middle Ages and which excluded any possibility of the transmigration of the soul. The immortality of the soul, implied in this doctrine, as well as her classification as substance, as individual being, results from an argument, which was well-known in the Middle Ages and which presupposes Ibn Sīnā's distinction between essence and existence: even someone, who is born completely developed, but who is not conscious of his body, already has knowledge, some kind of a 'first intuition' of his individual being. This individual being, the essence 'being man', does not require as a condition existence, which is merely something accidental. Therefore, quiddity – comparable to the universals of the philosopher Ockham, who is influenced here by Ibn Sīnā – can exist either as something visible or as general concept in the imagination or finally as something, whose existence is possible, without being bound to the concrete reality or to the imagination. Thomas Aquinas, in his *De ente et essentia*, spoke of fundamental definitions of things, e. g. as 'being' *ens*, because they have 'being' and not because the are 'being'. Only God is the pure being, in which things 'participate'. In a critical manner, this was further developed and modified by Meister Eckhart (d. 1328) and Raimundus Lullus (d. 1316) (on Raimundus see Daiber 2004a; shorter English version in Daiber 2005).

Within the context of his epistemology and his proof of God's existence from the contingency of the beings, Ibn Sīnā (Daiber 2004b) developed his doctrine of creation, which was echoed frequently in the Middle Ages – especially in Thomas Aquinas – but which was also criticised greatly. The divine cause is the only necessary being by itself. What is created receives its being from this necessary being by itself. Therefore, it is composed from essence and existence and is by itself only something potential. Ibn Sīnā's Neo-platonic doctrine of the eternity and necessity of the creative activity of the divine One and his doctrine of the solely indirect creation through creative intellects result in the assumption, that God does not create the individuals and does not know their acts. This has been discussed and criticised a large deal in the Middle Ages. Thomas Aquinas in particular denied Ibn Sīnā's Neo-platonic system of emanations and blamed him for his doctrine, that God does not know the particulars but only their general structures. At the same time, the scholastic philosophers received from Ibn Sīnā's epistemology, from his distinction between essence and existence, as well as from his doctrine of the soul and its individuation, decisive stimulations. Ibn Sīnā's thought and his adaptation of al-Fārābī's doctrines became known to the Middle Ages not only through Ibn Sīnā's main work *al-Shifā'*. Here, we must also mention a Muslim critic of Ibn Sīnā's philosophy, al-Ghazzālī, Latin Algazel, who died in 1111. He was often classified by the scholastics as a pupil of Ibn Sīnā. As preparatory work to his work *Tahāfut al-falāsifah* ('The incoherence of the philosophers'), he wrote a description of Ibn Sīnā's philosophy (including al-Fārābī's ideas), the *Maqāṣid al-falāsifah* ('The intentions of the philosophers'). This book was translated into Latin in Toledo at the end of the eleventh century by 'Magister Johannes', together with 'Dominicus Archidiaconus' (apparently Gundissalinus) under the title *Summa theorice philosophie*. Al-Ghazzālī's own ideas became known to the Middle Ages not before the fourteenth century, namely through the Latin translation of Ibn Rushd's *Tahāfut al-Tahāfut* ('The incoherence of the incoherence'), a critique of al-Ghazzālī's *Tahāfut al-falāsifah*.

Mainly the doctrines of al-Ghazzālī's 'Incoherence of the Philosophers' caused the scholastics of the Middle Ages to explain Ibn Sīnā in a different manner or to criticise him. Al-Ghazzālī refutes, above all, the following doctrines as unbelief: the eternity of the world without beginning; God's knowledge of the particulars in an universal manner and individual immortality of the soul without resurrection of the body. The last mentioned doctrine contradicts the Islamic doctrine of the resurrection of the body. Here, the Christian dogma of the resurrection of the dead was not only discussed in the Middle Ages with close reference to the New Testament (1. Cor. 15), but reflects also arguments forwarded by al-Ghazzālī in his critique of Ibn Sīnā.

Above all, al-Ghazzālī's theories of causality caused in the Middle Ages many discussions (Perler, Rudolph 2000). Al-Ghazzālī's *Incoherence of the Philosophers* was apparently already known before the appearance of the Latin translation of Ibn Rushd's critique, his *Incoherence of the Incoherence.* Scholars in Spain, for instance, could refer directly to Arabic sources. Quite a lot of Arabic texts seem to have been known to the famous Raimundus Lullus in Mallorca (c. 1235–1316), a critic of Averroes. Lullus composed an Arabic compendium of logic, which is orientated at al-Ghazzālī's *Intentions of the Philosophers*. It is preserved only in a Latin translation *(Compendium logicae Algazelis)* and in a Catalan translation based on it. Such a direct contact and access to the Islamic philosophical tradition – eventually also in an oral exchange of ideas – was, of course, rather an exception.

Most important for the transmission of Islamic philosophical traditions to the Latin Middle Ages became Ibn Rushd, known to Latin medieval Europe as Averroes. He was born in 1126 in Cordova, Spain, and died in 1198 in Marrakesh, Morocco. This philosopher and jurist became known in medieval scholastic thought above all as commentator of Aristotle. A primary role in the dissemination of Ibn Rushd's doctrine in the Middle Ages was played by the Latin translation of his already mentioned refutation of al-Ghazzālī's *Incoherence of the Philosophers*, the *Destructio destructionum*, written around 1180/81. This Latin translation was completed in 1328 by Calonymus Ben Calonymus Ben Meir from Arles in southern France. Besides Ibn Rushd's *Great Commentary* on Aristotle's *On the Soul* and on Aristotle's *Metaphysics* it became one of the most important sources of Averroism in the Middle Ages. Initially, Ibn Rushd kept to Ibn Sīnā's doctrine of God and creation. Later on, however, he abandoned the Neo-platonic doctrine of emanations, which Ibn Sīnā had combined with it and became a severe critic of Ibn Sīnā's philosophy and its model, al-Fārābī. His own model is Aristotle, whose teaching he tried to explain through commentaries. Nevertheless, Ibn Rushd remained obliged to al-Fārābī's and Ibn Sīnā's concept of religion as mirror image of philosophical truth. Consequently, there is strictly speaking no conflict between philosophy and religion. This arises only if texts are not interpreted literally. In the case of difficult texts, the demonstrative method of philosophers is required. Otherwise we must assume that these texts do not indicate whether they should be explained literally or allegorically, i. e. by applying the method of *ta'wīl*.

Apart from the complex philosophy-religion and apart from the doctrine of the intellects and in connection with it the denial of the individual immortality of the soul, the Middle Ages paid much attention to Ibn Rushd's refutation of al-Ghazzālī's criticism of causality, as they found it in Ibn Rushd's *Destructio destructionis*. Ibn Rushd's manner of arguing is often rather complicated and not always plausible. In view of the complexity of Ibn Rushd's manner of thinking and in view of the diversity of other Islamic philosophers, who were accessible in Latin translations, it is not amazing, that medieval philosophers since the thirteenth century took up Ibn Rushd's thoughts in different ways. This observation renders the classification of scholastic philosophers as 'Averroists' more difficult. It is, therefore, problematical to confine the concept of 'Averroism' to those scholastics, who follow Ibn Rushd's doctrine of the intellect, precisely of the unity of the material intellect, the *intellectus materialis* or *possibilis*.

'Averroism', in a broader sense, can already be found among authors who since 1225 composed treatises on the soul. Among those who declared themselves as adherents of Ibn Rushd we find John of Jandun, who taught about 1310 at the University of Paris, or, before him in the thirteenth century, Ferrandus de Hispania. Other scholars in the thirteenth century, like Thomas Aquinas, his teacher Albertus Magnus or Siger of Brabant, refer to Ibn Rushd mainly as commentator of Aristotle, without devoting themselves completely to the philosophy of Ibn Rushd. Moreover, the development of a uniform 'Averroism' was slowed down under the impression of the condemnation of 'Averroistic' doctrines by the bishop Stephan Tempier in 1270 and 1277 in Paris, as mentioned earlier. Tempier had condemned those thoughts of a 'radical Aristotelianism' (van Steenberghen), mainly by Siger of Brabant, which were considered to be incompatible with the Christian revelation and faith and which included 'Averroistic' interpretations. However, no uniform 'Averroism' is to be found. In fact, even central themes of so-called 'Averroism', for example the doctrine of the intellects, which often is called 'monopsychism', and the thesis of the 'double truth', which, in fact, are absent in Ibn Rushd's doctrine of the identity of philosophy and religion, reveal varying tendencies and interpretations, which do not harmonise with the actual intentions of Ibn Rushd.

A glance at the whole range of Islamic thoughts, which entered scholastic philosophy in the Middle Ages and which was criticized, gives an idea of the Islamic contribution to medieval thought: Islamic philosophers stimulated the development of scientific argumentation and the formation of scientific terminology in theological doctrines of the Middle Ages. Through Latin translations of Arabic adaptations by al-Fārābī, Ibn Sīnā, al-Ghazzālī and Ibn Rushd of logical and scientific works by Aristotle, scholastics became acquainted with the art of argumentation and definition, but also with encyclopaedic knowledge of a multitude of considerations in the field of physics and metaphysics. These considerations are concentrated upon: 1) the concept of God; 2) the eternity of the world; 3) the causality, and 4) the doctrine of the intellect and the soul and its immortality. As a by-product and because of a misunderstanding of Ibn Rushd, the theory of the double truth was discussed and the scientific character of theology and its relation to philosophy. Christian theology of creation and Islamic reflection on God's almightiness formed the starting-point of a discussion, which tried to clarify the relation between God, universe and man. The answer offered a hierarchic principle of order in the universe, in which the individuality of man did not receive much free play. As an intellectual being, he is subordinated to the divine active intellect, which, according to Ibn Rushd, actualises what man shares with the whole humankind. As creature of the nature, he is subject to the principle of causality, and herewith ultimately dependent upon the divine first mover. Ibn Rushd and Ibn Sīnā do not follow al-Ghazzālī's orientation, which considers the principle of causality incompatible with God's almightiness. Ibn Sīnā follows here more Neo-platonic doctrines of emanations, whereas Ibn Rushd is mainly shaped by Aristotle, without completely being free from Neo-platonic influence. This becomes evident from Ibn Rushd's doctrine of the active intellect and of the so-called 'monopsychism'. This restriction of individuality was of great consequence for one field of Islamic philosophy, which scarcely received attention among scholastics, i.e. Islamic political philosophy. Al-Fārābī's political writings were not translated into Latin. However, Ibn Rushd's commentary on Plato's *Republic*, which was written because of the lack of an Arabic version of Aristotle's *Politics*, was translated into Latin relatively late – in the fifteenth century – by Elias of Crete, and half a century later by Jacob Mantinus. Both translators used an Arabic-Hebrew version. The Arabic original of this Hebrew version from the fourteenth century is lost. This shows in an exemplary manner the importance of the medieval-Hebrew transmission for our knowledge of Islamic philosophy and for the spread of Islamic political theories in the Middle Ages.

The significance of the Islamic intellectual tradition today

We might end now our survey with an outlook on today. In our own times, Islamic philosophy and the history of sciences in Islam are receiving a new rank. They are estimated as a continuation of Greek philosophy and sciences only insofar, as they appear as a continuation of that seeking after truth, wisdom and scientific progress, which had its origin in ancient Greece. Here, the comparison of sources, of Greek, Arabic, Latin and Hebrew sources, as well as research into the history of the influences of ideas, appear as a hermeneutic way to the finding of truth. We should stress the importance of medieval Jewish and Christian scholastic thought in the Middle Ages for the interpretation of Islamic philosophy. Greek-Syriac-Arabic translations and adaptations of philosophical and scientific texts, as well as Latin and Hebrew versions and adaptations based on Arabic become indispensable tools for the reconstruction and for the 'understanding' of Islamic thought and its diversity. Islamic philosophical-scientific thought turns out to be a historical example of an occupation with problems and recognitions of human thinking. Islamic thought, as part of the universal history of ideas, its mediating role between antiquity and the Middle Ages, hints at the coherence of philosophy and sciences, of philosophy and metaphysics, or Islamic theology. In this way, it can continue to be a source of knowledge, not only in Europe. The history of Islamic thought is not only part of a description of errors of human thought on its way towards the increase of knowledge. Just as little as the occupation with Islamic thought can be motivated by romantic enthusiasm for 'Eastern wisdom', as we find it in the German romanticism of the 18th and 19th centuries and as it might motivated orientalists until the twentieth century, and beyond.

Islamic thought requires and trains the reflection upon contents and methods, as they appear to be exemplified in history. To reflect on them again is a constant challenge to the capacities of the human mind, its creativity and fantasy. The problem of originality and independence of Islamic thought, which has been discussed by Muslim and non-Muslim scholars again and again, looses thus much of its significance.

References

Akasoy, Anna Ayşe 2006: Philosophie und Mystik in der späten Almohadenzeit. Die Sizilianischen Fragen des Ibn Sabʿin. Leiden, Boston: Brill (Islamic Philosophy, Theology and Science. Texts and Studies 49).

Al-Hassan, Ahmad Y.; Hill, Donald 1986: Islamic Technology: An Illustrated History. Cambridge: Cambridge University Press.

Al-Sayed, Sahira A. 1973: A Lexicon and Analysis of English Words of Arabic Origin. PhD dissertation, University of Colorado at Boulder.

Allard, André 1996: The Influence of Arabic Mathematics in the Medieval West. In: Encyclopedia of the History of Arabic Science, ed. Roshdi Rashed, vol. 2. London, New York: Routledge, 539–580.

Al-Balkhī, Abū Maʿshar [Albumasar], ed. Richard Lemay 1995–1996. Liber introductorii maioris ad scientiam judiciorum astrorum, 9 vols. Naples: Instituto Universitario Orientale.

Benhamouda, Boualem 1996: L'origine arabe de la langue française. Paris: Dialogues.

Beshara, Omar Saleh 1977: Ibn al-Haytham's Optics: A Study of the Origins of Experimental Science. Minneapolis, Chicago: Bibliotheca Islamica.

Borzsák, J. 1981: Avicennas Qanun im westlichen Ärztekanon. In: Acta Antiqua Academiae Scientiarum Hungaricae 29, 65–72.

Burnett, Charles 1988: Hermann of Carinthia. In: Peter Dronke (ed.), A History of Twelfth-Century Western Philosophy. Cambridge MA: Cambridge University Press, 386–404.

Cannon, Garland Hampton (with Alan S. Kaye) 1994: The Arabic Contributions to the English Language: An Historical Dictionary. Wiesbaden: Harrassowitz.

Corriente, Federico 1999: Diccionario de arabismos y voces afines en iberorromance. Madrid: Gredos (Biblioteca románica hispánica 5, Diccionarios 22).

Daiber, Hans 1990: Lateinische Übersetzungen arabischer Texte zur Philosophie und ihre Bedeutung für die Scholastik des Mittelalters. Stand und Aufgaben der Forschung. In: J. Hamesse, M. Fattori (ed.), Rencontres de cultures dans la philosophie médiévale: traductions et traducteurs de l'antiquité tradive au XIVᵉ siècle. Louvain-la-Neuve, Cassino, 203–250.

Daiber, Hans 1991: The Qur'an as Stimulus of Science in Early Islam. In: Islamic Thought and Scientific Creativity 2, no. 2, 29–42.

Daiber, Hans 1993: Science and Technology versus Islam: A Controversy from Renan and Afghani to Nasr and Needham and its Historical Background. In: Annals of Japan Association for Middle East Studies 8, 169–187.

Daiber, Hans 1994: L'incontro con la filosofia islamica. In: Pietro Rossi, Carlo A. Viano (ed.), Storia della filosofia, vol. 2: Il medioevo. Rome, Bari, 180–195.

Daiber, Hans 2004a: Raimundus Lullus in der Auseinandersetzung mit dem Islam. Eine philosophiegeschichtliche Analyse des "Liber disputationis Raimundi Christiani et Homeri Saraceni". In: Matthias Lutz-Bachmann, Alexander

Fidora (ed.), Juden, Christen und Muslime. Religionsdialoge im Mittelalter. Darmstadt: Wissenschaftliche Buchgesellschaft, 136–172.

Daiber, Hans 2004b: The Limitations of Knowledge According to Ibn Sina: Epistemological and Theological Aspects and the Consequences. In: Matthias Lutz-Bachmann, Alexander Fidora, Pia Antolic (ed.), Erkenntnis und Wissenschaft. Probleme der Epistemologie in der Philosophie des Mittelalters. Berlin: Akademie Verlag, 25–34.

Daiber, Hans 2005: Raimundus Lullus' Dispute with Homer Saracenus in the Year 1307. An Inquiry into their Theological Positions. In: Maria Isabel Ripoll Perelló (ed.), Actes de les Jornades Internacionals Lullianes "Ramon Llull al s. XXI". Palma, 1, 2 I 3 d'abril de 2004. Palma de Mallorca: Universitat de les Illes Balears, Servei de Publicacions i Intercanvi Científic, 259–264.

Daiber, Hans 2007: Weltgeschichte als Unheilsgeschichte. Die arabische Übersetzung von Orosius' Historiae adversus paganos als Warnung an die Muslime Spaniens. In: Christian North – Muslim South. The Iberian Peninsula in the Context of Cultural, Religious and Political Changes, 11th–15th Centuries [proceedings of a conference, 20–23 June, Frankfurt am Main]. In print.

Daiber, Hans 2008: Islamic Thought in the Dialogue of Cultures. Innovation and Mediation between Antiquity and the Middle Ages. Sarajevo, in print (with a Bosnian translation).

Fierro, Maribel 2005: ʿAbd al-Rahman III, the First Cordoban Caliph. Oxford: Oneworld.

Gutas, Dimitri 1998: Greek Thought, Arabic Culture. The Graeco-Arabic Translation Movement in Baghdad and Early ʿAbbasid Society (2nd–4th/8th–10th Centuries). London, New York: Routledge.

Halleux, Robert 1996: The Reception of Arabic Alchemy in the West. In: Encyclopedia of the History of Arabic Science, ed. Roshdi Rashed, vol. 3. London, New York: Routledge, 886–902.

Harley, J. B.; Woodward, David 1992: Cartography in the Traditional Islamic and South Asian Societies. Chicago, London: University of Chicago Press (The History of Cartography II/1).

Haskins, Charles Homer 1924: Studies in the History of Mediaeval Science. Cambridge MA: Harvard University Press.

Hugonnard-Roche, Henri 1996: The Influence of Arabic Astronomy in the Medieval West. In: Encyclopedia of the History of Arabic Science, ed. Roshdi Rashed, vol. 1. London, New York: Routledge, 284–303.

Huff, Toby E. 1993: The Rise of Early Modern Science. Islam, China, and the West. Cambridge: Cambridge University Press.

Jacquart, Danielle 1996: The Influence of Arabic Medicine in the Medieval West. In: Encyclopedia of the History of Arabic Science, ed. Roshdi Rashed, vol. 3. London, New York: Routledge, 963–984.

Kaye, Alan S. 2005: Arabic Loanwords in English. In: Leila Abu-Shams Pagés, Jordi Aguadé, Angeles Vicente (eds.), Sacrum Arabo-Semiticum. Homenaje al profesor Federico Corriente en su 65 aniversario. Zaragoza: Instituto de

Estudios Islámicos y del Oriente Próximo, 223–234 (Serie estudios árabes e islámico 6).
King, David A. 1999: World-Maps for Finding the Direction and Distance to Mecca. London, Boston, Cologne: Brill (Islamic Philosophy and Science. Texts and Studies 36).
King, David A. 2005: In Synchrony with the Heavens. Studies in Astronomical Timekeeping and Instrumentation in Medieval Islamic Civilization I. II. Leiden, Boston: Brill (Islamic Philosophy, Theology and Science 55).
Kunitzsch, Paul 1959: Arabische Sternnamen in Europa. Wiesbaden: Harrasowitz.
Kunitzsch, Paul 1983: Glossar der arabischen Fachausdrücke in der mittelalterlichen europäischen Astrolabliteratur. Göttingen: Vandenhoeck & Ruprecht (Nachrichten der Akademie der Wissenschaften in Göttingen.1: Philosophisch-historische Klasse 11).
Kunitzsch, Paul, 2005. Zur Geschichte der "arabischen" Ziffern. München: Bayerische Akademie der Wissenschaften (Sitzungsberichte der Bayerischen Akademie der Wissenschaften, Philosophisch-Historische Klasse).
Lanteri, Lorenzo 1991: Le parole di origine araba nella lingua italiana: con l'arabo nella lingua sarda, l'arabo nel ladino della Val Gardena. Appendice: 60 arabismi in lingue europee. Padua: Edizioni Zenetel Katrib.
Lemay, Richard 1962: Abu Maʿshar and Latin Aristotelianism in the Twelfth Century. The recovery of Aristotle's Natural Philosophy through Arabic Astrology. Beirut: American University of Beirut (Publication of the faculty of Arts and Sciences, Oriental Series, 38).
Lindberg, David C. 1976: Theories of Vision from Al-Kindi to Kepler. Chicago, London: University of Chicago Press.
Lindberg, David C. 1996: The Western Reception of Arabic Optic. In: Encyclopedia of the History of Arabic Science, ed. Roshdi Rashed, vol. 2. London, New York: Routledge, 716–729.
Lombard, Maurice 1975: The Golden Age of Islam. Amsterdam: Markus Wiener Publishers.
López Alvarez, Anna María; Palomero Plaza, Santiago (ed.) 1996: La escuela de traductores de Toledo. Toledo: Diputacion Provincial de Toledo.
Mayerhöfer, Josef (ed.) 1961: Lexikon der Geschichte der Naturwissenschaften, vol. II: art. Alchemie. Wien: Brüder Hollinek, 172–175.
Millás Vallicrosa, José Maria 1943–1950. Estudios sobre Azarquiel. Madrid, Granada: C.S.I.C. Instituto Miguel Asín.
Needham, Joseph 1962: Science and Civilization in China: Physics, vol. IV. 1. Cambridge: Cambridge University Press.
Needham, Joseph 1980: Science and Civilization in China, 7 vols., vol. V. Cambridge: Cambridge University Press.
Osman, Nabil [3]1992: Kleines Wörterbuch deutscher Wörter arabischer Herkunft. München: C. H. Beck Verlag.
Perler, Dominik; Rudolph, Ulrich 2000: Occasionalismus. Theorien der Kausalität im arabisch-islamischen und im europäischen Denken. Göttingen: Vanden-

hoeck & Ruprecht (Abhandlungen der Akademie der Wissenschaften in Göttingen. Philologisch-historische Klasse, 3. Folge, No. 235).
Rashdall, Hastings 1987a: The Universities of Europe in the Middle Ages, 3 volumes, ed. F. M. Powicke and A. B. Emden, vol. II (Italy – Spain – France – Germany – Scotland). Oxford: Oxford University Press (reprint).
Rashdall, Hastings 1987b. The Universities of Europe in the Middle Ages, 3 volumes, ed. F. M. Powicke and A. B. Emden, vol. III (English Universities – Student Life): index s.n. astronomy, alchemy, anatomy, Aristotle, mathematics, medicine. Oxford: Oxford University Press (reprint).
Saliba, George 2007: Islamic Science and the Making of the European Renaissance. Cambridge MA, London: The MIT Press.
Schipperges, Heinrich 1964: Die Assimilation der arabischen Medizin durch das lateinische Mittelalter. Wiesbaden: Franz Steiner Verlag (Sudhoffs Archiv. Beihefte 3).
Schramm, Matthias 1963: Ibn Al-Haythams Weg zur Physik. Wiesbaden: Franz Steiner Verlag.
Schramm, Matthias 2001: Frederick II of Hohenstaufen and Arabic Science. In: Science in Context 14, no. 1–2, 289–312.
Sezgin, Fuat 1970: Geschichte des arabischen Schrifttums. Vol. III. Leiden: Brill (Medizin – Pharmazie, Zoologie – Tierheilkunde. Bis ca. 430 H.).
Sezgin, Fuat 1978: Geschichte des arabischen Schrifttums. Vol. VI (Astronomie bis ca. 430 H.). Leiden: Brill.
Sezgin, Fuat 2000: Geschichte des arabischen Schrifttums. Vol. X and XI (Mathematische Geographie und Kartographie im Islam und ihr Fortleben im Abendland. Historische Darstellung. Part 1 and 2). Frankfurt an Main: Universität Frankfurt, Institut für die Geschichte der Arabisch-Islamischen Wissenschaften.
Sguaitamatti-Bassi, Suzanne 1974. Les emprunts directs faits par le français á l'arabe jusqu'á la fin du XIIIe siècle. Thesis, Universität Zürich. Zürich: Juris-Verlag.
Ullmann, M.; Mojtowytsch-Wielandt, Rotraud 1983: Wörterbuch der klassischen arabischen Sprache. Vol. II/1. Wiesbaden: Harrassowitz.
Vegas Gonzalez, Serafin 1998: La escuela de traductores de Toledo en la historia del pensamiento. Toledo: Concejalía de Cultura.
Vernet, Juan (ed.) 1983: Nuevos estudios sobre astronomía española en el siglo de Alfonso X. Barcelona: Instituto de Filologia, Institucion "Mila y Fontanals", Consejo Superior de Investigaciones Cientificas.
Wasserstein, David 1990–91: The Library of Al-Hakam II Al-Mustansir and the Culture of Islamic Spain. In: Manuscripts of the Middle East 5, 99–105.

Further reading
(in addition to the publications mentioned in the list of references)

D'Alverny, Marie-Therese 1982: Translations and Translators. In: R. L. Benson, Giles Constable (ed.), Renaissance and Renewal in the Twelfth Century. Cambridge MA: Harvard University Press: 421–462 [repr. in: D'Alverny, Marie-Therese 1994: La transmission des textes philosophiques et scientifiques au moyen âge, ed. Charles Burnett. Aldershot: Variorum (Collected Studies Series v. CS 463)].

Daiber, Hans 1999: Bibliography of Islamic Philosophy 1999, 2 vols. Leiden, Boston, Cologne: Brill, index s.n. "science" (Handbook of Oriental Studies I. 43, 1–2).

Daiber, Hans 2007: Bibliography of Islamic Philosophy. Supplement. Leiden, Boston: Brill, index s.n. "science" (Handbook of Oriental Studies I. 89).

Daiber, Hans 2004: The Struggle for Knowledge in Islam: Some Historical Aspects. Sarajevo (pp. 52–66: The Way from God's Wisdom to Science in Islam: Modern Discussions and Historical Background) [German version, with bibliographical supplement: Daiber, Hans 2003: Von der Weisheit Gottes zur Wissenschaft. In: Evangelium und Wissenschaft 42, 3–13].

Daniel, Norman 1975: The Arabs and Mediaeval Europe. Beirut: Librairie du Liban; London: Longman.

Dunlop, D. M. 1966: Arabic Science in the West. Karachi: Pakistan Historical Society (Pakistan Historical Society Publications 35).

Jolivet, Jean 1988: The Arabic Inheritance. In: A History of Twelfth-Century Western Philosophy, ed. Peter Dronke. Cambridge: Cambridge University Press, 113–148.

Lindberg, David C. 1992: The Beginnings of Western Science. Chicago, London: University of Chicago Press.

Millas-Vallicrosa, J. M. 1963: Translations of Oriental Scientific Works (to the End of the Thirteenth Century). In: The Evolution of Science, ed. Guy S. Metraux and François Crouzet. New York: New American Library, 128–167.

Steinschneider, Moritz 1956: Die europäischen Übersetzungen aus dem Arabischen bis Mitte des 17. Jahrhunderts. Graz: Akademische Druck- und Verlagsanstalt.

Thorndike, Lynn 1923: A History of Magic and Experimental Science during the first thirteen Centuries of Our Era. Vol. 1 and 2. London: Macmillan & Co.

4

Muslim Communities of the European North-Eastern Frontiers: Islam in the Former Polish-Lithuanian Commonwealth

Ataullah Bogdan Kopanski

Abstract

When talking about the historical presence and contribution of Islam in Europe and its interactions with non-Muslims, the fate of the Eastern European Muslims – one of the continent's oldest Islamic communities – is often overlooked. Since the end of the fourteenth century the Polish-Lithuanian Muslims were mostly professional soldiers of the Polish-Lithuanian, Saxon, Prussian and Russian monarchies, partially incorporated into the Polish-Lithuanian nobility (szlachta). After the end of World War I, the Polish charismatic strongman, Marshal Józef Piłsudski, ordered the formation of the famous all-Muslim cavalry squadron, the 'Vilnian Ulans'. Recently, among the approximately 50,000 Muslims of the contemporary Republic of Poland, descendants of those Tatar warriors comprise less than 10 percent of the rapidly growing Islamic communities in this very new member of European Union. These 'Old Eurasian Muslims' constitute a distinctive ethnic community in present-day Poland. Their long and complex story is closely correlated to the history and heritage of the Ottoman multiethnic, multicultural, and tri-religious Islamic Commonwealth. According to the statistics from the Muslim communities in the ex-Soviet republics of Lithuania, Belarus and Ukraine, there are almost 400,000 Muslims in the former 'Eastern Frontiers' (Kresy Wschodnie), i. e. of what was once Greater Poland. In the ancient past of western Eurasia, it had been Germanic tribes and, later on, during the Middle Ages, Prussian Lithuanians, who had been forced to move from their ancestral homelands by waves of post-Scythian nomads from the Eurasian heartland. During our own times, waves of Muslim refugees and pauperised seekers of better life conditions and liberty have significantly increased the number of Muslims in what was known to the Ottomans as 'Lehistan' (the 'land of Lehs', i. e. the Poles), present-day Poland, Ukraine, Belarus, and Lithuania. The author's at times somewhat passionate comments provide nevertheless a good insight as to how the historical (as well as present) encounter of Eastern Europe with Islam is currently perceived by Polish scholars.

Introduction

Relations with the *Dār al-Islām*, the world of Islam, have always played a significant role in the history of Poland, Lithuania, Belarus, and Ukraine. For centuries, this ancient Sarmatia, dominated by the early medieval *Lehites* – identified by the Renaissance annalists with the ancestors of Polish aristocracy – shared common borders with the Islamic states of the Crimean Khanate, the khanate of the Golden Horde (Tatar: *Altın Orda*) and the Ottoman State, the latter having been the most powerful of all pre-modern Muslim dominions. Muslims from this 'Islamic Eurasian Belt' frequently settled down in the late medieval Kingdom of Poland and the Grand Duchy of Lithuania, which were ruled in union by the Lithuanian Jagiellon dynasty. Islamic civilisation penetrated this 'aristocratic republic' (Pol.: *Rzeczpospolita szlachecka*) via the Black Sea, the steppe, and the Danubian lands. A quasi 'Jewish Triangle' of post-Khazarian Bessarabia and the 'Wild Fields' *(Dzikie Pola)* comprised of the most violent zones of the Ukraine, which means quite literally 'frontier land'. It was contested ferociously by both the Muslim Turks and Christian Slavs, often to the disadvantage of the remnants of ancient Dacians and Romanised Vlachs. It was also a zone of banditry, where the presence of Cossacks was often equivalent to freedom to plunder, appalling serfdom, a rapacious economy of greed, Polish magnates called *żubry kresowe* (lit. 'border buffaloes') managed by hired local Jewish usurers and land renters. A combination of all of these 'liberties' ignited the sixteenth-century popular endemic risings of oppressed Ukrainian bondsmen against Poles and Jews. The Muslim Crimea, the Balkans, and the Danubian protectorates were natural havens for fugitives, dissidents, rebels, converts, and 'guest-workers' from the Polish-Lithuanian Commonwealth. Moreover, vice versa, many Muslim refugees, mercenaries, captives, insurgents, and pauperised princelings or dispossessed khans from the destabilised Kipchak tribes found asylum in the Polish-Lithuanian Commonwealth.

Early encounters

Already in the ninth and tenth centuries, the primitive Polish, Russian, and Prussian tribes had enjoyed a lucrative trade relationship with the Muslim big powers of the time, in particular with Khwarizm, *al-Andalus* (Muslim Spain) and the Abbasid Caliphate. The massive influx of Arab silver *dirham*s to then still pagan Poland, Silesia, and Rus during those centuries confirms the vigour of a nefarious slave-trade of Slavs – known to the Arabs as *al-Ṣaqālibah*. This trade was controlled almost entirely by the pan-continental trade enterprise of the 'Rahdanite' Jews – medieval Jewish merchants – and partially by the Rus – both Turkic and Nordic slave-hunters – who established their own *entrepôts* in Eastern Europe and were ruled by a dynasty descending from the legendary Swedish Viking Rurik and his warriors, known as Varangians. Interestingly, the earliest Muslim sources identified both *al-Urdmaniyyūn* (Norsemen) and the Turkic Itil Bolgars as *al-Rūs*.

Eastern Europe's intensive trade contacts with the world of Islam are particularly well-documented in the field of numismatics. The standard Muslim silver coin of 2.97 g was equivalent to one-tenth of the gold *dīnār* of 4.25 g, minted after the first monetary reform in the Umayyad Caliphate – or somewhat more 'practically', to the value of a poorly-fed Slavic slave sold by Jewish slave-dealers in Toledo, Cordoba, Ray, Baghdad, Palermo, or any other Muslim metropolis of the time. Inscription of the *shahādah* (the Islamic 'testimony of faith', i. e. 'There is no god but Allāh and Muḥammad is the Messenger of Allāh') or brief qur'ānic verses on the Islamic silver *dirham*s or gold *dīnār*s were ambiguous for the illiterate pagan or Christianised Polanes, Pomeranes, Vislanes, Opolanes, Masovians, Bobrzanes, Odrzanes, Golenshitze, Sorbes, Lutitzes, Veletes, and other 'Lehitic' tribes. However, the Arabic letters guaranteed that the coins were genuine and accepted by the merchants from the Muslim hinterlands. In particular, the coins minted by the Spanish Umayyad caliph Hishām II (r. 976–1009) and the Abbasid caliph al-Manṣūr (r. 754–775) are frequent numismatic components of the early medieval hoards unearthed in Poland, the best example being the deposit of Muslim silver coins from the village of Ochla in northern Poland). The famous Arab demographer al-Mas'ūdī (d. 956) was one of the first Muslim writers who mentioned in his *Murūj al-dhahab* or 'Golden Meadows' the names of the north-western Proto-Polish *al-Ṣaqālibah.* He referred to some of them as *al-Sarabiyyūn*, i. e., 'Serbs'. During the time of the four Rightly Guided Caliphs, i. e., between the 630s and 660s, the 'White Serbs' *(Bely Srbi)* and the 'White Croats' *(Bely Khrbati)* left Lower Silesia and the area of the Upper Vistula River and were hired by the Byzantines as mercenaries. They were allowed to settle down in the area that had belonged to the Illyrians, one of Europe's most ancient ethic groups of Europe, where Byzantine power was badly weakened by peasant revolts, religious strife, and invasions of Avars and Bulgars from the Bolga/Itil Basin. The Serbs became the Byzantine 'Servi', i. e., 'slave-soldiers' converted to Orthodox Christianity (note that the Cyrillic letter *b* corresponds to Latin *v*). This model of Byzantine 'state-owned slave-soldiers' and mercenaries from the Barbarian North of the 'Seventh Climate' was subsequently imitated by the Umayyad and Abbasid Caliphs who also had their own *Ṣaqālibah* troops and Varangian-like bodyguards. These Serbian slave-soldiers and captives turned into a Byzantine elite corps, a kind of medieval 'Gurkha regiment'. They also served as an attractive military model for the Muslim Seljuk *atabeg*s in *their* 'frontier lands', known as *Uç*. The Seljuks trained the captured, hired or purchased Turko-Ugric Kipchaki and Slavic-Finnic-Nordic Rus, transforming them into *'Mamluks'*, the Islamic version of 'slave-soldiers'. In the post-Byzantine Balkans, they also became the pattern of the later Ottoman system of *devşirme* – the systematic abduction of young boys from conquered Christian lands by the Ottoman sultans as a form of regular taxation in order to build a loyal slave army. Many of those boys became *içoğlan*s, literally 'boy servants', and worked in the *Enderun*, or 'Inner Palace', one of the three parts of Topkapı Palace, the residence of the Ottoman sultans in Istanbul. There, they received also the best education available in those days in order to advance later on to the highest ranks of the administrative or military hierarchy. Like the Mamluks and janissaries of the later Islamic sultanates, the Byzantinised and Christanised Serb slave-soldiers, too, became a formidable and defiant military force – in this case of Eastern Orthodox civilisation in the age of the Crusades against the Muslims.

The Spanish Umayyads used the Sephardic Jewish slave-dealers from Tortosa or Verdun, whereas the Abbasids of Baghdad used the 'Radhanites' as their spies to monitor the Barbarian zone of the 'Seventh Climate', in other words, the area between the lands of Roman-Catholic Franks and the Southern Steppe terrorised by the Khazar hordes. The trade passages of what became known to the Muslims of the time as 'Lehistān' – Poland, Lithuania, Belarus, and Ukraine – formed a strategic central link of the Silk Route connecting China with the lands of Franks, Norsemen, Danes, Anglo-Saxons, and Lombards. Ibrāhīm b. Yaʿqūb, a Jewish slave-dealer and spy from the Spanish Muslim city of Tortosa, wrote a special report on the military power of post-Great Moravian Bohemia and the northern neighbouring lands ruled by 'Mshka' (Mieszko), a barbarian prince of the *Polans.* Prince Mieszko accepted Roman-Catholicism in 966, after marriage with a Czech runaway nun, Dobravka, daughter of the Přemyslid duke Boleslav I the Cruel (r. 935–972). Mieszko's conquest of Silesia – always hotly contested by the Czechs and Germans – Kuyawia (a historical region, the northernmost part of Greater Poland) and Masovia (a geographical and historical region situated in eastern Poland) – both exposed to the annual raids of the then still staunchly pagan Prussians – and the lands of Vislans with their ancient post-Vandal fortified legendary stronghold *Krak*, allowed the ambitious and tough Polanian prince *(knez)* to unify the central realm of the 'Lehites' and to lay the foundations of *Wielkopolska,* 'Greater Poland'. Ibrāhīm b. Yaʿqūb's report, written in Arabic for the benefit of the intelligence service of Caliph al-Ḥakam II (r. 961–976), is one of the earliest historical confirmations of the existence of a Polish principality strong enough to defend itself against the Saxons, prowling Baltic Vikings, and other Slavonic-speaking tribal entities. The original version of Ibrāhīm b. Yaʿqūb's account is lost, but fragments of it survived in *Dhikr al-Ṣaqālibah* (Remembrance of the Slavs), a portion of a work by the Spanish-Arab geographer and historian Abu ʿUbayd al-Bakrī (d. 1094), and also in the encyclopaedia of the Persian geographer Ḥamd-Allāh Mustaufī Qazwīnī (d. c. 1340).

Jagiellons, Ottomans, and Tatars: The Great Time of the Muslim-Christian Encounter

In 1558, an anonymous Muslim chronicler from the Grand Duchy of Lithuania wrote during his pilgrimage to Mecca a unique treatise in Ottoman-Turkish, known to Polish and Tatar historians as *Risāle-i Tātār-i Leh* (Deliberation on the Polish Tatars). In Mecca, he dedicated his chronicle to Dāmād Rustam Pasha, from 1555 until his death in 1561 Grand Vizier of the Ottoman Sultan Sulaymān I 'the

Lawgiver' (r. 1520–1566; known and counted in the West as Sulaymān II 'the Magificent'). The author insisted that in medieval Lithuania, local Muslim Tatars constructed "poor, simple, and small mosques made of wood, without minarets and niches". He compared them to "similar mosques in villages of *Rumelī*", i. e., in the European parts of the Ottoman State. The unknown author of the *Risāle* reported also about existing mosques in Vilnus, the capital of Grand Duchy of Lithuania, in Kyrk Tatar (Sorok Tatary), Vakija (Waka), Yeni Shehri (Novogrodek) and Turk (Trokai) (Anonymous 965 A.H/1558 C.E., cited by Smirnov 1887: 56; see also Bartoszewicz 1860 and Muchlinski 1858). According to his narration, the ruler of *Lehistān*, i. e., Poland, had settled in Lithuania many Tatar refugees from the Golden Horde. The Polish monarch (probably the Lithuanian Grand Duke Yogaila (Władysław II Jagiełło, after his Roman Catholic baptism and coronation as Polish king; d. 1434) asked them for military aid against the crusading Teutonic Knights from eastern Prussia who frequently raided his dominions. The majority of these Tatar 'expatriates' escaped from the Kipchak Steppe, in present-day Central Russia, which was invaded and sacked by Tīmūr (known to the medieval West as 'Tamerlane'; d. 1405) during his war against Tokhtamysh (d. 1406), the last khan of the disintegrating White Horde. In 1380, Tokhtamysh became the powerful ruler of the vast Kipchak region, the westernmost Islamic realm of the original patrimony of Genghis-khan's eldest son, which stretched from the Lower Danube in Bessarabia to the Irtysh River in Siberia. This restored and Islamised Jochi *ulus*, as contemporaries called the lands of the Golden Horde, was populated by a boisterous multi-racial mould of nomadic, semi-nomadic, and pastoral peoples of Altaic, Caucasian, and Uralic origin – Volga-Kama Bulgars, Alans, Mordvins, Kankalis, Kirghizs, Kumans, Pechenegs, remnants of the Khazars and Ostrogoths, Slavs, Oguzes and Ongurs (eastern Magyars). All of them became summarily known as 'Kipchaks', the 'folks of the Steppe'. The territories of the Golden Horde reached as far as Khwarizm in Central Asia, whereas the northern Caucasus region and the Crimea marked their southern frontier. The Russian principalities and Finno-Ugric Mordva in the Far North formed the unmolested peripheral confines. Toward the west, pastoral Moldo-Wallachia (in Ottoman geopolitical vocabulary usually referred to *Bogdan ve Eflak*) with its arable grasslands often attracted invasions by the mounted tribes of the Steppe. Since times immemorial, this Eurasian pivotal heartland with its ancient trade routes and superb pasturages for horses was a constant war zone for Scythes, Sarmatians, Alans, Huns, Avars, Turks, and Mongols. In post-medieval times, the 'Wild Fields' (Pol.: *Dzikie Pola*) assumed this function for Poles, Crimean Tatars, and Russians, becoming the *Ukraina*, literally the 'frontier lands' of the Slavic Cossacks.

On 18 June 1391, the Golden Horde collapsed on the plains of Kunduzcha, east of the Volga River between Samara and Chistopol in what is now Tatarstan. Tokhtamysh escaped from the battlefield. According to the exaggerated account of the Timurid historian Sharaf al-Dīn ʿAlī Yazdī (d. 1454), a hundred thousand men and women lost their lives in this bloodshed. Some survivors found refuge in freshly Christianised Lithuania. The Lithuanian Grand Dukes were deceitful allies of the Golden Horde and their troops often participated in the civil wars between the ambitious khans of the Kipchaks. However, they at least accepted some of the survivors of the defeated powers of the Steppe.

Eleven years later, Tīmūr delivered his next deadly blow, this time to the Ottomans, the emerging great Muslim power in Anatolia and the Balkans. On 28 July 1402, his Muslim, mainly Turkic, troops defeated the likewise Muslim army of the Ottomans – hitherto thought of as invincible – and their Serb allies on the plains east of Angora (Ankara). Sultan Bāyazīd I (r. 1389–1402), referred to by the Turks as 'Yıldırım' (Thunderbolt), was captured and humiliated. Bāyazīd, whose janissaries and 'raiders' or *akıncıs* had just some years earlier smashed one of the greatest crusading coalitions of western Christendom at Nicopolis, on 25 September 1396, died in captivity. Surprisingly, the calamity in Asia Minor did not slow down the gradual Islamisation process in the Balkans which the Ottomans had initiated. As a matter of fact, the Ottomans were able to recover relatively quickly and embarked on establishing their *pax ottomanica* in Europe.

Sorok Tatary, a tiny village (in Eastern Slavic parlance meaning 'Forty Tatars'), is one of the oldest Muslim colonies built by these 'Tatar' survivors who had fled from Kipchak and asked the Lithuanian Grand Duke Vytautas the Great (r. 1401–1430), the cousin of Yogaila to whom we have referred earlier, for political asylum. According to the Lithuanian Catholic writer Michael Litwin, the author of *De moribus Tartarorum, Lithuanorum et Moschorum* (On the customs of the Tatars, Lithuanians, and Muscovites), written in Latin in 1550, Kyrk Tatar (Sorok Tatary) was founded by the "forty mighty son of Omeldash, sultan of Islam, who have been born in the same year to Omeldash's four wives and his thirty six slave-women". The original name of the settlement on the bank of the Waka River is derived from *kırklar*, meaning 'forty (persons)' in Turkish. The place was Russicised toward the end of the sixteenth century. In 1844, a Polish-speaking Lithuanian writer Jan Jaroszewicz recorded that Sorok Tatary or Kyrk Tatar was the cradle of four noble Muslim Tatar clans – Sobolewski, Bajraszewski, Tokosz, and Laszkusz, – which originated from four Tatar *agas* – Sobol, Bairash, Tigush, and Lashkut. However, but Polish historian Piotr Borawski insists that the name echoes the old Turkic legend about forty *kurhans* (graves) or *Kirktuba* in Matayas, Kirgizstan, where allegedly forty brothers died in a fratricidal battle. A wooden mosque in Sorok Tatary existed until 1945. The Soviet regime of Lithuania demolished this Muslim house of prayer in 1946 (Jaroszewicz 1844–1845: 1:121; Borawski 1977: 291–304; about the genealogy of the Muslim families of Sobolewski, Bajraszewski, Togosze, and Laszkucie see Dziadulewicz 1929).

In Muslim medieval sources, Grand Duke Vytautas is referred to as 'Amīr Wattad'. In 1395, several thousand Tatar Muslim warriors, led by Tokhtamysh – the already referred to defeated khan of the Golden Horde – escaped from Yeni Saray and crossed the borders to the Lithuanian Grand Duchy. Tokhtamysh himself was later murdered in Lithuania in 1407 and his thirteen sons tried to revenge his death (Kopanski 1992: 34). The fourteenth-century annals of the Polish-Ukrainian city of Lvov (the 'Lemberg' of the Habsburg monarchy) reported about well-established community of Muslim merchants and craftsmen who erected a brick-made mosque in the pivotal point of town, near the Dominican abbey (Jaszowski 1832; Borawski, Dubiński 1986, 18). Ian Dlugosz, a Polish Catholic chronicler of the fourteenth century, noted in his annals that "Tatar settlers in Lithuania enjoyed a freedom of their Mohammedan [Muslim] belief under the Grand Duke Vitautis [Vytautas], and they preserved their non-Christian outrageous [sic!] traditions" (Długosz 1869, 4, 32). Gilbert de Lannoy, a knight from Burgundy, who visited the Lithuanian towns in 1414, wrote in his chronicle that "a great number of Tatars live in several villages near Trokai [Troki], and inside the town, and they are not following the Lord Christ because they are Saracens". Four years later, Peter von Wormedith, a knight-monk of the Teutonic Order of the Virgin Mary, who resided in Livonia (modern Latvia), wrote in his letter to the Grand Master at Marienburg that in the city of Minsk a group of 400 Muslims built a wooden mosque. The Ottoman historian and traveller Evliya Çelebi (d. 1682) was convinced that during his time, at the beginning of the seventeenth century, more than 60 mosques existed in 'Lehistān' (Poland) and Lithuania, among them in Bazary (1685), Gudziany (1646–1690), Husseimiany (1671–1699), Ponary (1699), Prudziany (1558), Rejze (1558), Sienkiewicze (1699), Solkienniki (1615), Winksznupie (1558), Kiena (1615–1631), Lukiszki-Vilnius (1558), Mereczlany (1615–1699), and Niemiez (1684) (quoted in Borawski and Dubiński 1986, 60–61).

According to already mentioned *Risāle-i Tātār-i Leh,* "the Muslim frontiersmen in Lithuania were not Mongol heathens but gallant scions of the noble Turkic Seljuk *mīrzā*s". Many Muslim mercenaries led by Jānī Beg, the Tatar ally of the Lithuanian Grand Duke Olgerd in his war against the Polish kingdom, were the Turkic noblemen. Toward the end of the nineteenth century, the Polish Muslim writer Maciej Sulaiman Tuhan-Baranowski divided the Muslim colonists in Lithuania and Poland into three different ethnic groups. The richest and highborn Muslim *mīrzā*s are the 'Sarmatians' of Caucasian-origin from Dagestan. They were professional soldiers of fortune who joined the Lithuanian troops of Grand Duke Vytautas. Their leader, a prince by name of Temür (Tīmūr) Tuhan Beg, was the first commander of the Muslim mercenaries in Lithuania. He emigrated from the northern Caucasus region to Lithuania with his wife and two sons, Mīrān and al-Qadr. The former had married a daughter of the Polish Catholic nobleman *(szlachcic)* Baranowski and adopted her surname (Kruman 1896; Jasiewicz 1980).

The Ugro-Finnic, Turkic, Caucasian, and Altaic mixed marriages formed the second ethnic group among Polish-Lithuanian Muslims. They were the skilful craftsmen and farmers from the Volga River basin. The 'lowest' or the third caste of Muslim settlers in Poland and Lithuania were descendants of Tatar war prisoners and Nogay tribesmen captured by the Poles. Today, the Caucasians, Turks, Slavs, Altaic Mongols, and Ugro-Finns are completely hybridised. The Islamic faith – the most important indicator of their cultural identity – made those ethnoracial differences among Polish-Lithuanian Muslims an unimportant issue at the beginning of the nineteenth century. Many shamanist customs of the Nogay Tatars (rituals as such eating at the graves of relatives, the cult of dead ancestors, fortune-telling, the practise of magic through 'Islamised' talismans, or the so-called *duayki* and *hramatki*, etc.) survived among the Muslim Tatars in contemporary Poland, Lithuania, and Belarus, a circumstance that upsets the majority of well-educated Muslims in these countries (Konopacki 1962 and 1963).

After the defeat of the crusading Teutonic Order by a rather astonishing coalition of newly Christianised Lithuanians, Catholic Poles, Hussite Czechs, and Muslim Tatars (led by Jalāl al-Dīn Khān) at the encounter that is known in Polish historiography as the Battle of Grunwald and in Germany as the Battle of Tannenberg (1410), a second wave of Muslim Tatar colonists settled in Lithuania. They were mostly veterans of Grand Duke Vytautas' wars against the Teutonic Order. After the victory, they were granted land in Keidaniai (Kieydany), Dokszyce, Bazary, Korzysc, Dawgi, Birsztany, and Butrymance. Grand Duke Vytautas had been praised by Muslim settlers as protector of their Muslim liberties. In an epistle addressed to the Polish king Sigismund I the Old (r. 1506–1548) in 1519, Lithuanian Muslims described Vytautas of past memory as "a defender of Islam, whose name we respect like our caliphs" (Zdan 1930, 7, 530–601; Ochmański 1986, 82). The Polish Catholic chroniclers of the sixteenth century, Jan Krasinski, Martin Kromer, Matthias Miechovita, Matthias Strykovski, Martin Bielski, and Alexander Gwagnin portrayed Vytautas as the pro-Muslim prince who settled many Tatars in Lithuania. Gwagnin wrote in his *Description of European Sarmatia* that in 1396, Vytautas settled down in Lithuania numerous Tatar hostages and prisoners of war as well as their families from Kipchak, who later fought bravely for him under "the flags with Arabic letters". This chronicler described them as "the good farmers and fearless Muslim fighters who recognised the Polish king as their own ruler".

After the fall of Golden Horde, the Crimean khanate ruled by the Giray Khāns maintained separate diplomatic and economic ties with the Lithuanian-Polish dual monarchy. In 1511, Mengli Giray Khān abandoned his historical rights to Belorus and Podolia (Ukraine) for a controversial and temporal alliance with the Jagiellons, the ruling dynasty of the Polish-Lithuanian Commonwealth.

The Ottoman historian Munajjimbashī (Müneccimbaşi, d. 1702) conclusively indicated that during the reign of the first Muslim khan of the Golden Horde, Berke (or Baraka) Khān (r. 1257–1267), many 'Rūm' (i. e., Anatolian) Seljuk Turks from Konya and Oguz Türkmens settled in the Southern Ukrainian *Dzikie Pola* (the 'Wild Plains' referred to earlier). Berke Khān married a daughter of the Seljuk sultan. Their son, ʿIzz al-Dīn, received the Crimean towns of Solhat and Sudak (Ibn Baṭṭūṭuh's *Kiram*), and during his time, thousands of Anatolian Turks migrated to the Southern Ukraine. With the beginning of the fourteenth century, the Crimean Peninsula, previously inhabited by the Slavs, Germanic Ostrogoths, merchant colonists from Genoa, and nomadic Kumans (Polovtzy), was reported to be almost totally ethnic Turkic. The khans at Yeni Saray at the Volga River appointed Muslim custodians of the *Eski Kırım* (Turk.: 'Old Crimea') and the Steppe region. The Crimea was the hub of Islamic missionary activity in western Russia, Poland, Lithuania, and Belarus. The city of Solhat, with its picturesque mosques, *madras-*

ahs, and Sufi lodges and all their *mullahs*, *shaykhs*, *imāms*, and *qāḍīs*, served as the northern cultural metropolis of Islam. The first stone-made Friday mosque and *madrasah* in Solhat were built by Muḥammad Uzbek Khān (1313–1341) in 1314. Moreover, Baybars (r. 1260–1277), the famous Mamluk sultan of Egypt and Syria and scourge of the crusaders, who was born around 1223 on the Crimea, is said to have constructed a large mosque, the *Barbarsiyyah*, in Solhat.

Ḥājjī Giray I (r. 1449–1456 and 1456–1466) was the first independent Muslim ruler of the Crimean Khanate and the 'Wild Plains' of Southern Russia. He had been born in Trokai (Turki, Troki), Lithuania, and according to the Ottoman historian Ankaralı Ḥakīm Yaḥyā, he was poisoned in 1466, after his military support of Casimir IV Jagiellon (Grand Duke of Lithuania from 1440 and King of Poland from 1447, until his death in 1492), who fought against the invading troops of Aḥmad Khān (r. 1465–1481), the new ruler of revived Golden Horde.

In 1438, a large number of Ḥājjī Giray's followers settled down in Belarus and Lithuania. They established about 40 Muslim colonies, such as in Dowbuciszki, Iwie, Kleck, Lachowicze, Lowczyce, and Minsk. All those mentioned Muslim Tatar settlements had mosques, but almost all of them had been destroyed or misused during the Soviet occupation. Other medieval Muslim-dominated townships (Miadziol, Niemierow, Nieswierz, Orda, Sloboda Tatarska – lit. 'Tatar liberty' –, Slonim, Sobolnice, and Widze) lost their wooden mosques during World War I.

In 1454, Ḥājjī Giray made an alliance with the valiant Ottoman sultan Muḥammad II Fātiḥ (r. 1444–1446 and 1451–1481), the conqueror of Constantinople, and captured Kefe (Kaffa) from the Genoese. The Crimean Muslim troops led by Mengli Giray Khān (r. 1467–1476, 1475–1476, and 1478–1514), Ḥājjī Giray's successor, seized the city of Kiev in 1480, and decimated the Polish army of king John I Albert (r. 1492–1501) in Visnivietz (1494). By 1501, the Muslim forces of the Ottomans and their Crimean Tatar allies controlled almost the entire Ukraine. On 10 June 1502, the Crimean army, led by Mengli Giray, defeated the last khan of the Golden Horde, Sayyid Aḥmad II, who took refuge in Lithuania, where he was executed under the political pressure of Mengli Giray. After the victory of the Ottoman sultan Muḥammad IV (r. 1648–87) over the Polish-Lithuanian army in 1672, a large number of persecuted Ukrainian Muslims called *Lipkas* defected to the Ottomans. Hussein Murawski was appointed by the Ottomans as *bey*, or governor, of the captured Ukrainian fortress of Bar. Between 1680 and 1810, several thousands of Polish and Lithuanian Muslims emigrated to Bessarabia (Moldavia) and Dobrudja (Rolle-Antoni 1893).

The mass exodus of the Polish-Lithuanian Muslims to the Ottoman dominions was sparked by the prohibition of the building of new mosques and religious discrimination in public life in their home lands. However, in 1677, the Diet of Warsaw equalised the Muslim nobles with the Christian nobility, known in Polish as *szlachta*, and the Polish Muslims regained their old rights. Henceforth, the Muslims of the Polish-Lithuanian Commonwealth ignored these anti-Islamic laws and erected three new wooden mosques in Bohoniki, Kruszyniany (still existing in north-eastern Poland), and Studzianka. Until 1775, the construction of new brick-made mosques was banned in Lithuania and Poland. Back on 2 July 1609, a fanatical Catholic mob, incited by the bishop of Vilnius, had demolished a mosque at Trokai (Troki). Under the reign of the Swedish-born Sigismund III Vasa (King of the Polish-Lithuanian Commonwealth from 1587 to 1632, and King of Sweden from 1592 until he was deposed there in 1599), the Polish-Lithuanian Muslims suffered the worst persecutions. In 1616, the bishop of Vilnius, writing under the pen-name of 'Peter Czyżewski' published a very crude anti-Islamic lampoon, entitled 'Genuine Tatar *al-Furqān*, divided into 40 parts' *(Al-Furkan tatarski na czterdzieści części podzielony)*, in which he ridiculed the teachings of Islam, insulted the Prophet, and demanded the demolition of all mosques, as well as the enforced baptism of the Muslims in the Commonwealth. This piece, which can only be considered a part of the genre of Islamophobic hate-literature, appears to have attracted many Polish Christian bigots during those days as it was reprinted several times. Agitated by the anti-Islamic Catholic clergy, the Polish Parliament *(Sejm)* passed several anti-Muslim bills according to which Muslim men who dared to marry Christian women were to be executed. In 1655, Catholic troops attacked Muslim refugees and kidnapped several hundred Muslim children. Seventeen years later, the Polish Muslim troops rebelled against their Christian officers and numerous Muslim leaders took refuge in the realm of Islam, controlled by the Sublime Porte. Among them were Mirza Korycki, Ismail Sulimanowicz, Hussein Murawski, Dzafar Murawski, and others.

The maltreatment of the Muslims by their Christian overlords culminated in the so-called 'Mutiny of the Lipka Tatars' in the Ukraine which was led by Ali Kryczynski and Hussein Murawski, who served later as the dragomans for the Crimean khan Salīm Giray I (r. 1671–1678, 1684–1691, 1692–1699, and 1702–1704). Poland *lassa fessaque* – 'weak and exhausted' – suffered a crushing defeat by the Ottoman Turks and the Crimean Tatars in 1672 and was forced to sign the Treaty of Buchach. She had to pay the humiliating 'poll tax' *(jizyah)* along with the *kharaj* – a tax on agricultural land – amounting to 22,000 gold ducats annually and had to hand over both the Ukraine and Podolia to the Sublime Porte. Ali Kryczynski was installed by the Ottoman sultan as *bey* of the Ukrainian fortress of Bar (S. Kryczyński 1935a). In the fortified cities of Kamienietz Podolski and Bar two large Friday mosques were constructed. They were demolished after the return of the area of the Polish Christian administration. In 1763, the Ottoman envoy to Prussia, Rasmī ʿAẓmī Effendi, travelled across Poland, Lithuania, and Podolia, where he visited the fortress of Kamienietz Podolski which was in Muslim hands from 1672 to 1699. He was particularly moved by the sight of a ruined minaret with inscriptions in Arabic, including various qur'ānic quotations, and the *hijrī* year of its construction. He wrote in his diary;

> When I red this inscription, I uttered a prayer from my heart that it might please Allāh – Exalted is He – soon return these places to Islam, so that the word of Truth may resound from this minaret (ʿAẓmī Effendi 1303 A.H./1886 C.E., 27–28; see also Beldiceanu 1960, 1,127).

The construction of the first mosque in the western Ukraine was reported by Fulvius Ruggieri, the papal legate to Volhynia in 1565. He wrote that "in the city of Ostrog there is a Tatar mosque, and Ostrogski princes established in Volhynia many Tatar villages". Among the elites of the Muslim Tatars were the clans of Assanczukowicz (Hassancukivic), Bahrynski, Juszynski, Kadyszewicz, Korycki, Kryczynski, Lostayski, Lowczycki, Smolski, Shirinski, Talkowski, Taraszewski,Ulan, and Zawacki, who were descendants of ruling Crimean and Kipchak khans. They possessed many villages with Tatar inhabitants. Some of them, like Hussein Malikbashicz, who sold his estate to Ostaphy Wollowich in 1570, were indeed very rich persons (Czacki 1835, 2, 87–108; L. Kryczyński 1930a; Bandtke 1843, 117–127). In 1477, the Crimean Peninsula was controlled entirely by Aḥmad Khān, the ruler of Golden Horde. He nominated the young Jānī Beg Sulṭān as his 'deputy' khan on the Crimea, but the powerful Shīrīn clan, supported by the Sublime Porte, preferred the old Crimean khan Nūr Dawlat Giray (r. 1466–1467, 1474–1475, and 1476–1478). Several months later, the Ottoman-backed Mengli Giray returned to power in Bakhchyseray, and Nūr Dawlat Giray had been forced, together with his brother Aydar and a few *bohatyr*s or 'young brave hearts', to flee to the Kievian Ukraine. One of Nūr Dawlat's sons asked for political asylum in Poland, and the Polish-Lithuanian king Casimir IV bestowed to him the wooden castle of Punie. Nūr Dawlat's son accepted the Polonised name of 'Punski'. He bought several Lithuanian towns in the Trokai region and the villages of Dudziszki, Wyszkiszki, Rudniki, Waki, Rejze and Krzymanowiec. The Polonised Muslim princes *(kniazie)* of Punski's family enjoyed high esteem among Polish-Lithuanian Muslims. Punski 'squadron commanders' (Pol.: *rotmistrze*) led the Polish royal cavalry, and in 1568 one of them, *kniaz* Islam Janbekovich Punski, was appointed as supreme commander of all Tatar troops in the Polish army. In 1567, he was awarded by the king for his valour and heroism in the war against Moscovy and Sweden and received an estate in Januszkowo. However, toward the end of the seventeenth century, the Punski family left for to the Ottoman lands and this valiant Muslim clan died out in Lithuania.

When the Russians invaded Lithuania in 1500, Shaykh Aḥmad (r. 1499–1502), the ruler of the Golden Horde in Kipchak, offered military aid to Alexander Jagiellon (r. as Grand Duke of Lithuania 1492–1506 and as Polish king 1501–1506). Six years later, the Crimean Tatars invaded Lithuania, but they were repulsed by the local Tatar cavalry. The Crimeans lost more than three thousand men who were captured and settled in the Belorussian towns of Kleck, Nieswierz, Minsk, and Sluck. Among them was a rich *mīrzā,* Malik Pasha Shīrīn. He married a Lithuanian Muslim woman and received from the Polish monarch estates in Ledzinki and Kroszyn. Malik Pasha Shīrīn is recognised as a protoplast of the Polish Muslim clan Szyrinski. A Lithuanian rich owner of Tupaly, Sieyt (Said) Bachtiarowicz, protected his Crimean uncle Sulṭān Aḥmad Karachay (Karaczej) when the latter was captured by Polish troops.

After the fiasco of Crimean invasion, the Lithuanian lord *(kniaz)* Aidar Jepaczewicz Juszynski paid a high ransom for Murza Nursejc (Mīrzā Nūr Saʿīd), a son of ʿIzz al-Dīn Khān. In 1528, Murza Nursejc was appointed *ataman* or commander of Juszynski's Muslim troops in the Ukraine. In 1502, Mengli Giray of Crimea attacked Shaykh Aḥmad's starving Golden Horde in the southern Ukraine and Shaykh Aḥmad lost his power. He was detained by the Lithuanians in Trokai, where the Lithuanian Muslim *kniaz* Ahmet (Aḥmad) Ulan Assanczukowicz (Hassanchikovich) offered him protection or the so-called *'poreka'* (Old Pol. for 'trusteeship'). After twenty years of Lithuanian captivity, Shaykh Aḥmad and his oldest son Manṣūr returned to the Kipchak Steppe. His youngest son Aziubek Sulṭān decided to stay in Lithuania when the Polish king Sigismund the Old endowed to him seven hundred Christian serfs near the town of Ostryna. Aziubek Sulṭān adopted the surname 'Ostrynski' and founded one of the most famous Polish Muslim aristocratic clans. In 1553, he received new estates in Położno and Ryczyna.

When the Khanates of Kazan, Kasimov, and Astrakhan fell to the Muscovite Tsar Ivan the Terrible (r. [as tsar] 1547–1584), a large number of Muslim refugees moved from the Itil-Ural to Volhynia, Podolia and Crimea. In Catholic Poland and Lithuania, like in the Islamic state of the Crimean khans, the Muslim population lived under the jurisdiction of Islamic *sharīʿah* law. In the Ukraine, the Muslim Tatars served mostly in the private armies of Polish magnates. They established several Muslim urban colonies, the so-called *'kąty tatarskie'* (Pol. for 'Tatar corners') in Ostrog, Rozważ, Chorów, Podłuż, Płonne, Labuń, Stary Konstantynów, and Łuck. In 1659, the Volynian Muslim communities *(dzemiaty)* had with Ali Kryczynski and Mulla Ramazan Milkomanowicz their own delegates in the Polish Parliament (Jabłonowski 1893, Szymielewicz 1905].

In 1581, Antonio Possevino, the Jesuit legate, informed the pope in Rome that Lithuanian Muslims use to send their children to Arabia, where they are learning the language of the Qur'ān and the proper recitation of the Holy Book of Islam. Possevino organised Catholic missionary activities in the Lithuanian towns inhabited by the Muslims, but after several years of fruitless efforts, he recognised his failure and returned to Italy (S. Kryczyński 1935b). The Ottoman historians Mehmed (Muḥammad) Ağa Fındıklılı (d. 1726) and Evliya Çelebi (d. 1682) recorded that Lithuanian Muslims studied in Hedjaz, and the unknown author of the earlier referred to *Risāle* apparently had interviewed several Lithuanian pilgrims in Mecca and Medina.

Polish Muslims remember fondly King Sigismund II Augustus (r. 1548–1572) as the Christian ruler who infuriated his Catholic court by expressing in public "his love for the religion of Islam because its teachings and traditions are pure" (in Polish archaic vernacular: *Kocham ich i ich religie bo ona zasadza sie na czystości nauki obyczajów).* The last Jagiellon rulers of the Polish-Lithuanian Commonwealth established friendliest relations with the Ottoman State when compared with other periods of Polish history. King Sigismund I the Old, for instance, abolished the *kunica,* a weird levy on married Muslim daughters, whereas his son Sigismund II August invalidated the old law which did not allow a Muslim to witness against a Christian culprit (S. Kryczyński 1934).

Sigismund II August's 'pro-Islamic' policy, however, was reverted by Stephen Báthory (r. 1576–1586 as Polish king and 1571–1576 as Prince of Transylvania), who was elected Polish king after a tumultuous interregnum. In 1588, Báthory removed all Muslims from the Lithuanian administration. Some Polish Christian magnates built their own private prisons for Tatar captives, called 'tatarnie', where Muslim captives were tortured, branded, or mutilated. The Voivoda of Cracow, Stanisław Lubomirski, kept 'tatarnia' – Tatars – in his castle of Rzemień. He had used Muslim captives as a cheap labour force for the construction of numerous monasteries, castles, and churches throughout his domains. 'Killing fields' of Muslim prisoners existed also in a 'private city' that was owned by the powerful magnate Stanisław Żułkiewski.

Not all Polish magnates, however, were anti-Muslim fanatics. Some of them, like the Princes Mikołaj 'Black' Radziwiłł and Jan Albrecht Radziwiłł, protected the Islamic 'way of life' of their Tatar troops. At the beginning of the eighteenth century, several Muslim settlements were established on their Lithuanian domains. Many victimised Muslim Tatars settled in Kleck, Nieśwież, Słuck, Orda, Januszyny, Żuprany, Gieciszki, and Osmołowo under Radziwiłł protection, among them even the Tatar prince Zakariya Korycki who received the village of Iwanowo. King John II Casimir (r. 1648–1668) settled many Muslim war veterans in Belarus. In July 1551, the town of Oratov and the villages of Dulickie and Rastowice were settled by Tatar war veterans who had fought against the Ukrainian insurgents of Bohdan Chmielnitzky (1648–1655). In 1656, the Crimean khan Muḥammad Giray IV (r. 1641–1644 and 1654–1666) supported the Polish king against the Swedish invasion. In the Battle of Warsaw (28 July 1656) – although an overall victory for the invading Swedish and Brandenburg allies – the Crimean *aga* Subḥān Ghāzī and his 2,000 strong cavalry almost killed the Swedish king Carl X Gustav (r. 1654–1660). The Crimean Muslim allies of John II Casimir also raided Prussia where they are said to have killed about 20,000 people.

In 1679, the Polish King John III Sobieski (r. 1674–1696) settled his Muslim soldiers in the Lithuanian villages of Lebiedziew, Malaszewicze, Litwinki, Botczy, Kleszcze, Połatyce, Piaski, Zabiny, and Ruchowicze. The Polish king expressed his gratitude to Colonel Murza Krzeczkowski, a Muslim royal henchman who had shielded the king from a mortal blow of a Turkish sabre in the Battle of Parkany. The Polish shock troops were defeated in Moldavia, but Murza Krzeczkowski received the villages of Kruszyniany, Luzany i Bialgorce. Ramadan-Romanowski obtained Strudzianka. Two Muslim cavalrymen, Bogdan Kinski and Ghazi Sielecki, were rewarded with the villages of Bohoniki, Drahle, and Malawicze in the region of Podlasie.

However, in the 1710, the political and social situation of Muslims in Lithuania and Poland changed dramatically. Jan Scipio del Campo, a demagogue from Lida, described in the Parliament the Polish Muslims as a *gens infenssima*, a 'hostile tribe', which "must be expelled mercilessly from their possessions without any compensation" *(sine stipendio ex fundis possesis quam rigorississime caveantur)*. The persecution and harassment of the Tatar Muslims during the Polish Civil War of 1715 – a side event of the Great Northern War (1700–1721) – ignited their second mass exodus to the Ottoman-controlled territories of Wallachia, Dobrudja, and Moldavia, where they joined the army of the Sublime Porte.

The position of the Muslims improved again under the rule of Poland's 'Saxon kings' of the Wettin dynasty. Augustus II the Strong (r. as Polish king 1697–1704 and 1709–1733, as Frederick Augustus I, Prince-Elector of Saxony, 1694–1733) restored all Muslim *immunitates et libertates non obstantibus quibus vis privatis laudis, lege publica ventis invilabiliter*. His successor, Augustus III (r. as Polish king 1734–1763, as Frederick Augustus II, Prince-Elector of Saxony, 1733–1763), declared in his charter of 1736, that Muslim Tatars living in the Grand Duchy of Lithuania *iure terrestri gaudentes* ('who enjoyed the law of land possession') under the old rule of the Lithuanian Grand Dukes, will repossess *in toto* all lost obtained acreage (S. Kryczyński 1938; L. Kryczyński 1935a). In 1727, Augustus II awarded Mustafa Montusz by a new possession of the village of Ortel in Podlasie (north-eastern Poland). In 1744, Augustus III distributed the villages of Prusk, Wyczółki and Pisczac between the brothers Jan, Ali, and Shamil Czymabajewicz. Mustafa Ibrahimowicz received the village of Szypowicze. The Muslim settlers rebuilt destroyed mosques and established new *djemiaty*, or Muslim community, in Łowczyce, Dowbuciszki and Minsk Litewski. Due to a very small number of their own educated spiritual leaders, the larger Polish-Lithuanian Muslim settlements invited *imāms* from the Crimean Khanate. The first known Polish *qāḍī*, Hadji Chelebi Murzic was elected in 1594. He served as *imām* of the town of Dowbuciszki.

Eastern Europe's Muslims after the fall of the Polish-Lithuanian Commonwealth

After the fall of the Polish-Lithuanian Commonwealth as a result of the 'partitions' at the end of the eighteenth century, the Lithuanian Muslims recognised the *fatwā*s of the Crimean *muftī* of Simferopol. The Polish Kingdom was 'resurrected' as one of the results of the Congress of Vienna (1815). Ruled in 'personal union' by the Russian Tsars, this new construct became known as 'Congress Poland'. In fact, however, Poland had now become some sort of 'colony' of Tsarist Russia, a circumstance which resulted in the course of the nineteenth century in several rebellions from the part of the oppressed Poles, rebellions that were suppressed ruthlessly by the Russians.

Already after the lost insurrection of the ultra-Catholic anti-Russian Confederacy of Bar (1768) thousands of Polish insurgents who had fought against the Russian troops found asylum in the Ottoman dominions. The Sublime Porte never recognised the various late eighteenth-century 'partitions' of the territory of Poland between its Russian, Habsburg, and Prussian neighbours and even risked war with Russia. The symbolic empty sofa for 'the absent envoy of the Polish kingdom' in the Topkapı Palace was a reason of constant rage for the Russian ambassador to Istanbul. Thousands of Polish freedom fighters who were routed by the

Russian troops found asylum in the lands ruled by the Ottomans. Hundreds of them embraced Islam and joined the Ottoman army, among them General Jozef Bem (Murad Ferik Pasha), Ahmed Bey (Alexander Pulawski), Hidayet Bey, Sadik Pasha Czajkowski, and Emir Waclaw Rzewuski – some of the greatest Polish heroes (Dopierała 1988, passim; Łątka 1995).

In the first decade of the nineteenth century, a rich Muslim family Tuhan-Baranowski built a wooden mosque with a house for *imām* in their Lithuanian possession of Winkszniupie (Osipowicz 1868). Jakub Tarak Murza Buczacki (1745–1835) was one of the greatest patrons of Islamic life in Poland and Lithuania under the Russian yoke. He paid for the reconstruction of the mosque in Lebiedziew which was burned down during war. After the partition of Poland between Russia, Prussia and Austria, toward the end of the eighteenth century, he emigrated to Istanbul and later to Mecca and Medina, where he spent several years. After his return to Podlasie in Poland, he was nominated a judge in Malaszewicze, Lebiedziew, Biała Podlaska and Michałkow. In 1818, Jakub T. M. Buczacki was elected as a spokesman of both the Muslim and Christian inhabitants of Podlasie in the Parliament of the Polish Kingdom. Buczacki's son, Selim Murza Tarak Buczacki, translated the Qurʿān into the Polish language. The revised Polish translation of Islam's Holy Book, corrected by Selim's son Jan Tarak Murza Buczacki, was published in Warsaw in 1858 (S. Kryczyński 1935c).

The end of World War I saw the establishment of an independent Lithuanian state and a likewise independent Polish Republic, known as the 'Second Republic', 1918–1939', the latter being dominated by the charismatic strongman and war hero Marshal Józef Piłsudski (1867–1937). It was Piłsudski who ordered the formation of the famous all-Muslim cavalry squadron, the 'Vilnian Ulans'. The 'Second Republic' is generally perceived as a happy period in the history of the country's Muslims. In 1930, there were 17 mosques in the independent republics of Poland and Lithuania. However, this contrasted sharply with the situation in the Soviet Russian-held Crimea, where all mosques were destroyed by the Bolshevists. As a matter of fact, the Bolshevists only continued the work of their hated Tsarist predecessors, since –according to the Polish Muslim L. Kryczyński – there had been 1,556 Crimean mosques and 5,138 *imāms* in 1805, whereas already by 1914, only 729 mosques and 942 *imāms* had survived the Russian policy of 'de-Islamisation'. One of the oldest mosques in Sudak was converted into an Orthodox church as early as 1783.

Almost all Muslim communities in Lithuania and the Polish region of Podlasie built wooden mosques. They are examples of the oriental architecture in the northern lands. The most famous wooden mosque was constructed in the eighteenth century in the Lithuanian town of Dowbuciszki. This mosque survived World War I because the Russian Muslim general Sulaiman Mehmandar forbade his Orthodox Christian soldiers to burn it down. In 1856, Count Eduard Ivanovich von Totleben (1818–1884), a famous Russian general of German-Baltic descent, built in Kieydany (Lith.: Kedainai) a mosque for Turkish prisoners of war captured during the Crimean War. In 1930, the old and ruined wooden mosque in the then Lithuanian capital of Kaunas was replaced by the most graceful brick-made mosque in the northern Europe. In what was then known as the 'Little Tataria' of the Vilnius-Lukiszki area lovely wooden mosques served a large urban Muslim community until the outbreak of World War II in 1939 and Lithuania's occupation by the Soviets. Wooden mosques with a tiny minaret attracted the attention of famous Polish Muslim and Christian writers and ethnographers. Władysław Syrokomla (Ludwik Kondratowicz), Ali Woronowicz, J. W. Bandtke, J. Bohdanwicz, Cz. Jankowski, L. Kryczynski, and other described the Lithuanian, Belorussian and Polish mosques in Widze, Niekraszunce, Vilnius, Lowczyce, Niemierz, Nowogrodek, Dokszyce, Słonim, and Kiejdany (Syrokomla 1857–1860; Strykiewicz-Korzoń 1932; Talko-Hryncewicz 1924; Tuhan-Baranowski 1936; Woronowicz 1931, 1937; Reychman 1958; S. Kryczyński 1936, 1937a, 1937b; L. Kryczyński 1930b, 1934; Bohdanowicz 1936; Jankowski 1896–1900; Bajraszewski 1934; Połujański 1859; Zahorski 1910, 134). Their descriptions of the historical mosques in Poland and Lithuania are often the only existing evidences of these monuments of Islamic material culture, because during the Soviet occupation, almost all mosques were destroyed or misused by the Communist regimes.

When Adolf Hitler's armies invaded the Soviet Union in 1941, the Nazi administration rebuilt many Crimean mosques and rejuvenated the Islamic traditions of Crimea, but after the return of the Red Army, all restored mosques were razed to the ground by Stalin's police apparatus and all Crimean Tatars have been either massacred or deported to Central Asia. Recently, thousands of exiled Muslim Crimeans returned to their ancestral homeland and again the muezzin calls Muslims to the prayer in Bakhchyseray. The mosque in Yalta is still a hotel-cum-museum, where the 'Big Three', Stalin, Churchill, and Roosevelt, decided about the partition of post-war Europe. In Poland, however, the two 300-years old mosques in Kruszyniany and Bohoniki still serve as the centres of religious life for the local tiny Muslim congregation. New mosques had been built in the Baltic port of Gdansk (formerly known by its German name, Danzig), Warsaw, Cracow, Opole (formerly Oppeln in German), Wrocław (formerly Breslau in German), and Białystok. Following the fall of Communism in post-World War II Poland, in particular the years between 2001 and 2006, however, were characterised by open and venomous Islamophobia from the part of what is seen by many local Muslims as the 'new crusaders', secular extremists, and leftish or rightish *kulturkämpfer*. On the other hand, however, is believed that about 9,000 Polish ex-Christians and ex-agnostics have since then embraced Islam.

Eastern European Muslims between revival and prejudice, past and present

Unfortunately, this revival of anti-Islamic prejudice among certain segments of Polish society in newly independent Poland – now a member of NATO and the European Union – is nothing new in the history of Islamisation in Europe. Already the medieval and early modern periods witnessed frequent papal calls for the extermination of the 'wicked Turks, Saracens, and Moors', as well as for the annihilation of the *falsa secta Mahometa ferro ignique* (lit. 'by iron and fire'). During those days, a significant number of Christian refugees, fugitives, captives, and envoys of all Christian sects from the Polish-Lithuanian Commonwealth, embraced Islam when they entered the Ottoman dominions and refused to return to their native lands. Many oppressed Polish or Russian serfs found not only their way to a new faith – Islam – but also to new lucrative jobs in the rapidly expanding Ottoman State. Many Polish converts – often from well-known noble families, like Bielecki, Bialoskorski, Kamienski, Swiderski, or Cegielski – found a new and better life and high positions in Istanbul. Among them we come across Ibrāhīm Bey (Joachim Strasz), a powerful dragoman of Sultan Sulaymān I 'the Lawgiver', and Saʿīd Bey (Jan Kierdey), a translator of Sultan Salīm II (r. 1566–1574). Yodok Detius, a Polish Renaissance chronicler, reports about a nobleman, Laskowski, who rejected the Christian faith and embraced the 'Mohammedan errors'. Stanisław Orzechowski, a Polish demagogue, was infuriated by Elias, the son of the Wallachian *voivoda* Peter, who "went out of the Christian faith and had fallen into Mohammedan error". In 1633, Jędrzej Taranowski, the Polish envoy to the Sublime Porte, lamented in his poem that many famous Polish noblemen accepted Islam and Turkish way of life:

Przy boku ichoglani z handżary złotymi,	*Near* [the sultan] *içoğlan*s [servants] *with golden daggers,*
Ciebież to Kalinowski widzę między tymi	*I see you, Kalinowski, among them*
Albo piękna nadziejo Chmieleckich,	*Or you, beautiful hope of Chmielnicki's family,*
w ubiorze i tulipach spahijow tureckich!	*In garbs and turbans (tulips) of Turkish spahis* [horsemen]*!*
	(Taranowski 1633, 3)

Not all Polish Catholic writers were disturbed by the spread of Islam among the Poles in the Ottoman lands. Nicholas Rey (Reius), for instance, the greatest poet of the Polish Renaissance, praised the Islamic approach toward justice and the tolerance of the Ottomans. In his poem *Turczyn* (The Turk), he states enthusiastically:

Na wielkiej baczności ta święta królowa,	*Greatly alerted is this saintly queen,*
sprawiedliwość, co wszystkie stany równo chowa [...]	*There [i. e., in Turkey], all things are in strict order.*
Tam wszystko porządkiem można nazwać prawie [...]	*There [i. e., in Turkey], all things are in strict order.*
Skoro się okaże w kim co osobnego, to już go slawić, bogacić, by syna własnego.	*When somebody expose his uniqueness, momentarily they praise him, make him rich like the own son*

Najdziesz tam Francuza, i Hiszpana i Włocha,	*You find there Frenchman, Spaniard, and Italian,*
także Niemca z Węgrzynem, Polaków tych trocha	*also a German with a Hungarian, and a few Poles.*
	(Rej 1914, 322)

Interestingly, hundreds Christian peasant women from the Ukraine who were sold on the slave-markets of the Crimea and the Ottoman lands received a high education in private 'harem-schools' and became politically influential wives of powerful viziers, pashas and agas. One such captive – allegedly the daughter of an Orthodox priest from the Ukraine known as 'Roxolana'[1] – bewitched the old sultan Sulaiman Kanuni and became his *haseki-sultan*, a kind of *femme fatale*. The sultana Tarchan, a wife of Ibrāhīm I and mother of Muḥammad IV, too, was an ex-captive from Poland. Some of those Polish female 'Turkicised captives' *(poturchone branki)*, however, spied on their Muslim husbands and sent secret messages back to their native Poland. Many young Christian girls were even deliberately sold to the harems of the top-ranking Ottoman pashas to gather intelligence on prepared actions against Poland (Kopanski 1975, 1976, 1977). 'Marusia Boguslavka', for instance, a heroine featuring prominently in sixteenth-century Ukrainian *dumka* or 'epic songs', was the most celebrated anti-Turkish 'Mata Hari' from Podolia (Podhorodecki 1971, 285–286).

---

[1] Her name was very unusual for a Christian peasant girl from the Ukraine, which was inhabited in ancient times by the Alanic nomadic tribe of the *Roxolani*. Polish Renaissance writers, like the chronicler Martin Bielski and educated noblemen, who knew Latin, declared themselves direct descendants of the ancient Sarmatians or Lehites rather than of the of native peasant 'Slavs' (Davies 1986, 324; Zamoyski 1994, 107). 'Roxolana' – known in Ottoman history as Haseki Hürrem Sultan – was hardly a peasant girl; she herself claimed that she was the daughter of Polish King Sigismund, born to a 'noble woman of his true love'. In 1548, she and her daughter Mihrimah wrote from the Topkapı harem many letters to Italian-born pro-Turkish Queen Bona Sforza of Poland and her son, King Sigismund Augustus. Moreover, as 'Haseki Sultan', the mother of the sultan's first-born son, she had a negative influence on the deeply infatuated Sultan Sulaymān I 'the Lawgiver'. Her son, the notorious drunkard Salīm II 'the Sot', ruined all achievements of his great father and weakened the Sultanate. 'Roxolana' was highly educated and able to prevent or stop two invasions of Poland by the Ottoman armies led by her powerful husband. Polish foreign policy was manipulated during that time by a very crafty pro-Habsburg cabal which established a wide network of spies reaching from Istanbul to Cracow, then Poland's capital city. Was 'Roxolana' a Habsburg-installed snitch in the very secretive Topkapı Palace? At any rate, her letters, translated into the Polish language by the sultan's Polish-born dragoman Ibrāhīm Bey (Joachim Strasz) are preserved in AGAD, the *Central Archive of the Old Documents,* in Warsaw (*Archivum Koronne, dzial turecki, teczka* [Archive of the Crown, Turkish section] *157, nr. 302 (n, fol. 157, no. 302).*

One of the most bizarre result of this Polish-Ottoman historical symbiosis is the augury of Wernyhora, a legendary Ukrainian 'Nostradamus' who lived and 'prognosticated' during the anti-Russian Bar Confederation (1768–1772) which was supported by the Sublime Porte. According to his (several times 'actualised') oracle, Poland will be enslaved by Russia and she will regain her liberty only when the Turks and British together invade the Russian Empire (an, alas, unsuccessful invasion that took place during and after World War I, respectively), when "the Muslim horses will drink water from the Horyn river".

Muzułmanin na znak świętej zgody *Napoi konie u Horynia wody.*	*And a Muslim in an act of holy treaty will release his horses to drink water from the River Horyn* [Ukraine]). (Makowski 1995, 16, 17, 183; for similar 'prophecies' see Kulin 1943).

Despite the infamous claim of the Polish pro-Habsburg and papist factions of the past (and their successors of more recent ill fame) that Poland was *antemurale Christianitatis* – a 'bulwark of Christendom' – versus the Islamic Sublime Porte and the Crimean khanate (in resemblance to what is today perceived by some quarters as the 'Muslim flood' of immigrants), the historical destiny of independent Poland was always affiliated with the Islamic power of the Turks. Norman Davies described this symbiosis in his *The Heart of Europe:*

> Whenever Poland was hard pressed by the Habsburgs, or by the Muscovite Russians, the Poles would frequently pray for a Turkish campaign in the Balkans or on the Black Sea coasts. From the Battle of Mohacs in 1526 to the Treaty of Adrianople in 1829, the Ottomans provided the only regular counterbalance to Poland's more immediate eastern neighbours, and increasingly the only hope of relief [...]. Touchingly enough, the Ottomans did not forget their link with Poland. The 'Sick Man of Europe' remembered the Dead. Throughout the nineteenth century at the gathering of the Diplomatic Corps of the Sublime Porte, the Ottoman *chef de protocol* would call on His Excellency, the Ambassador of Lehistan, to step forward, and an aide would announce his regrets for the ambassador's temporary indisposition (Davis 1986: 346-347).

In the 1980s, during the US-supported resistance against the Soviet occupation of Afghanistan and the Communist puppet regime in Kabul, the Muslims of Poland – along with the absolute majority of the Poles – sympathised with the valiant Afghan patriots. Nowadays, the infamous presence of Polish troops in occupied Afghanistan and Iraq has once again united the Muslims of post-Soviet Poland with the majority of their Christian compatriots who demand the immediate withdrawal of the Polish contingents from the lands of the *Dār al-Islām*. Along with their Muslim brethren in other parts of the 'Old Continent' – in Bosnia-Herzegovina, Albania, Kosova, Bulgaria, Greece, and elsewhere – Poland's Muslim, too, can look back to a long history of multifaceted interactions with other Europeans, a history that was not always marked by conflict and bloodshed, a history should be remembered as it is a constituent part of the European heritage.

Appendix

Muslim population in the Polish-Lithuanian Commonwealth (544 families), 1528–1631

1528	*1631*
3,200 men and women (approximately)	9,050 men and women (approximately)

Muslim population in Poland, Lithuania, and Belarus between 1849 and 2005

Year	Population
1849	5,049 men and women
1851	5,788 men and women
1897	12,680 men and women
1939	1,500 men and women
1994	11,000 men and women
2005	51,000 men and women (including new converts and foreigners)

Sources: O. Gorka: Uwagi orientacyjne o Tatarach polskich i obcych. Zamosc, 1935. – idem: Liczebnosc Tatarow krymskich i ich wojsk. Warsaw, 1938. – K. W. Wojcicki: Wiadomosci o Tatarach i Dokumentacja Kierdeja o lustracji Tatarow z roku 1631, z metryki litewskiej, "Teka Wilenska", vol. 1–6. Vilnius, 1848–1858. – Statistics of the Russian Ministry of the Interior, Census of 1915.

References

Anonymous 965 A.H./1558 C.E.: Risāle-i Tātār-i Leh [in Ottoman-Turkish, cited by Smirnov 1887].

ʿAẓmī Effendi 1303 A.H./1886 C.E.: Sefāretnāme-i ʿAẓmī. Istanbul: Matbaʿ-i Ebuziyā.

Bandtke, J. W. 1843: O Tatarach mieszkańcach Krolestwa Polskiego [About the Tatars, the inhabitants of the Polish Kingdom]. In: Album Literacki. Warsaw: 117–127.

Beldiceanu, N. 1960: Les actes des premiers sultans conservés dans les. manuscrits turcs de la Bibliothèque Nationale Paris. 2 vols. Paris, The Hague: Mouton.

Czacki, T. 1835: O Tatarach. Pomniki historii i literatury polskiej [About the Tatars. Monuments of Polish history and literature]. Cracow: Wiszniewski 1835, 2, 87–108.

Bajraszewski, M. 1934: Tatarzy słonimscy [The Tatars of Slonim]. In: Życie Tatarskie 9, 12.

Bartoszewicz, J. 1860: Pogląd na stosunki Polski z Turcją i Tatarami, na dzieje Tatarów w Polsce osiadłych, na przywileje im nadane, jako też wspomnienie o znakomitych Tatarach polskich [Opinion on the relationship between Poland, Turkey, and the Tatars, on the history of the Tatars settling in Poland, and on the privileges obtained by them, and about the recollection of prominent Polish Tatars]. Warsaw.

Bohdanowicz, J. 1936: Przyczynek do monogorafii parafii muzułmanskiej w Dokszycach [Introduction to a monograph on the Muslim parish in Dokshitze]. In: Życie Tatarskie 5, 109–111.

Borawski, P. 1977: Z dziejów kolonizacji tatarskiej w Wielkim Księstwie Litewskim i Polsce, XIV–XVIIw [Civilisational picture of Lithuania from the earliest times to the end of the eighteenth century]. In: Przegląd Orientalistyczny 104, no. 4, 291–304.

Borawski, P.; Dubiński, A. 1986: Tatarzy polscy, dzieje, obrzędy, legendy, tradycje [The Polish Tatars: history, rites, legends, and traditions]. Warsaw: Iskry.

Davis, N. 1986: Heart of Europe. A Short History of Poland. Oxford, New York: Oxford University Press.

Długosz, I. 1869: Dziejów polskich ksiąg dwanaście [The twelve books on the history of Poland]. Cracow.

Dopierała, K. 1988: Emigracja polska w Turcji [Polish Emigration to Turkey]. Lublin: Polonia.

Dziadulewicz, S. 1929: Herbarz rodzin tatarskich w Polsce [The heraldry of Tatar families in Poland]. Vilnius 1929.

Jabłonowski, A. 1893: Etniczna postać Ukrainy [The ethnic shape of the Ukraine]. In: Kwartalnik Historyczny [Warsaw] 7, 14–32.

Jankowski, Cz. 1896–1900: Powiat oszmianski [The county of Oshmyan], 4 vols. St. Petersburg.

Jaroszewicz, J. 1844–1845: Obraz Litwy pod względem cywilizacyjnym od czasow najdawniejszych do końca wieku XVIII [Civilisational picture of Lithuania from the earliest times to the end of the 18th century]. Vilnius.

Jasiewicz, Z. 1980: Tatarzy polscy. Grupa etniczna czy etnograficzna? [The Polish Tatars. Ethnic or ethnographic group?). In: Lud [Wrocław, Poznan] 64, 145–157.

Jaszowski, S. 1832: Turcy i Tatarzy we Lwowie [Turks and Tatars in Lviv]. Lemberg (Lviv).

Konopacki, M. 1962: O muzułmanach polskich [On the Polish Muslims]. In: Przegląd Orientalistyczny 43, no. 3, 225–240.

Konopacki, M. 1963: Elementy folkloru Tatarow polsko-litewskich na pograniczu polsko-białorusko-litewskim [Elements of Polish-Tatar folklore in the Polish-Belorussian-Lithuanian Frontier]. In: Literatura Ludowa 7, no.1, 29–42.

Kopanski, A. B. 1975: Antynomie polityki zagranicznej ostatnich Jagiellonów wobec Turcji [Antinomies of the foreign policy of the last Jagiellons toward Turkey]. In: Przegląd Orientalistyczny 99, no. 3, 227–234.

Kopanski, A. B. 1976: Kwestia Turecka w sejmach polskich i pismach ulotnych XVI wieku [TheTurkish Question in the Polish parliaments and leaflets of the sixteenth century]. In: Przegląd Orientalistyczny 101, no. 1, 37–41.

Kopanski, A. B. 1977: Znajomość państwa tureckiego i jego mieszkańców [The knowledge of Turkish State and its inhabitants in the fifteenth and sixteenth centuries]. In: Przegląd Orientalistyczny 103, no. 3, 221–229.

Kopanski, A. B. 1992: The Broken Crescent. The Rise and Fall of the Muslim Crimea. Islamabad: Islamic Book Foundation.

Kruman, A. 1896: O Muslimach litewskich [On Lithuanian Muslims]. Warsaw.

Kryczyński, L. 1930a Dobra Łostajskie [The Lostay Estate]. Vilnius.

Kryczyński, L. 1930b: Zabytki orientalne w Wilnie [Oriental monuments in Vilnius]. In: Przegląd Islamski 4, 4–7.

Kryczyński, L. 1934: Historia meczetow w Łowczycach i Nowogródku [A history of the mosques in Lovchytze and Novogrodek]. In: Przegląd Islamski 3–4, 15–17.

Kryczyński, L. 1935: Tatarzy polscy a Wschód muzułmanski [The Polish Tatars and the Muslim East]. In: Rocznik Tatarski [Vilnius] 2, 1–143.

Kryczyński, S. 1934: Zygmunt August a tatarzy litewscy [Sigismund August and the Lithuanian Tatars]. In: Przegląd Islamski 3–4, 8–10.

Kryczyński, S. 1935a: Bej barski. Szkic z dziejow Tatarow polskich w XVII w. [The Bey of Bar. A sketch from the history of the Polish Tatars]. In: Rocznik Tatarski [Vilnius] 2, 229–301.

Kryczyński, S. 1935b: Nieudana misja katolicka wśród muzułmanów litewskich w XVI wieku [The failed Catholic mission among the Lithuanian Muslims in the sixteenth century]. In: Przegląd Islamski [Warsaw] 3–4, 11–14.

Kryczyński, S. 1935c: Życiorysy zasłużonych muslimów [Biographies of reputable Muslims]. In: Rocznik Tatarski [Vilnius] 2, 407–418.

Kryczyński, S. 1936: Meczet w Niekraszuncach [The mosque in Nyekrashuntze]. In: Przegląd Islamski 1–3, 12–13.

Kryczyński, S. 1937a: Historia meczetow w Wilnie [A history of mosques in Vilnius]. Vilnius.

Kryczyński, S. 1937b: O ratowaniu zabytkow tatarskich [On the protection of Tatar monuments]. In: Życie Tatarskie 10, 4–7.

Kryczyński, S. 1938: Tatarzy litewscy – próba monografii historyczno-etnograficznej [The Lithuanian Tatars. An attempt of an ethno-historical monograph]. In: Rocznik Tatarski [Vilnius] 3, 1–318.

Kulin, M. J. 1943: Proroctwa i przepowiednie dotyczące wojny obecnej [Prophecies and oracles on the current war]. Baghdad, London.

Łątka, J. S. 1995: Agent Księcia Adama [Agent of Prince Adam]. In: Rocznik Tatarów Polskich [Gdansk and Torun: Adam Marszalek] 3 (Autumn – Winter 1995), 17–48.

Makowski, S. 1995: Wernyhora. Przepowiednie i legenda [Vernyhora. Oracles and legend]. Warsaw: Czytelnik.

Marcinkowski, C. 1997: Notes on the Ottoman-Habsburg Antagonism in South East Europe and Its Climax during the 17th Century. In: Al-Shajarah 2, no. 1, 103–138.

Muchlinski, A. 1858: Zdanie sprawy o tatarach litewskich [Information on the Lithuanian Tatars]. In: Teka Wilenska [Vilnius] 6, 1–137.

Ochmański, J. 1986: Dawna Litwa. Studia historyczne [Old Lithuania. Historical studies]. Olsztyn: Pojezierze.

Osipowicz, A. 1868: Meczet w Winksznupiu [The mosque in Winkshupye]. In: Tygodnik Ilustrowany, 19 December, no. 51.

Podhorodecki, L. 1971: Tatarzy [The Tatars]. Warsaw: KiW.

Połujański, A. 1859: Wédrowki po guberni Augustowskiej w celu naukowym odbyte [Journeys in Augustow province, performed for scientific reasons]. Warsaw.

Rej, M. 1914: Zwierciadło [Mirror]. Cracow: Oficyna Wydawnicza Narodowa.

Reychman, J. 1958: Zabytki Islamu w Polsce [Islamic monuments in Poland]. In: Euhemer [Warsaw] 5–6: 17–25.

Rolle-Antoni, J. 1893: Dzieje osadnictwa tatarskiego na woloskim pograniczu [History of the Tatar settlement in the Valachian Frontier]. In: Sylwetki i Szkice historyczne i literackie [Cracow] 9, 241–385.

Smirnov, V. D. 1887: Krymskoe khanstvo pod verkhovenstvom otomanskoi porty do nachala XVIII veka, (The Crimean khanate under the rule of the Ottoman Porte until the beginning of the eighteenth century]. St. Petersburg [in Russian].

Strykiewicz-Korzoń, T. 1932: Szkic historyczny o Tatarach litewskich w Minsku Litewskim i jego okolicach [Historical sketch of the Lithuanian Tatars in the Lithuanian [sic!] city of Minsk and its country]. In: Rocznik Tatarski 1, 165–179.

Syrokomla, W. 1857–1860: Wycieczki po Litwie [Excursions in Lithuania], 2 vols. Vilnius.

Szymielewicz, M. 1905: Litowskiye tatary [The Lithuanian Tatars]. Vilnius [in Russian].

Talko-Hryncewicz, J. 1924: Muslimowie czyli tak zwani tatarzy litewscy [Muslims, or the so-called Lithuanian Tatars]. Cracow.

Taranowski, J. 1633: Przewa Żna legacya [Important delegation]. Cracow: Officina Sw.Blazeya.

Tuhan-Baranowski, S. 1936: Tatarzy na Litwie [The Tatars of Lithuania]. In: Zycie Tatarskie [Vilnius].

Woronowicz, A. 1931: Cmentarz muzułmanski w Widzach [The Muslim graveyard in Vidze]. In: Przegląd Islamski 1–2, 16–17.

Woronowicz, A. 1937: Przyczynek do historii meczetow w Polsce [Prolegomena to the history of mosques in Poland]. In: Życie Tatarskie 12, 1–6.

Zahorski, W. 1910: Przewodnik po Wilnie [Guide of Vilnius]. Vilnius.

Zamoyski, A. 1994: The Polish Way. A Thousand-Year History of the Poles and their Culture. New York: Hippocrene Books.

Zdan, M. 1930: Stosunki litewsko-tatarskie za czasów Witolda wielkiego księcia Litwy [The Lithuanian-Tatar relationship during the time of Vitold, the Grand Duke of Lithuania]. In: Ateneum Wileńskie [Vilnius] 7, 530–601.

5

Multiculturalism and EU Enlargement: The Case of Turkey and Bosnia-Herzegovina*

Muhidin Mulalić

Abstract

The twenty-first century is usually seen as a century of multicultural diversity. Multicultural diversity as such originated and has always been flourishing in the Eastern and Mediterranean civilisations. Historically speaking, the West began to encounter multicultural diversity on a global level only after the fall of Muslim Spain and in the following centuries, as a result of the explorations and discoveries of the New World and the colonial process. The acceleration of multicultural diversity reached its climax in the past century as a result of migrations, the globalisation process, and especially due to the Western push for open market economies. In the past, the reactions to this type of multicultural diversity, however, have left a black mark on the pages of Western history, in the light of the harassment and expulsion of the Muslims and Jews from Spain, the persecution of the Protestants, the near extinction of the indigenous peoples in the New World and the destruction of the European Jews. As a result of the American and French Revolutions, such historical outcomes resulted in a kind of 'multicultural rethinking' in the West, with the climax and more practical implementations after World War II. For the past few decades Europe had been a 'champion of multicultural diversity'. However, the past decade has been a decade of gradual decline of multiculturalism and the current major predicament of the European Union appears to be how to address the 'side effects' of multicultural diversity, among them the burning question of legal and illegal immigration. In addition and closely related to this issue, Europeans seem to be increasingly worried about how to integrate 'their' Muslim minorities inside and outside the confines of the Union. The author's objective in this essay is to discuss the question as to whether and how an admission of Turkey

* An earlier version of this paper was presented by the author at the "International Conference on East-West Relations in the 21st Century", International University of Sarajevo (IUS), Sarajevo, 14 February 2008.

and Bosnia-Herzegovina to the European Union could enrich and strengthen European multicultural diversity.

Eastern and Western multiculturalism: a historical analysis

The twenty-first century is a usually portrayed – especially by scholars and policymakers in the West – as a 'century of multicultural diversity'. Such an emphasis projects the idea of the West as the sole guardian of multiculturalism, the yardstick being its secular culture. However, the very valuable (and often different) historical multicultural experiences of both East and West need to be considered more carefully. A clearer understanding of those experiences could provide us with a more appropriate understanding of the role of multiculturalism in the 'rise and fall' of civilisations, empires, and states. It is also worthwhile to consider the multicultural experiences and realities of the Ottoman Empire and Bosnia-Herzegovina which could become the ground for new multicultural understandings and future pattern of coexistence. Besides, our aim is to examine how the accession of both Turkey and Bosnia-Herzegovina into the European Union (EU) could actually enrich and strengthen multiculturalism. In this regard, we shall also address the role of global geopolitics, conflict resolution, multicultural coexistence, and Muslim minorities.

A clear understanding of the historical and cultural heritage is vital, not only for researchers, but also for the wider audience, regardless of their religious, cultural, or historical orientations. Such an understanding is essential in order to do away with stereotypes and prejudices that are widespread in our modern times and could also inevitably enhance multi-religious, multi-cultural and multi-historical tolerance and understanding. Besides, the preservation of cultural and historical heritage is also crucial for the people who share the same experiences of the past, because their identity and self-esteem are based on and derived from their language, religion, culture, and history. History and culture, therefore, have a role to play in the projection of individual, social, religious, and cultural identity. As a matter of fact, it is history and culture or a cumulative experience, which tells us who we are. In this regard it is significant to ask: what has been the place of multiculturalism in the Eastern and Western civilisations? Is the twenty-first century indeed a century of multicultural diversity? Does multiculturalism, as repeatedly emphasised in the West, go beyond its supposedly Western origins? (Werbner 1999).

Multiculturalism as an idea began in the Near East, and one of its earliest proponents was Cyrus the Great (r. 559–529 BCE), the founder of the Achaemenid Persian Empire. Cyrus the Great and his perceptions of multiculturalism and religious tolerance and understanding towards the Hebrews are clearly illustrated in several passages of the Bible. Upon his conquest of Babylon, Cyrus, whom the Hebrews praised as the 'Lord's anointed', supported the return of the Hebrews to their homeland. Furthermore, he ordered the reconstruction of the Temple in Jerusalem at his own expense. Numerous other examples show Cyrus' view of multiculturalism and religious and racial tolerance towards those ruled by him. The Persians are proud to represent multicultural concept as illustrated in a unique *bas relief*, which portrays a four-winged, crowned figure. The two horns of the crown are mentioned in the Bible, whereas the design of the sculpture has an Egyptian element, and the costume is Babylonian, while the wings are Persian symbols (Root 1979, 131).

Multiculturalism was also predominant in the philosophical ideas of Socrates and Diogenes. When someone asked Diogenes what country he came from, he replied "I am a citizen of the world" (Pangle 1998). An idea of multiculturalism was also propagated by Alexander the Great of Macedon (r. 336–323 BCE). He was obsessed with Greek culture and the Eastern administrative advances and values. Therefore, he contributed much to the bridging of Greek and Eastern cultures, a practice continued by the Romans (Pocock 1992). Among the various cities founded by him throughout his empire was the city of Alexandria in Egypt which soon became a centre of science and scholarship. Being a cosmopolitan city, Alexandria attracted intellectuals, artists and traders regardless of their culture, ethnicity, and religion.

The approach of the Romans toward their civilisation can be considered as in line with the philosophy of Zeno of Citium (334–262 BCE), the founder of the Stoic school of philosophy. Zeno, proponent of human brotherhood and equality, held the belief that the world is a single community (Pocock 1992). Such an idea of 'world community', internationalism and cosmopolitanism was indeed the main characteristic of the *Pax Romana,* which was a symbol of human progress, development, and multicultural diversity. Roman civilisation united cultures, religions, diverse ethnic groups, and languages on a global scale. Such diversity continued to flourish in the East under the Byzantine civilisation. Although the Byzantines gave preference to one particular religion – Christianity – many diverse ethnic groups with their cultures were essential parts of their civilisation.

By the coming of Islam, multiculturalism in the Near East as such did not cease to exist. Beforehand, it is important to stress the universality of the religion of Islam and its inclusiveness, which does not recognise race, ethnicity, skin colour and nationality barriers as divisive factors. Islam fosters and even encourages pluralism and multicultural coexistence. The Stoic idea of the 'world community' was indeed reemphasised by the religion of Islam. Islamic civilisation in the course of its spread through the continents had to encounter diverse tribes, races, nations, religions, civilisations, cultures, and languages. Such diversity became the essential part and the major drive for the flourishing of the Islamic civilisation. Instead of destroying multicultural diversity, Islamic civilisation preserved several aspects of Greco-Roman Hellenism, its sciences, literature, language and philosophy, and various notions of the Jewish, Persian and Christian cultures, religions, and languages (Mulalić 2005). Besides, although Arabs, Persians, Mongols, Turks, Indians, and all the other 'Islamised' peoples placed themselves firmly within Islamic civilisation, all of them managed to preserve their particular cultural identities.

That is why until today the Muslim world has been both, mono-religious (due to the religion of Islam) and multicultural (due to inclusiveness and preservation of different races and cultures within Islamic civilisation).

The history of the Muslims in general can be considered as an expression of religious and multicultural tolerance and understanding. Muslims, who understood and applied their religion, did not mistreat people of other faiths. Based on the teachings of the Qur'ān, 'People of the Book', the Jews and Christians, enjoyed freedom of worship. Sir Thomas Arnold in his monumental work on the spread of Islam explored the tolerance that was shown by Muslims towards the Jews and Christians (Arnold 1974, 48). In the two cosmopolitan cities of Cordoba and Baghdad, for instance, Christians and the Jews were prominent scholars and civil servants, yet they were practicing their own religions, cultures and customs. They were judged according to their own religious laws, an approach which reached its climax in the Ottoman *millet* system, which will be discussed in the following part of the paper.

In the West, after the fall of the Roman civilisation, multiculturalism and the idea of the global world community had almost disappeared. Centuries of multicultural intolerance would pass until the West would rethink Roman multiculturalism. Germanic culture and ethnicity contributed to the emergence of the nation states. At several instances, religious intolerance caused the emergence of decades of religious wars. Such ethnic, religious, and national regionalism was cemented by the Treaty of Westphalia of 1648, which ended the Thirty Years' War. Intolerance and divisiveness even increased after the Enlightenment with the emergence of secularism, which became the bitter enemy of all but liberalism. Secular intolerance together with 'social Darwinism' caused revolutions, western imperialism and, ultimately, the horrors of two world wars.

Considering psychological theories of remorse and guilt, it is not strange that after so much intolerance and destruction, the West changed its course. Tolerance and understanding as a result of remorse and guilt were formalised, institutionalised, and – more importantly – implemented only after World War II. As a result of organised labour migrations to the West and the emergence of multicultural, multiethnic and multi-religious societies in Europe, there emerged a need to accommodate such diversity. Therefore, only by the early twentieth century Europe became a 'multicultural continent', if one is to exclude the Muslim presence of past memory in Spain and the Jewish presence in Europe. In addition, Europe also became for some time a model of multicultural understanding and coexistence, which was another reason for mass migrations to the Old Continent.

Taking into consideration multiculturalism as a historical phenomenon, one has to consider that it is not a Western invention, as presented very often quite dogmatically by certain quarters. Yet under a very strong Western influence, many believe that Western countries alone have been bastions of multiculturalism. Our foregoing analysis has already pointed out that this is not in accordance with the realities of history. As a matter of fact, most of the Western countries have been experimenting with multiculturalism only for the past fifty or so years. Besides, it is important to mention that Europe has managed to fulfil some historical preconditions, such as political and economic stability and prosperity, which contributed towards the emergence and flourishing of multiculturalism.

Therefore and in the light of the fulfilment of those historical preconditions, one can not expect from 'new democracies' such as Turkey and Bosnia-Herzegovina to foster ad hoc functioning multiculturalism because of the lack of certain political and economic predicaments. As a matter of fact, the to a certain extend successful experiments in countries like Britain and the Netherlands are currently seriously shaken up, not because of political and economic challenges, but because of the inability of the 'indigenous' masses to accept multiculturalism and coexistence. Therefore, in spite of all charters, conventions and laws regarding multicultural coexistence, intolerance in Europe has actually increased over the past decade and is today at an alarming stage.[1] Why does Europe face such multicultural predicament? Why do many European scholars and policymakers consider multiculturalism a 'failed mission'? In answering such questions and connected to what has been discussed above, the problem of cultural clash and cultural dominance should be considered more carefully than done in the past. Western cultural supremacy is in theory presented as universal while all the other cultures, including the previously mentioned historical multicultural experiences, are simply discredited. Unless all cultures are accepted on an equal basis and unless unquestionable tolerance is shown to all cultural practices without applying superiority and inferiority approaches, European multiculturalism is destined to fail.

Ottoman and Bosnia-Herzegovina multicultural experience

With their shared historical and cultural experience, Turkey and Bosnia-Herzegovina, in turn, have much to offer to enrich the present world in terms of applied multiculturalism. Their experiences as well as their geographical location make both countries very unique in meeting multicultural requirements.

To begin with the Ottoman Empire, since its expansion it included a variety of ethnic and religious groups. In spite of their often hostile attitude towards the Ottoman 'infidels', many non-Muslim historical accounts show that Ottomans did

---

1 The following titles, written by 'prominent' scholars, imply a significant degree of intolerance: *The Myth Of Islamic Tolerance; Eurabia and The Decline of Eastern Christianity Under Islam; Slave Soldiers and Islam; Religion of Peace? Why Christianity Is and Islam Isn't; The Truth About Muhammad: Founder of the World's Most Intolerant Religion; The Sword of the Prophet: History, Theology, Impact on the World; American Jihad: The Terrorists Living Among Us; Militant Islam Reaches America; Londonistan; Eurabia: The Euro-Arab Axis; Religion of Peace? Islam's War Against the World; Islam and the Jews: The Unfinished Battle; Islam Unveiled: Disturbing Questions About the World's Fastest Growing Faith.*

not intervene in the affairs of their non-Muslim subjects. Moreover, Armenian, Georgian and Greek reports mostly affirm – although there do exist certain reports related to Ottoman mistreatment of non-Muslim minorities – kindness, fairness, freedom and justice to all communities under Ottoman rule. Being a multicultural empire, the Ottomans as a result developed the very unique *millet* (Ottoman-Turk., from Arab. *millah*) or the 'community system'. Although this system existed to a certain extent among previous Muslim empires, the Ottomans are credited for its institutionalisation. In order to implement justice in the state towards so many diverse multicultural groups, the Ottomans divided communities according to their religion and developed a system based on the relationship between members *within* such communities, as well as with other religious groups and with the state. The Muslims were organised as the *millet al-islām* – regardless of their race, language or culture. Therefore, Turks, Arabs, Kurds, Albanians, Bosnians and others, whose cultures and languages differed, were sharing *one* particular *millet*. The non-Muslims, too, were organised according to their religion and, therefore, the Orthodox, Catholic and Jewish communities or *millets* existed side-by-side.

It is significant to mention that it had been the Ottoman sultan Muḥammad II Fātiḥ (r. 1444–1446 and 1451–1481, 'Mehmed the Conqueror') who initiated the establishment of the *millet* system after his conquest of Constantinople in 1453. The *millet* system was based on religious adherence, rather than ethnicity or geographical location. Mehmed's *millet* system determined how the Ottoman Empire would administer diverse ethnic and religious groups for almost five centuries. *Millet* status was later granted to *all* other non-Muslim communities, who were represented and enjoyed freedom, justice and security. The Ottoman state controlled the most essential state affairs while the *millets* had jurisdiction over education with the medium of instruction of community's choice, social security, welfare system, health, religious affairs and family laws. Each *millet* had its own law courts over which the state did not have authority. However, the non-Muslims were only subjected to the state's penal code and they had to pay the poll-tax (Arab.: *jizyah*) in return for protection as well as the canonical land tax (Arab.: *kharāj*). It is important to mention that by the time of the Ottoman *tanzimat* or reform period, in the 1860s and 1870s, the *millet* system was reorganised in order in to meet the demands of the multi-religious and multicultural communities of the state. Such an arrangement, however, did not prevent many non-Muslims from holding key positions in the Ottoman Empire (On the *millet* system see Braude and Lewis 1982, 1, 1–34; Jelavich 1983, 1, 49–50). In particular during the fifteenth and the sixteenth centuries, life was prosperous for all citizens in the Ottoman Empire, thus the main criteria for the fostering of multiculturalism and inter-communal relations was fulfilled.

One interesting historical incident, which is closely related to the rights of the minorities, was the Ottoman kindness shown to the Jews who were fleeing from the Spain during the time of the *reconqusita* which resulted ultimately in the end of Muslim rule on the Iberian Peninsula. Jewish refugees found a safe heaven in the Ottoman Empire after they had faced the consequences of the infamous Edict of Expulsion of 1492. It is also worth mentioning that Spanish-speaking Jewish refugees made also their way to present day Bosnia-Herzegovina, bringing with them the collection of Passover meditations later known as the *Sarajevo Haggadah*. Moreover, in particular the Jewish cemetery in Sarajevo provides historical evidence of European Jewish migrations to Bosnia-Herzegovina during the Ottoman period. Gravestone inscriptions suggest that European Jewish migrants to Bosnia-Herzegovina included Spanish, Polish, Czech, and Hungarian Jews (on multicultural coexistence in Spain prior to the *reconqusita* see Menocal 2002, 11–12). This example would suggest that the Muslim lands were the places where non-Muslim minority rights were granted and enforced the state, as it is today the case with the Western countries.

Multi-religious and multicultural tolerance and understanding on behalf of the Ottoman Empire can be also inferred from Sultan Mehmed II's pledge in Bosnia-Herzegovina in 1463, which granted freedom, safety and security to the Bosnian Franciscans (Donia, Fine Jr. 1994, 64–65). Similar tolerance was expressed towards the Armenian Christians by Sultan Salīm I 'the Grim' (r. 1512–1520) and Sultan Maḥmūd II (r. 1808–1839) in 1517 and in 1830, respectively (Braude, Lewis 1982, 1, 388).

By the end of the nineteenth century, it had become clear that the reforms of the Ottoman *tanzimat* period had been were unable to deal with economic decline, serious shortcomings of the administrative structure of the state, and the subsequent breakdown of public order. Therefore, with such predicaments, multiculturalism began gradually to decline. Reforms in the educational, administrative, economic, military, and political aspects of life also disrupted the *millet* system. Due to the influence of nationalism, the Ottomans attempted to promote 'Pan-Ottomanism' whereby the divisions of the society into Muslim and non-Muslim would gradually disappear. By that time, the main task of the *millets* was seen as promoting loyalty to the Ottoman Empire (Çolak 2006).

What is usually described as the 'decline' of the Ottoman Empire could be closely related to the rapid spreading of nationalism during the nineteenth and early twentieth centuries. Historically speaking, nationalism affected not only the disintegration of the Ottoman Empire, but also that of Austria-Hungary and Tsarist Russia. As a result, multinational and multicultural disappeared form the maps. Various peoples which previously had been under the Ottoman Empire – Bulgarians, Romanians, Greeks, Serbs, Bosnians and Albanians – aimed at national unification and self-determination based not on religion but common language, history, culture, and geography. Therefore, religious identity under the Ottoman *millet* system was replaced by very strong sense of Ottoman, Serbian, Albanian, Greek, Bulgarian and other nationalisms. Nationalism – at times very dogmatic – from the part of former non-Muslim subjects of the Sublime Porte was often based on the epic folk songs, glorifying the struggle against 'the Turk' (Details in Judah 1997, 73–89). The literary works of Balkan authors, such as those of Ivan Gundulić *(Osman)*, Ivan Mažuranić *(Smail Aga's Death)*, Petar Petrović Njegoš *(The Mountain Wreath)*, and Ivan Vazov *(Under the Yoke)*, were purposefully written to portray

Muslims and Ottoman Turks as uncivilised. Driven by fanatical waves of nationalism, Ottoman minorities, all too often with the tacit or open support of several European powers, revolted openly against the Ottoman Empire. Peaceful coexistence of the diverse groups of people within the Ottoman Empire soon turned into bloody ethnic conflicts. In the Balkans and Anatolia, ethnic conflicts resulted in the death, expulsion and dislocation of millions in the century that preceded the end of the Ottoman state in the aftermath of World War I. During those ethnic conflicts, Turks, Greeks, Serbs, Bulgarians, Albanians, Jews, Bosnians, Armenians and Arabs were equally victims.

Historical multicultural experience is very much an integral part of Bosnia-Herzegovina. Since its early history, the country was connected to different empires and civilisations that left a great mark on its history, culture, religion and overall its identity. What is now Bosnia-Herzegovina was part of the Roman, Byzantine, Serbian, Ottoman and Habsburg empires. However, of all those civilisations and powers, it had been the Ottomans who had left the greatest mark on Bosnia-Herzegovina (on Bosnian Muslim identity see Velikonja 2003, 19). The Ottomans deeply influenced – between the country's conquest in 1463 until its annexation by Austria-Hungary in 1878 – Bosnia-Herzegovina's culture, language, arts, architecture and religion.

In Bosnia-Herzegovina's towns and cities, the *Bascarsija* or 'oriental bazaar', is the legacy of the Ottoman Empire and one of the greatest examples of multicultural inclusiveness. Throughout the country, the Old City is usually the place where one can find a Serbian Orthodox Church, the Roman Catholic Cathedral, a Jewish synagogue and a mosque – houses of worship of communities which all flourished under Ottoman rule in Bosnia-Herzegovina. The most important characteristic of the Old City is its market which was the place where all groups freely came together to buy and sell (Karahasan 1994, 3–16).Such coexistence contributed to significant oriental influence on local Bosniak, Croat and Serb culture, language, literature, customs and practices. During the Ottoman period, Bosnia-Herzegovina did not encounter the brand of internal religious warfare based that cause the deaths of millions elsewhere in Europe in the course of history. That is why Sarajevo, the capital city of Bosnia-Herzegovina, became also known as the 'Jerusalem' of Europe (based on the etymology of 'Jerusalem', often referred to as 'City of Peace').

In 1918, after the break-up of the Austro-Hungarian Empire, the Kingdom of the Serbs, Croats and Slovenes emerged. However, the kingdom was conceived as a Christian state, where minorities were second-class citizens. Due to agrarian land reforms, once wealthy Bosnian Muslim landowners became the most impoverished social group. After the creation of the Yugoslavia, the communists created yet another artificial 'identity' in Bosnia-Herzegovina, equally neglecting the identities of Serbs, Croats, and Bosniaks. The creation of this forced 'common identity' resulted in the suppression and, in some cases, destruction of the diverse realities which formerly existed in Bosnia-Herzegovina. In the former Yugoslav republics, a national 'common identity' was articulated, instead of true multiculturalism. Due to this scenario, various types of nationalists revived their ideologies and began articulating only their distinctive particularities. Serb, Croat and Bosniak politicians used highly nationalistic rhetoric and connected it with myths of the past, thus ultimately contributing to the bloody 'Balkan Wars' of the early 1990s (for sources highly critical of historical nationalist mythmaking see Oberschall 2000).

A wrong approach towards multiculturalism, emphasising differences rather than common traits in both Turkey and Bosnia-Herzegovina continues to pose a major challenge. One keep in mind that after the disintegration of the Ottoman Empire, the secular republican state of Turkey inherited the Armenian, Kurdish, and (later on) Cypriot problems. Similar could be said with regard to Bosnia-Herzegovina, where prejudice and interethnic strife has not only let to civil war, but is also still crippling any future progress and a possibility of joining the EU.

The foregoing discussion suggested that the running of multicultural states – such as the Ottoman Empire and Bosnia-Herzegovina – had been a rather painful experience. Similarly, the problem of minorities with a different cultural background is one of the major challenges faced by modern nation states. Since it is not possible to provide each community with *complete* self-determination it is important to develop innovative and sustainable means of multicultural and multiethnic coexistence in order to put national coherence on a more durable footing. In this regard, many people tend to view history as a burden and the main contributor to multicultural misunderstanding because differences are deeply rooted in history, religion, culture and language. Although this is only partly true, one has to consider also the role of history in providing us with a useful experience in dealing with multicultural diversity. Therefore, the Turkish and Bosnia-Herzegovina experiences could be very useful when addrssing the issue of redefining multicultural coexistence. Such an experience would imply that nationalism is the main enemy of multiculturalism. Here, our main aim was not to provide us with practical solutions to the multicultural challenges of today, but we certainly cannot neglect that such experiences contain also many lessons that merit our careful attention.

Challenges and prospects for multiculturalism and EU enlargement: the role of multiculturalism and geopolitics in conflict-resolution

Turkey and Bosnia-Herzegovina are situated on the borders of civilisations that are usually referred to somewhat sloppily as 'Western' and 'Eastern' (Vali 1971, 44). Very often, such borders were, as Huntington (1993, 1998) argued, 'fault lines' dividing civilisations. However, this 'fault line' thesis, which refers also to supposed 'future battle lines' between civilisations, has also been heavily criticised (Sen 2006, Berman 2003). Yet, what are the future prospects, and is it possible to turn such borders of between a new 'Iron Curtain' between the east and the West into bridges in order to unite world's diverse civilisations? Taking into consideration distant and recent historical complexities, this question in itself is indeed very complicated. This author should like to argue that the particular geographical positions of both Turkey and Bosnia-Herzegovina could be used to link rather than to separate diverse civilisations (Ramizer 2007).

As matter of fact, Ottoman expansion and engagement with the great powers of Europe had made the Sublime Porte politically and militarily a part of the European family. As early as in 1856, the Ottoman Empire had joined the 'Concert of Europe' when it fought alongside with Britain and France in the Crimean War. By that time, Ottoman foreign policy was clearly directed towards a rapprochement with Europe, a feature that becomes also apparent when considering the efforts of reformers of the *Tanzimat* period towards modernising the legal and internal structures of the ailing Ottoman Empire, then perceived in the West as the 'Sick Man of Europe'. Later, during the early republican era, complete Westernisation was one of the main agendas of Kemal Atatürk's policies. Since then, especially since 1963, Turkey has continued to turn to the West and has aimed at joining what is now the European Union. Without any doubt, both geography and history play significant roles in the international relations between East and West. In this regard, the Turkish geographical location at the crossroads of civilisations could be used either as a barrier, as in the past, or as a bridge (Ó Tuathail, Dalby 1991, 3). Some Western scholars, however, have argued that Turkey's supposed 'otherness' would make here geographically, culturally and historically 'alien' and even 'hostile' to the West (see, for instance, Robins 1991, 3).

After World War II, and especially during the 'Cold War', Turkey, due to her geographical location between two continents, became of particular strategic interest to both NATO and the Soviet Union. The West saw Turkey as vital for defending its 'soft flank' in Southeast Europe (Azbet, Müftüler-Baç 2000). In light of her rather confrontational experiences with Russia which date back far into the eighteenth century, Turkey joined NATO in 1952, and until the 1990s Turkey perceived itself as a key country defending Western Europe against what was perceived a threat from the part of the former Soviet Union. Since the fall of the 'Iron Curtain' and the EU enlargement towards Eastern European former socialist states, however, Turkey's strategic importance to the West has diminished (Bilgin 2004). Many Western policymakers and strategists tend to see Turkey today as a separating wall between the EU and Asia. Some would even assert that Turkey does not belong to any particular region because it is somehow 'in between'. Would Turkey thus become once again a 'curtain' or rather a bridge between the Middle East and Europe?

Due to its historical background and unique geographical position, Turkey continues to face at times rather strained relations with both Greece and Cyprus – both countries being members of the European Union. However, it could also be argued that Turkey's geographical location and her historical and cultural connections with Europe (in particular the Balkans), the Caucasus, and the Middle East could also be used to bridge rather than to divide and separate these diverse worlds. This author strongly believes that with a Turkish EU membership 'fault lines', as Huntington coined them, could well become meeting points of diverse cultures and civilisations. Such a 'civilisational dialogue' would also be useful in order to resolve Turkish differences with the EU, and in particular with Greece and Cyprus, as those differences are all too often loaded with emotions and mutual misperceptions that are rooted in the experiences of the past (Onis 2006). Secondly, since Turkey is located at the crossroads of international politics, she can also play a leading role in the future EU integration process of the Balkan states, especially that of Bosnia-Herzegovina, due to its historical and cultural connections with the region. Turkey could well become a leading model for new Balkan applicants to EU. Turkey is indeed ahead in meeting EU criteria for full membership because of its successful reforms in the past few years, not to mention her fast growing economy (Aybet 2006). Thirdly, the Turkish strategic location could be useful when thinking of mediating between the Muslim world and the West. Therefore, the Turkish geographical location should perhaps not be considered a 'problem', as some scholars argue, but rather on the contrary, in today's global world without borders it should be considered a real asset, a 'bridge of multicultural diversity' rather than a divisive factor.

Bosnia-Herzegovina, in turn, became in history the 'front line' between Byzantine Orthodoxy and Western European Catholicism, a 'front' which run partly along the river Drina, which today constitutes Bosnia-Herzegovina's eastern border. This division was geographical, cultural, linguistic and religious. The climax was reached with the 'Great Schism' of 1054, the quasi 'official' date for the split of Christianity into Eastern Orthodox and Western Catholic Christianity. A particular Bosnian brand of Christianity, known as the Bogomils or 'Bosnian Church', emerged as a result of such division (Malcolm 1996, 27–42). Prior to the coming of the Ottomans, medieval Bosnia-Herzegovina cherished religious tolerance and coexistence among these three different Christian faiths (for and excellent study on Bosnian unity in religious diversity see Mahmutcehajić 2000). Just like Turkey, Bosnia-Herzegovina too saw itself between two major civilisations – Eastern Orthodox Christianity and Western Catholic Christianity.

After the arrival of the Ottomans on the Balkan scene and the subsequent Islamisation process, Bosnia-Herzegovina became once more another dividing point, this time between the Muslim Ottoman Empire and Western Christendom. Many medieval authors considered this new frontline yet another feature of the supposedly 'perennial struggle' between Christianity and Islam, an attitude that has largely prevailed up to our own timers considering the fact of Bosnia-Herzegovina's mixed population of Muslims, Catholic and Orthodox Christians. This 'mixture', however, can also be considered a 'multicultural asset' which manifested itself during most periods of the country's history various facets of interaction. This valuable historical multicultural experience provides therefore some important lessons related to the current issue of 'civilisational dialogue'. Instead of the still prevailing phobias and rather negative views of the (Ottoman) past by mainly non-Muslim quarters in most of the Balkan countries, however, this past should rather be considered as a an example of the *constructive* engagement of the world of Islam with the West – based on the earlier outlined historical realities of

Ottoman tolerance and leniency towards their non-Muslim subjects. Therefore, in order to counter certain post-Cold War geopolitical strategists who still view history as a potential for renewed 'clashes' (Huntington 1998, Barber 1995, Pearse 2004, Lewis 2002), one should rather envisage possibilities of dialogue that are based on the historical consciousness of cross-cultural geographical regions like Turkey and Bosnia-Herzegovina. Of special interest is the anser to the question whether Bosnia-Herzegovina would be able to function as a bridge between the Muslim and Western worlds?

During World War II, Bosnia-Herzegovina was a battleground where Germans, Croats, Serbs and the Partisans – the local resistance fighters – fought over the control of the country. In the course of the war, Serb and Croat nationalist pretensions on Bosnia-Herzegovina were great. As a result of the emergence of post-World War II Yugoslavia, Bosnia-Herzegovina was once again seen as a block between the 'mainland' Serb and Croat territories, respectively. The quasi inter-communal 'borders of separation' that existed *de facto* within Bosnia-Herzegovina itself (especially in the minds of people) resulted ultimately in the 'Bosnian War', the bloody showdown between Serbs, Croats and Bosniaks (Torsti 2004). The present-day political predicament of the current Balkan states suggests that only a *true* multicultural survival of Bosnia-Herzegovina would be able to avoid a repetition of the tragic events of the early 1990s. Only the future will show whether Bosnia-Herzegovina would be able to function as a bridge between Serbia and Croatia.

Multicultural coexistence in Turkey and Bosnia-Herzegovina

It would be very subjective to claim that Turkey and Bosnia-Herzegovina have fulfilled their responsibilities in terms of multicultural coexistence. One of the main criteria for Turkish EU membership, as clearly stated at the EU Helsinki Summit of 1999 and the Copenhagen Summit of 2002, is meeting basic minority and human rights standards, whereby strong nationalistic feelings could be checked and balanced (Toktaş 2006). Similarly, in Bosnia-Herzegovina, there is a need to bring to justice war criminals or to improve cooperation with the war crimes tribunal in The Hague and to eliminate expressions of extremist and excessive nationalism, which has been equally featured by all involved ethnic groups.

The necessity to preserve of the rights of ethnic or religious communities within the state and their cultural, linguistic, historical, and religious heritage and identity should not be questioned. As we have seen, in history, recognition of such diversity was precisely the case with the Ottoman *millet* system. Today, this is also one of the agendas of the EU, and especially the practices in Britain and the Netherlands has shown what would be possible of all parties involved contribute sincerely. However, although during the past years many minority rights and human rights standards met, both countries still have a long way to go. In some EU countries, certain political parties foster even fears among the public, and, by doing so, are undermining multiculturalism. Especially European political parties from the conservative and right-wing spectrum should make a significant shift from their current attitudes on immigrants with a 'different' (as a matter of fact non-Christian) background and should instead foster what this writer would like refer to as 'true multicultural democracy'. Such a shift should also involve a more constructive and perhaps even encouraging view in terms of the EU accession of Turkey and Bosnia-Herzegovina, two countries with a historical and cultural background that sets them apart from the Western European 'Occident', or the *Abendland*, as the Germans would say.

Turkey is indeed a very unique place where, due to her rich historical and cultural experience, many identities continue to flourish side-by-side. One has to keep in mind that Turkey – although being a Muslim-majority country – is nevertheless a secular state. The earlier referred to Turkish Westernisation process has contributed towards the emergence of a secular identity which is still widespread in present-day Turkey, even among observing Muslims. Moreover, Turkey is still, to a certain extent, a multi-religious state where Muslims, Christians, Jews and other followers of other faiths live together in relative harmony. In this regard, it is very important to mention that Turkey, too, has also to deal with the rise of Muslim revivalism. As a result, Islam became an integral part of the public political discourse whereby Islamic-oriented political parties – a *novum* in republican Turkey – have reappeared on the political scene. In the view of this writer, this currently emerging 'Turkish synthesis' of secularism and Islam might also be able to offer political conflict resolution strategies between secularists and Islamists in other Muslim countries (on the role of the Justice and Development Party (AKP) in moving Turkey towards EU membership see Insel 2003). Finally, Turkey has been dealing with the 'Kurdish problem' within her borders. All this combined would suggest that Turkey is very rich in terms of her diversity, a circumstance which should be used to unite the nation rather than to divide it. Only sincerely applied (and lived) multiculturalism could provide appropriate and workable solutions to arising internal issues, whereby *unity in diversity of identities* should become the backbone of the Turkish state. Besides, globally speaking the "[...] Turkish Model, as a model of a secular, multi-cultural society appeared to increase particularly in the novel global context of the post-September 11 era during which cross-civilizational dialogue was imperative for global peace and security" (Onis 2006, 280).

Similarly, multiculturalism might also be the solution to the present-day Bosnia-Herzegovina predicaments. The EU should foster the implementation of the Dayton Peace Agreement and the return of refugees to their homes so that multi-ethnic and multicultural villages, towns and cities can again flourish as they did before the war. Secondly, it is very important to acknowledge the existence of multiple identities that enrich rather than pose a threat to the country. Only such diverse identities can connect citizens of Bosnia-Herzegovina with those of neighbouring countries in particular and of the EU in general. Multicultural identity should become a common identity while multiple identities should be cherished by all Bosnia-Herzegovina citizens. Serious preference should be given to the *institutionalised* fostering of multiculturalism – not only for the sake of the very survival of Bosnia-Herzegovina as a state but for the survival of global multiculturalism as a whole.

EU multicultural crisis and Muslim minorities

In the foregoing discussion, we have argued that multiculturalism and the meeting of EU criteria and standards could help both Turkey and Bosnia-Herzegovina to resolve their internal problems. Both countries could also form a very unique identity that bridges cultural, religious, ethnic, linguistic and secular dimensions. Due to their historical multicultural and, more importantly, their geographical position, both countries could be helpful in integrating Muslim minorities that are currently living in EU member states.

Large minorities originating from both countries are present in many EU countries. They happen to be institutionally very well-organised and connected with their home countries. The organisations of those immigrant communities are often both religious-based and nation-based. As such, they act as a bridge between the host country and their place of origin. Two major Turkish organisations that are already active in the EU include *Diyanet* (Directorate for Religious Affairs) and *Milli Görüş*, the latter being one of the major, if not the major, religious movement, among Turkish immigrants in Western Europe (Avci 2005). The self-declared main objective of these organisations is to assist the full integration of Turkish minorities in EU countries as well as to foster better understanding between Turkey and the EU at last. Although Bosnia-Herzegovina's immigrant community in the EU countries is small, compared with the Turkish presence, its systematic organisation structure could be useful for resolving Muslim minority challenges faced by EU countries. Moreover, this writer would also like to argue that centuries-old religious institutions of Turkey and Bosnia-Herzegovina could also prepare Muslim minorities living in the EU to become useful and good citizens. Therefore, in order to assist the integration process, certain aspects that are in conformity with EU legal standards – such as part of Islamic personal law – could well be institutionalised in the EU with the help of Turkey and Bosnia-Herzegovina, two moderate Muslim countries.[2]

In order to avoid the impression of appearing as a largely 'Christian club', the EU should perhaps be more sincere in its approach towards the flourishing of multiculturalism. Since cultures should not be permitted to clash, the EU would do well to foster the existence and cooperation of all cultures on the equal basis. However, the recent spread of 'Islamophobia' (and even 'Europhobia') through some

---

2 Two main proponents of institutionalisation of Islam in the EU are Professors Fikret Karcic and Mustafa Cerić, the latter being the Grand Mufti of Bosnia-Herzegovina since 1999 and a major international figure in interfaith dialogue.

rather irresponsible parts of the media has seriously put to question the EU's true intentions in promoting multicultural equality (Savage 2004). Conspiracy theories are currently blossoming on both sides of the fence. Perceptions of Western civilisation as supposedly superior vis-à-vis 'others' appear to project 'secular culture' as the *only* measure of 'true' multiculturalism. At times, such (mis)treatment of other civilisations results in clashes over certain cultural and religious norms (for patterns of Western cultural supremacy theories see Bowen 2004). Besides 'secular extremism', the EU is currently facing the revival of several brands of extreme nationalism which is running against the idea of 'multicultural democracy'. The rise of nationalistic political parties and the growing intolerance against minorities are major predicaments of the EU project.

Concluding remarks

This essay has tried to provide researchers and policymakers with some ideas in terms of addressing present-day multicultural challenges. The future of multiculturalism in Europe might also be of strategic relevance in terms of security and political stability. This author has argued that historical multicultural experiences – in particular those during the Ottoman period – could, to a certain extent, be taken as yardsticks when addressing and trying to solve current issues. The main agenda should be the prevention of actual 'cultural clashes' by just and equal treatment of all parties involved. In the past, the emotional projection of the supposed mono-cultural superiority of one particular social group – be it by promoting 'social Darwinism', extreme nationalism, secularism, and religious fanaticism of any type and brand – has been a major source of conflicts. This writer tried to present a reappraisal of the historical multicultural experience by relating it to geopolitics and conflict resolution. He has argued that geographical particularities should, at times, be considered as a bridge rather than as a divisive factor. In this regard, Turkey and Bosnia-Herzegovina could play a significant role in internal and as well as global conflict resolution if admitted to the EU. With an EU membership ticket and with the backing of the EU, both countries would be in the position to foster better multicultural coexistence *within* their borders, by at the same time assisting the EU in dealing with issues connected to the integration of European Muslim minorities.

References

Arnold, Thomas 1974: The Preaching of Islam. New York: AMS Press.

Avci, Gamze 2005: Religion, Transnationalism and Turks in Europe. In: Turkish Studies 6, no. 2, 201–213.

Aybet, Gülnur 2006: Turkey's Long and Winding Road to the EU: Implications for the Balkans. In: Journal of Southern Europe and the Balkans 8, 65–83.

Azbet, G.; Müftüler-Baç, M. 2000: Transformations in Security and Identity after the Cold War: Turkey's Problematic Relationship with Europe. In: International Journal 55, 567–582.
Bal, Idris 2000: Turkey's Relations with the West and the Turkic Republics: The Rise and Fall of the Turkish Model. Aldershot, Burlington: Ashgate Publishing Ltd.
Barber, Samuel 1995: Jihad vs. McWorld: Terrorism's Challenge to Democracy. London: Transworld.
Berman, Paul 2003: Terror and Liberalism. New York: W. W. Norton & Company.
Bilgin, Finar 2004: A Return to "Civilizational Geopolitics" in the Mediterranean? Changing Geopolitics Images of the European Union and Turkey in the Post-Cold War Era. In: Geopolitics 9, no. 2, 269–291.
Bowen, John R. 2004: Does French Islam Have Borders? Dilemmas of Domestication in a Global Religious Field. In: American Anthropologist 106, no. 1, 43–55.
Braude, Benjamin; Lewis, Bernard (eds.) 1982: Christians and Jews in the Ottoman Empire. The Functioning of a Plural Society, 2 vols. New York: Holmes and Meier.
Çolak, Yilmaz 2006: Ottomanism vs. Kemalism: Collective Memory and Cultural Pluralism in 1990s Turkey. In: Middle Eastern Studies 42, no. 4, 587–602.
Donia, Robert J.; Fine Jr., John V. A. 1994: Bosnia and Hercegovina: A Tradition Betrayed. New York: Columbia University Press.
Huntington, Samuel 1993: The Clash of Civilizations? In: Foreign Affairs 72, no. 3, 22–49.
Huntington, Samuel 1998: The Clash of Civilization and the Remaking of World Order. London: Touchstone Books.
Insel, Ahmet 2003: The AKP and Normalizing Democracy in Turkey. In: South Atlantic Quarterly 102, 293–308.
Jelavich, Barbara 1983: History of the Balkans, 2 vols. Cambridge: Cambridge University Press.
Judah, Tim 1997: The Serbs: History, Myth and the Destruction of Yugoslavia. New Haven CT, London: Yale University Press.
Karahasan, Dzevad 1994: Sarajevo, Portrait of an Internal City. In: idem (trans. Slobodan Drakulic), Sarajevo, Exodus of a City. New York: Kodansha International.
Lewis, Bernard 2002: What Went Wrong? New York: Oxford University Press.
Mahmutcehajic, Rusmir 2000: Bosnia the Good: Tolerance and Tradition. Budapest: Central European University Press.
Malcolm, Noel 1996: Bosnia: A Short History. New York: New York University Press.
Marcinkowski, Christoph 2001: Leaving the Gazi's Path: Turkey's Evaporating Eastern Dreams. In: Journal of Diplomacy and Foreign Relations [Kuala Lumpur] 3, no. 1, 104–107 [review of Idris Bal 2000: Turkey's Relations with

the West and the Turkic Republics: The Rise and Fall of the Turkish Model. Aldershot, Burlington: Ashgate Publishing Ltd.].

Marcinkowski, Christoph: From Suspicion to Trust: Rephrasing Contemporary Greek Foreign Policy. In: Journal of Diplomacy and Foreign Relations [Kuala Lumpur] 4, no. 2, 122–125 [review of Achilleas Mitsos and Elias Mossialos (eds.) 2000: Contemporary Greece and Europe. Aldershot, Burlington: Ashgate Publishing Ltd.].

Menocal, Maria Rosa 2002: The Ornament of the World: How Muslims, Jews, and Christians Created a Culture of Tolerance in Medieval Spain. Boston: Back Bay Books.

Mitsos, Achilleas; Mossialos, Elias (eds.) 2000: Contemporary Greece and Europe. Aldershot, Burlington: Ashgate Publishing Ltd.

Mulalić, Muhidin 2005: Alija Izetbegovic: A Study of a Modern Muslim Thinker. In: Journal of the Pakistan Historical Society 53, no. 4, 25–44.

Ó Tuathail, Gearóid; Dalby, Simon (eds.) 1991: Rethinking Geopolitics. London: Routledge.

Oberschall, Anthony 2000: The Manipulation of Ethnicity: From Ethnic Cooperation to Violence and War in Yugoslavia. In: Ethnic and Racial Studies 23, 982–1001.

Onis, Ziya 2006: Turkey's Encounters with the New Europe: Multiple Transformations, Inherent Dilemmas and the Challenges Ahead. In: Journal of Southern Europe and the Balkans 8, 279–298.

Pagden, Anthony 2000: Stoicism, Cosmopolitanism, and the Legacy of European Imperialism. In: Constellations 7, no. 1, 3–22.

Pangle, Thomas L. 1998: Socratic Cosmopolitanism: Cicero's Critique and Transformation of the Stoic Ideal. In: Canadian Journal of Political Science 31, no. 2, 235–262.

Pearse, Meic 2004: Why the Rest Hates the West: Understanding the Roots of Global Rage. Downers Grove IL: InterVarsity.

Pocock, J. G. A. 1992: The Ideal of Citizenship Since Classical Times. In: Queen's Quarterly 99, no. 1, 33–55.

Ramizer, Martin 2007: Peace Through Dialogue. In: International Journal of World Peace 24, no. 1, 65–79.

Robins, Philip 1991: Turkey and the Middle East. New York: Council on Foreign Relations Press.

Root, Margaret Cool 1979: The King and Kingship in Achaemenid Art. Leiden: E. J. Brill.

Savage, Timothy M. 2004: Europe and Islam: Crescent Waxing, Cultures Clashing. In: The Washington Quarterly 27, no. 3, 25–50.

Sen, Amartya 2007: Identity and Violence: The Illusion of Destiny. New York: W. W. Norton.

Toktaş, Şule 2006: EU Enlargement Conditions and Minority Protections: A Reflection on Turkey's Non-Muslim Minorities. In: East European Quarterly 40, no. 4, 489–513.

Torsti, Pilvi 2004: History Culture and Banal Nationalism in Post-War Bosnia. In: Southeast European Politics 5, no. 2–3, 142–157.
Vali, Ferenc A. 1971: Bridge Accross the Bosphorus. Baltimore: Johns Hopkins University Press.
Velikonja, Mitja 2003: Religious Separation and Political Intolerance in Bosnia and Herzegovina. Austin TX: Texas University Press.
Werbner, Pnina 1999: Global Pathways: Working Class Cosmopolitans and the Creation of Transnational Ethnic Worlds. In: Social Anthropology 7, no. 1, 17–35.

6

Between the Muslim World and Europe? A Brief Note on the Balkan Muslims

Mesut Idriz

Abstract

This brief but nevertheless insightful viewpoint by a contemporary Macedonian Muslim scholar addresses the issue as to how many Southeast European Muslims might see themselves and their own cultural and historical traditions within contemporary Europe. It offers also a concise overview on some current trends among them, such as Sufism, but refers also to the dangers of extremism in the wake of disappointed post-Balkan Wars and post-Iron Curtain hopes and the unsolved question of identity.

The two peninsulas and the coming of Islam

It is a well-known fact that the religion of Islam was introduced to Europe mainly through two peninsulas, namely the Iberian and Balkan ones. Interestingly enough, the advance of Islam towards Europe did not proceed beyond those two peninsulas. As for why Islam did not/could not go beyond these two points is still a matter of question and discussion. Perhaps this consequential issue should continue to be the subject of somewhat more in-depth analysis from the part of scholars and students of history as no one so far has examined it in a satisfactory manner. In the following, we do not intend to contribute new ice-breaking results. We rather would like to address the issue from a somewhat different perspective in order to demarcate some of the distinctive features of Islam in contemporary Southeast Europe.

The Balkans Muslims in history

The Iberian Peninsula was under Muslim rule for about five centuries, beginning from the early coming of the Muslims in the eighth century – instead of 'conquest' in the pertinent Arabic literature often referred to as *futūḥāt* ('liberation', lit. 'opening') – until the era of the Crusades and lastly the coming of the Spanish Inquisition. Thereafter, Muslims lost their wing in the Iberian Peninsula and the number of Muslims there began to decline drastically and finally almost disappeared.

The Balkan Peninsula, on the other hand, experienced Islam and was ruled by Muslims for over 650 years, beginning with the early Ottomans in the fourteenth century until the final stage of the collapse of their power in Europe in the early 1900s. From this time onwards, Muslim rule became extinct in any part of the Balkan Peninsula. In other words, Muslim rule in Europe as a whole became nonexistent.

However, in contrast to the Iberian Peninsula, the number of Muslims on the Balkans in the post-Ottoman period in the territories ruled by their Christian successor states did not decline significantly. They continued to live in Albania, Macedonia, Kosova, Bosnia and Herzegovina, Bulgaria, and – numerically to a lesser degree – in north-eastern Greece, southern Serbia, in the northern and north-eastern parts of Montenegro, and in South and Southeast Romania.

The fact that the Balkan Muslims fall geographically under Europe and that they are ontologically within the confines of that continent raises the following question: Are the Balkan Muslims a bridge or a barrier between Muslim world and the West, non-Muslim Europe in particular? In the following, we would like to contribute our own thoughts on this controversial issue.

Going back to medieval history, the Christian Orthodox Byzantine Empire and parts of the Balkans were – because of their relative proximity to the Middle Eastern 'homelands' of Islam – exposed to Islam at an early stage, perhaps as early as during the tenth century. The early Balkan Muslims were generally members of Asiatic tribes which settled for a variety of reasons in different parts of the Peninsula. A continuous Muslim presence in the Balkans, however, began only with the arrival of the Ottomans in the fourteenth century. Although the Ottoman State has to be considered a Muslim 'Empire' (in Ottoman-Turkish referred to as *Devlet-i 'Âliye*, lit. the 'August State'), it was shaped by three distinct traditions: the traditional Islamic conception of statehood as exemplified by the Abbasids, Byzantine elements, and the heritage of the Central Asian pre-Islamic Turkic origins. The Islamic foundations of the Ottoman State conditioned the strict distinction between Muslims and non-Muslims. The two non-Muslim monotheistic religions, recognised as such by the qur'ānic tradition – Christianity and Judaism – enjoyed official protection, and thus to a great extent 'toleration' (Arab. *samāḥah*) by the Sublime Porte. Non-Muslims were allowed to continue practicing their religion. Some scholars have claimed that one church was confiscated and converted into a mosque in each town (Balič 1997, 77–78). Contrary to this, however, the large number of archival documents and architectural monuments serves as evidence against these erroneous claims. For instance, as I have been trying to show elsewhere (Idriz 2002), none of the churches in the city of Manastir (today Bitola, Macedonia) was converted into a mosque.

On the other hand, although Ottoman rule in the Balkans established Muslim authority over a large number of Christians it did not lead to their forced conversion or substantial assimilation. Following the conquest of Constantinople, present-day Istanbul, in 1453, the Orthodox Church in the Balkans was formally reorganised, its jurisdiction and property were confirmed, and it was allowed to protect Christian communities there (Lapidus 1988, 247, 309).

When dealing with the issue of the Balkan Muslims, it is also important to recognise just how diverse these populations are. Although the majority of them originate from the fourteenth century onwards, they can in no way be described as homogeneous. While studying the process of Islamisation in the Balkans, three points need to be remembered. Firstly, the people of this area, both Muslims and non-Muslims, lived for centuries side by side together in villages and towns. Secondly, the impact of Ottoman institutions, laws, and legal infrastructure in society as a whole was great. Finally, the sophisticated Ottoman culture that was being perceived and emulated as being a 'prestige culture' by the indigenous peoples inevitably had an impact on the local culture as well – and consequently on religion itself.

As a matter of fact, contemporary Europe as a whole hosts various Muslim communities which are originating from different parts of the world, such as from the Maghreb countries, the Indian subcontinent, Turkey, and other parts of the world. Yet, those communities are not to be considered indigenous Muslims of Europe. In contrast to this, the Southeast European Muslim communities, particularly the Balkan Muslims, are indigenous people.

In addition to the prevailing four main linguistic groups (i.e. Albanian, Slavic, Turkish and Romanian-speaking), the Balkan Muslims are divided along national and/or ethnic lines, such as Albanians, Bošniaks, Pomaks, Turks, etc. The great majority of them are Sunnite Muslims attached to the Ḥanafī *madhhab* or 'school' of jurisprudence. In terms of adherence to Sufi or 'mystical' orders or movements, some of them belong to the Bektashis (in particular in Albania and Kosova), the Mevlevis (predominantly in Bosnia) or Alevis (especially in Bulgaria and Greece). This explains why in regions such as western Macedonia, southern Kosova, the Rhodopes (Greece, Bulgaria) and Dobrudja (Romania), several different Muslim populations co-exist. It is in these regions too that ethnic identities remain most fluid, and competition between ethnic entrepreneurs is liveliest.

The fate of the Balkan Muslims after the Ottoman collapse

There are differences when considering the aftermath of the Christian 'reconquests' of the lands of the Iberian and Balkan Muslims, respectively: The particularly brutal Spanish Inquisition was clearly targeting Muslim minorities and crypto-Muslims on the Iberian Peninsula after the Christian 'Reconquista' and was conducted in a loud and explicit manner. In the Balkans, in turn, the persecution or maltreatment of Muslims by the new non-Muslim local political environment after the collapse of Ottomans during the late nineteenth and early twentieth century took place for the most part in a silent and political manner. A large number of the Balkan Muslims left their homelands and migrated to different parts of the world, mainly towards the East such as Turkey, Syria, and Jordan, etc. In order to restrain and refrain the Balkan Muslims from leaving their homeland and migrating to other destinations, the leading *'ulamā'*, or Muslim clerics, of the Balkans issued, though not written, oral *fatwās*, or religious verdicts. Since laymen were generally perceived to have no particularly high intellectual capacity and understanding of the Religion of Islam, their *'ulamā'* applied a metaphorical interpretation of religion, implying that if the Balkan Muslims left their homeland and migrated to different countries, they would have committed a 'sinful' or 'unlawful' *(ḥarām)* act, as a layman would be more cautious of not committing sin as it has religious connotations. However, if the *'ulamā'* would simply have implied a somewhat weaker expression such as "don't leave your homeland and migrate to another place" then the layman would perhaps not have paid attention and would not have been too cautious about any consequences. In other words, the specific term *ḥarām* has a religious implication.

However, this particularly religious feature did not fully prevent local Muslim inhabitants from emigrating. At the present, in Turkey, for instance, there are more than five million Balkan Muslim immigrants, in Syria and Jordan over a hundred thousand, not to speak of other places. Following their massive migration during the early twentieth century, urban Muslim elites have practically disappeared from the eastern Balkans (Bulgaria, Greece, and Romania). In the western Balkans (Bosnia-Herzegovina, Albania, Kosova, and western Macedonia), the urban Muslim presence dating back to the Ottoman period is still perceptible, but there are deep rifts within the Muslim communities in these areas between secularised urban populations on the one hand, and rural or neo-urban populations attached to traditional religious and cultural practices, on the other (Bougarel 2005, 7).

The geographical distribution of the Muslim populations in the Balkans is very uneven. Up to 1991, the only Balkan state where a majority of the population (roughly 70 percent) had an Islamic cultural background was Albania. With the break-up of Yugoslavia, two other political states or quasi-states with a Muslim majority appeared: the so-called 'Bošniak-Croat Federation'-one of the two entities of Bosnia-Herzegovina where approximately 75 percent of the population is Muslim, and the Serbian province of Kosova, whose final status is still uncertain, and where some 90 percent of the population is Muslim. There are also large Muslim minorities in Macedonia (33 percent), in what was was until June 2006 Serbia-Montenegro (4.5 percent, without Kosova), and Bulgaria. Greece and Romania have relatively small and very localised Muslim populations in Western Thrace and Dobrudja (1.5 percent and 0.2 percentr, respectively) (Bougarel 2005, 7–8).

From a religious point of view, the most immediate consequence of the withdrawal of the Ottoman Empire was the creation of Islamic religious institutions limited to the respective territories of the new (now non-Muslim dominated) Balkan states. At that time, that is to say from the early twentieth century onwards,

Balkan Muslim communities tended to structure themselves around their religious institutions – mainly *madrasah*s (religious schools), *waqf*s (inalienable religious endowments), and *sharīʻah* or religious courts – and to negotiate their allegiance to the dominating political power or the government of the day on a clientelistic basis. The two relative exceptions were Albania, a country with a Muslim majority in which the Sunni elites conserved most of their political power, and Bosnia-Herzegovina (which was since 1878 under the Habsburg Empire and, subsequently a part of Yugoslavia) were the Muslim community created its own political party in 1906 and mobilised itself in the 1930s to defend Bosnia-Herzegovina as a distinct territorial entity (Bougarel 2005, 9).

However, with the installation of new Communist regimes in Yugoslavia as well elsewhere on the Balkans, following World War II all the above religious institutions were abolished, and between 1945 and 1990 the Balkan Muslims were condemned to isolation (in particular in Bulgaria and Albania) – with some exception with regard to Yugoslavia, where the doors of the mosques were left open and a few new links developed between the local Muslim community and the outside Muslim world. After the collapse of the Communist regimes and especially after the break-up of Yugoslavia, the situation of the Balkan Muslims took different directions and forms. It goes without saying that, aside from the local Muslims, Christians too – both Catholic and Orthodox – experienced a revival of their religious activity and self-consciousness with the appearance of democracy in the successor states of former Yugoslavia and in the former Soviet bloc countries of Southeast Europe.

It is worth to note that although the Muslim World has made efforts to improve the lot of the Balkan Muslims those efforts were mostly perceived by them as empty promises, lacking any kind of systematic approach. Along with this, various Islamic movements from outside to the Balkans tried to get a foothold in the region. Although their efforts with regard to the Balkan Muslims were often based on good intentions and had indeed brought about some good results, in particular in terms of humanitarian and moral support, they were not free of shortcomings. At times, certain problems occurred, which caused ruptures in the local Muslim communities, such as the issues of the practicing of different 'schools of jurisprudence' or 'legal rites' (Arab. *madhāhib*), different perceptions of *ḥalāl* and *ḥarām* (licit and illicit), and matters pertaining to creed (Arab. *ʿaqīdah*). Especially the latter became relevant in terms of certain influences from Shiʿite Iran. The issue of polygamy, too, which is sanctioned by Islam but hardly practised among the Muslims of Southeast Europe, arose, aside from other matters.

The Balkan Muslims and the contemporary Muslim world

In terms of contemporary Islamic influences arriving from outside the region, two different trends and quasi-doctrinal fashions had been discernible: Neo-Sufī tendencies, coming mainly from Turkey, and to some extent, from Iran, and neo-

Salafīsm, derived for the most part from the Arab world, mainly from Saudi Arabia. Efforts to influence the local Islamic scene have been made mostly through Muslim NGOs, which often used – and continue to use – humanitarian aid as an incentive to encourage people to fulfil certain acts that are perceived as religious duties (wearing the veil, attending informal religious education classes etc.). All of them contribute to the circulation of new religious doctrines coming from the Arab world and challenge the former monopoly of the Ḥanafi *madhhab*, as well as the religious legitimacy of the heterodox practices of Balkan Islam. These new doctrines are also spread trough books and pamphlets translated from Arabic, videos and websites, and the young *'ulamā'* returning from Muslim universities in the Persian Gulf countries. This new generation of *imāms* plays an increasingly important role in local religious life through their preaching activities in mosques and the teaching in some small *madrasah*s funded by the Gulf countries.

At times, those developments are referred to as 'imported Islam' or 'Wahhābī Islam', in contrast to a supposedly 'heterodox' and tolerant 'local' version of Islam. However, the view of a 'wahhabisation' of Balkan Islam conceals what seems to be the real issue. The label 'neo-Salafists' would perhaps be more appropriate and is a reminder that from the start of the twentieth century onwards the development of Balkan Islam has been influenced by various religious doctrines from the Muslim world. It is more than true that they misused their presence. This has become obvious through many conflicts, as those problems were of a subjective nature that was reflected on the surrounding, local setting. Almost none of the projects of those associations were fully implemented. Aid that was forthcoming from those associations and organisations came with religious and cultural limitations that were specific to each small 'team'. One imagine three or four persons coming from Algeria, Sudan, or Egypt working in an unknown surrounding, not being familiar with the native languages, traditions, and cultures …

With regard to the relations between the Balkan Muslims and the outside Muslim World on any official level one notes that they had been highly limited and ended to some extent in failure. Projects, like the establishing of hospitals, institutions of higher education, banks, and other social and infrastructural complexes have been discussed at length, but many of them have been delayed or left in limbo without further development.

An excessive focus on Wahhābī influences thus masks the fact that they too are part of the internal diversification of Balkan Islam and are confronted with other external influences, most notably from Turkey and its multiple religious movements and actors. Turkish political and religious actors play a very specific role in the Balkans, because of Turkey's geographical proximity and its various links with the region's Muslim populations, which are not only historical in nature but which are pretty much alive through family connections between Turkey and the Balkan Muslims.

At the particularly religious level, however, the most active Turkish actors are without doubt movements with no direct links to the State. The Fethullah Gülen movement which displays certain affinities to Sufism as opened several Turkish-run or controlled colleges and institutions of higher learning in the Balkans, among them the new International University of Sarajevo in Bosnia-Herzegovina which is basically an institution with a rather 'secular' curriculum. Turkish business companies too – often somehow connected to the Gülen movement and acting in unison with it – began to establish universities (the one in Sarajevo that had been just mentioned, as well as in Skopje, the capital of Macedonia). Moreover, various Turkish Sufi orders have developed close links with their Balkan counterparts. Similarly, the main Turkish Islamist and nationalist parties maintain regular contact with some political and religious representatives in the countries of the Balkan Muslims.

With the exception of Turkey, other organisations and associations from the rest of the Muslim World have hardly ever engaged in the local mass media, although the newspapers and other media continue to play an important role in society. Even worse, those organisations and associations did not pay enough attention to the cultural and institutional religious space and rather appeared to be interested merely in enlarging their particular spheres of interest while neglecting the needs of the local Muslims.

Perspectives

The Balkan Muslims have come a long way since the arrival of democracy in their countries during the early 1990s. There can be no doubt that the foreign influences that we have tried to outline above – in particular those with a particularly political background – are worth of careful monitoring in order to ensure the maintenance of peace, stability, and interfaith harmony in the region and beyond. However, it should be kept in mind that Muslim life in the contemporary Balkans – as elsewhere for that matter – displays today a diversity that should be considered an asset rather that a threat to a multicultural Europe that is taking shape before our very eyes.

References

Balič, Smail 1997: Der Islam und seine geschichtliche Bedeutung für Südosteuropa (mit besonderer Berücksichtigung Bosniens). In: Hans-Dieter Döpman (ed.), Religion und Gesellschaft in Südosteuropa. München: Südosteuropa-Gesellschaft, 71–86.

Bieber, Florian 2000: Muslim Identities in the Balkans before the Establishment of Nation States. In: Nationalities Papers 28, no. 1, 13–28.

Bougarel, Xavier 2005: The Role of Balkan Muslims in Building a European Islam. In: European Policy Centre Issue Paper [Brussels] 43, 1–25.

Idriz, Mesut 2002: Manastir in the Second Half of the 18th Century. A History of a Balkan City with Special Reference to Ottoman Judicial Records. Unpublished

PhD dissertation. Kuala Lumpur: International Institute of Islamic Thought and Civilization, ISTAC.

Lapidus, Ira 1988: A History of Islamic Societies. Cambridge: Cambridge University Press.

7

Muslim Intellectual Responses to Modern Western Science and Technology: Between Ottoman Westernisation and Post-Colonial Islamisation

Osman Bakar

Abstract

The main aim of this essay is to discuss several aspects of the Muslim intellectual and political responses to the rise of modern European science and technology in the seventeenth century and its continuing dominance of the global scientific and technological culture ever since. Befitting the status of the Ottoman state as the most scientifically and technologically advanced and the most powerful in the Islamic world during the whole period under consideration until its dissolution in 1922 the author focuses on the Ottoman response to modern Western science and technology. The various facets of the Ottoman response, which is still largely unknown, including to contemporary Muslims, could provide important lessons for the current worldwide Muslim attempts at dealing with their lack of progress in science and technology. In particular, we need to know more about the intellectual pattern of Ottoman scientific thought and its state science and technology policy, particularly its technology transfer policy, as the state seeks to respond to Western superiority in these fields. On both issues, this paper shall provide a preliminary discussion. The author emphasises the fact that the spirit of the Ottoman science and technology policy could only mean more modernisation and westernisation of its society and yet remaining unsuccessful in bridging the technological gap with the West. Just to show how much post-Ottoman and post-colonial Muslim thinking on modern science and technology has developed over the decades, this paper presents the intellectual perspectives of the contemporary Muslim intellectual movement associated with the Islamisation of knowledge agenda. Although this movement is concerned with all the sciences, the discussion shall be limited to the field of natural sciences, the main concern of this paper. The philosophical perspectives of contemporary Muslim critics of modern Western science and technology, of whom Seyyed Hossein Nasr is the most articulate, vocal, and well-known, may be viewed as a pertinent commentary on the Ottoman response.

Introduction

When considering the issue of the Ottoman policy in terms of science and technology, it is crucial to arrive at a proper understand as to why – with increasing modernisation and westernisation of Ottoman society as dictated by the policy during the later period of the empire – the state remained unsuccessful in bridging the scientific and technological gap with the West. Interestingly, governments of the post-Ottoman and post-colonial Islamic world have not abandoned this failed policy. Partly in critical response to this failure, however, there have emerged in the post-colonial era currents of thought that argue for a veritable Islamic response to modern science and technology. The most well-known of these responses, which we propose to discuss here, is associated with the 'Islamisation of knowledge' intellectual movement which emerged in the 1970s. Although this movement is concerned with the issue of Islamisation of ideas in all the sciences, we shall limit our discussion to the field of natural sciences, which is the main concern of this paper. For the purpose of our discussion, we have decided to concentrate on the intellectual responses of Seyyed Hossein Nasr as he is generally regarded as the most vocal, articulate, and influential contemporary Muslim critic of modern science and technology. Nasr's philosophical critique of modern western science and technology, shared by many others, may be viewed as a pertinent commentary on the Ottoman response.

Islamic science and the rise of modern Western science and technology

The foundations of modern science and technology were laid down in Europe in the course of the seventeenth century. We now know fully well that this so-called modern science and technology was in many respects new to Europe, but it was certainly not entirely new in the history of mankind. A significant part of it was inspired by and borrowed from Islamic intellectual culture and Muslim achievements in science and technology. Traditional Islamic science was, in fact, the most important non-Western science to have influenced the birth and growth of modern European science. As such, in both its foundation and characteristic features, this new European science and technology displayed a striking continuity and similarity with Islamic science and technology it had begun to surpass and which was by then at least nine centuries old. The continuity and similarity was more apparent in some sciences than in others.

One of the major elements common to both traditional Islamic science and modern European science was the acceptance of a rational foundation for the study of the universe and the study of man. Both sciences demonstrated a positive attitude toward the place and role of the world of nature and of intellect and reason in the life of man. However, the two sciences appealed to different metaphysical considerations for their positive treatment of nature and intellect-reason. Another important element shared by the two sciences was the deeply rooted appreciation in society of the experimental method of scientific inquiry.

If we are to go along with many Western claims in the past, then experimental science had to seen as a novel invention at the hands of Europe of the sixteenth and seventeenth centuries. However, contrary to these claims, historians of Islamic science have shown that this science had been practicing the experimental method of inquiry centuries ahead of Europe, that is, if we exclude the Iberian Peninsula under Muslim rule from the early eighth to the fifteenth century. As far as empirical science is concerned, clearly there was continuity between Islamic science and modern Western science. If the widespread use of empirical methods were to be presented as one of the prominent features of the modernity of science, then it was not the West but Islam that had created this particular element of modernity.

There were, however, notable discontinuities between the two sciences. As the new European sciences developed over the last four centuries through what twentieth-century historians of Western science have termed a series of 'scientific revolutions', it parted ways with Islamic science, adopting a new spirit of scientific inquiry and new philosophical attitudes toward knowledge, the world of nature, and the religious worldview. Similarly, there were notable discontinuities between Islamic technology and modern European technology, especially as the latter came to be developed after the Industrial Revolution in the late eighteenth and early nineteenth centuries, heralding the age of mechanisation of both man and society.

Ottoman science as an important chapter of Islamic science

In the same seventeenth century that had witnessed the rise of modern science and technology in the West we saw the beginning of a gradual decline of Islamic science when measured both against the development of the former and against its own 'golden age' from the tenth to the fifteenth centuries. A few words need to be said about the periodisation of Muslim innovation and stagnation in science and technology[1] as this issue is closely related to the periodisation of Muslim responses to modern Western science and technology. In identifying the 'golden age'

---

1 One periodisation of the historical development of Islamic science and technology has been provided by Al-Hassan and Hill 1986, 19–21 and 280–283. In their view, there are three distinct stages or periods in the evolution of Islamic science and technology. The first period covering the eighth and ninth centuries is one of transition and assimilation, leading to the emergence of Islamic science. The second coinciding with the tenth and eleventh centuries is characterized by the prevalence of scientific innovation. The third, a much longer period spanning five centuries or more from the twelfth to the sixteenth or seventeenth century is one of innovation in both science and technology. In our view, however, the above characterization of the three periods in question may be accepted as valid only if we are to understand them not in a mutually exclusive sense but rather by way of emphasizing the different intensity of innovation that characterized each period. Evidently, technological innovation is discernable in each of the three periods.

of Islamic science and technology with the historical span of six centuries from the tenth to the fifteenth century, we are abandoning the earlier view of historians of this science that posited and limited its 'golden age' to the tenth century.

We further maintain that Muslim innovation in both science and technology continued to be visible beyond the 'golden age' for another two centuries or so, although its pace of development then appeared to have slowed down. Contrary to the widely held view in the West that Islamic science went into sharp decline in the eleventh century if not altogether coming to a halt, it was actually noted for many more scientific accomplishments right up to as late as the sixteenth century. If we are just thinking of Islamic technology, which historically has always followed its own inner logic and course of development independently of Islamic science, then we are confronted with a period of innovation, development, and vitality that outlasted scientific innovation by two centuries.

Studies of Islamic science of the later period – our 'post-golden age' period – appear to lend strong support to the view that it was not until the seventeenth century that Islamic science stopped innovating. From the sixteenth to the eighteenth century there were three major centres of Islamic science, namely Ottoman Turkey, Safavid Iran, and Mughal India. Of the three, Ottoman science was perhaps the most advanced and also the most well-known. Ottoman science, whose origin can be traced to the foundation of the Ottoman state at the turn of the fourteenth century, was an important chapter in the history of Islamic science. Although in both theory and practice its philosophical orientation was continuous with Islamic science of the earlier period, Ottoman science exhibited several new features, the most important of which was perhaps the adoption of Ottoman-Turkish as a major language of science and technology alongside Arabic and Persian.

In the vast Ottoman dominions, Islamic science found a new lease of life and, since the fifteenth century, became the most developed and innovative in the Islamic world, just as the Ottoman Empire itself had become the most powerful of the Islamic states. The current view is that Ottoman Islamic science reached its peak in the sixteenth century, only to decline in the following century (McClellan III, Dorn 1999, 194). Although there might well have been limited progress and isolated advances in one or two branches of Islamic science in the three regions in question, such as in medicine, the general trend in scientific activity was discernable. Everywhere in the Islamic world Islamic science was in decline. The declining trend continued right down to the post-World War II period when the liberation of Muslim lands from Western colonial rule helped to check and reverse this trend. However, post-sixteenth century Islamic science did not completely die out. Many branches of traditional Islamic science still survive to this day. In the field of technology, however, the picture was far more complex.

Ottoman science and modern Western science in competition

The West's first taste of superiority over the Islamic world – and the rest of the globed – was in technology, not science. More precisely, it was in military technology. Moreover, understandably, it was in the military sector that European technology first penetrated Ottoman society. The West appeared to have achieved that technological superiority during the second half of the fifteenth century, if not earlier. By contrast, this superiority in science did not materialise until much later in the seventeenth century when the foundation of modern science was already well in place. Even then, the West's superiority over non-Western science was by no means total so as to embrace all of the then known branches of science. In some scientific fields, like medicine, traditional Islamic science still commanded an intellectual lead and influence, not just in the Islamic world but also in the West. It took at least another century before modern Western science could declare a total supremacy over the traditional sciences.

In military affairs, the West's superiority over Islam which was then its most powerful rival was made possible thanks to its innovations in gunpowder and firearms technology. Some historians of technology have attributed this Western superiority to the 'gunpowder revolution' that swept Europe in the fifteenth century (McClellan III, Dorn 1999, 194). It was not long before that Europe began to reap the harvest of its military technological innovations. Its newfound cannon power was able to inflict two major losses on the Islamic world, one being the fall of Granada in 1492, leading to the expulsion of Islam from the Iberian peninsula, the other, the fall of Malacca in the Far East to the Portuguese in 1511. These almost simultaneous clippings of both the western and eastern wings of the Islamic world led to its gradual weakening as a global force and as a civilisational bloc distinct from and in competition with the Christian West, although the Ottoman Empire, centred in Anatolia, continued to flex its muscles as a contemporary superpower until at least the end of the seventeenth century.

The above-mentioned historic twin events also marked the beginning of the rise of European states as global powers that were able to gradually dominate the Islamic world and subsequently to colonise most of its lands. By the eighteenth century, the West's technological lead on the Islamic world had widened to the point of giving the former a military and economic superiority that proved highly consequential for their global relationships. It is interesting to note that the Muslims had actually preceded the Europeans in the use of gunpowder and artillery technology. Some Western historians even believe that "the transfer to Europe of knowledge about gunpowder and cannon took place by way of Spain" (Al-Hassan, Hill 1992, 114–115).

Understanding the Ottoman response to modern Western science and technology

Of great interest to us here is the development of Muslim responses to the growing Western superiority in military technology. The first Muslim response came from the Ottoman Empire. The source of this response is not surprising since Ottoman Turkey was Europe's next neighbour and was battling it on many fronts. Turkey therefore had a very good practical reason for taking a deep interest in European military technological development. For the sake of the security of its large Empire, the Sublime Porte had to keep a constant watch on European advances in military technology to prevent the balance of power tilting permanently in Europe's favour. From the fifteenth century until its collapse as a result of World War I, the Ottoman Empire was the most powerful state in the Islamic world. Up to the end of the sixteenth century, it was also more powerful than any of the European states. It reached its zenith under the rule of Sultan Sulaymān I 'the Lawgiver' (r. 1520–1566; known and counted in the West as Sulaymān II 'the Magificent'). The turning-point of Ottoman fortunes only came in the wake of a series of defeats suffered at the hands of Western Christian forces, one of them being the naval battle in the Bay of Lepanto in Greece (1571). Yet another major defeat occurred in 1683 at the Siege of Vienna. In particular this disaster was to lead to more defeats, resulting subsequently in the 1699 Treaty of Karlowitz which resulted in significant territorial losses for the Ottomans on the Balkans – the first time ever in their history that the Sublime Porte had to make such a concession. Given the significance of that defeat, historians have taken the date 1683 as the beginning of a new era in Ottoman history that lasted until 1826 when its legendary elite corps, the Janissaries corps was disbanded (on the Janissaries, see Goodwin 1997). The subsequent era has been described as one of stagnation in Ottoman power. However, it was actually a period of 'decline' when viewed in relation to both the 'golden age' of Ottoman power and the steadily growing Western power. The post-1826 period was even much bleaker and, in fact, catastrophic for the shrinking Empire, as it fared worse than the stagnation period.

There is an important reason why we are concentrating on the Ottoman experience insofar as their responses to modern Western technology are concerned. If we take into account the whole of their experience covering the three qualitatively different periods of their history – the period of 'rise and growth', the period of 'stagnation', and the period of 'decline' – and set this against the background of a West ascending to world supremacy, we would find these experiences to be fairly representative of the Islamic world as a whole. To know the pattern of past Muslim responses worldwide to modern Western technology it would be enough to look at the Ottoman experience during the three periods in question.

Here we have in the Ottoman Empire the most advanced and the most powerful Muslim state in the world – militarily, economically, and culturally – that had tasted both successes and failures in its arms race with the West. At first, during the period of 'rise and growth', the Ottoman state succeeded in making itself competitive in the race. Then, during the periods of 'stagnation' and 'decline', it lost the race despite embarking on a policy of technology transfer from the West. The same fate was sealed on the race in other sectors of technology, although Western superiority in non-military technology was achieved later than in the military sector. In mining technology, for instance, as late as in the seventeenth century, the Ottomans were still as advanced as Europe (Ihsanoglu 1992a, 25). However, having lost the technology race the Ottoman state found itself in every possible disadvantageous situation that could happen to a weak and defeated nation, as had also been experienced by the rest of the Islamic world.

The crucial question is why the Ottoman state had been quite successful in meeting the challenge of Western military technology from the fifteenth to the seventeenth century, but failed miserably in the task from the last few decades of the seventeenth century onwards? This is obviously a question that cannot be satisfactorily answered until more comprehensive research has been done, not only on the state and development of Ottoman technology in each period, but also on the corresponding Western technological development. Moreover, many other issues are involved. Among the major ones are issues of the Ottoman state in terms of technology and military policy, the state of its economy, the quality of its political leadership, the state of bureaucracy and corruption, not to mention the views and attitudes of the religious establishment. All these issues were interrelated and interdependent.

In the case of the Ottoman Empire, the issue of interrelatedness and interdependence of all sectors of national affairs assumed a critical importance, at least for two reasons. First, the state was very much a centralised authority, whose enduring power and well-being could only be sustained if the unity of the empire's extensive dominions was guaranteed. Second, an even more important reason, the Ottoman state had to remain faithful to the unifying principles of Islam as embodied in the *sharī'ah*, the body of Islamic religious law. As elsewhere in the Islamic world, Ottoman political legitimacy was founded on the idea of the all-embracing authority of the *sharī'ah*. In theory, the *sharī'ah* provided the mechanism for the cohesiveness of state and society, the common thread linking state-power with religious authority, and the underlying unity of state-policies and enterprises and the various functional groups in society. In the final analysis, the issue of the degree of interrelatedness and interdependence of things in society boils down to the issue of the quality of the relationship between spiritual authority and temporal power. This means that in practice the effectiveness of the *sharī'ah* in delivering the stated societal goals depended a lot on who was at the helm of temporal power, and, just as important, on who was wielding spiritual authority. It is important to know what these two most important branches of Muslim leadership were thinking about on the issue of the Ottoman response to Western technological superiority.

The practice of the state patronising science and technology had been around in the Islamic world since the eighth century, several centuries earlier than in the West. The practice became more intensified in the subsequent centuries, right up to the peak of Ottoman power and beyond. With continuous patronisation by the state it is permissible to speak of a state science and technology policy within

Islam that has its own history of ups and downs or changing fortunes over the centuries. New outbursts of scientific and technological activities that accompanied new and enlightened patronisation efforts suggested one thing. There was a causal relationship between the two societal phenomena. Patronisation was crucial to the progress of science and technology in classical Islam, just as it proved to be true later in the case of the modern West where and when it took new dimensions and importance. It seems certain that the decline of the patronisation of science and technology in the Islamic world after the seventeenth century constituted one of the major factors for the decline of Islamic science during the period in question (Osman Bakar 1997, 239–242).

A viable and prudent science and technology-policy necessitates an effective patronisation by the state. However, such a patronisation would not come about unless there is an enlightened political leadership that sees wisdom in its pursuit. Moreover, patronisation would also necessitate a national treasury that is sufficient enough to finance science and technology projects favoured by the state. Therefore, in trying to fully understand the successes and failures of the Ottoman responses to Western technological superiority in general and its military technological superiority in particular, it is not enough to see the issue of response as simply one of how to make possible a technology transfer from the West. In itself, technology transfer was not the real issue, nor was it problematic for the Ottomans. The Ottoman state was well-disposed to accepting foreign technology for its needs. At various stages in its history, both during its 'rise and growth' and during its 'stagnation' and 'decline', it had been actively importing Western military technology and techniques.

From the eighteenth century onwards, the Ottoman state even went to the extent of employing European military experts and technicians to train its military personnel on how to use the newly imported war technology. Despite these significant measures, which could easily be construed as either desperate acts or a readiness to embrace a more extensive modernisation and Europeanisation from the part of the Ottomans, the state failed to arrest the widening gap in military technological capability separating it from its European rivals. Clearly then, there was no lack of trying on the part of the Ottoman state to bridge the gap and to catch up with the West. However, the failure of the military technology policy embarked on since the eighteenth century to produce the intended results only went to show that the technology transfer policy by itself would be inadequate to effectively help the state overcome the challenge of Western technological superiority.

The Ottoman technology transfer policy in the military sector has to be seen and evaluated in the broader context of its technology-policy covering all sectors of life. This is important, since a successful military technology transfer presupposes the state's self-sufficiency in most, if not all, of the critical allied sectors of technology. Apparently, throughout much of the eighteenth century, the Ottoman state failed to produce self-sufficiency in several strategic sectors of technology allied and deemed vital to the latest war technology. According to Ihsanoglu (1992a, 28), after the Russo-Turkish War of 1768–1774, a decisive conflict that brought the southern Ukraine, northern Caucasus and the Crimea within the orbit of the Russian Empire and which also featured the greatest naval defeat (Battle of Çesme, 1770) suffered by the Ottomans since Lepanto, "[...] the gunpowder which was produced in the Ottoman land was only good for the ceremonial cannon shots; in order to meet their military needs the Ottomans were obliged to buy gunpowder from foreign countries at a high price".

Lessons from Ottoman modernisation and westernisation

The Ottoman experiences in modernisation and westernisation in general, and in technology-transfer in particular, offer many useful lessons for students of cross-cultural technology-transfer and the cultural context of technology. We may state here two of the most important of these lessons. First, modern technology, when pursued according to its own logic of development and progress, is bound to destroy traditional technology, arts, and crafts. This is because modern technology keeps demanding more and more of the cultural space from society for itself at the expense of traditional technology, not to speak of the demand on its physical space. If a state's technology policy is to fully support the pursuit of modern technology but to leave traditional technology to develop on its own without any state support, then there could be no hope of survival for the latter form of technology. As modern technology generates its open-ended list of demands on societal space, and with the state acceding to them, traditional technology finds itself marginalised to an ever greater degree until it could hardly find a breathing space – if it survives at all.

Modern technology's logic of development and progress is such that not only it drives traditional technology into extinction, but it also leads eventually to the 'technologisation' and mechanisation of society itself. In addition, we are now even witnessing the global phenomenon of the mechanisation of man himself. Theoretically speaking, this 'cultural catastrophe' could only be avoided if the state has an effective policy on the preservation of traditional technology and a wise approach toward the appropriation and acculturation of modern technology within the framework of its value system. Beginning in the eighteenth century, the Ottoman state followed the path of a progressive modernisation of technology, starting with the military sector and then expanding into the industrial and other sectors. With its bureaucracy and upper classes emerging as the main agents of modernisation and westernisation, the Ottoman state was to witness the gradual transformation of the traditional Turkish city landscapes toward the modern western concept – a concept which, among other things, involved the westernisation of architectural technology and aesthetics as well as urban design.

The second lesson to be drawn is that technology is not neutral with respect to values. The transfer of technology from one culture to another results either in the acculturation and domestication of the imported technology without undermining the indigenous value system or in the gradual replacement of the indigenous technology system and its supporting value system by the new technology system, generated by the imported technology and its inherent values. The first result would be a rare success to which we have previously referred in terms of the conditions for it to happen. The second result was what happened as a matter of fact to Ottoman society. As one contemporary Turkish academic has put it, the eighteenth-century Ottoman experience on urban restructuring in the European manner with the help of modern technology led to the realisation that the new urban structure necessitated both physical and social transformations which resulted in value-conflicts with the traditional social order (Tanyeli 1992, 355). In the Ottoman case, this means a conflict between the Islamic values underlying the traditional social order and the modern European values underlying the new technological social order, values which were made largely possible by the unhindered flow of modern technology. When development and progress begin to be measured in terms of the physical and social transformations that must accompany the application of modern technology, then it is perfectly understandable why Islam itself begins to be viewed as an obstacle to progress, as it was, in fact, seen by many members of the modernised and westernised Ottoman intelligentsia and bureaucracy.

The Ottoman response to modern scientific thought

In the field of science, the Ottomans became first acquainted with modern Western scientific ideas, concepts and theories in the seventeenth century following the translation into Ottoman-Turkish of a number of European works, particularly those dealing with astronomy, cosmography and geography. The first known European work to be translated – under the flowery title *The Mirror of the Heavens and the Purpose of Perception* – was *Nouvelle théorie des planètes* by the French astronomer, Noël Durret (d. ca. 1650). Its translator was Tezkireci Köse İbrahim Efendi, a Hungarian convert who settled in Istanbul (for more details of this work see Ihsanoglu 1992b, 68–76). It was the first book to introduce Copernican astronomy to Ottoman science. Through this translation, Ottoman seventeenth-century scientists were also able to learn about the astronomical ideas and observations of Tycho Brahe and Johannes Kepler. In contrast to Europe, where Copernicus caused much dispute, the Ottomans embraced the new theories wholeheartedly.

Other translations followed, further disseminating modern scientific ideas and theories in Ottoman society. Of special interest to us from the point of view of our discussion of religion and science is the Ottoman response to Copernican astronomy which had generated a great controversy and heated debates between its proponents and opponents. The early Ottoman response in the eighteenth century to the heliocentric theory associated with Copernicus appeared to be mixed and low-keyed. There was both opposition against and support for the theory. The kind of intellectual agitation, excitement and tension that gripped the post-Copernican West was, however, not to be seen in Ottoman society. While the debate in the West had degenerated into an ideological clash of worldviews that was of a major religious and philosophical significance – between the geocentric model defended by the Church and the heliocentric system defended by science – the Ottoman response to the heliocentric theory was to treat it mainly as a scientific issue (Ihsanoglu 1992, 75). As clearly pointed out by George Saliba, a leading historian of Islamic science, the best proof that the Western debate on the theory was more philosophical and religious than scientific in nature is the fact that the issue of its scientific novelty was hardly discussed (Saliba 1992, 145–147). However, if the mathematical and scientific justification of the theory had been discussed in light of the sophisticated pre-Copernican mathematical models of the planetary system developed by Muslim astronomers in Marāghah (Iran) and Damascus several centuries earlier, then, in Saliba's words, "a lot of the novelty of his [i. e. Copernicus's] astronomy would fade away" (Saliba 1992, 147).

Ottoman scientists generally adopted a cautious attitude toward Copernican astronomy. Their relative lack of enthusiasm for the new astronomy was largely influenced by their belief that they were in possession of a more advanced practical astronomical knowledge than the West. Thus, the issue of compatibility between their astronomical tables in current use and those of modern Western astronomers, for instance, surfaced as a major restraining influence on their reception of the new astronomy. Once this practical concern was removed, the initial hesitancy to embrace the theory gave way to acceptance. However, this was not to happen until the mid-nineteenth century after the new astronomy had been introduced into the Ottoman educational system following its modernisation. Moreover, this happened only after attempts had been made to persuade the larger public to accept the 'Islamicity' of the heliocentric theory. All these incidences seem to suggest that there must have been also a significant religious opposition to the theory. The Ottoman attachment to the traditional brand of Islamic astronomy was not to be completely severed until the second half of the nineteenth century.

Post-colonial response: a case for the Islamisation of the sciences

By the turn of the twentieth century, we could see tremendous developments and progress in the transfer, appropriation, and cultivation of modern Western science and technology in the Islamic world, particularly in the heartland of the Ottoman world, in what was to become republican Turkey, as our previous discussion has clearly shown. The growing forces of modernisation and westernisation in the Islamic world had made such a development possible. As the twentieth century progressed, numerous factors – political, economic, educational, and military – arising mainly from the ultimate collapse of what was left of the Ottoman Empire in 1922 and the resulting political and intellectual relations between the Islamic world and the West forced the former to be more conscious of the latter's superiority in science and technology. Mainly motivated by the consideration of science as a source of physical power rather than of truth, Muslim voices championing modernism grew louder as decades went by. Muslim learning and acquisition of modern science and technology as a necessary condition for their success in competing with the West became a fundamental article of faith for all Muslim modernists and reformers fighting for liberation and political independence from their colonial powers.

As political power in the post-colonial Islamic world fell into the hands of people with similar ideological persuasions and frame of mind (secularism, nationalism, westernisation, and – at times – various brands of socialism), various Muslim states sought to promote modern science and technology as a major pillar of national development and progress. However, intellectually, they hardly portrayed the image of a Muslim nation independent of the West. The way they understood science and technology, approached it, taught it, and applied it was a complete imitation of the West. There was no awareness of the deep relevance of their own religious and cultural tradition to the successful development of science and technology. Not surprisingly, their uncritical pursuit of modern science and technology has brought about many problems and posed increasing challenges to Muslim life and thought. Moreover, despite the pursuit of more and more learning and acquisition of modern science and technology in the post-colonial era, the Muslim world-community (Arab. *ummah*) does not appear to be any closer to the declared goal of bridging the scientific and technological gap between the Islamic world and the West, as every generation of Muslim modernists and reformers over the last two centuries has hoped for.

In discussing the post-colonial Muslim intellectual response to modern science and technology, it is the other points of view critical of the 'official' and dominant position that we wish to consider. These 'other viewpoints' are largely inspired by the varying and, at times, diverse understandings of Islam and their implications for Muslim life and thought in the contemporary world. Muslim critics of the pursuit of modern science and technology in the Islamic world have pointed to a number of its negative consequences on Muslim life and thought. One of the most important of these consequences is the secularisation of Muslim minds. How to stem this tide of secularisation in Muslim societies by at the same time achieving balanced scientific and technological progress has become the major concern of contemporary Muslim intellectuals and thinkers. This intellectual concern was articulated in different ways in the writings of a number of scholars, which appeared in the second half of the twentieth century. These writings – although often proceeding from different perspectives and premises, attempt to inspire what is often referred to as 'Islamic revival', a tendency which first manifested itself in the 1970s and which is now seen as entering a new phase of development.

The current intellectual concern in question is directed at broader issues pertaining to Islam and contemporary civilisation than just the issue of Islam and modern science and technology. One of these issues is the 'Islamisation of knowledge' debate, which is closely related to the issue of the 'Islamicity' of modern knowledge in all academic disciplines. In other words, the issue of Islam and modern science and technology has been conceived as a special case of a larger issue, namely, the compatibility between Islam and the whole of modern knowledge. It is, however, an important point to be noted here that, while on the one hand the present Muslim concern with Islam and modern science and technology has to be seen as a logical continuation of all the previous attempts at overcoming the challenges modern science and technology has posed to Muslim societies, on the other hand it has a new significance conferred by the 'fresh' vision of Islam and science displayed in some of the writings of contemporary scholars. It is this fresh vision of Islam and science and technology that we wish to highlight in this section.

Before doing this, we wish to offer a few remarks on the contemporary intellectual movement concerned with the idea of Islamisation of knowledge. The significance of this idea to the Muslim community, in particular its *practical* implications for Muslim education, cannot be overemphasised. So appealing was this idea of Islamisation of knowledge to a great multitude of Muslims that it has led to the birth of many innovative Islamic educational institutions in various Muslim countries during the last decades. Perhaps the most significant of these institutions was the series of Islamic universities established under the patronage of the Organization of the Islamic Conference (OIC), the largest international body catering to the interests of the entire Islamic world, including Muslim minorities worldwide. The idea of Islamisation of knowledge was first widely promoted in the 1970s on the basis of the writings on Islam of such scholars as Seyyed Hossein Nasr, Syed Muhammad Naquib Al-Attas, and Ismail Raji al-Faruqi. An important international event which greatly contributed to the popularity of this idea was the First World Conference on Muslim Education held at Mecca in April 1977 (for all the works of the three afore-mentioned scholars that are relevant to the issue of Islamisation of knowledge see the bibliography of our new edition of *Tawhid and Science,* Osman Bakar 2008).

We wish to avoid here discussions of the controversial issue of the origin of this idea. In the context of the objectives of our present paper, what we seek to emphasise instead is the core concern of this idea and its implications for the Muslim discourse on Islam, science, and technology and the contemporary Muslim quest for an *authentic* Islamic science. The intellectual program of the Islamisation of knowledge agenda is basically concerned with the challenge of modern thought in all its dimensions in light of the teachings and practices of Islam. It is based on the conviction that, in light of its worldview and value-system, Islam has its own philosophy and vision of knowledge and its own views on how best to organise, prioritise, and apply knowledge – not only for the benefits of Muslims but also for the benefits of the rest of mankind. The fundamental aim of the Islamisation of knowledge is to create a knowledge-system in which there is compatibility and harmony between revealed religion and human knowledge and to provide ethics of knowledge that could ensure the wise production, use, and application of knowledge in society.

The intellectual movement spearheading and championing the cause of Islamisation of knowledge is now nearly four decades old. A number of academic institutions and organisations have been established over the years with the expressed view of realising its very aims. Of particular prominence are the International Institute of Islamic Thought (IIIT) founded by the late al-Faruqi and based in Herndon, Virginia, in the United States, and the International Institute of Islamic Thought and Civilization (ISTAC) in Kuala Lumpur, founded by Al-Attas but institutionally treated as part of the International Islamic University of Malaysia (IIUM) which, too, was established in dedication to the idea of Islamisation of knowledge. Academic and scholarly meetings have been held pertaining to various aspects of the Islamisation concept, books and papers published, and journals established. The discourse has produced several distinct intellectual positions or schools of thought on the meaning and significance of Islamisation of knowledge. Although this discourse has been partially documented by several scholars, much of what has transpired since the 1970s is yet to be documented and made known to the larger public. More importantly, a critical evaluation of the successes and failures of this intellectual movement is yet to be undertaken (for the most comprehensive account of the discourse available so far see Stenberg 1996; see also Wan Mohd Nor Wan Daud 1998).

Nasr's Islamic critique of modern science and technology

A very important component of the Islamisation of knowledge agenda is the Islamisation of the sciences, both the natural (including the mathematical) and the social – the latter, in fact, constituting its core. Since our primary concern in this paper is with Islam and science understood in its limited sense, that is, as referring to the natural and mathematical sciences, it is to the well-articulated views of Nasr we should turn if we intend to discuss the depth and breadth of the contemporary Muslim discourse on the Islamisation of science and the related issue of Islamic science. This is because no other Muslim scholar has written as much as he has on this subject. Moreover, almost paradoxically, it is his traditional approach to Islam and science that is offering a fresh vision of the relationship between the two.[2] The clarity of the conceptual relationship between science and traditional metaphysics is perhaps the most striking thing in this fresh vision.

In the post-colonial period, one of the most well-known of Muslim intellectual responses is undoubtedly the one articulated by Nasr and his intellectual school. The philosophical position established and articulated by Nasr – currently a University Professor of Islamic Studies at George Washington University in the United States – is well-known both in the Islamic world and in the West.

---

[2] We have listed in the bibliography of Osman Bakar 2008 all of Nasr's works dealing with the subject of Islam and science and technology. His latest work (Nasr 2007) addresses the problems and dilemma of contemporary Muslims in the field science and technology in a more comprehensive and contemporary manner than any of his other writings.

It is not an exaggeration to say that, through his numerous writings, not to mention the countless public lectures he has delivered throughout the world over the last five decades, Nasr has provided the most comprehensive intellectual response to modern science and technology that a Muslim scholar has ever presented in the entire history of the debate in question. Nasr's critique of modern science is profound and based on sound scholarship. He displays in his critique a deep knowledge of both the history and philosophy of modern western scientific thought and the Islamic scientific tradition in the light of which he has urged Muslims to study and evaluate modern science.

Nasr's philosophical position on modern science and technology is very clear. It may be summarised as follows:

(1) Modern science is not the *only* legitimate science of the natural order, but is *a* science of nature, legitimate only within the premises of its assumptions of the nature of both the known object and the thinking subject;

(2) Islamic civilisation cannot simply emulate Western science and technology without necessarily destroying itself; to those who know well both the religion of Islam and the nature of modern science, it is very clear that modern science is a direct challenge to the Islamic worldview;

(3) Modern science and technology is not neutral or value-free; it imposes on man the worldview and the value system of its creators.

Accordingly, Nasr argues, Muslims must confront modern science and technology with a deep sense of intellectual and moral responsibility and integrity in the light of the Islamic intellectual tradition. He wants Muslims to master the modern sciences, and not to shun them. However, at the same time, he urges Muslims to come up with a positive Islamic critique of modern science on the basis of the Islamic intellectual tradition, not only concerning what it is, but also concerning what it is not. As he sees it, it is the sacred duty of Muslim scholars, intellectuals, and scientists to create an *authentic* contemporary Islamic science.

Nasr has been characteristically consistent and steadfast in his critique of modern science and technology in the last fifty years. The intellectual contours and philosophical perspective of his critique have remained unchanged during all these years. Every now and then, it would appear that his writing seeks within this perennial philosophical perspective to expose more and more of what he strongly believes to be the destructive and dehumanising aspects of modern science and technology. Many Muslims do agree with his views, but there are also many others who have criticised his alternative to modern science and technology – an *authentic* Islamic science – as being 'backward looking' and too impractical to be implemented in the contemporary world.

Any attempt at a complete Islamisation of science worthy of the name must aim at two things: one is a comprehensive and profound critique of modern science that is well-documented; the other would be an exposition of the general principles of Islam relevant to all the sciences and an exposition of the specific principles of each science, whether these are derived from the general principles or otherwise. Through his numerous writings, Nasr has largely succeeded in realising both aims. Certainly, he has succeeded in marshalling an array of profound arguments that lay bare the limitations and shortcomings as well as the extravagances of modern science as a science of nature without denying its achievements. These critiques of modern science are necessary to the task of clearing the intellectual ground for the creation of an *authentic* Islamic science in the contemporary world. As for the second aim, Nasr's contribution to its realisation is rather extensive. He has given an exposition of most if not all of the Islamic principles needed for the Islamisation of the sciences. The only thing is that this exposition is scattered in his different writings, as different sets of principles have been treated in separate works, as dictated by their respective objectives and orientations.[3] However, some other people with the right interest and capability can always help with the task of identifying and enumerating these principles and applying them concretely to the different branches of science. Still, there is a lot more work to be done. For one thing, the Islamisation of the various sciences is yet to be translated into practical shape in the form of textbooks and methods of instruction appropriate for each level of education.

Nasr has often argued that the traditional cosmological sciences play a very important conceptual role in any veritable attempt to Islamize the sciences. These sciences would serve as a common foundation of all the sciences. In this regard, he has contributed a great deal to the Islamisation of the sciences. His early book, *An Introduction to Islamic Cosmological Doctrines*, which was based on his doctoral thesis completed in 1958 and first published in 1964 by Harvard University Press, provides a wealth of knowledge concerning Islamic cosmological doctrines that are ultimately based on the teachings of the Qur'ān. Nowhere in the book is to be found the word 'Islamisation', but it would be wrong to infer from this mere fact that this pioneering work on Islamic science has nothing to do with the idea of Islamisation of knowledge which we have just explained. In fact, Nasr has discussed in the book the meaning of 'Islamic', which is a key term in the conception of Islamisation, as applied to science, and also the cosmological doctrines.

The central goal of Islamisation is to produce things Islamic. The right definition of the term 'Islamic', or, what amounts to the same thing, the right criterion of 'Islamicity', then becomes crucial. In accordance with his traditional universal perspective – which is in conformity with the qur'ānic idea of *tawḥīd* (oneness of God) as the core message of all the prophets and messengers of God – he views the formula of *tawḥīd* as the most universal criterion of orthodoxy in Islam or the 'Islamicity' of things. In his words, the fact this "[...] doctrine may be said to be Islamic affirms this unity in one way or other" (Nasr 1978, 5).

The adoption of this universal criterion of 'Islamicity' enables Nasr to integrate knowledge from the pre-Islamic sciences into his conception of Islamic science. It is the same criterion that would enable contemporary Muslim scholars to select the most worthy elements from modern and contemporary science for integration into

---

3 Nasr's most recent work (2007) would be of further help to those interested in understanding his contribution to the Islamisation of the sciences.

the 'new Islamic science' with intellectual confidence and clarity of purpose. The appeal of Nasr's idea of an *authentic* Islamic science lies precisely in his definition of the term 'Islamic'.

Concluding remarks

There is an urgent need to undertake a deeper study of the Ottoman and other Muslim responses to modern science and technology with the view of deriving useful lessons from their experience. The contemporary Islamisation of modern science, understood in the sense we have just explained, would be enriched by our studies of past Muslim experiences. Our own view is that Islamisation would be the most apt intellectual response for Muslims to adopt toward science. Only through Islamisation can Muslims achieve true scientific and technological progress and at the same time retain and even fortify their Islamic intellectual, moral, and spiritual outlook. Its success will have a great significance not only for the revival of the Islamic intellectual tradition but also for the future development of modern science itself. Today, many scientists are earnestly searching for new paradigms for the natural sciences. Islam can once again play its providential universal role of providing the essential ingredients for these new paradigms and solving the numerous problems that now confront modern science but which the secular West has proved impotent to solve. However, the success of the Islamisation of the sciences depends a great deal on the concerted and coordinated efforts of all Muslim intellectuals.

References

Goodwin, Godfrey 1997: The Janissaries. London: Saqi Books.

Al-Hassan, Ahmad Y.; Hill, Donald 1992: Islamic Technology. An Illustrated History. Cambridge: Cambridge University Press.

Ihsanoglu, Ekmeleddin (ed.) 1992a: Transfer of Modern Science and Technology to the Muslim World. Proceedings of the International Symposium on Modern Sciences and the Muslim World. Istanbul: Research Center for Islamic History, Art, and Culture.

Ihsanoglu, Ekmeleddin (ed.) 1992b: Introduction of Western Science to the Ottoman World: A Case Study of Modern Astronomy, 1660–1860. In: Ihsanoglu 1992a, 67–120.

McClellan III, James E.; Dorn, Harold 1999: Science and Technology in World History. Baltimore, London: The Johns Hopkins University Press.

Nasr, Seyyed Hossein 1978: An Introduction to Islamic Cosmological Doctrines. London: Thames & Hudson.

Nasr, Seyyed Hossein 2007: Islam, Science, Muslims and Technology: Seyyed Hossein Nasr in Conversation with Muzaffar Iqbal. Petaling Jaya: Islamic Book Trust; Alberta: Al-Qalam Publishing.

Osman Bakar 1997: The History and Philosophy of Islamic Science. Cambridge: The Islamic Texts Society.

Osman Bakar 2008: Tawhid and Science: Islamic Perspectives on Religion and Science. Kuala Lumpur: Arah Publications.

Saliba, George 1992: Copernican Astronomy in the Arab East: Theories of the Earth's Motion in the Nineteenth Century. In: Ihsanoglu 1992a, 145–155.

Stenberg, Leif 1996: The Islamization of Science: Four Muslim Positions Developing an Islamic Modernity. Stockholm: Almqvist & Wiksell.

Tanyeli, Ugur 1992: Transfer of Western Urban Planning Concepts and Techniques to Turkey, 1718–1840. In: Ihsanoglu 1992a, 345–363.

Wan Mohd Nor Wan Daud 1998: The Educational Philosophy and Practice of Syed Muhammad Naquib al-Attas: An Exposition of the Original Concept of Islamization. Kuala Lumpur: International Institute of Islamic Thought and Civilization (ISTAC).

Part III

Contesting Worldviews, Contesting Civilisations?

8

Islamism, Women, and Political Participation: Comparative Perspectives

Nilüfer Narlı

Abstract

The issue of Islam and politics and its reflection in a vibrant global movement have dire implications for women's movements not only in the Muslim world, but also for the Muslim diasporas in North America and Western Europe. Islamism, feminism, and Islamic feminism have been mobilising women and are currently shaping their political attitudes and patterns of action. Two critical questions that are emerge from this context shall be addressed in this paper: Firstly, what are the current trends in terms of political participation of Muslim women in Islamic civil society as well as in political parties? Secondly, what are the gains of Islamic activist women? In order to find appropriate answers, the paper examines the political participation of Islamic women within the context of Turkey, Egypt, and Tunisia. In all three countries, Islamism, feminism, and Islamic feminism have become strong forces – vis-à-vis certain secular counter measures taken by the respective governments – and they have shaped the political and religious attitudes of women. Turkey shall be the central focus for analysing the variations in 'Islamic' and 'Islamist' women's political participation and for drawing lessons for the future. It shall be demonstrated that Islamic women have not yet achieved much in terms of participation in formal politics. Nevertheless, there are indications of powerful new demands by Islamic women in Turkey as well as in many other countries of the Muslim world for stronger representation in the formal decision-making process.

Introduction

This paper aims to analyse current trends in terms of political participation of Muslim women in Islamic civil society and political parties by referring to Turkey, Egypt, and Tunisia as case studies. Islamism, feminism, and Islamic feminism have shaped the political and religious attitudes of women in those three countries.

In the following, special attention shall be paid to Turkey in order to make out the variations in 'Islamic' and 'Islamist' women's political participation.

Throughout this paper it shall be distinguished between Islam as a religion and Islamism as a political ideology, and between a 'Muslim', an 'Islamist', and an 'Islamic woman'. A 'Muslim woman' may be pious and practice religion or may be a believer who does not observe all rituals regularly. For an 'Islamic woman', however, not only piety but also a strong religious identification and conduct of life in accordance with Islamic values and morality are important. Islamism, on the other hand, indicates a *political* consciousness rather than a *religious* one, and is a deliberate attempt to transform Islam from religion into ideology. An Islamist is not only a pious Muslim who follows religious observances as part of religion and folk culture; she/he also *politicises* Islam and, therefore, rejects the idea of religion being limited to belief, prayer, ritualistic acts of worship, and private consciousness. The Islamist therefore tends to reject secularist models on the grounds that Islam is both religion and state (Arab. *dīn wa dawlah*). On the other hand, the Islamist is also very likely to consider the necessity of a gradual progress towards the ideal Islamic state and may be willing to undertake any type of action that is justified in terms of 'Islamic' morals.

Both feminist and Islamist movements have an impact on women's political participation as many women have been mobilised by various secular and Islam-oriented political parties and groups within the last two decades in the Muslim world. Both movements gained momentum in the 1980s, and their influence on state, society, and gender has since then increased. Islamism and feminism are not novel movements. They emerged during a comparatively early period of time when what could be considered 'state feminism' was part and parcel of post-colonial national ideology in many Arab countries, whereas Islamism has its roots in the early twentieth century. Some would argue that Islamism has failed (Roy 1994, 2004, 2007). Within this line of thought it would not be significant to analyse the impact of Islamism on women's political participation. In the view of the present writer, Islamist politics have adjusted to changing conditions and benefited from social changes that had occurred in many Muslim countries. Islamist movements have lost their revolutionary character and they have also changed in form by transforming from political movements into religious ones with strong emphasis on Islamic morality. Moreover, they resist less to modernisation unless it contradicts Islamic family values and morality defining the conduct of women. In addition, Islamist movements have transformed themselves into Islamic movements aiming at the 'Islamisation' of society at large. They have also broadened their appeal to various segments of society in that they expanded their support from the newly urbanised lower classes to the urban middle and upper middle classes. They have succeeded in bringing Islam into mainstream socio-cultural life. Finally, they have created platforms to exchange ideas with diversified political groups, which provide common ground for secular and Islamic feminist women.

The Arab world and parts of Asia currently witness a variety of attempts to promote women's rights from within the Islamic framework, and many women in the

Muslim world are utterly convinced that at its core, Islam sanctions full equality between the genders. To make their arguments credible within the broader Muslim community, Islamic feminists need to be able to refer to Islamic traditional sources. In Turkey, many Islamist and Islamic women share this tendency. Yet they are also largely influenced by secular feminist ideas.

Why Turkey, Tunisia, and Egypt?

This paper selects Turkey, Tunisia, and Egypt because of four major reasons. First, the governments of those three countries have taken measures against Islamist political agendas, such as preventing the foundation of any political party that is taking Islam as a reference. In Turkey and Tunisia, public affairs have been conducted in accordance with secularist principles that are laid down in their respective constitutions, and there are constitutional safeguards against Islamist political activities and additional measures restricting the display of Islamic symbols (i.e. head scarf) in public buildings, for instance. In Egypt, the government has taken certain 'secularising' steps in recent years despite Islam being one of the sources of the country's legislation.

The second reason, which applies more to Egypt and Turkey, is the increased visibility of Islam in social life and the participation of Islamist and Islamic political parties in parliament. In both countries, Islamic groups have 'theoretically' the constitutional means to work *within* the system and to achieve representation in parliament. In Turkey, the ruling Justice and Development Party (Turk. *Adalet ve Kalkınma Partisi*, abbr. AKP), coming from Islamist roots yet currently distancing itself from political Islam, gained electoral victories in 2002 and 2007. In Egypt, the Muslim Brotherhood, an Islamist group, gained about 20 percent of the seats in the relatively fair elections that were held in late 2005. In both countries, the issues of social and political reforms and – in the case of Egypt – religious reforms, as well as the prospect of Islamists sharing political power have been debated widely. In Tunisia, Islam has gained visibility in social life, yet Islamist or Islamic political parties have no constitutional channel to be active in formal politics, and thus there is no representative of any Islamic party in parliament.

Closely related to the revival of Islamic consciousness in Turkey, Tunisia, and Egypt, as well as being their third common denominator, is the dynamic interaction between feminism, Islamism, and Islamic feminism. In Turkey and Tunisia, a strong secular feminist movement and Islamism have been the two challenging movements that have affected gender relations since the early 1990s. While secular feminism has evolved and has been institutionalised in Tunisia in the face of a growing Islamist movement that had been strengthened by trans-national Islamist dynamics, Egypt does not feature a strong 'home-grown' secular feminism, but rather Islamic feminism. Also in Egypt, the Islamists and Islamic feminism have been the two challenging movements that have affected gender relations since the early 1990s. Differently from Egypt, in Turkey and Tunisia the new wave of feminism of the 1980s, which has grown independently of state feminism, has created strong women's rights lobbies that are demanding changes in the law to eliminate gender discrimination. Turkey and Tunisia have been quite successful in this regard, to wit the adoption of the Personal Status Code (PSC) of Tunisia, which became a model for the region, and Turkey's elimination of all types of discrimination against women in civil and criminal law after a series of reforms carried out since the mid-1990s.

The fourth reason for the choice of those three countries is related to the increased visibility since the early 1990s in all three countries of religion and religious symbols in social and political life, in particular the headscarf. This visibility – together with the politicisation of the issue of the 'headscarf ban' – can also be noticed when looking at several other Muslim countries and countries with strong Muslim minorities. As in the Middle Eastern countries, in many Asian countries, too, the wearing of the headscarf appears seems to be on the rise (for the case of Indonesia see Brenner 1996). In Turkey, where many newly urbanised young women have already 'converted' to a 'modern Islamic dress-code' in the 1990s, a survey conducted by KONDA, Turkey's most trusted public opinion survey group, revealed that between the years 2003 and 2007, the proportion of women covering their head increased from 64.2 percent to 69.4 percent (Erdem 2007). Many observers have noted the dramatic increase of women donning the headscarf in Tunisia within the last three years. In Egypt, there is no law banning the headscarf, while it is banned in Turkey and Tunisia for women working in the public sector. As such, in both Turkey and Tunisia, the headscarf issue has been highly politicised and mobilised a large number of women to take a political stance. It has also been linked to the local human rights situation and connected to the global human rights agenda. Islamist women human rights groups have been fighting against the ban on wearing the headscarf in public institutions. In Turkey, various Islamic NGOs and especially the women section of the human rights organisation *Mazlumder* have taken a radical posture. In Tunisia, Monjia Abidi, Chairperson of *Women against Torture*, publishes articles that criticise the ban (see, for instance, Abidi 2004).

The issue of women and politics has attracted more attention as the headscarf issue has become a controversial matter after the headscarf was banned in public buildings in Turkey (at public universities in 1989 and enforced after 1997) and Tunisia (2006). By the late 1980s, for instance, the headscarf had become a contentious issue in Turkey. In the 1990s more women began to don the headscarf along with a long coat. The 1997–1999 resistance by university students against the headscarf ban mobilised a large number of supporters who took part in numerous demonstrations that continued until the victory of the AKP in the November 2002 elections. Tarhan Erdem's nationwide 2003 survey showed that almost 70 percent of women in Turkey covered their head (Erdem 2003). In 2006, another survey conducted by Ersin Kalaycıoğlu, a Turkish political scientist and former President of Istanbul's private Işık University (2004–2007), and Ali Çarkoğlu, an Associate Professor in the Faculty of Arts and Social Sciences of Istanbul's private Sabancı University, showed that 65 percent of the sample supported the idea of lifting the ban on the headscarf at universities. The symbolic functions of the headscarf in the power struggle between the Islamists and those holding a secular worldview, as well as the fight between modern and religiously conservative styles of life need attention. In April 2007 it was this power struggle that created a government crisis and the government decided to hold early elections in July that year (Kalaycıoğlu and Çarkoğlu 2006).

In Turkey, at the dawn of the general elections of 2002, the headscarf issue divided the society along Islamist/secularist lines. As a political symbol, it mobilised support for the AKP, a party which supported the hopes of the Islamic grassroots for lifting the ban on the headscarf in public instructions. The AKP, however, did not do much in practise for lifting the ban during its first terms (2002–2007), yet the hopes for a lifting of the ban did not die. The issue created a crisis in 2007 when the then cabinet minister Abdullah Gül, who has a background of Islamic political activities and whose wife is 'covered', was nominated as a presidential candidate in April that year. In response to his candidature, several mass rallies in April and May protested against the perceived threat of an 'Islamisation' of society and public policy. Soon after, a large rally took place in Ankara on 14 April 2007, and at least 800,000 demonstrators gathered in Istanbul in defence of the secular republic on 29 April. Turkish media estimated that more than one million people took part in the rally at the Çağlayan neighbourhood in Istanbul's Şişli district where the most striking phenomenon was the larger number of women demonstrators and several women making speeches in support of Turkey's secular system. In Ankara and Istanbul, flag-waving protesters shouted, "Turkey is secular and will remain secular". Others chanted: "The roads to Çankaya [the presidential palace] are closed to *imāms* [Muslim clerics]". At the Istanbul rally, they expressed their commitment to democracy by exclaiming: "Neither *sharī'ah* nor coup d'état, but a fully democratic Turkey", in reference to the statement of 27 April 2007 that had been posted on the website of the Turkish armed forces hours after the Turkish parliament had held a first round of voting in the presidential elections in which Foreign Minister Abdullah Gül was the only candidate. On that night of 27 April, during which the voting had taken place, the military stepped in and voiced its opinion on the issue at hand via the Turkish General Staff website (Türk Silahlı Kuvvetleri 2007). The memo signalled that the Turkish Armed Forces – as 'guardian of the state's secular character' – would uncompromisingly defend the principle of secularism. Following the overwhelming victory of the AKP, which polled 47 percent of the total votes in the July 2007 elections, Gül was elected in August that year as the eleventh President of the Republic of Turkey on the third try after he failed to obtain the votes of 367 members twice. The AKP had made a compromise in electing a non-Islamist Speaker of Parliament, but as a matter of fact the party had managed to push through its own candidate for the of office of the country's Head of State rather than seeking a consensus on the issue. Subsequently, the sight of a Turkish First Lady covering her head was celebrated across Muslim countries at a time of 'globalised' Islamic consciousness.

Conceptual considerations

This paper is structured by analytical categories adapted from Vicky Randall that define the major forms of political participation: 'conventional' and 'less conventional' (Randall 1987, 50–60). Based on this scheme, conventional formal institutionalised means of political participation and action include voting, activity in electoral campaigns, being a member of a political party or interest group, performing institutionalised political action by working in party organs and by becoming a deputy, involving in 'communal activities' in the sense of contacts of citizens with government officials on matters of general interest and 'particularised' citizen-government contacts on matters of concern to a specific individual or group (Randall 1987, 55). They are all constitutional political activities that are organised by political parties or legitimate interest groups and organisations. Not all political systems and social groups provide the avenues of political participation within the context of formal institutionalised politics. Hence, there would be a need for 'less conventional forms' of participation which include ad hoc participation, or other forms of "participation in political campaigns that are short-lived, throwing up makeshift organizations and tending to rely on direct tactics such as pickets, squats and self-help projects" (Randall 1987, 58). The less conventional forms of political participation also include (violent) political action within the context of politically motivated underground scenarios, such as urban and revolutionary guerrilla movements and all other types of anti-regime activities. Therefore, not all means employed are by necessity always constitutional with many activities organised outside the legal framework, up to the sphere of terrorism.

If we were to compare the situation in our three countries in terms of possible forms of political participation, we would perhaps arrive at the following scheme:

Types of women's political participation: Turkey, Tunisia and Egypt

countries	*less conventional*	→	*conventional*
Turkey	islamist (illegal)	islamic (legal/illegal)	secular (legal)
Tunisia	islamist (illegal)	islamic (illegal)	secular (legal)
Egypt	islamist (illegal)	islamic (legal/illegal)	semi-secular (legal)

a) Women's participation in 'conventional politics'

In Turkey, the number of women in elected offices was relatively low till the July 2007 elections. The proportion of female members of parliament rose from 4.4 percent to 9.8 in the Turkish Grand National Assembly. The female proportion amounted to 0.5 percent in local governments (Marmara Stratejik Araştırmalar Vakfı 2007). In the executive branch, including the top administrative positions such as ministries, the female rate was 7 percent in the 2005–2006-period. It began to decline recently, and males have been replacing women bureaucrats according to a survey by Narınç Ataman. According to Ataman's study, all 25 undersecretaries are men; out of a total number of 85 assistant undersecretaries, only 2 are women. In the public sector, out of a total number of 139 general directors, there are only 8 women, and out of a total number of 363 assistant directors, only 36 are women (as reported by Yetkin 2007). Women are also loosing ground in the decision-making organs of the executive branch. Likewise, their representation in the decision-making organs of political parties is lower compared to that of men, despite a fact of a relatively large number of Turkish women who are members in political parties (see below).

In Tunisia, the number of women in elected offices is relatively high. In the Chamber of Deputies their proportion was 22.8 percent and in the Upper House it was 3.4 in 2004. In the local governments, the female proportion was 21.6 percent. There was a fair representation of women in the executive branch: two women cabinet ministers, five women Secretaries of State, an advisor to the President of the Republic, and a female provincial governor (TunisiaOnline 2007).

In Egypt, the proportion of women in parliament is rather low with only 2.0 percent. In the Upper House it is 6.8 percent. In the 2002 local elections, 774 women won seats for local government councils, and of these 750 were candidates of the ruling National Democratic Party. It should be mentioned that in Egypt, the constitution does guarantee some sort of multi-party system. In practice, however, the National Democratic Party is the long-time ruling party and is dominant in the Egyptian political arena, whereas opposition parties have only a very slim chance to win any election. In January 2003, President Mubarak issued a decree whereby he appointed a female judge to the Constitutional High Court – for the first time in Egypt's history. The High Judicial Council had nominated lawyer Tahani Al Jebali to this position. Two other women were appointed as members to the panel of Constitutional High Court Commissioners (United Nations Development Programme. Programme on Governance in the Arab Region [UNDP-POGAR] 2007).

b) Women's participation in 'less conventional politics'

Women have taken part in legal and semi-legal Islamist activities in Turkey, Egypt, and Tunisia, whereas women in Turkey and Tunisia have taken part in legal and illegal protests against the ban on headscarves. In Turkey the headscarf ban protests go back to the late 1980s when thousands of women organised sit-in protests throughout the country's major cities. In Tunisia, the protest against the headscarf ban is a recent phenomenon. In January 2007, an Algerian-based Islamist group issued a statement to protest against the ban on wearing headscarves (Black 2007). Islamist women joined the protest by gathering in front of the university, donning headscarves (for more details and on militant Islamism in Tunisia see InternetHaganah, 2007). Some of the home-grown radical Islamist groups have developed links to international extremist networks, including Al-Qaeda. On 5 January 2007 *Gulf Times* (quoted in Black 2007), reported that "[i]n the first week of January 2007, the Moroccan government announced the dismantling of an alleged 62-person terrorist cell". According to the same source and based on statements made by the government, this cell had "ideological links with and financial and logistical support from international terrorist groups" including al-Qaeda and the Salafist Group for Call and Combat (GSPC)" (Black 2007). In Turkey, in the late 1990s, many Islamist groups conducted illegal and even terrorist activities with the help of female members (e. g. though what is known as the 'Turkish Hizbullah', a largely ethnic-Kurdish Sunnite militant organisation that arose in the late 1980s in response to alleged Kurdistan Worker's Party [PKK] atrocities against Muslims in south-eastern Turkey, where is has been proposed that the group is seeking to establish an independent Islamic state). In Egypt, Islamist women have been active in several semi-legal and illegal political activities.

Women and the 'New Islam' movements in Turkey, Tunisia, and Egypt: Creating space for 'conventional politics'

The new Islamic movements, which promote a particular brand of religious morality in order to 're-educate' society towards what they perceive to be the 'true' version of Islam, have also created space for Islamic women to take part in formal politics. In Turkey and Egypt, as many Islamists have adopted a new approach and new terminology to define their political rhetoric and their relation to Islam, many Islamic women have expanded their participation in political parties and NGOs. In Turkey the ruling AKP presents itself as 'conservative Muslim' or 'conservative democratic', referring by this to a particular 'conservativism' in terms of leading a moral and religious personal lifestyle. However, they (still) consent fully with democratic norms. This parallels a shift of emphasis from the part of the Islamists from politics to individual morality, as they appear to have lost their interest in the State. Islamist and Islamic women are becoming highly visible in political parties and civil society associations in Egypt and Turkey, as what can be considered the 'New Islam movements' create more space for their activities. In Tunisia, however, Islamic and Islamist women in formal politics are not visible and many of them prefer to remain a low profile.

Two trends are striking when we try to analyse the directions of change in terms of actions and ideological debate featured by Islamist women in Turkey and Egypt: first, Islamic and Islamist women undertake many activities in the public spheres that were once exclusively occupied by men (Hafez 2003). These activists work to enhance the wellbeing of the larger community in the name of Islam in order to make its members become 'better Muslims'. They organise training sessions for women, carry out community projects and educate women in the skills necessary for employment. Through their activism, they have become visible in many sections of society. They are very likely to be aware that they are contesting male power in the public sphere. This trend has advanced within the last ten years. Secondly, Islamic and Islamist women try to broaden their ideological outlook.

Many Islamic and Islamist women have sported an interest in a gentler, more progressive version of religion, in what we refer to as 'New Islam'.

Similarly, many Islamist women are attempting to argue for women's rights from *within* an Islamic framework, even though secular feminist ideology has had an impact on many of the individuals that are active in Islamic and Islamist groups. In Egypt, for instance, IslamOnline (IOL) hosts a website where one can find debates on 'New Islam'. Some of the debates on women aim at bridging the 'ideological gaps' between the secular women's movement, Islamic feminism, and the Islamist women's movement. While this 'bridge-building' is evolving, it can also be observed that Islamists are becoming less defensive and more open-minded while reconciliation between Islamists and secularists is maturing, according to Dalia Yousef, age 27, an Egyptian lady, who defines herself as a 'Muslim activist'. In describing her rapprochement to the secularists, she underlined that working at IslamOnline (referred by her as "her dream") has broadened her outlook to forge common ground with the secularists. She added: "The women's movement was secular. And the Islamists were reactionary and defensive. I think we Islamists are becoming more broad-minded and more sophisticated. Now we admit there are problems, and we're trying to see how we can solve them. That may bring the two sides closer, at least among the young generation" (Kristianasen 2005). Similar tendencies of 'reconciliation' can also be made out in Turkey.

While Islamist and Islamic women are becoming highly visible in political parties and civil society associations in Egypt and Turkey, in Tunisia, however, they are less visible and prefer to stay underground. President Ben Ali has been determined to maintain the restrictions on the spread of ideas or signs and religious symbols which could strengthen the country's outlawed Islamic opposition movement *Al-Nahḍah* (Arab. for 'renaissance' or 'awakening'). In 1990, Tunisia's main Islamist movement was banned soon after the war erupted between the radical Islamists and the state in Algeria. In recent years, new restrictions were introduced after observing an increase in the number of women wearing headscarves at the very beginning of the twenty-first century. According to a BBC report in 2006, "Police in Tunisia have been stopping women on the streets and asking them to remove their headscarves and sign pledges that they will not go back to wearing them" (Saleh 2006). Nevertheless, in Tunisia, Islamic women have challenged their relatively secular sisters by promoting Islamic morality and Islamic feminism.

Turkey, a case of its own …

In the 1960s and 1970s, Turkey's centre-right political parties and the ultra-nationalist Nationalist Movement Party (MHP) have not been able to provide the appropriate means and channels for female participation in party politics. Likewise, the pro-Islamic National Salvation Party, founded in 1973, did not have any vision and room for female activism in the party.

This was to change in the early 1980s. Firstly, the Motherland Party (Turk. *Anavatan Partisi*, abbr. ANAP), founded in 1983, invited women to be active at the grass-root levels and to join the party ranks as actors in decision-making organs. Many upper-middle class professional women were active in decision-making organs and they even gained seats in parliament and positions in the executive organs after ANAP had won in the 1983 elections. On the other hand, numerous the first or second-generation urban women from the lower middle classes undertook various activities at grass-root party politics.

The late 1980s also saw the political mobilisation of a large number of women from the middle and lower-middle Islamist class, as well as by centre-right and pro-Kurdish political parties. Since then their number has been increasing, with many more newly urbanised women joining political parties and civil society associations. However, the level of female participation in interest groups and in institutionalised party politics, as well as their numbers in the decision-making organs is often lower than those of men. In Turkey, the representation of women in the decision-making organs of associations, unions, syndicates, bar associations, and of various chambers of professions is significantly lower than that of men. Women also feature a lower proportion of total party membership than men. This particularly applied to Islamist and ultra-nationalist parties that resisted female representation in the higher ranks and in parliament until the 1999 elections.

The 1999 general and local elections which both were held on the same day (18 April) had led to some increase in the female representation both in parliament and in local governments. Their number in parliament rose from 1.8 percent in 1991 to 4.18 percent (23) in 1999 and their representation in local governments also increased and reached 0.55 percent. But there were no female city mayors, apart form some female mayors who made it to leading administrative positions on the district and sub-district levels. There was a further increase in female parliamentary representation after the 3 November 2002 general elections, reaching 4.4 percent. In the Turkish Grand National Assembly, out of a total number of 550 seats, 24 were occupied by women (AKP: 13; Republican People's Party [Turk. *Cumhuriyet Halk Partisi*, abbr. CHP): 11]. There are differences in the level of female parliamentary representation across the political parties. Until the 1999 elections, none of the Islamist parties (including the now defunct Welfare Party [Turk. *Refah Partisi*, abbr. RP] and the Great Union Party [Turk. *Büyük Birlik Partisi*, abbr. BBP]), as well as the Turkish nationalist Nationalist Movement Party (MHP) had female representation in the parliament, nor did they list female candidates to contest for local elections. However, the centre-right, centre-left, and Kurdish nationalist parties have always listed female candidates to contest for general and local elections, and they have had female parliamentary representation, up to the level of women cabinet members. In the 2002 general elections, almost all the Islamist, pro-Islamic, and nationalist parties listed female candidates, however, without placing them at the top of their lists, as the data on the location of female candidates in the lists prepared by the political parties for the November 2002 general elections showed clearly. However, parties with a more or less social-democratic orientation, as well as those of the left and centre-right spectrum frequently gave the first three top listings to them to them. Similarly, in the March 2004 local elections the centre-left parties listed a higher number of women candidates, compared with the AKP and the Felicity Party (Turk. *Saadet Partisi*, abbr. SP; for a comparison of the political parties with respect to the number of listed candidates and the number of women mayors see Kindira 2004).

Not only gender policies of political parties vary with differences in party typology and ideology. Studies also show that the women members of the Islamist/ultra-nationalist parties, the leftist/social-democrat parties, and the centre-right parties differ significantly in terms of political socialisation and recruitment channels, in the worldviews adopted, and in the ways in which political functions are carried out (KASHAID 2000).

The background of Turkey's women in 'less conventional politics'

Turkey has a tradition of female participation in less conventional politics, including taking part in urban guerrilla movements, student protests, and in clandestine leftist activities in the 1970s. *Ad hoc* political activity, which was introduced by the leftist groups in the 1970s and then advanced by Islamic parties in the mid-1980s, included community actions and self-help projects targeting the welfare of the slum people and raising their political consciousness. The pro-left female actors of ad hoc politics were more frequently urban and modern female university students from the middle classes, who identified themselves as 'progressive'. Among them, there was no woman with what could be considered 'Islamic tendencies'. The legal arrangements made after the 1980 coup aimed at suppressing less conventional political activities and at preventing the participation of women and the youth in conventional party politics. The military government outlawed the formerly organised youth and women sections of political parties that had been active in both institutionalised party politics and in *ad hoc* politics.

Islamist and Islamic women in 'less conventional politics' before the 1980s

In Turkey, there are various examples of less conventional forms of political activities undertaken by Islamist women. Women's participation in the Islamist movement, which is organised through associations, foundations, political parties, informal groupings and clandestine groups, began in the form of informal political participation in the early 1970s. Often the wives and the daughters of male Islamists became involved in Islamist political activities as auxiliaries to men. Yet there were a few activists, including public figures, preaching to groups of women to raise their 'Islamic awareness'.

Islamist and Islamic women in 'less conventional politics' after the 1980s

Until the mid-1980s, Islamist women did not hold formal memberships in associations or political parties. Neither did they work in campaigns as actively as they do today. Nevertheless, they were able to mobilise their kinship groups and neighbourhood networks each time the Islamist men asked them to poll support for the party. Since the late 1980s, the involvement of women in the Islamist movement has grown and taken many forms with increased participation in public life and conventional party politics. They mobilise people by their effective educational and propaganda activities and by fundraising. They also conduct self-help projects with the aim of reaching the disadvantaged and the 'oppressed' people. Furthering their activities beyond institutionalised party politics, many of them have been found marching and demonstrating in the street in protest of perceived injustices, and some gather and disseminate news or distribute leaflets. Street activism included also the organising of nation-wide demonstrations, sit-in protests, and the nation-wide hand-in-hand campaigns to resist the headscarf ban in the late 1980s and later between 1997 and 1999, which can be seen as an important symbol for the ongoing power struggle between Islamists and secularists in Turkey.

The mid-1980s marked the beginning of female involvement in 'less conventional' Islamist as well as in 'formal' political activities. Until that time, Islamist women did not hold formal memberships in associations or in political parties. Neither did they work in campaigns as actively as they do today. Since the late 1980s, however, the involvement of women in the Islamist movement has grown and taken many forms with increased participation in public life and conventional party politics, as many of them joined the now defunct Welfare Party. They mobilise people by their effective propaganda activities and fundraising. They also conduct self-help projects with the aim of reaching the disadvantaged and the 'oppressed' lower strata of society.

Increased female activism in 'conventional' and 'less conventional politics' in the 1990s

From the early 1990s onward, the female participation in *ad hoc* political action (e. g., short-lived self-help projects and community actions, etc.) and conventional party politics increased with the rise of the Islamist movement and women's increasing participation in the Islamist and pro-Islamist parties, associations and foundations. Islamic civil society expanded rapidly with the increased number of voluntary associations, foundations and informal groupings since the late 1980s (Türkiye Ekonomik ve Toplumsal Tarih Vakfı 1996: 12–14). A large number of civil society organisations is led either by Islamists or by the groups that are organised on the basis of primordial identity, sentiments and ties, such as ethnic, sectarian, regional, religious identities and sentiments (for the role of primordial ties in Islamist associations and other organizations see Narlı and Nari 1999). The increased interest of Islamic women in NGO activities motivated many Islamist, ultra-nationalist, and centre-right parties, including the Motherland Party and True Path Party (Turk. *Doğru Yol Partisi*, abbr. *DYP*), to welcome the political activism of Islamic women, in particular in grassroots politics. Fieldwork data from 1998 and 2002 reveal a number of patterns in the political preferences of Islamic women. A pious woman with a low level of Islamist tendencies is prone to join a centre-right party. A religiously conservative Sunnite woman upholding strong nationalist ideas will tend to support the Great Union Party if the Islamic component of her ideology has a higher leverage. On the other hand, a Kurdish-nationalist Islamic or a religiously conservative woman from the eastern and south-eastern provinces is more likely to prefer the pro-Kurdish People's Democratic Party (Turk. *Halkın Demokrasi Partisi*, abbr. HADEP). The political attitude of Kurdish women was studied by the present contributor when she was comparing the political participation of women in various political parties in Turkey (Narlı 2002).

Despite the initiation of female participation in grassroots party politics, when growing numbers of women were recruited into the Welfare Party (1983–1998), the party nevertheless excluded women from decision-making organs and from parliamentary representation. It confined them to the 'women's commission'. On the other hand, female participation grew in grassroots party politics, in *ad hoc* actions (constitutional and unconstitutional), and in 'less conventional' Islamist political activities (e.g. joining the Islamist student movements).

The Virtue Party (Turk. *Fazilet Partisi*, abbr. FP, operative until 2001), which moderated the Welfare's Party's more radical Islamist ideology, brought a change in its profile of female members. Non-Islamist women who were distinguished by their non-Islamic outfit, rhetoric and political objectives joined the party and took part in the party's decision-making organs. They gained parliamentary representation following the 1999 general elections. Women in the higher ranks were not selected from among the Islamist women who started their political careers in the informally organised women's commission and played vital roles in grassroots party politics. This was true also of the Islamist Great Union Party.

With the foundation in 2001 of the currently ruling AKP – which further moderated its Islamist politics and adopted a quasi-liberal party program – the participation of Islamic women in grassroots party politics was accompanied by an increase in the number of non-Islamic women in the party's decision-making organs. Despite the contribution made by Islamic women to grass-roots politics in the 2002 election campaign, only non-Islamic women gained parliamentary representation. Meanwhile, in the SP, which was also founded after the closure of Virtue Party, the level of female activism and participation in grassroots party politics declined and there was a decrease in the number of women in party's decision-making organs. Later in 2004, the SP began to give importance to female political mobilisation again despite its stronger religious conservatism, compared to the AKP. In the 2007 general elections, the AKP listed 62 female candidates for the total number of 550 seats. Although a significant number of women (26) from the AKP list were elected into parliament, none of them had previous experience in doing Islamic politics. They are often urban middle and upper middle class professional women or entrepreneur women.

The mid-1980s marked the beginning of female involvement in Islamist political activities. Subsequently, growing numbers of women were recruited into the Welfare Party and became active in its women's commission. Although the party excluded women from decision-making organs and from parliamentary representation, female participation grew in grassroots party politics, *ad hoc* actions, clandestine activities, and Islamist student organisations. As we have seen earlier, under the Virtue Party (1997–2001), for instance, also non-Islamist women had been included in the party's decision-making process (see table 1 for the political parties mentioned above).

Islamic women in nationalist parties

In the 1990s, the Nationalist Movement Party (Turk. *Milliyetçi Hareket Partisi*, abbr. MHP, also translated as 'Nationalist Action Party') featured an increased number of religiously conservative and Islamic women in constitutional grassroots party politics through their activities in the party's women commission and *ad hoc* activities that were considered constitutional. Yet both the Islamic and non-Islamic female members were from the party's decision-making process and from parliamentary representation until the late 1990s. In the 1999, 2002, and 2007 elections, the MHP listed women candidates who were secular nationalist and highly educated women.

The Kurdish nationalist party HADEP, which had included a large number of women in the decision-making organs since its foundation, also initiated many Islamic women in its grassroots activities in response to the increased influence of the Islamist movement in Turkey in the 1990s. Many of those women participated in spontaneous and extra-constitutional actions, in addition to the party's constitutional activities. The likewise pro-Kurdish Democratic Society Party (Turk. *Demokratik Toplum Partisi*, abbr. DTP), which eventually replaced HADEP, has not made specific reference to Islam in its program, and it did not include Islamic women in its grassroots activities. In the largely ethnic Kurdish Southeast of the country, the secular, leftist, and Kurdish nationalists support the DTP while Islamic Kurds and religiously-oriented ethnic Turks have been supporting the AKP since 2001. Islamic Kurdish women are no longer active in the Kurdish nationalist parties.

The centre-right parties: Motherland Party and True Path Party

A larger female participation in grassroots party politics and an increasing role of women in decision-making processes appear to characterise the female participation patterns in both the Motherland Party (ANAP) and True Path (DYP).

Both parties recruited Islamic women to be active in their particular grassroots politics in response to the increased influence of the Islamist movement in Turkey in the late 1990s. The Motherland Party had been particularly successful in mobilising many religiously conservative women in Istanbul from the mid-1980s till late 1990s, as observed in several studies on female political participation that are based on field research.

Before the snap elections of 22 July 2007, in May that year, the two centre-right parties, ANAP and DYP, had decided to merge in order to form a new party – the Democratic Party (Turk.: *Demokrat Parti*, abbr. DP). In their election campaign, they highlighted the importance of secularism in Turkey as well as their respect for religion and piety. However, in the 2007 elections, the new party did not manage to jump over the 10-percent hurdle and thus did not achieve representation in parliament.

Perspectives and global trends in the political participation of Islamic women and lessons learned from the Turkish experience

Islamic politics, which has become very vibrant since the early 1980s, is a global phenomenon. As such, it has dire implications for feminist and women's movements not only in the countries of the Muslim world but also in the Muslim diaspora communities of North America and Western Europe. Many Muslim women, who have decided to 'convert' to a 'more Islamic' lifestyle and cover their head, reconstruct their self by redefining their identity. They perceive themselves as 'modern Muslim women' who are different from their mothers and they distance themselves from the past. They see themselves different from their traditional mother-role in that they have taken up many activities within the public domain and participated in redefining (and reshaping) society along lines that are perceived by them as 'Islamic'. They often differ from their lower middle class provincial or rural mothers in that they have gained social mobility within the last two decades as Islamic networks have managed to translate their solidarity and power with their families into political power and monetary gains. In several interviews, Islamic and Islamist Turkish women have differentiated their way of life and the style of head-covering from that of their mothers. They increasingly perceive themselves as what could be referred to as 'modern Islamic women in action'. Moreover, they take part in various political activities ranging from petition drives to sit-in protests against the war in Iraq, to street rallies in protest over perceived injustices. Here, the question is to what extent they have changed from the roles of their traditional-minded mothers in terms of the level of participation in formal political decision-making?

The Turkish experience reveals also that Islamic and Islamist women from newly urbanised middle classes have become very active in Islamic and Islamist politics through their diverse forms of political participation. However, female participation in institutionalised party politics and civil society and their numbers in the decision-making organs are lower than those of men, and they feature a lower proportion of total membership than men. Yet, they are not highly discontented with such gender discrimination, as they feel victorious over the secularists and they are aware of the rewards their family and kin have gained over the past decade. Even the disenfranchised Islamist women, who are more discriminated by the socio-economic discrepancies and who face contradictory demands made on them by Islamic men in positions of authority, appear to prefer silence. They are not disturbed to observe that urban upper middle class non-Islamist women are often favoured by Islamic parties when it comes to parliamentary representation.

Educated and professional yet non-activist women appear to be welcome in all political parties in Turkey. Prior to the 2007 elections, the ruling AKP, for instance, gave signals that women candidates, many of them upper middle class professionals adopting some sort of modern way of life, would be given top placements in the lists for the coming general elections. However, all parties excluded women activists who in the past had contributed to the women's right movement, such as Canan Arın, Seyhan Ekşioğlu, Nazik Işık, and Selma Acuner, who applied for candidacy on the respective lists. Many Islamic women were also excluded from the listing as candidates.

Despite the lower representation of Islamic women in the formal political processes, there are, nevertheless, indications of powerful new demands from their part and from their sisters in other Muslim countries. Such demands could undermine male-dominated party politics if they are well-articulated and allied with the feminist demands from various circles. They suggest new moral imperatives and values that the political parties may no longer be able to satisfy unless they change their attitudes towards women.

Such a likely development appears to be the key if grassroots women in Turkey and elsewhere in the Muslim world want to challenge male-dominated leadership in political parties and discrimination against disadvantaged women at large. In articulating and justifying their new demands, they may very well adopt a combination of Islamic and universal concepts.

Appendix

Table 1: Right and Centre-Right Political Parties by Type and Dates of Existence

Islamist parties	Nationalist parties	Centre-right parties
Welfare Party, RP, 1980–1998	Nationalist Movement Party, MHP, 1983 – present	Motherland Party, ANAP, 1983 – present
Virtue Party, January 1997 – June 2001	People's Democratic Party, HADEP, 1993 – March 2003 (pro-Kurdish)	True Path Party, DYP, 1983 – present

Islamist parties	Nationalist parties	Centre-right parties
Great Union Party, BBP, 1993 – present	Democratic Society Party, DTP, 2003 – present (pro-Kurdish)	
Felicity Party, SP, July 2001 – present		
Justice and Development Party*, AKP, August 2001 – present (pro-Islamic, but defines itself as a conservative centre-right		

Table 2: Political Parties in Parliament by Number of Seats after the 2007 General Elections

Justice and Development Party (AKP)	340
Republican Party People's (CHP)	98
Nationalist Movement Party (MHP)	70
Democratic Society Party (DTP)	20
Democratic Left Party (Turk. *Demokratik Sol Parti*, abbr. DSP)	13
Great Union Party (BBP)	1
Freedom and Solidarity Party (Turk. *Özgürlük ve Dayanışma Partisi* abbr. ÖDP, a socialist party)	1
Independents	5
total	548

Table 3: Number of Women in Parliament by Political Parties after the 2007 General Elections

Justice and Development Party (AKP)	26 (doubling the previous number of its female deputies)
Democratic Society Party (DTP)	8 (out of 20)
Nationalist Movement Party (MHP)	2 (out of 70)
Democratic Left Party (DSP)	1 (out of 20)
Republican Party People's (CHP)	7 (out of 98)
total	44

References

Printed sources

Brenner, Suzanne 1996: Reconstructing Self and Society: Javanese Muslim Women and "The Veil". In: American Ethnologist 23, no. 4, 673–697.

Hafez, Sherine 2003: The Terms of Women's Empowerment: Islamic Women Activists in Egypt. Cairo: The American University in Cairo Press (Cairo Papers in Social Science 24, Series 4).

Kalaycıoğlu, Ersin; Çarkoğlu, Ali 2006: Türkiye'de sosyal tercihler araştırması [Social preferences in Turkey]. Unpublished research report, joint project of Işık and Sabancı Universities, Istanbul.

KASHAID [Kadının Sosyal Hayatını Araştırma ve İnceleme Derneği] 2000: Kadının sosyal hayata katılımı ve siyasal mobilizasyonu [Women's participation in political life and their mobilisation]. Ankara: Ankara: Kadının Sosyal Hayatını Araştırma ve İnceleme Derneği ve Veri Araştırma A. Ş.

Narlı, Nilüfer 2002: The Role of Islamist Women in Political Parties in Turkey. Paper presented at the conference "Women in the Global Community", organised by Fulbright Program, 18–21 September 2002, Boğaziçi University, Istanbul.

Narlı, Nilüfer; Nari, Yaşar 1999: Türkiye'de hemşehri derneklerinin siyasete katilması ve demokratikleşme sürecine etkileri: Bursa örneği [The political participation of hemşehri associations and democratisation in Turkey: The case of Bursa]. In: Yeni Türkiye [New Turkey], Year 5, vol. 1, no. 29 (Eylül/Ekim [September/October]), 176–184.

Randall, Vicky [2]1987: Women and Politics: An International Perspective. Chicago: Chicago University Press.

Roy, Olivier 1994: The Failure of Political Islam. Cambridge MA: Harvard University Press.

Roy, Olivier 2004: Globalised Islam: The Search for a New Ummah. New York: Columbia University Press.

Roy, Olivier 2007: Secularism Confronts Islam, tr. George Holoch Jr. New York: Columbia University Press.

Türkiye Ekonomik ve Toplumsal Tarih Vakfı, 1996: Sivil Toplum Kuruluslarıı Rehberi [Civil society guide]. Istanbul: Tarih Vakfı Yayınları.

Internet resources

Abidi, Monjia 2004: State Feminism and the Right to Dress. URL: http://www.prohijab.net/english/tunis-hijab-news3.htm (accessed on 12 December 2007).

Black, Andrew 2007: The Reconstituted Al-Qaeda Threat in the Maghreb. In: Terrorism Monitor 5, no. 2. URL: http://www.jamestown.org/terrorism/news/article.php?articleid=2370242 (accessed on 12 December 2007).

Erdem, Tarhan 2003: Türban dosyası [Turban file]. In: Milliyet, 27–29 May 2003. URL: http://www.milliyet.com.tr/2003/05/27/guncel/agun.html (accessed on 17 December 2007).

Erdem, Tarhan 2007: Türbanın hızlı yükselişi. In: Milliyet, 3 December 2007. URL: http://www.milliyet.com.tr/2007/12/03/guncel/agun.html (accessed on 17 December 2007).

InternetHaganah 2007: Statement from the Jihadi Brothers in Tunisia. 9 January 2007. URL: http://haganah.org.il/harchives/005849.html (accessed on 14 December 2007).

Kindira, Zübeyir 2004: Yerel yönetimde kadının adı yok [Women have no place in local governments]. In: Sabah, 2 April 2004. URL: http://arsiv.sabah.com.tr/2004/04/02/siy105.html (accessed on 14 December 2007).

Kristianasen, Wendy 2005: New Presidency, Changing Nation. Egypt: Islamic Sisters Advance. In: Le Monde Diplomatique, September 2005. URL: http://mondediplo.com/2005/09/12woman (accessed on 14 December 2007).

Marmara Stratejik Araştırmalar Vakfı 2007: Ulusal kadın politikası 2007–2011 eylem planı [National women policy and action plan 2007–2011]. URL: http://www.marmaragrubu.org/gallery/2007-2011UlusalKadinPolitikasi.doc (accessed on 14 December 2007).

Saleh, Heba 2006: Tunisia Moves Against Headscarves. In: BBC News [online version], 15 October 2006. URL: http://news.bbc.co.uk/2/hi/africa/6053380.stm (accessed on 17 December 2007).

TunisiaOnline 2007. Tunesian Women in Figures. URL: http://www.tunisiaonline.com/women/women4.html (accessed on 14 December 2007).

Türk Silahlı Kuvvetleri [Turkish Armed Forces] 2007: Genelkurmay Başkanlığı [General Staff], 2007. URL: http://www.tsk.mil.tr (accessed on 17 December 2007).

United Nations Development Programme. Programme on Governance in the Arab Region [UNDP-POGAR] 2007: Democratic Governance, Gender, Algeria. URL: http://www.pogar.org/countries/gender.asp?cid=. (accessed on 14 December 2007).

Yetkin, Murat 2007: Bütçe, anayasa ve kadın hakları [Budget, constitution, and women's rights]. In: Radikal, 5 December 2007. URL: http://www.radikal.com.tr/haber.php?haberno=240774 (accessed on 14 December 2007).

9

Islam as Social Capital: Reinventions of Nationhood in an Age of Economic Globalisation*

Wazir Jahan Karim

Abstract

The Malaysian discourse on 'Islam Hadhari' or 'Civilisational Islam' offers a development perspective to the theory of practical religion. In terms of the growing global divide between fundamentalism and modernity, the discourse on 'civility' in the implementation of the tenets of faith provides a neutral ground for those Muslims who are concerned with the advancement of productive life in an increasingly global domain. The discourse is also closely associated with the concept of 'tamaddun', the Arabic (and Malay) term for 'civilisation', where Muslims are encouraged to accommodate to cultural diversity and multiculturalism without losing perspective of their commitment to productive welfarism. The writer argues that the concept of 'Civilisational Islam' reinvents nationhood in a developing economy to face the challenges of economic globalisation, offering an alternative to economic liberalism. At the same time, it enriches the drive towards netting relationships in ways beyond the enclaves of ethnicity and religion. In Malaysia, where Malay ethnicity is closely bound to an Islamic consciousness, the idea that faith itself can be a driving force for change and social transformation proposes a social vibrancy in nation-building. Thinking beyond the social realities of mundane life, to the infinite challenges of production, energised by faith, provides an idealised alternative to economic liberalism which can bring Islam into a less defensive relationship with modernity.

---

* An earlier version of this chapter was first presented on 25 February 2005 as a seminar paper at the Institute for Southeast Asian Studies (ISEAS) in Singapore under the title "Macro-Economic Trends and Civilisational Islam in Southeast Asia". It has since been updated for inclusion in this book.

Introduction

Alternative approaches to economic globalisation (Mander, Goldsmith 1996; Tabb 2004; Krugman 2005) have been proposed by experts on international political economy who have consistently described the fallacy of 'equal advantage' and the lack of transparency of its global agenda. Economic globalisation is advanced capitalism which ensures the optimisation of markets for industrialised and post-industrialised economies, providing maximum advantage to the most developed economies which have already advanced technologies to manage and control global wealth and in the process, secure geo-political and economic dominance (Stiglitz 2002, Sennet 2006). The concern for widening economic disparities and differential wealth between the most developed and least developed economies (Cavanagh, Mander 2002; Tabb 2004; Kimbrell 2002) have led developing nations to draw upon indigenous knowledge and social capital, when possible, to harness a competitive economic spirit. Malaysia's contribution to an alternative model is the development of an economic policy to increase the 'advantage of the disadvantaged', through reinforcing the special position of the 'bumiputeras' (Malay for 'sons of the soil', i. e. the Malays and various other indigenous ethnic groups) who have been economically marginalised during the colonial era of British rule, between 1786 and 1957. However, forces linked to religious fundamentalism, political party extremism and ethnic conflict continue to divide the nation. These issues have been partly addressed by drawing the attention of Muslims and non-Muslims to the discourse on *Islam Hadhari*, 'Civilisational Islam', which challenges extremism and certain narrow-minded interpretations of orthodoxy by providing a more congenial approach to Islam which is development-oriented and practical enough to provide a space for non-Muslims to participate in the exercise of nation-building.

The discourse on *Islam Hadhari*, usually translated as 'Civilisational Islam' or 'Islamic civil society', was introduced in 2004 to encourage greater compatibility of interests among Muslims and between Muslims and non-Muslims. Its effectiveness may be too soon to evaluate, but a commentary on Malaysia's constant attempt to reinvent itself, in the face of regional and global competition, may be timely. This chapter discusses Malaysia's alternative to economic globalisation, as a strategy of social reconsolidation or enrichment of social capital through the economic rationale of redistributive wealth. It proposes that spiritualism and economic rationalisation may be compatible with the generation of material wealth while material wealth itself is necessary to enable its redistribution through productive welfarism. It also proposes a more dynamic synergy between faith and economics and a more accommodating, cosmopolitan environment for all communities to work together and seek better livelihoods.

Alternatives to economic globalisation are not so much anti-global in oppositional terms but anti-liberal vis-à-vis the critical understanding of the historic privilege of the indigenous (privileged indigenisation) and its marginalisation throughout the nation's economic history. At the same time, there is a concern for equal citizenry and equal opportunity for all citizens regardless of faith and origin. Tabb (2004, 1) discusses the "disjuncture between understandings of the world political economy among elites, social movements of global civil society, mainstream social scientists and critical realists" and this discussion, to a certain extent, comments on this disjuncture by explaining how Malaysia attempts to reinvent nationhood to generate social capital for a more globally competitive economic environment. In doing so, it suggests its own constraining position in economic globalisation without formally opposing it. It also opposes the idea that economic globalisation can be stopped or that wealth distribution will be equitable within national populations, once its effect is instituted in trade and monetisation. Indirectly, it envisages a problematic disadvantage among its predominantly faith-minded citizens, in particular Muslims, who are cynical of Western secularism and liberalism. Hence, whether it is an alternative development strategy or a preparatory project to maximize the 'advantage of the disadvantaged', the discourse is worth a comment in the context of the uneven economic growth of the region, in particular the economics of ASEAN.

Unresolved issues of development

Southeast Asia's political leaders had prioritised agendas which have become familiar universals in the wake of economic globalisation.[1] Among the major thrusts of Southeast Asian leaders are strengthening indigenous production capacities to-

---

1 The present Prime Minister of Malaysia is one in a line-up Prime Ministers and Presidents in Southeast Asia who were recently elected: Dato' Seri Abdullah Ahmad Badawi was sworn into office in March 2004 after an overwhelming victory for the National Front, or *Barisan Nasional*, the alliance of political parties that had been in power since Malaysia obtained its independence from Britain in 1957. On 20 September 2004, Indonesia welcomed a new face in the name of Susilo Bambang Yudhoyono. Megawati Sukarnoputri's Nationhood Coalition lost its popular support for it only secured 39 percent of the 92 percent counted ballots with Yudhoyono leading by a clear 61 percent. Thailand's deposed Prime Minister Thaksin Shinawatra, elected for the first time in September 2001 and again in February 2005, was also a new champion of development. He was determined to prove that political stability in the South can be achieved if education is standardised by the State and if opportunities for new wealth through globalisation are given to the majority living below basic needs. His efforts, however, bore no fruit and a coup removed him from office in 2006. Last but not least is Southeast Asia's smallest nation, Singapore, where the country's third Prime Minister, Lee Hsien Loong, was sworn in on 12 August 2004. The son of the pioneer Prime Minister Lee Kuan Yew, he has given priority to issues of globalisation, defence and security, population growth and water resources. In his first National Day Rally Speech on 1 September 2004, he referred to 'openness and dialogal communication between leaders and citizens'. It seems that the first wave of authoritarian democracies in Southeast Asia must give way to liberal democracies for these nations to be better prepared for economic globalisation.

wards greater equity and balance between micro and macro-scale operations in rural and urban areas. Countries which depend on low-end unskilled and semi-skilled labour, such as Malaysia and Singapore, are making major efforts to reduce the dependence on unskilled and semi-skilled foreign labour from countries such as Indonesia, Vietnam, and the Philippines. For the most, major concerns include eradication of poverty and underemployment, good corporate and public governance, and greater transparency in political and public decision-making.

One of the expected outcomes of economic liberalism is religious moderation, multiculturalism and cosmopolitanism, prompting a healthy participation in local and global civil society. Another hopeful result is the end of violence through tripartite cooperative and reciprocal dialogue with public, corporate, and non-governmental agencies. Also in the package is a passive endorsement of the ideals of democracy with a caution on the use of the terminologies 'Western-style', or 'liberal', to justify national structures and systems instituted through political history. Having played on home turf for so long, most Southeast Asian leaders who have been democratically elected are aware of the bitter consequences of failure to contain rising economic differentiation in globalisation. Unresolved issues of poverty, migration, regional imbalances in development, and ethnic differentiation by economic classes harbour the seeds of discontent (Frank, Amin, Arrighi, Wallerstein 1990). Not everyone can impose its own 'moral economy' (Scott 1976) or be a 'rational peasant' overcoming a political culture of oppression (Popkin 1979). The scale of differential wealth is now so large, it is part of the consciousness of the poor and not something easily ignored through foot-dragging or fatalistic ideas of self-deserving hardship. In these small family and community-based Southeast Asian nations, things economic and social go hand in hand to form practical networks of cooperation in daily life. Dislocated families and fractured networks encourage alternative forms of regrouping and – in the context of poverty and unemployment – can have dire consequences on civil society.

The ingredients of a productive society participating in global competitiveness is not simply derived from economic liberalism- opening markets, making exports more competitive through pricing or ending protective tariffs for fundamental industries. 'Thatcherism' (Evans 1997), 'Reaganism' (W. Williams 2003), and 'Mahathirism' (Hilley 2001) had a common principle in the privatisation of public enterprises and the rise of foreign capital in public enterprises.[2] This was based on the guiding philosophy of macro-economic planning, that if governments 'took care of the big things, the small will take care of themselves'. However, in the smaller economies of Southeast Asia, Malaysia in particular, a significant amount of social engineering had been done (in Malaysia, prompted by the ethnic riots of 13 May 1969) to 'take care of the small things', less the marginalised farming and urban working communities become completely incapacitated in their attempt to

---

2 'Reaganism', 'Thatcherism', and 'Mahathirism' had a common concern for the privatisation of public goods and services and the corporatisation of public enterprises as globally competitive businesses.

keep up with the new demands of work and enterprise in the metropolis.[3] Human labour is not only an asset if it serves the needs of the global enterprise, it must also be a strategy for socio-economic mobility. To achieve this, human labour must be transformed into talent and human capital. Hence, to engineer social change to advance human capital further, Malaysia has embarked on a project of building social capital through Islam, in the hope that this might invigorate the population to become more hardy, competitive, and resilient to change. If more Malay Muslims were to realise that they were connected, netted, and wired to a global pool of talent, Muslim or otherwise, a sentiment of confidence and self-worth could develop in them. They could, like anyone else, be capable of social and economic achievements which are astounding. They would, indirectly, be reproducing those incredible moments in pre-colonial history of civilisation when Islam was a Renaissance-like experience, invigorated with the spirit of creative science, arts, and existential intellectual activity. Hence, the Abdullah Badawi government in Malaysia has made human capital a priority agenda for Malay Muslims, without discounting the positive value of spiritualism (popularly referred to in Malay as *nadi insan*), to think beyond the boundaries of ethnicity, language, and faith and to be confident to place the world at their feet.

One of the major thrusts of Malaysia' macro-economic policy is to transform Malay Muslims into urban cosmopolitan multi-linguistic people who can take better advantage of the challenges of a faceless but netted global enterprise, when online forms for employment, services or resources sought are 'secular' – disinterested in an applicant's ethnic origins, gender, or religion. In this context, the utilisation of Islam as a tool of social change in economic globalisation may be useful to Muslims who have through socialisation come to define religion through ethnicity. To promote better understanding of Islam as a geo-political ideology which embraces multiculturalism and cosmopolitanism as a form of socio-economic livelihood which enriches thought and action, knowledge, and practical life is a hazardous task, in a world where foreign interests and intervention have sparked sectarian conflict and tribalism. Economic liberalism and capitalisation of the primary resources of Muslims in the Middle East, for instance, has also opened the corridors to the past, enabling people to reconsolidate current interests with former passions, frozen through draconian military or colonial governments. Malaysia, however, despite her constitutional democracy, faces a current problem of 'divide and rule' through ethnic politics, a residue of its economic history, when

---

3 The ethnic riots of 13 May 1969 were provoked by the victory of the Chinese-dominated oppositional Labour Party in Kuala Lumpur. Apparently, the Malays were insulted with boos and bottles by the victorious Chinese crowd. Subsequently, the Malays rioted, under the slogan of *selendang merah* (Malay for 'red slash'). Since Malays were on the offensive, the death toll of ethnic urban Chinese were higher, amounting to hundreds. This led to the resignation of Malaysia's first Prime Minister, Tunku Abdul Rahman, and the formulation of the New Economic Policy in 1970, under the leadership of Tun Abdul Razak, to help Malays overcome rural and urban poverty

the British sought Southern Indian (Tamil) and Southern Chinese workers for their plantations, tin mines, and construction industry. Furnivall (1960), writing mainly on Burmese and Indian colonial history, describes this specialisation of migrant labour as conforming to two of the three principles of economic progress which is 'the survival of the cheapest' and the 'desire of gain'. The third principle, "that progress is conditional on the observance of certain social obligations", translated mainly as welfare, was never properly instituted by the British colonial administration, although education was a priority in the preparation of locals as administrators of the colonial civil service. Malays were generally reluctant to leave their lands to work in colonial sectors of the economy, but this has made them dependent on work in the public services.

Over 171 years of colonial rule, from 1786 to 1957, Malaysian Muslims have gradually moved towards a more corporate competitive mentality. Sharing a political economy where history has defined the land as their very own *(tanah Melayu)*, they see themselves to be 'custodians' of a country they have had to share with Chinese and Tamil migrants (Karim 2008).[4] Adopting the colonial 'divide and rule' principle of governance, ethnic based parties have been formed where positions of leadership are distributed according to demographic representation, under an umbrella multi-ethnic alliance called the 'National Front' or *Barisan Nasional* (BN). As 'technopreneurs' they are sophisticated commission agents, bringing Chinese capitalists closer to government contracts through contacts and connections. The Chinese and Indians of Southeast Asia have always ruled local economies by harnessing indigenous social capital and increasingly expanding their enterprises overseas to compete in the global market (Suryadinata 2007a, 2007b). They are survivors and have always had to work hard to achieve results through engagement in economic production. In Malaysia, Indians, for the most part Tamils, have perfected the art of salesmanship as intermediaries of powerful Malay politicians and bureaucrats, in the past traditionally labelled in Malay the *saudagar raja*, 'King's merchant'. Indian Muslims and Hindus are best at the enterprise of networking and score high on business confidence and respectability. Northern Malays popularly refer to this art of being able to convince someone to do any kind of business with them as *boria,* meaning 'anything goes, without a designed modus operandi'. The new generation of Indian professionals, however, is visible in the legal, engineering, and medical professions and they are increasingly famed for their services in media and communications. The majority of Tamil workers continue to be working class citizens of the metropolis as second and third-generation descendants of indentured labourers who served for a couple

---

4 The discussion on Malay identity by this writer as 'Statehood' in Chapter One of *Straits Muslims: Diasporas of the Northern Passage of the Straits of Melaka*, a book edited by her and forthcoming in 2008 (Asia-Europe Institute, University of Malaya), explains the idea of Malay central leadership under a physical territorial entity equivalent to the State but mentions the Malay concern for symmetrical relationships of reciprocity. Hierarchies encourage shifting alliances and changing loyalties.

of centuries in British-owned plantations and worked laboriously on roads and railways. Together, many different ethnic groups have developed their own unique contributions to the local economy 'globally' (colonisation was a global capitalist endeavour), necessitating an ideological discourse which can accommodate these economic transformations on a global scale.

Islam Hadhari or 'Civilisational Islam'

Against this very colourful entry into economic globalisation is Malaysia's proposition of 'Civilisational Islam' or *Islam Hadhari.* There is life beyond being a Malay and beyond being a Muslim, a worldview which Indian Muslims, professing to be 'Malay' are comfortable with, but which renders an unease in Malays who believe that they have always had to accommodate 'others', thus having been most 'civil' throughout their history. Malay consciousness of trusteeship of the State, a 'brown Man's burden', is not so much founded in institutionalised discrimination of 'migrants' but more to bring about the realisation in 'the other', that they are embedded in a Statehood where history has provided them with the political privilege of defining the rules of multiculturalism (Karim 2008). However, although Islam has always been an added source of strength to define Malay identity, it has usually functioned as political capital to harness male leadership at all levels of governance (Karim 1992). Its contribution as a source of social capital in multiculturalism, beyond the Malay state, has not been clearly defined. In the current revitalisation of nationhood, it draws upon the enrichment of working relationships, where all kinds of netting possibilities, among citizens and between citizens and non-citizens can develop. One does not need to be a Muslim to do business with Muslims, but one has to develop the embedded Islamic spirit of practice of fair trade and reciprocal profits. This contradicts the philosophy of economic liberalism and economic globalisation which is based on the principle of 'competitive advantage'. Islam enables competition with fair advantage where, for example, usury or high interest and taxation may place a partner at a significant disadvantage. Generally, however, reflecting on the ease with which Malays have done business with Hadrami Arab, Persian, and Indo-Persian traders throughout Southeast Asian history (Clarence-Smith 2000, Ho 2006, Karim 2008), the association of enterprise with cultural and spiritual vibrancy is not something new.

The five principles of *Islam Hadhari* have since been elaborated by supportive scholars like Mohd Kamil Haji Abdul Majid (2005) and others, among them Farish Noor (2004). Basically, those principles are: the foundations of knowledge in civilisations, balanced development, prosperity as a way of life, good and preventive health, and a spiritual lifestyle. The philosophy of combining these principles is balancing fundamentalism *(salafiyyah)* with change or renewal *(tajdīd)* and balancing core principles and values *(thawābit)* with changing perspectives *(mutaghayyirāt)*. Islam has to be understood in its totality *(shumūl)* and not decontextualised by quoting from singular remote texts without their own historicity.

Farish Noor (2004) however, states that Islam is about overcoming the trails and tribulations of humankind in its singular state and essence and does not address ethnicity or communalism. Hence, without stating any kind of reference to multiculturalism or social stratification, Islam is essentially concerned with justice and equality in its appeal. It does not need to address its connectivity to multiculturalism since it transcends cultural diversity into the realm of faith.

Why then does a government invite a public debate in a spiritual issue on the relationship between religion and economics which is bound to create disagreement among its Muslim followers? The realities are obvious, that people, whether Muslim, Christian, Hindu, or Buddhist, do in different situations and contexts carry their ethnicity and culture into their belief systems. The adoption of a more holistic approach in practical Islam is believed to lead Malaysian Muslims towards a more globally enriching experience – in particular one which transcends ethnicity. Muslims can move beyond the experience of understanding of 'being a Malay' towards a 'global player' of sorts, interacting and networking with other competitors. It also promotes closer partnerships with Muslim countries and business relationships which may have been avoided, such as trade with embargoed Muslim countries. It does not, however, need to promote prosperity or balanced development if it has promoted principles of social justice. The assumption of reformist religions is that once justice is served everything else will fall in place and all will prosper.

However, the concept of 'Civilisational Islam' is open to debate. Does it imply that Islam had no 'civilisation' in the first place, thus making it necessary for Malaysia to establish a connection between the two? This may not be the assumption of the discourse, although the term *tamaddun*, 'civilisation', which more closely links Islam to the rise of urban civil society and cosmopolitanism, might have been more appropriate. It merely states a public position of a religion which has dictated the lives of millions of believers, sometimes towards change and at other times away from change, towards social stagnancy. For example, the belief that an 'Islamic Republic' is a direction towards progress may also be interpreted as a direction towards social stagnancy. Civilisations transform and reinvent themselves. They die when there is obsessive conformity to traditions which are socially unacceptable or outmoded. By associating Islam with a civilisational discourse, it clearly states a position towards change, a more open, moderate and progressive position which suits the trends of economic development in a culturally diversified nation.

Why then do Malaysian Muslims need to be taught again the art of holistic and cosmopolitan living? Perhaps because a fatalistic complacency has set in among Muslims, disillusioned with the growing economic dominance of Western powers that there is no future except in the presence of faith. Reminding Muslims to revitalise *tamaddun* and the potential of a global civil society through *tamaddun* prepares them for a future compatible with the way the rest of the world is going. The future is no longer about developing a holistic consciousness of being, through Islam, but using Islam as a geopolitical and social strategy to work with others to do better. Thus the spirit of Malaysia's 'Civilisational Islam' is not unlike Weber's discourse on the "Protestant Ethic and the Spirit of Capitalism" (1905, 1992).[5] Weber argued that Calvinism in the United States spearheaded the rise of capitalism. It enabled followers to apply themselves rationally to acquire wealth and that this experience made them one of the 'elected' few to see the path of heaven in the afterlife. The 'rationalisation of action', however, was implied in the spirit of competitiveness and was not clearly stated as a principle of faith. Malaysia's 'Civilisational Islam' has an embedded logic of rational thought and action but does not provide a strategy for the afterlife. If any, it implies that self-initiative and industry *(ikhtiyār)* in this world is spiritually sanctioned by Islam. The afterlife should not be a preoccupation of mind and body. Islam should be a driving force of achievement. It is about reaching a higher level of global competitiveness, but where success should be shared to institute social and economic equality. Success enables a higher degree of redistribution of wealth which is necessary to keep people happy. The definition of 'happiness' however has transgressed quantifiable measurements of 'wellbeing' (Frey and Stutzer 2002) in terms of material and physical factors and pose relative discrepancies of experience in time and place.

Multiculturalism, however, is the greater area of concern of Malaysians who equate social equity with the rights of citizenry. Malaysia's economic development strategies of poverty eradication are for all Malaysians, but ideas of 'Civilisational Islam' may be challenged by Chinese and Indian Malaysians who feel that the systems of distribution of public resources and services were not equitable in the first place. The relationship between 'Civilisational Islam' and the 'special position' enjoyed by the Malays is unclear, but what is apparent is the view that Malay leadership, in its promotion of multiculturalism, enables greater autonomy of origin and identity than cultural assimilation in other ASEAN countries. Minorities in Malaysia tend to see Malays as accommodating to cultural diversities but stubborn about their political history and rights of rule. The right to institutionalise Islam is constitutionally provided, but a modern democracy requires a discourse which is acceptable among citizens which have chosen to retain their ethnic identities, based in their rights of origin from different nation-states. Hence, a more heterogeneous society has not emerged in any other part of Southeast Asia. Malaysia's policy of social integration rather than assimilation (as in Thailand, Indonesia, Myanmar, and others) has enabled a plural society to emerge where all ethnic groups are free to claim their rights of origin, practice their ethnic languages and dialects and uphold their chosen religions.

In the context of development, citizens are also free to explore options of economic liberalism in privatisation and globalisation. However, it may be a disadvantage in the long run for Malays to hold on to the idea of guardianship over 'national possessions'. Entry into the global market challenges the idea of guardianship over land and resources. The global arena of tangible assets, through acqui-

---

5 Weber's 'Protestant Ethics' describes the early phase of capitalism in America, under the surge of migrants seeking fame and fortune in the Americas.

sitions and mergers, introduces another phase in ownership of land and resources. The notion of 'Civilisational Islam' indirectly distances Malaysian Muslims from the idea of belonging to a land where territorial boundaries merge with selfhood. Instead it embarks on a more generic notion of 'freedom', to be free to move beyond the physical boundaries of nationhood, to seek success in a world without borders. Hence, in terms of *economic* globalisation, 'the small things' may not survive when global policies of the World Trade Organisation (WTO) go into full bloom in the next decade. Small people and small nations can be easily subsumed under mega deals where multinational corporations like Exxon-Mobil own assets many times larger than those of Southeast Asia put together. If Southeast Asian nations are unable to manage issues of socioeconomic hierarchies among citizens as well as multi-level acquisitions and mergers among corporations, political autonomy may be compromised. The government envisages a problem and is preparing Malays for a future where issues like 'ownership, 'leadership', and 'authority' may be more imaginary than real and more porous than absolute.

The discourse on the *tamaddun* also questions an absolute dependency on the fundamentals of Western ideals of economic liberalism, designed to promote the interests of financial capitalists. What is 'liberal' and 'advantageous' to developed economies may be confining and disastrous to the less developed. The Sierra Club activists of alternate globalisation (Mander, Goldsmith 1996) refer to economic liberalism as 'corporate colonisation'. Foley (2006) refers to 'free trade' as an 'economic theology', bound to the 'bible' of Adam Smith's *The Wealth of Nations*. The economies of Thailand, Indonesia, and the Philippines went into free fall in 1997 at the height of the financial crises when the Thai baht was devalued and foreign investment pulled out overnight. It took more than four years for these economies to recover from the recession which hit them and the policies of the International Monetary Fund (IMF) and the World Bank were unable to save the jobs of millions of production and service workers who were destitute overnight, unable to support their families for even a meal a day. Two years of demonstrations, riots, interethnic strife, and religious extremism saw the downfall of the IMF-bound governments of Suharto in Indonesia and Estrada in the Philippines, while Malaysia's Tun Dr Mahathir Mohamad became a national hero with his defiance of the forces of global financing. His controversial pegging of the Malaysian *ringgit* against the US dollar and tight controls on foreign capital speculation choked the breath from the Kuala Lumpur Stock Exchange (KLSE) but saved the Malaysian economy from going into free fall. He defied the IMF by increasing rather than decreasing public borrowing. He mooted the idea of creating reserves from local public savings, established *Danaharta* as an asset management company to buy up fundamental stocks of Government-linked Corporations (GLCs) and propped up thousands of jobs in the production and service sector.[6] Singapore, too, used up its national reserves to prevent massive deployment from industries

---

6 This move also enabled Tun Dr Mahathir Mohamad to secure Malaysian ownership of asset-rich companies linked to public services, like water, energy, and transportation.

hit by the recession and went on a comprehensive retraining exercise of retrenched workers caught in the wave of corporate bankruptcies.

Economists like Paul Krugman (2005) and Jeffery D. Sachs (2003a, 2003b, 2005) who have critically argued against liberalism in an emerging global economy, conceded that smaller nations caught at the threshold of the politics of global capitalisation, somehow have to come up with their own economic solutions for long-term survival. However, Sachs (2005) also argued that the World Bank and donor nations must change in their orientation towards profits. As Director of the Earth Institute at New York's Columbia University and former Special Advisor to the UN General-Secretary, Mr Kofi Annan, on the 'Millennium Development Goals' (MDGs), he argued that capitalist policies of global organisations were crippling to poorer nations. Poorer nations were led into economic globalisation without understanding the long-term issues of sustainability in development. Malaysia's preparation for 'sustainable globalisation', through the enrichment of social capital can be achieved through formal education and lifelong learning, but with the Islamist opposition through *Parti Islam SeMalaysia* (PAS) prescribing other definitions of Islam, the idea of 'Civilisational' Islam may encourage Malays and Muslims to rethink the role of religion, both spiritual and practical. If any, it may prepare for the possible scenario, where the only assets one can depend on would be the knowledge of survival. The religion of Islam cannot be an instrument for global survival, but can only be grounded in the belief that the world has opened up all kinds of new possibilities for Muslims to enrich themselves, through knowledge acquisition, accumulation and sharing among a diverse local and global population, making it more resilient to total immersion in a global system dictated by Western corporatism.

Qualifying economic globalisation through 'Civilisational Islam'

Malaysia's 'Civilisational Islam' can be viewed as a development strategy in a world of infinite possibilities and obstacles. It introduces a development approach to Islam to suggest its compatibility with – although not entirely supportive of – economic globalisation. It does not, however, suggest that there is a 'global Islam' which has converged with Western capitalism. It avoids this interpretation and instead supports the idea of universals in belief between spiritual consciousness and economic moderation. There is a strong idea of regeneration of fundamental values of family, charity and welfarism. Therefore, it does frown upon unfair practices of usury or profiteering in advanced capitalism, without mentioning its dysfunction in social and economic life. It proposes that progress is not only about the private accumulation of wealth. Indeed, the enrichment of the rich and the impoverishment of the poor run contrary to the grain of *tamaddun*. It upholds social and democratic principles without mentioning them and supports state-sponsored and productive welfarism without giving it this particular name. The discourse is similar to Sen's idea of 'development as freedom' (1999) when the poor are liberated from destitution and have more choice to direct their lives. Hence, its economic policies, in providing safety nets for corporations to enable them to keep Malaysians employed, may run contrary to IMF-dictated global policies of downsizing, delayering and refinancing in times of deflation, but provides a humanistic approach to working people with families to support. At least, the rich can prop up the poor and the poor can regain the ability to move on.

According to Datuk Dr Abdullah Mohd. Zin, Minister in the Prime Minister's Department for Religious Affairs, *Islam Hadhari* is a *development* strategy, based on the rational and progressive principles of the religion of Islam. This approach links Islam to the past and present alike, without breaking away from the fundamentals of the Qur'ān and the Sunnah, the recorded 'way of life' of the Prophet. In an interview with the *New Straits Times* (1 August 2004) he states, "It emphasises wisdom, practicality and harmony. It encourages *wasatiyah* or a balanced approach to life". Hence, individuals must not only be spiritually strong but economically independent and self-reliant with vision and the ability to face the challenges of a global age. According to the Minister, the BN-government has always placed an emphasis on economic development, but it is more concerned now with developments within the Muslim community which in some sectors have come to emphasise the afterlife to the total rejection of the contemporary. In *Islam Hadhari*, the concepts of moderation and modernity are avoided since these are usually linked to Western civilisation. A balanced or harmonious view of life is preferable. For example, currently, he argues that there is a lack of sympathy and understanding of the problems of Muslim women in society. To illustrate this, *sharī'ah* judges often base their judgments solely on the role and position of Muslim women at the time of the Prophet (Aminah Wadud 1999, Milallos 2007). This, however, is very difficult to comprehend and accept. On the contrary, during our times it is imperative that Muslims are more tolerant and concerned for social equity regardless of gender, ethnicity, and religion. Hence, education and economic development are the keys to progress, but these must be upheld in a holistic and comprehensive way to cover all aspects of day-to-day and practical life. Religious education must address contemporary socioeconomic developments in the Muslim world or Muslims would progressively fall behind other ethnic groups in their strife towards prosperity.

It may be difficult for non-Muslims to understand the need and purpose of a practical Muslim discourse which is state-sponsored, but world events have placed Muslims and Muslim-majority countries in Southeast Asia and the Middle East on the defensive (Desai, Tauris 2007; Ben-Ami 2007). Terror acts of suicide bombings have become a way of life for disillusioned Muslims, and there is the danger of a silent majority rejecting Islamic discourses which are seen to compromise with Western values of modernity and progress. It is challenging to come up with statements which are advocating progress rather than modernity, since one of the outcomes of modernity is the globalisation of Western institutional reform, including the democratisation of nation-states, and liberalisation of developing economies. However, the focus on the afterlife as a solution to the miseries of the present has its own pitfalls (Sen 2006). It is too extreme a reaction to the global phenomena of modernity. Martyrdom *(shahādah)* in the form of suicide bombing is only concerned about the afterlife. What about 'present life'? Should it not be important to enrich the future generations of Muslims to think for themselves what progress is, in the context of a culturally diverse global society? Should they not think about 'moving on', if not beyond the boundaries of faith but to unbounded boundaries, where these boundaries can be elastic enough to absorb the diversity of global life? As an illustration, to say that the canonical tithe *(zakāt)* must be paid in bags of rice would relate Islam only to its past (aside from the fact that 'rice' would refer to a purely Southeast Asian rather than the originally Middle Eastern context). The past and the afterlife must be addressed in relation to the present since the present is where Muslims are now and the future where they are going to be. The immediate future rather than heaven is the venture into the global world. Heaven belongs to the realm of 'infinity' – the future in the afterlife.

Unfortunately, some have argued that the *Islam Hadhari* discourse was introduced to lead Muslims away from militancy. This would have been the case if the root causes of militancy in Islam were known and clearly understood. If youthful Muslims see militancy as the last resort to reform and change, it may be seen to be compatible to *Islam Hadhari.* What needs to be done, however, is to associate *Islam Hadhari* with poverty eradication of the marginalised Muslim communities of the country and region. Other than indigenous minorities, the next impoverished communities are Malay Muslim farmers and fishermen, living on the margins of development. To state that there must be balanced development is another way of stating that there must be poverty eradication, but balanced growth must be sustainable for poverty eradication programmes to be taken seriously. Farish Noor (2004) states, that the Malaysian Government must make up its mind whether it wants Islam to move more towards socialism or capitalism. With economic trends moving closer to capitalism on a global scale, it can be assumed that 'Civilisational Islam' renders an invisible hand of approval to global forces of change prescribed for the developing world. In 'Civilisational Islam', this global force of change, however, like a benefactor, should be benevolent. Can we put back the humanism in economics (Rawls 1971, Kolm 1997) or is it a foregone conclusion that this is only possible if justice transcends enterprise?

Reviewing the battered Muslim populations of Southeast Asia, we see that nearly 90 percent of Indonesia's 238 million people are Muslims, whereas more than 50 percent of them are living on the poverty line. Indonesia's two largest religious organisations, *Nahdatul Ulama* (NU) with a membership of 30 million and *Muhammadiya* with a membership of 20 million, have given support to President Susilo Bambang Yudhoyono for a moderate progressive approach to Islam. Malaysia, with her 25 million citizens of which about 60 percent are Muslims, is also concerned for peaceful development as shown in the support given to the *United Malay National Organisation* (UMNO), the country's largest political party, in the 2004 elections. Muslims form a minority of 3.3 million people in Buddhist Thailand, 3.9 million in the Catholic Philippines, and about 500,000 in Chinese-dominated Singapore. Their minority status in Singapore, Thailand, and the Philippines coincides with a new growing consciousness among Muslims and participation of extremist elements in militant activities. The common denominator appears to be economic imbalances in growth and development. Hence, support for peaceful resolutions will be sustained as long as these populations believe that their leaders will deliver the cargo. It seems that the issue at stake is essentially about faith – not so much in religion, but in political leadership. Hence, 'Godism' is not about God but about holding on to the sanctity of justice.

The Indonesian Foreign Minister, Hassan Wirajuda, stated on 27 September 2004 at the plenary of the 59th United Nations General Assembly that

> [...] the global coalition to defeat terrorism [...] must address the root causes of terrorism: the grievances and the poignant sense of injustice that drives human beings to such depths of despair, they would carry out the most heinous acts of mass murder and destruction (United Nations 2007a).

Alberto Romulo, the Foreign Secretary of the Philippines, echoed this concern at the same debate:

> A new kind of peace [...] for a new kind of war [...], a global alliance to remove poverty as a breeding ground for resentment and conflict [...]. Conflicts should be addressed before terrorism can begin to define or exploit the conflict (United Nations 2007b).

Speaking for Malaysia, the Prime Minister, Dato' Seri Abdullah Ahmad Badawi, then Chairman of the 57-member Organisation of Islamic Conference (OIC), expressed his view that the 'war on terror' was tainted by anti-Muslim bigotry. He said;

> Most damaging of all is the linkage between international terrorism and Islam [...]. We need to clear the confusion of linking the problems faced by some Muslim countries with Islam the religion (United Nations 2007c).

Pakistan's President Parvez Musharraf, a key US-ally in the 'war on terror', warned of an 'iron curtain' falling between the Islamic world and the West, with Muslims feeling unjustly treated in international disputes (United Nations 2007d). Lastly, at the same debate, the Chinese Foreign Minister, Li Zhaoxing, stated that "only when the root cause of terrorism is eradicated can people live in peace and tranquillity again" (United Nations 2007e).

Despite these pleas for a humane approach to the war on terrorism, one observes more countries treating Muslim minorities as potentially dangerous and a threat to national security. Where Islam is the majority population, as in Malaysia and Pakistan, there is the same sentiment of disapproval for Muslims who sympathise with the problems of Muslims in other countries and who offer their knowledge to combat isolation or oppression. 'Civilisational Islam' is about sharing ideas on progressive education, both scientific and social, through peaceful interventions. It does not support radical interventions through militancy but through building and strengthening institutional structures in civil society.

Is the Malaysian government introducing these new development models to remove the influence of PAS on Muslims? The overwhelming victory of UMNO in the 2004 elections in Malaysia would indicate that the Government does not see PAS to pose a threat on Malay political unity. There are, however, new ideologues in the UMNO Youth Division who want to see Islam develop a competitive edge against Western economic and political dominance and who believe that smaller Muslim nations can make profound contributions in social capital and develop a 'Muslim Renaissance' in civil society. Disenchantment with Muslim leadership in the Middle East and its continued dependence on the United States as the prime mover of trade and industry may be some of the underlying issues prompting Malaysia to take a lead, but another, very real, fear factor is the mounting prejudice against Muslims, branded as terrorists and militants by Western media. Lulled into sleep by ideas of the afterlife, Muslims on the East Coast of Malaysia have not resorted to militancy or violence, but have been cautioned against participating in development. A field visit to Terengganu (2006), for instance, showed that the activities and mega-enterprises of Malaysia's wholly state-owned oil and gas company *Petronas* have had little impact on the local people of there, except for rising prices of food and services.[7] Their quality of life remains poor, without adequate infrastructure, housing, or income-generating activities. Except for State-managed tourist enterprises, traditional family-based *batek* industries, and tiny-scale food industries, all large-scale and successful businesses associated with domestic or foreign tourism are owned by ethnic Chinese or foreign companies. According to Malay anthropologists and sociologists working on development projects run by *Kolej Ugama Zainal Abidin* (KUZA, recently absorbed into *Universiti Darul Iman* at Kuala Terengganu), Malays in Terengganu seem to be reluctant to make the quantum leap into large-scale operations, being concerned for loyalty to traditional customers linked to friendship and kindred ties and also uncertain that they can attract and sustain new customers from outside the state and region.[8]

Their social and economic encapsulation in tradition has upheld a stagnation in business practices which somehow has been justified by a sense of 'spirit de corps' in poverty. This comes close to the 1960s neo-Marxist analysis of the 'peasant ethics' and 'the image of limited goods' by Potter, Diaz and Foster (1967), according to which a sense of comfort is developed from everyone being equally

---

7 The East Coast Development Corridor, announced in late 2007, partly attempts to address the problem of uneven development in Malaysia, but it is unknown if the jobs which are being created can absorb East Coast Malays effectively. Economic differentials may escalate if low-end jobs are occupied by locals while professional positions are occupied by outsiders.

8 Discussions were held with Dr Ramle Abdullah, then Director of Research at the KUZA College in April 2004 in conjunction with the 'Conference on Methodologies and Ethics of Field Research', organised by the college.

poor in close group cultures. Eventually traditional farming communities deny the need to seek new alternatives in productive life. Hence, Malaysia and other developing nations in Southeast Asia need to seriously address poverty and economic development through their own social frameworks. An agenda for social change has to be properly executed before further development policies are implemented in underserved areas. *Islam Hadhari* provides a congenial philosophical emotion for social change, but it does not address the link between poverty and the social framework of economic stagnation.

Poverty at the margins of economic globalisation

Southeast Asia's solution to underdevelopment, especially in the troubled South of Thailand, the Philippines, and rural areas of Myanmar, Cambodia, and Vietnam, is the creation of wealth through local-level development. Since government-monopolies have not really done much to uplift local populations from poverty, it is hoped that economic liberalisation and privatisation will. Since 1 January 1995, the *World Trade Organisation* (WTO) has replaced the *General Agreement on Tariffs and Trade* (GATT) in providing rules for international trade. Since 1948, GATT completed several rounds of trade negotiations which ended with the Uruguay Round (1986–1994) and the creation of WTO. Its agreements cover trade in services, traded inventions, creations, and designs (intellectual property). WTO is the only international organisation dealing with rules of trade between nations, and at its heart are legal documents, negotiated and signed by most of the world's trading nations. The organisation's main objective is to ensure economic liberalisation based on transparent, predictable, and legal rules which are globally binding. WTO also negotiates for effective dispute settlements between and among trading nations. Among the fundamental principles of WTO are the following:

- globalisation is associated with economic and trade liberalisation,
- reduction of Protectionism (duties, tariffs, subsidies),
- regionalisation must allow for multilateralism.

In the case of developing and least developed countries, this requires the following commitments:

- macro-economic stability must be ensured in short-term capital flow,
- enhancement of Foreign Direct Investment (FDI),
- development of Human Resource Capabilities in new areas of specialisation-biotechnologies, Information and Communications Technology (ICT) tools and applications, global laws of trade patenting and intellectual property,
- maintain political and social stability, including land, oil, and water management, and exploitation and control over ideological warfare and militancy,
- development of good citizenry and promotion of the advancement of a global civil society,
- strategic branding of products and services including social systems and ideologies.

For the developed nations, globalisation assumes the following economic gains with conditions attached to global profiteering:

- enhancement of markets and investments in the Asia-Pacific and African regions with adequate labour protection,
- increase in capitalisation offset by phenomenal gains in outsourcing may lead to little domestic employment, whereas higher economic growth without the creation of new jobs does not enhance human development,
- advantage in bio-patenting and intellectual property may lead to new forms of control over environmental resources of the least developed and developing,
- higher risks in capitalisation in countries which are politically unstable,
- development of new niche areas for short-tem gains in investment and stocks.

In the case of the least developed nations, which include all of the new members of ASEAN (Vietnam, Myanmar, Cambodia, and Laos) and most of the countries in Asia and the Pacific region, Africa and Latin America, the WTO provides flexibility in the implementation of agreements, such as the imposition of import duties on newly emerging industries and protective tariffs for farmers and small businesses. However, the question whether these forms of special assistance and trade concessions for least developed nations are enough to prevent them from selling out their assets and resources for quick gains of economic growth which may not be sustainable in the provision of productive human capital in the long-term continues to be a matter of grave concern. While it is well known that protectionism may render local industries obsolete faster than liberalisation, it is still necessary to review the increasing plight of rural populations who are unable to grasp some of these critical changes that are taking place in local development which invariably have an impact on their income and quality of life.

The Asian Development Bank (ADB) study *2005 International Comparison Program (ICP) in Asia and the Pacific: Purchasing Power Parity and Real Expenditure* showed average per capita earnings in Asia to be highest in Singapore and Hong Kong with Malaysia at the sixth place. The Price Level Index or the ratio of Purchasing Power Parity (PPP) to the exchange rate showed Nepal to be one of the poorest economies with low purchasing power. The study highlights huge inequalities in living standards in the Asia-Pacific region. The average Singaporean earns more than 60 times the average Vietnamese, nearly 80 times the average Laotian, and nearly 92 times the average Cambodian does. In terms of life expectancy, the average Cambodian woman can expect to live up to the age of 55 and a man until 52, while in Thailand women can live up to 71 and men to 67. In Malaysia, life expectancy exceeds these ASEAN countries, at 76 for women and 72 for men (Asian Development Bank 2007).

The linkage between investors' confidence and political leadership is so direct that economists should begin to consider socio-political capital as a factor of production and not only an index of international trade. Indulgence in radical politics leads to pull-outs, boycotts, embargos, and even strikes, hurting the economy beyond repair and this in turn stimulates individuals who have suffered pay cuts and layoffs to participate in radical politics. The root causes of militancy are not necessarily grounded in indigenous structures of poverty themselves, but in external forces of economic and military intervention, generating a vicious cycle of action and reaction to policies which work against the poor. Indigenous poverty which has not reached the pressure point of destitution or starvation may lead to radicalism, although not necessarily militancy. However, externally-driven policies that support military action against radicalism will always lead to militancy. When people begin to realise that their governments are not acting independently against them and are dictated by foreign pressure, they often tend to resort to activities which are more tactical and invisible since they know they will be defeated in an open war of words or action. This is when militancy becomes terrorism. Terrorism is the beginning of the end, the end of faith in political leadership and the substitution of religion for 'Godism' based on the maxim 'In God we trust and in God we submit at will'. Most religions convey the same sentiment, but Islam articulates this very clearly – 'surrender to God for the afterlife is near'.

Post-socialist countries in Southeast Asia – Vietnam, Cambodia, Laos – are now preoccupied with fighting a different kind of war against poverty. Religion has always been remote in the lives of the common people who have been starved of faith under socialism and the common process of healing is now profit-driven. God is wealth, no doubt, and 'Godism' is about putting things right again for faith in God to have any added value in life-style or psychological wellbeing. God is a luxury waiting to happen. The long-drawn misery of losing family, community, land, and resources brought on a loss of faith in leadership, both political and spiritual, and torture, starvation and death lead usually to a poor understanding of the relationship between the divine sphere and the people. It is impossible to speculate if the Buddhists in the three mentioned Southeast Asian post-socialist countries have any nostalgia for the divine leadership of the Buddha under the circumstances faced by them. They would have welcomed some sort of 'radical Buddhism', but this would not have helped them in the fight against poverty at the end of the long wars engulfing Vietnam and Cambodia. The wars have contributed to economic stagnancy, but they recuperated to a fair extent by successfully converting their rural economy to labour-intensive export-oriented industries in rice, textiles, and craft. Tourism has also been a contributing factor in providing new employment to the more skilled and educated urban work force. The ASEAN-market, through the ASEAN Free Trade Agreement (AFTA), has made them beneficiaries of regionalisation. However, with more capital inputs from more competitive companies wanting to have a share of the cheap but productive labour and land of these newly blossoming ASEAN rice bowls, there must be more measures to protect the transfer of capital and technology into other multinational corporations or MNCs which may not be as concerned for domestic equity as they are for efficiency. All this translates into wealth and eventually a different understanding of the notion of God, something more secular than profane and indeed closer to what has been defined as 'Civilisational Islam' within the context of Malaysia.

However, one should not rule out the link between radicalism and militancy so easily in globalisation, for even without foreign pressure to use military action against resistant movements, globalisation will be perceived as a foreign incursion upon indigenous rights if it does not win the fight against poverty. A point of concern is the impact of private or government monopolies in poverty-stricken areas in Southeast Asia which have traditionally been the centres of resistance and rebellion articulated through messianic cults. The indifference of local and national governments to social equity has been a major contributory factor and the spread of networks of resistance across local communities, another. 'Godism' may have gone global, but along with it is the language of resistance to make God relevant to practical life. This phase, however, does not render faith as 'civilisational', but rather 'radical' and, in extreme conditions, even 'militant'. Globalisation, through the movement of MNCs into traditional bases of agriculture and industry, needs to be carefully monitored for fear of massive displacement from traditional sectors without sustainable alternatives in human resource development and employment.

Southern Thailand in particular is a region to watch as incidences of bomb attacks are received by a stronger military presence and hardening of punishment. This echoes the situation in the Middle East, especially in Palestine and Iraq, where more than 50 percent of the population are unemployed, due to war and occupation. In Southern Thailand, it now appears that militants are drawn to the global tools of resistance movements by deploying suicide bombers, conducting kidnappings and hijackings, and posting conditions of release of hostages on websites. The destructive use of global tools of communication in everyday resistance movements is a manifestation of the downside of globalisation, and this may escalate as economic and political globalisation takes its natural cause. Hence, a discussion of the spread of wealth through globalisation and liberalisation of the world economy must also include a discussion on the spread of violence and militancy through globalisation and the protection of global interests of world powers through trade embargos and military occupations. Separatist movements which are usually explained as internal civil disorders by national governments, such in the case of Chechnya (Russian Federation), Acheh (Indonesia), Mindanao (Philippines), and Patani (Thailand), also result in escalating violence as financial and military support becomes global.

The separatist movement in Southern Thailand, for example, had been dormant for several years until the US-led occupation of Iraq prompted sporadic attacks on security stations and public buildings. Thai intelligence (*New Straits Times*, 27 September, 2004) reports that there are now at least 10,000 volunteer militants who have accepted the franchise of destruction of public and private property and attacks on security forces in Southern Thailand from want of something better to do.[9] The ideology is still separatism but the modus operandi has become global.

---

9 The high rates of unemployment in Patani and the other Muslim-dominated areas in Southern Thailand – largely founded in discrimination, neglect, and underdevelopment – are also said to be a major cause of local unrest and terrorism. A vicious cycle of poverty, violence, and unemployment has resulted, where acts of terrorism provide some kind of activity with a promise of food and shelter.

The underlying cause is still poverty and underdevelopment and alienation from development which has increasingly taken the form of large-scale tourist and industrial projects of no benefit to local people, except in the provision of casual work or unskilled labour. Education, both secondary and tertiary, continues to be underdeveloped, causing a rise in the preference for fundamentalist education in Islam. This long-lasting ideological struggle between political and economic globalisation on the one hand and terrorism on the other may become a way of life expressing the mood of new age wars of the twenty-first century. It may become part of the structure and form of globalisation itself that every action creates a reaction and a reaction further action. The magnitude of this problem on a global scale is worrisome since the majority of people want wealth to come with peace and not violence.

Southeast Asian nation-states which include significant regions occupied by cultural minorities such as Northern and Southern Thailand, Southern Philippines, Eastern Indonesia and North Sumatra (Acheh), should in particular address the socio-cultural and political sensitivities of the people of these regions and embark on special problems to overcome economic poverty and cultural alienation. On the other hand, Singapore, which has the highest per capita income in Southeast Asia, and Malaysia, which has a conservative count of 250,000 people living below the poverty line, have stabilised economic growth by addressing the problems of sustainable development through mass education and human resource development.

Netting wealth in under-developed regions in Malaysia and Southeast Asia

Hicklin, Robinson, and Singh (1997, 10), writing for the IMF, state that Southeast Asia's strong economic fundamentals – in particular, those of Singapore and Malaysia – have the following foundations:

- financial policies oriented towards macro-stability, keeping inflation low and external imbalances under control,
- market-friendly and outward-oriented, with liberal external regimes that maintain generally strong competitive positions,
- careful government interventions in a number of areas, such as antipoverty programmes, unleashing a powerful circle of government spending (especially in education and health), productivity, and growth that helped ensure the economic and political sustainability of the reform process in these countries,
- willingness to adjust policies flexibly and quickly in response to challenging economic circumstances, allowing a rapid transformation of economic structure while maintaining intact strong macroeconomic fundamentals.

Although all Southeast Asian countries generally subscribe to the above practices to a greater or lesser degree, it is argued that the least developed countries, in particular Myanmar, Cambodia and Laos will eventually subscribe to the above practices to a greater degree once they believe in the benefits of economic liberalisation in a post-socialist region which has generally subscribed to the ideology of social engineering in macro economic development. However, these countries should continue to develop strong social equity strategies through social engineering especially in affirmative action in education, health and human resource development among cultural minorities which are increasingly frustrated by low public investments in infrastructure, education, health agriculture and industry. Since the problems of minorities and border populations spill over into neighbouring countries and cause significant regional instability, ASEAN should develop an index of economic development which clearly shows *sub-regional inputs* of capital including FDI's, into infrastructure, education, health, industry, agriculture, social development and other public services to evaluate and monitor areas which continue to be underserved. Only in this way can sustainable local-level development be instituted in a growing climate of economic globalisation in the region.

Going global in ICT seems to be a contradiction in terms since the internet is essentially a global tool for communications, resource, and research. However, the global ICT scenario continues to be dominated by large technology MNCs such as Oracle, Satyam, Microsoft, Infosys, Intel, Nokia, IBM, ands others. Southeast Asian countries lack home-made success stories, although there might be many young unknown 'technopreneurs' who have yet to catch the eye of officials and academics to be in a position to influence the growth of human capital in ICT. Malaysia's Multi-Media Super Corridor (MSC) promotes MSC-status companies by quantifying total sales output, number of patents files, jobs created and technological competitiveness but worldwide recognition is gained only when a larger pool of local talent can compensate for the poorer infrastructure found in Malaysia outside towns and cities. The ICT infrastructure found in Bangalore, India, is said to be poorer than that of Kuala Lumpur or Putrajaya, but the surplus of expertise in India more than compensates for the rush to use India as a base for telework outsourcing and vendoring in hard or software. According to N. R. Narayana Murthy, the founder and chairman of Indian technology giant Infosys Technologies Pte Ltd., "Going global means developing a global mindset. If you want to develop, you must accept the principles of globalisation. The principles of globalisation means sourcing capital from where it is most available, producing where it is most profitable, without being constrained by national boundaries" (*The Edge Malaysia*, 13 September 2004: 6).

In Malaysia, the National Economic Action Council special consultancy team on globalisation, headed by Mahani Zainal Abidin, believes that trade liberalisation under the WTO in 2005 may lead to the removal of tariffs and subsidies, but other kinds of incentives can be enhanced, such as human resources and research and development capabilities (UNCTAD, Kuala Lumpur, on *World Investment Report*, 22 September, 2004). Hence, it is no longer a question of setting one nation against another in global competitiveness, but of ensuring that the leadership of a nation generates the right kind of economic, social, and political environment for new knowledge to effectively lead the underdeveloped masses to greater wealth. This means that a nation must not only be concerned with the development of human capital or the flow of foreign direct investments or FDI's, but the *equita-*

ble distribution of ICT resources throughout the nation and region. The digital, gender, and class divide aggravates the diasporas of cheap labour which are easily exploitable by global and local corporations (M. Williams 2003, Karim 2007).

The Fifth Asia-Europe Meeting (ASEM) held at Hanoi on 7 October 2004, addressed some of these issues. At the end of the dialogue, the 39-members, consisting of the European Union countries, the European Commission, the ASEAN countries, and China, Japan, and South Korea, agreed on three documents: the 'Chairman's Statement', the 'Hanoi Declaration on Closer ASEM Economic Partnership', and the 'Dialogue Among Cultures and Civilisations' (*New Straits Times*, 6 October 2004). Hence, it is apparent that the agenda of Malaysia's 'Civilisational Islam' proposes a closer synergy between knowledge as an integral source of social capital and the rise of indigenous entrepreneurship based in business and commercial networks in economic globalisation. Closely related to the global knowledge agenda is the concern to make faith a savvy experience in the pursuit of wealth, ultimately resulting in the departure from poverty. Since Muslims are most likely to question this, Malaysia has engaged Muslims in a discourse of Islam as a *practical* religion. The end objective is the engagement of people with a clear notion of a *productive* life where resources are better shared.

Some of the reasons why anti-capital and anti-globalisation sentiments continue in the age of ICT (Rifkin 2000, Angell 2000) are to be sought in the phenomenal contrasts in production of knowledge of the information and communication sciences. This has led to the capturing of global ICT technologies and services by MNCs on the one hand and the displacement of clerical, administrative, and production workers through delayering caused by heavy capital investment in ICT on the other. While outsourcing is capable of generating employment in poorer countries with surplus knowledge workers, it is incapable of generating equitable wealth, as long as knowledge acquisition remains a private profitable enterprise and a component of high-end capital. Trends towards the 'casualisation' of labour, poor legal representation of workers, and sudden dismissals with pullouts, as well as relocation exercises, may even contribute to massive destitution on a phenomenal pace. Leading New Age thinkers, among them Angell (1995), refer to it as "an oversupply of humanity". What is needed are massive inputs in education and human resource development which should not necessarily be a sole concern of national governments. MNCs should also play a major role in the qualitative improvement of human capital in countries which ensure them profits so that economic gains can be better distributed within a globally productive society (Angell 2000). This is usually argued through research and development (R&D) investments. R&D in product development and patenting has a narrow range of beneficiaries and benefits mainly those professionals and specialists who are already in the same line of businesses, but R&D in more generic areas of education, housing, environment, culture, politics, and law may have a far wider impact upon local populations and contribute to regional stability and security. Hence, it is insufficient to channel global efforts in R&D into global enhancement of capital and technology, but regional, national, and local issues must be addressed since they hinder the equitable spread of global wealth and security especially in the increasingly productive societies in Asia.

Privatisation, Anti-Trust and Anti-Monopoly Regulation in the World Trade Organisation (WTO)

The impact of private or public government monopolies on poverty-stricken areas may be catastrophic if the overriding concern is profit and competitiveness. With economic liberalisation, anti-monopoly laws upheld by the WTO may be enforced enabling external MNCs to bid for public and private projects in underserved areas. These projects may have massive capital inputs, but they do not necessarily improve the economic and social life of the poor. On the contrary, they may prolong poverty through a postponement of professional, technical, or lifelong education in the rush to procure quick jobs to overcome poverty. Furthermore, local political and public intervention may develop as MNCs develop projects which exploit natural resources or casual engendered labour. Hence, legislation is the only way to protect the interests of small landed farmers or landless businessmen. Southern Thailand, the Southern Philippines, the east coast of Malaysia, Sabah in Malaysian-Borneo, as well as Vietnam and Cambodia in particular will be more seriously affected by these changes as competitive pressures reduce the involvement of the public sector in the economy in favour of the public sector.

While anti-monopoly or anti-trust laws are being firmed up, there is much concern for the future of small businesses and farms, and these must be protected against capitalist excesses. Government-linked companies or GLCs can be given a certain amount of monopoly in poverty-stricken areas if they also implement a social safety net system to protect local people against unforeseen economic disasters or periods of recession and unemployment. The construction of public amenities, such as housing, transport infrastructure, schools, and hospitals must be also given priority to improve the quality of life of the people. On the other hand, organisations like the WTO must be able to anticipate the negative impact of globalisation and liberalisation on the rural poor and invest expertise to resolve the widening gap in income and quality of life of the rich and poor within and across countries in the least developed and developing areas of member countries. Surges of new competition may force local populations to sell out, mortgage land or migrate to urban centres. This will not only have negative repercussions on the economy, but will also destabilise existing social and political systems which have so far rendered a fair amount of cohesion and cooperation in day to day life.

Therefore, it is desirable that developing and least developed countries urge the WTO to link the status of 'most favoured nations' to the existence and spread of underserved areas, in particular where underdevelopment has shown visible signs of political and social destabilisation and where the marginalisation of minorities has caused significantly wide income gaps and social differentials of income and quality of life. However, these nations must be able to show sufficient antipoverty projects and programmes, including social safety nets, to be able to benefit from such a status. Projected targets of economic growth must be discriminatory to show serious attempts at levelling socioeconomic differences within these 'most favoured nations'.

The economic advantage which developed nations have over Asia may not be as critical an issue as the advantage which some sectors of the population have over marginalised communities which may be the majority population in some geographical areas. The spread of economic opportunities nationally and regionally must be in proportion to the spread of the new global and national wealth emerging from the link between the two. Hence one can see that the most troubled areas in Southeast Asia are linked not so much to the unequal spread of capital development, human resources, and technology transfer between the advanced nations of the West and Southeast Asia, but the marginalisation of large sectors of productive society from national and regional development, leading to economic, social, and political instability. The consequences of this may be disastrous to regional security, affecting the flow of foreign direct investments into the region.

Returning to our earlier discussion of the role to be played by *Islam Hadhari*, There can be no doubt that the vast majority of the world's more than one billion Muslims are peaceful citizens who can merge into a global productive life-style quite easily without guilt or self-censorship. However, since Islam has come to be associated with terrorism, the radical forms of Islam which have intensified since 9/11, have been justified by the situation in occupied Palestine and what is perceived by them as the quasi-colonisation of Muslim lands and resources in Southeast, Central, and South Asia. American and British economic domination through the use of military intervention has evoked former images of Western supremacy over Asia, although this does not mean that Muslims agree to terrorism as the ultimate form of resistance. The most moderate voices to Islam are actually located in Southeast Asia – in particular in Malaysia and Indonesia – and the success of the newly elected governments of Abdullah Badawi and Susilo Bambang Yudhoyono against fundamentalist hardliners is evident of the reconciliatory mood in Southeast Asian Islam. However, moderates say that the situation in Iraq has put them on the defensive. Says Hafiz Hussian Ahmed, a Pakistani cleric and Member of Parliament, "The US and its allies must realise that by occupation, by killing and dishonouring Muslim women – such as in the Abu Ghraib jail in Iraq – they are sowing the seeds of hatred" (*New Straits Times*, 13 September 2004, 41).

While many strategies are being developed by governments to combat the growing tide of resentment of Muslims against political, economic, and social marginalisation, Malaysia seems to be very keen to globalise its own brand of Islam, 'Civilisational Islam', to combat growing trends towards fundamentalism and to inspire them to make wealth and not war. The flow of foreign direct investment is measured nationally, but data on regional location of FDIs in terms of rural and urban investment is not available for countries where rural populations are still largely poor, as in Malaysia, Thailand, Indonesia, and the Philippines, and where fundamentalism tends to go hand in hand with rural poverty.

The World Investment Report 2004 (UNCTAD) states that the top ten recipients of FDI-flows in developing Asia for 2003 and 2003 are China, followed by Hong Kong, Singapore, India, South Korea, Azerbaijan, Malaysia, Kazakhstan, Brunei, and Thailand. Four of these ten countries are from Southeast Asia but investments are mostly in ICT products and services, manufacturing, and retailing, located in towns and cities. These FDI-flows are unlikely to trickle down into rural areas and more likely will encourage rural-urban migration and displacement of families when jobs are opened up in urban centres. Local investments in rural areas are low except in the field of agro-manufacturing which continues to be dominated by entrepreneurs from the city. Land transfers from rural to urban entrepreneurs occur on a large scale, a scenario aggravated by migration, shortage of labour, unsuccessful business ventures, and bank mortgages.

Needless to say, investments alone are not enough and a changes in the mindset of rural farmers and businessmen may be necessary to enable them to deal with the forces of globalisation. Fatalism may become a fatal attraction, and nothing may be gained from what has been lost. As farmers are forced to leave the countryside to seek casual employment in towns and cities, a surge of new capitalist owners of the rural countryside may materialise, which in years to come may lead to total alienation of local people from their land. MNCs make further gains when migrant workers serve the casual labour market in the city. Therefore, in the context of Malaysia, any concept of 'Civilisational Islam' must include tertiary or technical education and human resource development to enable local people and their children to sustain productive livelihoods from the rural sector as farmers and entrepreneurs.

Conclusion

The 'Millennium Summit', a meeting attended by many world leaders between 6 and 8 September 2000 at the UN Headquarters in New York City, endorsed a world policy on the eradication of poverty, aiming at reducing the incidence of income-poverty in developing countries from 30 percent to 15 percent until 2015. Unfortunately, since then, the number of people remaining in poverty has not significantly decreased and has remained at 1.2 billion or a fifth of the world's population.

Although it has become part of 'New Age Social Sciences' to discuss poverty and globalisation by a flip of the coin as two inevitable global trends, there has been little connectivity made between the new international political economy and its formalisation through world financial organisations, like the IMF and the World Bank, which support what this writer would like to refer to as 'instituted corporate colonialism'. Globalisation has and will be part of the scenario of trade and politics between the developed and lesser developed economies of the world. What is needed, however, are theories to show how globalisation does cause inequality, underdevelopment, and poverty, and whether this is a consequence of the rules of management of the global economy that are now dictated by financial institutions favouring the developed.

There are examples where nations have embraced globalisation, maintain high productivity and low inequality. Canada and Taiwan are two clear examples. Singapore is another country which has managed to check urban poverty by rapid retooling in global industries. Yet in neighbouring Indonesia, workers are daily campaigning for a minimum wage of US$ 130 per month, which is the salary of an Indonesian domestic worker in Malaysia, where all costs of accommodation, food, transport, recreation and personal artefacts are absorbed by the employee. Malaysia has also one of the lowest inflationary levels in Southeast Asia, keeping well below 3 percent for the last ten years. However for 2008, the Malaysian Institute for Economic Research (MIER) forecasts an inflationary level of above 3.2 percent, with a rise in petroleum prices of 30 percent above the levels of 2007. It is obvious that countries like Malaysia, Indonesia, and the Philippines, as well as the newly admitted ASEAN members, will have to be concerned with rising income inequality, since this will contribute to long-term problems of poverty. The issue of Indian minorities in Malaysia, for instance, demanding a review of economic policies to ensure equal rights for all citizens, is a symptomatic expression of embedded poverty. The Ninth Malaysia Plan acknowledges the need to redefine poverty levels (the agreed poverty line for 2007 having been RM 1,200), although it does not yet endorse programmes such as the restructuring of wages of the unskilled and semi-skilled, social welfare, and social safety nets. Average income figures can no longer reflect the *real* socio-economic constraints of low-income families living under the pressure of inflation and changes in lifestyle.

Many social scientists would accept the argument that the state of *'homo hierarchicus'* is inevitable within and among nations. As the conquest of markets of the least developed and developing nations of the world becomes more complete, it remains even more doubtful if globalisation can benefit everyone and every nation equally. Economists may prove that this can happen through a sound theoretical review of development theory and global economics but the spread of social capital in a nation is a determinant of equitable rise of wealth. The ingredients that make up a nation-state are unique to the culture, development history, and politics of communities of a particular country. However, if the combination of factors which determine national wealth can be built into a theory of economic growth, then economic models should be more sustainable and adjusted according to the prevailing conditions which make them work. A more resilient workforce, higher levels of literacy and specialisation, and greater need for economic democratisation should require a discourse of *practical* religion to merge with economic initiatives. This can reduce the competitive edge which other groups have over the Malays.

In Muslim developing nations, the road to equitable economic growth through good governance may be hastened if tribalism and patriarchy are removed from Islam and Islamic civil society put to the test. Malaysia seems to be concerned to take the lead in disseminating ideas on 'Civilisational Islam', which links Islam directly to economic parity in development without necessarily equating Islam with secularism. A social and cultural ideology is used to revitalise and synergise a society to global competitiveness. The doomsday prediction of Muslim societies as being incompatible with the West and Western-style liberal democracies and trade is refuted through sustainable economic growth with global competitiveness rather than isolation. This is, in a way, the Muslim 'Protestant Ethics', a Weberian approach to social transformation in an increasingly global world.

Backed by sound fiscal policy, equitable labour markets, careful trade regulation and international controls on short-term capital flows to reduce volatility of local markets and commodity prices, sharp investment and recession-induced inequalities in income may help to bring about macroeconomic stability and with it political stability. In the long run, this may actually reduce the growing use of terrorism to resolve internal and external grievance against states. To prevent internal intervention in politics and the use of military force to forcefully democratise Muslim and post-socialist nations, the WTO should work closely with the United Nations to reduce foreign intervention in local politics through conventional forms of military warfare. Instead of embargos and military strikes, the policies of ASEAN should be emulated where inclusion rather than exclusion is used as a policy of containment. In order to achieve equitable globalisation, nations must resort to other ideologies beyond those contained in macroeconomic theory, as long as these are compatible with the social fabric of civil society. Support for well-intended policies can only be obtained through political action which shows sympathy for public opinion. The release of the former Deputy Prime Minister of Malaysia, Anwar Ibrahim, by the Federal Court on 2 September 2004, for instance, two days after Independence Day, was said to be timely executed since it reflected an independent judiciary system. The KLSE soared 2.6 points, brought on by a surge in foreign investors, reflecting a positive link between corporate and political culture and the judicial independence with investors' confidence. Concern for public opinion gives policies a boost, but the synergy between a state-driven ideology and social acceptance must be revealed in more tangible gains in social equity.

There is awareness that economic growth is about social equity and not only holistic globalisation. Setting high standards of domestic public, corporate, and civil governance so as to be more resilient to those imposed forms of global organisations like the WTO and the IMF is important, but translating this into tangible forms of social equity is the future challenge. As the understanding of globalisation becomes more holistic and comprehensive, developing nations prepare for more domestic reform. Malaysia, however, believes she has to synergise ideology with practical life. The public has to be convinced that state-instituted Islamic ideology can and will be effectively executed for social equity, or they may believe that it is yet another move to defend existing structures of ownership and capitalist enterprise – or in other worlds, that *individuals* have to change rather than *systems* which divide them.

References

Printed sources

Aminah Wadud 1999: Qur'an and Woman: Rereading the Sacred Text from a Woman's Perspective. London: Oxford University Press.

Angell, I. 1995: Winners and Losers in the Information Age. In: LSE Magazine 7, no. 1, 10–12.

Angell, I. 2002: The New Barbarian Manifesto: How to Survive the Information Age. London: Kogan Page.

Ben-Ami, S. 2007: Commentary on Jihadists. In: South China Morning Post, 11 April, 13.

Castells, M. 1989: The Informational City. Information Technology, Economic Restructuring, and the Urban-Regional Process. Oxford, Cambridge MA: Blackwell.

Castells, M. 2001: The Internet Galaxy. Reflections on the Internet, Business and Society. Oxford: Oxford University Press.

Cavanagh, J.; Mander, J. 2002: Alternatives to Economic Globalisation: A Better World is Possible. San Francisco: Berrett-Koehler Publishers.

Cornia, G. A.; Court, J. (eds.) 2004: Inequality, Growth and Poverty in the Era of Liberalization and Globalization. Oxford: Oxford University Press.

Cornwell, B. 2007: The Protestant Sect Credit Machine: Social Capital and the Rise of Capitalism. In: Journal of Classical Sociology 17, no. 3, 267–290.

Desai, M. 2006: Rethinking Islamism. The Ideology of the New Terror. London: I. B. Tauris.

Evans, E. J. 1997: Thatcher and Thatcherism: The Making of the Contemporary World. London: Routledge.

Farish A. Noor, 2004: Malaysia's Badawi Encounters His First Hurdle. In: Daily Times [Lahore, Pakistan], 2 October, 1–2.

Frank, A. G.; Amin, S.; Arrighi, G.; Wallerstein, I. 1990: Transforming the Revolution: Social Movements and the World System. New York: Monthly Review Press.

Foley, D. K. 2006: Adam's Fallacy: A Guide to Economic Theology. Cambridge MA: The Belknap Press of Harvard University Press.

Frank, G. A. G. 1998: ReOrient: Global Economy in the Asian Age. Chicago: University of Chicago Press.

Hicklin, J., Robinson, D.; Singh, A. 1997: Macroeconomic Issues Facing ASEAN Countries. Washington DC: International Monetary Fund.

Hilley, J. 2001: Malaysia: Mahathirism, Hegemony, and the New Opposition. London: Zed Books.

Ho, E. 2006: The Graves of Tarim: Genealogy and Mobility Across the Indian Ocean. Berkeley CA: University of California Press.

Frey, B.; Stutzer, A. 2002: Happiness and Economics: How the Economy and Institutions Affect Well-Being. Princeton NJ: Princeton University Press.

Karim, W. J. 2008: Asia-Pacific Childhoods in an Age of Globalisation: Systemic Relational Analysis in the Study of Migration and Social Nets. In: D. Behera, R. Waterson (eds.), Changing Asia-Pacific Childhoods. London, New Delhi: Longmans Pearson (in press).
Kimbrell, A. (ed.) 2002: Fatal Harvest. The Tragedy of Industrial Agriculture. Washington DC: Center for Food Safety.
Kolm, S.-C. 1997: Modern Theories of Justice. Cambridge MA: MIT Press.
Krugman, P.; Obstfeld, M. [7]2005: International Economics. Theory and Policy. New York: Addison Wesley.
Mahathir Mohamad 2002: Globalisation and the New Realities. Kuala Lumpur: Pelanduk Publications.
Mander, J.; Goldsmith, E. 1996: The Case Against the Global Economy and For a Turn Towards the Local. San Francisco: Sierra Club Books.
Milallos, T. R. 2007: Muslim Veil as Politics: Political Authority, Women and Syariah Islam in Acheh. In: Contemporary Islam 1, no. 3, 289–301.
Plant, R. 1984: Equality, Markets and the State. London: The Fabian Society (Fabian Society Tract No. 494).
Popkin, S. L. 1979: The Rational Peasant: The Political Economy of Rural Society in Vietnam. Berkeley CA: University of California Press.
Potter, J. M.; Diaz, M. N.; Foster, G. M. (eds.) 1967: Peasant Society: A Reader. Boston: Little, Brown and Company.
Redfield, R. 1960: The Little Community and Peasant Society and Culture. Chicago: University of Chicago Press.
Rifkin, J. 2000: The Age of Access: The New Culture of Hypercapitalism, Where All of Life is a Paid-For Experience. New York: Tarcher Putnam.
Sachs, J. D. 2005: The End of Poverty: Possibilities of Our Time. New York: Penguin Press.
Sen, A. K. 1999: Development as Freedom. Oxford: Oxford University Press.
Sen, A. K. 2006: Identity and Violence: The Illusion of Destiny. London: Penguin.
Sennet, R. 2006: The Culture of the New Capitalism. New Haven CT: Yale University Press.
Scott, J. C. 1976: The Moral Economy of the Peasant: Rebellion and Subsistence in Southeast Asia. New Haven CT: Yale University Press.
Stiglitz, J. 2002: Globalisation and its Discontents. London: Penguin.
Suryadinata, L. 2007a: Indonesia's Foreign Policy under Suharto: Aspiring to International Leadership. Singapore: Marshall Cavendish International.
Suryadinata, L. 2007b: Understanding the Ethnic Chinese in Southeast Asia. Singapore: Institute of Southeast Asian Studies.
Wallerstein, I. (ed.) 2005: The Modern World-System in the Longue Durée. Boulder CO: Paradigm Publishers (Fernanad Braudel Center Series).
Tabb, W. K. 2004: Economic Governance in the Age of Globalisation. New York: Columbia University Press.
Weber, M. 1992: The Protestant Ethic and the Spirit of Capitalism, tr. T. Parsons. London: Routledge.

Williams, W. 2003: Reaganism and the Death of Representative Democracy. Washington DC: Georgetown University Press.

Williams, M. 2003: Gender Mainstreaming in the Multilateral Trade System. A Handbook for Policy-Makers and Other Stakeholders. London: Commonwealth Secretariat.

Internet resources

Asian Development Bank 2007: Purchasing Power Parities and Real Expenditures. URL: http://www.adb.org/Documents/Reports/ICP-Purchasing-Power-Expenditures/default.asp (accessed on 9 January 2008).

Karim, W. J. 2002: Ethics for a Global Civil Society: Non-Western Perspectives. URL: http://www.globalknowledge.org/gkii/ncw_social_culture_a.pdf (accessed on 9 January 2008).

Marwaan Macan-Markar 2004: The March Towards a More Moderate Islam. In: Asia Times, 24 December. URL: http://www.atimes.com/atimes/Southeast_Asia/FL24Ae01.html (accessed on 8 January 2008).

Mohd Kamil Hj Abdul Majid 2005: Memahami Pendekatan Islam Hadhari. URL: http://www.pensabah.gov.my/dasar/Islam_Hadhari.htm (accessed on 8 January 2008).

Myers, B. 2004: ASEAN's Great Divide. In: The Cambodian Daily ASEAN Supplement. URL: http://www.camnet.com.kh/cambodia.daily/asean/3.htm (accessed on 8 January 2008).

Sachs, J. D. 2003a: Globalization and Inequality (video of a panel discussion, 24 February 2003). URL: http://www.columbia.edu/cu/news/vforum/03/globali zation_inequality/ (accessed on 8 January 2008).

Sachs, J. D. 2003b: Ending Global Poverty. Transcript of the speech at the Hilton Foundation Conference "Humanitarian Intervention Today: New Issues, New Ideas, New Players", New York, 24 September 2003. URL: http://www.stwr.net/content/view/65/37/ (accessed on 8 January 2008).

United Nations 2007a: Statement by Dr. N. Hassan Wirajuda, Minister for Foreign Affairs, Republic of Indonesia. URL: http://www.un.org/webcast/ga/59/state ments/indoeng04927.pdf (accessed on 9 January 2008).

United Nations 2007b: Statement by H. E. Dr. Alberto G. Romulo, Secretary of Foreign Affairs, Republic of the Philippines. URL: http://www.un.org/webcast/ga/59/statements/phieng04927.pdf (accessed on 9 January 2008).

United Nations 2007c: Press Release GA/10263. URL: http://www.un.org/News/Press/docs/2004/ga10263.doc.htm (accessed on 9 January 2008).

United Nations 2007d: Address by General Pervez Musharraf, President of the Islamic Republic of Pakistan. URL: http://un.org/webcast/ga/59/statements/pakeng040922.pdf (accessed on 9 January 2008).

United Nations 2007e: Statement by Li Zhaoxing, Minister of Foreign Affairs of the People's Republic of China. URL: http://un.org/webcast/ga/59/statements/chieng040927.pdf (accessed on 9 January 2008).

10

Islamic Economics: An Approach to Development Alternatives in Muslim Societies

Amer Al-Roubaie

Abstract:

During the last few decades, substantial literature has been written about the role of Islamic economics in the development of Muslim societies. Presently, the income gap between Muslim and non-Muslim countries is widening, reflecting the extent of economic disparity and extreme poverty. Despite attempts to reengineer their economies and alleviate poverty, Muslim countries have failed so far to bring about satisfactory socio-economic progress. This is despite their aggregate rich resource endowment, financial capabilities and human capital potential. For over fifty years, Muslims have employed theories and models mainly resembling an approach to development in Western societies. These models and theories have proven to be inadequate to formulate planning strategies and construct policies capable of promoting change and sustaining development in the developing countries. Experience with development has shown that economics alone is not sufficient to enhance societal progress. In other words, economic development is a process of structural changes that require political, social, technological, scientific, as well as economic ingredients. Similarly, indigenous development constitutes locally-made decisions that comport with the cultural and environmental requirements of the society. Islamic economics underscores the importance of the Islamic fundamentals of justice, freedom and equity in societal change. Development in Islam comprises sharing of resources to ensure equity and fair distribution of income and wealth. Unlike capitalism, Islam discourages monopolistic control of resources by giving priority to meeting basic needs of the society and increasing participation in production processes. The aim of this paper is to highlight the importance of socio-economic development in Islam by reflecting on the current challenges facing Muslim societies including poverty, globalisation, environmental degradation, knowledge, and human development.

Introduction

The period following the Second World War has witnessed radical socio-economic changes at the level of both national economies and international markets. The end of the war brought hopeful prospects that international cooperation and development assistance would create new opportunities, especially for developing countries, by giving them greater access to global markets and providing them with better conditions for technology transfer and exports of manufactured products. Being subjected for so long to colonial trading systems, many of these countries developed dual economic structures creating very few forward and backward linkages. In addition, high levels of commodity and marketing concentration in trade subjected the economies of these countries to instabilities brought about by market imperfections and crop failures at home and business fluctuations in Western countries. As a consequence, with the exception of a few countries in Southeast Asia like Malaysia, the economic situation in developing countries remained inadequate for meeting basic needs. International income inequalities increased to the extent that in the year 2006 the United States, with less than 5 percent of the world's population, earned more income than all developing countries combined. Similarly, income inequalities within nations and regions widened to the extent that the average income in high-income countries is more than 80 times higher than the average income in the least developed countries.

In recent years, globalisation has begun to introduce new rules which, in turn, are changing existing trade relations by promoting a knowledge-based economy for increasing access to global trade and investment. Unfortunately, many of the developing countries, including Muslim nations, are lacking adequate technological capacities to speed up the process of development and take advantage of globalisation. The hostile Western attitude toward development in Muslim countries has been so far expressed by economic sanctions, boycotts, export restrictions, and financial appropriations and restrictions.

In the new economy, attention has been shifted towards production for export by encouraging nations to liberalise trade and privatise local economies for attracting foreign direct investment (FDI) and stimulating domestic production. The new economy, driven by globalisation, is distinguished by knowledge-based features which require high-quality labour, sound managerial and organisational structures, and substantial investment in research and development. Unfortunately, very few developing countries are in a position to meet the challenges of globalisation due to financial and technological constraints. In other words, most developing countries are in a disadvantage position to compete in the global markets due to capacity limitation, market imperfection, and inadequate institutional infrastructure.

This paper aims at highlighting development alternatives by examining the attributes of the Islamic economic system and its contribution to socio-economic development in Muslim societies. In these countries, economic growth remains unsatisfactory to eradicate poverty, enhance global competitiveness, improve living standards, create indigenous knowledge and sustain development. Although

Islamic economics is still in its infancy, there are several important features which could be discussed in the light of the existing challenges facing Muslim countries. Good management of natural resources and sound investment in human capital would induce rapid changes to enable these countries to leapfrog by bypassing several developmental stages. Efforts to adopt some of the economic fundamentals brought by the *sharī'ah* could provide alternatives for the current materialistic and secular models of Western development. In Islam, development is people-centered, aiming at increasing human capabilities to make decisions and to fully participate in the process of development.

Economic development

For several decades since independence from colonial rule, the Muslims' experience with development has not been satisfactory. Per capita income among Muslims is the lowest among all world regions reflecting the extent of poverty and low living standards. As Table 1 illustrates, on average, a Muslim earns about $US 1,650 compared to $US 36,487 in high income countries and $US 7,439 worldwide. Globally, the share of all Muslim countries combined in total global gross national product (GDP) accounts for about 5.5 percent despite their rich resource-endowment and huge financial capabilities. Table 1 also shows that the combined GDP of all Muslim countries accounted for less than that of Germany in 2006. Similarly, the share of Muslim trade in total world trade, particularly production and export of manufactured goods and services, represents less than 5 percent of world volume reflecting low productivity and weak competitiveness in global markets. Economic development constitutes process of structural changes which require efficient managerial, organisational and administrative mechanisms to make decisions and implement programs. Ultimately, however, the goal of economic development is to enhance people capabilities to participate in decisions making through the creation of a suitable environment capable of increasing productivity, improving labour flexibility, building technological capacity and promoting economic growth.

The new paradigm on 'Rethinking Bretton Woods' outlines the objectives of development, as stated by two economists, Griesgraber and Bunter:

> The goal of development is to create conditions that will enable each human being to realize her/his potential for political, social and economic fulfilment in a manner consistent with the common good. Individual rights, duties and participation are central to this process and to its goal. The first priority is the eradication of poverty, empowering people to gain a measure of control over their own lives and to obtain the resources to meet their basic needs in an ecologically sustainable manner. Genuine development is essentially a grassroots, bottom up process, growing from the base with local communities being key players. Economic activity should be managed

Table 1: Macroeconomic Indicators for Various Regions, 2006

region	*GDP (US$, billions)*	*percent of World*	*GDP per capita (US$)*	*total exports (US$, millions)*	*total imports (US$, millions)*	*percent of high-tech exports in manufacture exports*
world	48,481.8	—	7,439	12,063,483	12,278,444	22
low income	1,562.3	3.2	650	323,706	388,830	4
middle income	9,415.4	19.4	3,051	3,305,551	2,934,082	21
high income	37,528.9	77.4	36,487	8,435,922	8,960,432	22
M. East & N. Africa	771.2	1.6	2,481	280,881	210,805	3
United States	13,446.0	27.7	44,970	1,037,320	1,919,574	32
United Kingdom	2,425.2	5.0	40,180	443,358	600,833	28
Germany	3,018.0	6.2	36,620	1,112,320	910,160	17
Japan	4,900.0	10.1	38,410	647,137	577,472	22
Muslims	2,500.0	5.2	1,650	978,085	733,345	—

Source: World Bank, World Development Report 2008 (Washington: World Bank, 2007)

> by human beings, within the bounds of the fragile and exhaustible environment. The market may be a means to achieving these goals, but it is not an end in itself (Griesgraber, Bunter 1966, xiv–xv).

Historically, underdevelopment in Muslim societies is attributed to a complex combination of economic, political, social, scientific and external factors. Early colonial powers encouraged production, mainly primary products, for exports which caused the deterioration of the terms of trade and increased dependency on world markets. In addition, the decline interest in scientific research and knowledge-creation weakened the ability of Muslim countries to diversify economic structure and build viable economies. As a consequence, orientation towards international trade created dual economic structures weakening in the process the contribution of the leading sector from producing sufficient linkages to stimulus the economy, i.e. the failure of development in these countries could be attributed to a set of historical, cultural, social, economic, political and external forces which prevented these countries from taking advantage of the rapid transformation brought about by the industrial revolution and scientific development especially in Europe. As Ira Lapidus explains:

> [t]he legacy of eighteenth and nineteenth-century historical change, however, is not a unilinear movement toward modernization, but a heritage of

> continuing conflict in Muslim countries over political, economic, and cultural goals. Political decline and European intervention have led to a struggle among political elites, scholarly (ulama) and mystical (Sufi) religious leaders, and revivalist movements for political and social power. While secularized political elites tend to favor modernization in Western forms, and the redefinition of Islam to make it consistent with modern forms of state and economy, religious reformers espouse the revitalization of moral values and formation of new political communities on Islamic principles (Lapidus 2002, xx).

In recent decades, substantial attention has been given to development studies. Not only national governments and non-governmental institutions have become active precipitants in the debate about various aspects of development, but also international institutions, Western governments, environmentalists, academicians, social workers, students and women groups. Adding credit to these efforts, the World Bank and the International Monetary Fund were established in the mid-1940s to provide developing countries with financial and technical assistance in order to implement programs for alleviating poverty, increasing productivity, and accelerating growth. Most recently, the United Nations adopted the Millennium Development Goals (MDG), to achieve several development objectives including eradicating extreme poverty, promoting universal primary education, reducing child mortality, improving maternal health, ensuring environmental sustainability, developing global partnership, and enhancing gender equality. So far, however, these developmental efforts produced limited results in many of the developing countries. As Jeffrey Sachs points out, "the greatest tragedy of our time is that one sixth of humanity is not even on the development ladder. A large number of the extreme poor are caught in a poverty trap, unable on their own to escape from extreme material deprivation" (Sachs 2005, 19). The economic condition for many people worldwide remains far below the minimum requirements to satisfy basic human needs. The complex nature of developmental processes implies that external solutions are not necessarily sufficient to remedy the challenges facing many of the developing countries. The failure of these countries to reengineer their economies and activate manufacturing production reflects the inability of national policies and international programs to stimulate economic growth and eradicate poverty. Western development theories maintain that "the path to modernisation of the underdeveloped countries lay in their adoption of Western values, techniques and institutional structures, which meant that they must at the same time reject their own supposedly incompatible social institutions and lifestyle" (Hedley 2002, 44).

Economic development involves different stages of technological application and scientific testing which require highly skilled labour and professionals in several fields. Development must create indigenous environments capable of solving some of the domestic problems facing Muslim countries. Sustaining long term economic growth requires sound investment in human capital and good management over macroeconomic variables. Priorities to achieve such objectives must be given to projects that generate high backward and forward linkages. Outward looking policies could encourage production for exports but not necessarily create a balance between demand for domestic production and demand for foreign markets. The economy, driven by globalisation is identified with knowledge creation and information dissemination. Unfortunately, most Muslim countries lack adequate technological capacity to increase connectivity, absorb knowledge and induce rapid socioeconomic transformation. Not only has knowledge become an important factor in production, but also a powerful tool for wealth creation.

In this age of global integration, it is vital to build technological capacity capable of increasing global linkages to absorb knowledge and produce quality products. As a consequence, the objective of development in Muslim societies must be oriented towards full utilisation of human and natural resources to balance between domestic requirements for satisfying basic needs and production for global markets. Due to their rich resources endowment and large financial capabilities, Muslim countries could have comparative advantage in production and exports of several commodities. However, Muslims need to increase cooperation and adopt unified policies to encourage specialisation in production and improve global competitiveness. Globalisation, driven by liberalisation and privatisation, could increase uncertainty about future economic prospects in developing countries. In most developing countries, including Muslim nations, the productive structure is relatively weak to absorb global shocks and manage globalisation. In addition, the power of the state over the management of the economy is expected to weaken due to its inability to exercise full control over macroeconomic variables.

Low per capita income in Muslim countries hinders attempts to speed up the process of modernisation by making development more difficult. The present economy driven by globalisation is a knowledge-driven economy which requires not only applying and absorbing knowledge but also creating knowledge. Supporting such an economy underscores the importance of building technological and human capital capacities capable of speeding up the process of change and accelerating economic growth. At this stage of their development, capacities to absorb knowledge in most Muslim countries are still inadequate to enhance productivity and support rapid socio-economic growth. Unlike 'high human development' countries, the economies of Muslim countries are oriented towards production and export of primary products which are subject to a wide range of fluctuations. Instability in export earnings and a high degree of marketing concentration in trade could have negative consequences by subjecting the economies of Muslim countries to fluctuation in global demand for primary products. Under such circumstances, development becomes highly sensitive to external forces the control of which is beyond Muslim countries.

Western developmental theories are output-centred, emphasising output per person as a measure of development. Such an approach undermines the importance of indigenous factors such as social, cultural and religious elements in the process of development. Moreover, the Western economic approach pays little attention to the distribution of income and wealth among members of the society. Concentration of wealth in a few hands reduces the velocity of circulation of money in the economy and, therefore, weakens the roles that aggregate demand plays in stimulating economic growth. In contrast, the Islamic economic system provides conditions that create a balance in society by introducing mechanisms for sharing resources in an equitable manner, i. e. the existing of monopolies or excessive control by a few over resources is not permitted. Economic justice underscores the importance of equal opportunity to all citizens to ensure that individuals live a happy and prosperous life. The concept of brotherhood in Islam implies that resources must be organised, managed and distributed through participation and cooperation of all members of the Muslim community.

Economic development is about people and their well being, and therefore development will not be able to fulfil its objectives unless it takes into consideration the people and the environment they live in. The process leading to change must allow people to fully participate in decision making regarding allocation of resources as well as in getting a fair share from the fruits of development. Most people look forward toward better improvement in living standards and in having equal opportunity to participate in the overall decisions that influence the lives. Development is a process of structural changes aiming at serving multi-dimensional purposes comprising all aspects of human live. Human development underscores the importance of institutions for providing the necessary means to improve the living conditions.

Islamic economics

Throughout history the rise of civilisation has been greatly influenced by a nation's economic power and its financial capability to facilitate growth in trade, factor mobility and industrialisation. As a field of study, economics is concerned mainly with the allocation of society's resources to improve man's welfare and also to ensure that resources are equitably distributed among members of the society to bring about fairness in production and consumption of these resources. However, in capitalism, allocation of resources is left to individuals and private entrepreneurs who are motivated by maximising profit or return on investment. It is assumed that individuals act in a rational manner by making decisions in their best interest whereas the interest of the society is served through the invisible hand or the rational activities of various individuals. On the other extreme lies communism in which individuals are denied ownership of means of production and final decisions concerning allocation of resources rest with the government. In other words, economic development is left either to the willingness of individuals to invest and earn profit or to decisions made by governments driven by military and political considerations with little attention paid to the economic interest of the nation. Without supervision and accountability, the market may not function on its own to serve the interest of society. Market imperfections and the exploitive nature of business could lead to mismanagement of resources and increase income inequalities in society. The Islamic economic system imposes certain restrictions on what society can produce by giving priority to the production of goods and services that are directly related to human development. In Islam, resources are considered as God's bounty to man and, therefore, the return on investment in these resources should not only be measured in terms of material welfare, but also in terms of spiritual elements. From an Islamic point of view, economic development is synonymous with knowledge and happiness to ensure what is called in Arabic *falāḥ*, success. Material gains may satisfy man's physical needs but may not make him happy. The principles of the Islamic economy are derived from the teachings of the *sharī'ah* and are based mainly on ethical and moral guidelines to alleviate poverty and to strengthen economic justice. In other words, the objective of maximisation is not limited to a material gain alone but includes the social, ethical, educational and religious aspects as well. The Islamic approach towards economy ensures economic and financial stability by prohibiting interest and usury and maintaining good management over monetary variables.

Islam rests on the concept of *tawḥīd* or 'oneness of God' which requires submission to the will of Allāh as shown in the Qur'ān and the *Sunnah* or teaching of the Prophet. Man acts as a *khalīfah* or vicegerent of God on earth and, therefore, is entrusted with the task of managing productive resources in the best possible manner for his material satisfaction but within the limit set by moral law. It is, therefore, incumbent upon man to organise, manage and utilise effectively these resources to ensure that both humans and animals can maximise the benefit from the use of these resources. Unlike capitalism where ownership is absolute, control over resources in Islam must be subservient to the welfare of the society. In other words, monopolies and absolute ownership of natural resources violate the teaching of the *sharī'ah*. The interest of society is given priority over the interest of the individual by imposing ethical and moral guidelines in relation to production, consumption and distribution of resources. Fulfilment of these principles not only rests with the state but also with individuals through active participation in decision making, planning, organizing, managing and making decisions to increase productivity of these resources. In this regard, strict conditions are adopted to ensure the compliance of the *sharī'ah* concerning meeting the society basic needs, production of illicit or non-*ḥalāl* products, and prohibition of interest payments and enhance efficiency. As stated by Farhad Nomani and Ali Rahnema,

> [t]he laws of Islam, co-ordinating an Islamic Society, are therefore divinely pre-ordained. The fact that these laws were communicated through revelations implies that they are not subject to human reason and interference. The Shari'a, as a comprehensive and coherent body of legal injunctions, is complete. It constitutes the commands the prohibitions of God and is therefore binding and incumbent upon all believers (Nomani, Rahnema 1995, 1).

There are several features that distinguish the Islamic economic system, including individual liberty, right to property, economic inequality within natural limits, social equality, social security, wider circulation of wealth, prohibition of accumulation of wealth, prohibition of anti-social institutions and social and individual welfare (Afzal-ur-Rahman 1990). The Islamic economic system perceives change as a balancing factor between the material and spiritual activities in life. In Islam, economics endorses a moderate solution to the economic problem aiming at establishing a balanced system for ensuring equal opportunity, prohibiting exploitation, reducing monopolistic control, creating knowledge, promoting just distribution and sustaining development. In other words, development is not only concerned with production of material output but also comprises social, cultural, environmental and human elements. Islamic economics views development as a comprehensive approach the impact of which includes all human endeavours. In other words, development cannot be separated from other components of the Islamic system. This inseparability underscores the importance of coordination and planning with regard to allocation of resources for meeting society's basic needs. Human capital is derived from investment in skill production and knowledge creation. The return on investment depends largely on the quality of decisions as well as on the institutional structure needed for implementing various developmental projects. This is to confirm the proposition of the pre-eminent medieval Muslim theologian and thinker al-Ghazālī (d. 1111) which states that both knowledge and action are important for promoting development (Faris 2002).

The ultimate objective of the Islamic economic system is to meet human demand for necessities. These represent the goods and services which are required for achieving people requirements such as fulfilling religious duties, population growth and family support, and purification of soul. In addition to the essentials, the Islamic economic system also provides goods that facilitate productivity growth such as computers, transport equipments, agricultural tools and capital goods. In this way, the Islamic economy enjoys better means for distributing income and wealth among people by preventing resources from being concentrated in a few hands which may be used for production of luxury products the consumption of which will be limited to a small group. In short, the fundamentals of the Islamic economic system go beyond physical production and wealth concentration to comprise principles derived from Islamic jurisprudence, the system of *tawḥīd* and the knowledge of modern economic system. Islam promotes human progress by endorsing a number of commands and restrictions covering all aspects of human life. It is a practical system which is suitable for encouraging production and providing incentives to work hard.

As a field of study, the interest in Islamic economics springs from the failure of development theories in Muslim counties to achieve satisfactory economic growth. Historically, economic concepts and issues were discussed by a number of early Muslim scholars but no concrete methodology was developed to define the functioning of the economic system. Abū Yusūf (d. 798), al-Shaybānī (d. 804), Abū Ubayd (d. 838), al-Māwardī (d. 1058), al-Ghazālī (d. 1111), and Ibn Khaldūn

(d. 1406) discussed broad issues related to markets, prices, state revenues and expenditures, money, economic fluctuations and inflation. The economic ideas of these scholars were derived from the teaching of the *sharī'ah* comprising ethical and moral values which Islam introduces for conducting economic transactions. Most of the concepts have parallel meaning in present-day economics reflecting the understanding of early scholars in terms of business life and the workings of the market. Since their early history, Muslims were concerned with the allocation of resources in promoting development and increasing living standards. Labour is given special treatment as a determining factor in production. For example, Ibn Khaldūn made it clear that labour is the source of value of the goods and services produced, and, therefore, market prices should reflect the cost paid to support labour. In today's economics, labour cost represents a major share in total cost of the good produced. Similarly, al-Ghazālī discussed economics from a religious point of view by reflecting on man's character and pattern of conducts. Al-Ghazālī's approach is unique in the sense that both knowledge and action are important for fulfilling man's duties. These two ingredients still represent the main backing of the contemporary economic system both locally and globally. An economy driven by globalisation is a knowledge-based economy in which knowledge plays a critical role to enhance the capability of man to achieve the main objective in life. Al-Ghazālī recognised that man can achieve *falāḥ* in the Hereafter through his worldly actions. He states that man must strive through his own work to meet his basic essentials in life. In the present debate about Islamic economics, work is regarded as a form of worship through which man can achieve *falāḥ* in both worlds (Al-Roubaie: Islamic Economics […]. Unpubl.).

In an Islamic society continuous planning and good managerial supervision of the economy are essential for ensuring flexibility and avoiding obstructions by foreign markets. Enforcing such market flexibility and managing globalisation requires the building of efficient institutions capable of constructing practical policies and making sound decisions. The use of fiscal policy, for instance, to supplement *zakāt*, the canonical 'alms tax', can be enforced by imposing new taxes or by reallocating investment resources through incentives and subsidies to increase social capital. The Islamic economy postulates workable measures to redistribute income and reduce inequalities among members of the community, i.e. it provides a variety of apparatuses to encourage the utilisation of human and natural resources by emphasising private ownership, competition, investment, profit-making and the right to engage in business for personal gain. The Islamic economy has the tendency to minimise the risk of business fluctuations via voluntary expenditures including *zakāt*, *awqāf* ('pious foundations'), charity, and spending 'in the way of Allāh'. These expenditures reduce business cycles by preventing the economy from experiencing recessions or depressions. In an Islamic economy, economic growth is driven by expenditures of the voluntary sector which ultimately stimulates economic activities and increase employment opportunities. In addition, the prohibition of interest rates in financial transactions reduces the burden of debt which prevents the national economy from overspending.

The concept of development in Islam

Development represents a comprehensive approach to societal changes aimed at improving man's material conditions as well as enhancing his spiritual life. In this sense, the goal of development is to advance such Islamic fundamentals as social justice, equality, freedom and rights and dignity by providing such basic needs as food, shelter, clothes, education and health. As a way of life, Islam requires that development ultimately be guided by these fundamentals to create a just and moral society. For the society to function, however, Islam demands the establishment of efficient institutions, enforcement of moral and ethical standards, electing responsible leaders, and allowing the participation of public in the process of development. As Syed Kholi points out,

> [t]hrough development, though, a society could achieve the growth it aspires, however, the potential confusion between the concept of development and the Western civilization, or its features, should be avoided; otherwise, society may turn to a consumer of goods and services without acquiring the capabilities to be sophisticated from the viewpoint of production. In other words, such a society would be deprived of the foundation as well as the basic factors of a technologically advanced society that produces goods rather than just consumes them. Thus the Western theories on economic development are inappropriate to the present conditions of the developing countries (Kholi 2000, 98).

At present, poverty remains one of the most serious challenges facing Muslims everywhere. Islam equates poverty with sin and therefore, eradicating poverty is a religious duty at both individual and state levels. As a consequence, development in Islam aims at increasing investment opportunities to enhance productivity and increase human capabilities to contribute to the process of development. In other words, development advances those qualities, which constitute the essence of man, so that the more they are developed the more, he lives in peace with himself. To live in complete harmony with this natural essence, and thus to be fully human, man must direct all his activities towards the serving of God. In this respect, the Islamic concept of development cannot be measured in terms of per capita income as in the case of the pertinent Western literature. In addition to the material improvement, the Islamic approach to societal change requires the development of man's conscious understanding about the nature of God, brotherhood, the *ummah* or Muslim community, and the universe at large.

During the past few decades, Muslims employed Western economic methodologies to promote societal changes in their societies but failed to achieve satisfactory rates of socio-economic progress, to eradicate poverty and improve their quality of life. In Islam, access to society's resources is a divine right to be utilised by all individuals in the interest of the community. Islam views resources as God's bounty to His creatures for enabling them to live meaningful and fulfilling life. It is incumbent upon man, therefore, to properly manage, organise, and develop these resources if he seeks Allāh's pleasure. The Qur'ān states: "It is He [i. e. Allāh] Who has made the earth manageable for you, so traverse ye through its tracts and enjoy of the sustenance which He furnishes" (Qur'ān 67:15). This means that man cannot claim absolute command over resources on earth since ownership belongs to Allāh, neither is he allowed to exploit these resources for his own personal benefit whereas the majority remains in need, i. e. man becomes an agent, his sole responsibility being to develop these resources in a manner to increase his own benefit.

From an Islamic perspective, development has been given much broader meaning to include not only the production of material goods, but also to enlarge people capabilities for participating in decision-making. As a process of structural change, development serves to increase man's happiness through increasing knowledge, enhancing moral and ethical practices and sustaining economic growth. Consequently, allocation of resources in a Muslim society must be directed at implementing the Islamic fundamentals of justice, freedom and equity. The concept of *khalīfah* in Islam authorises man to become His vicegerent responsible for the allocation of resources in a manner in which all members of the community benefit from it. As God's bounty, access to resources should not be limited to privileged groups or individuals in order to avoid monopoly, waste and excessive exploitation. In Islam, ownership of means of production is permissible but should not violate public interest. Resources are entrusted to man to develop, manage and organise so as to increase their productivity and enhance their contribution to economic development. Khurshid Ahmad (1994, 20) argues that development in Islam is driven by the Islamic philosophy of *tawḥīd* or God's oneness and sovereignty *(rubūbiyyah)* or divine arrangements for nourishment, sustenance, and directing things towards their perfection, *khilāfah* or 'vicegerency' and *tazkiyah* or 'purification' (i. e. of the soul) plus growth. These Islamic principles constitute fairness and justice by endorsing equity as an important pillar of development. Equity in production and consumption removes all forms of injustices and discriminatory practices among members of the community. In Islam, equity in distribution exhibits individual efforts, skills, knowledge and motivation, i. e. rewards must be measured by individual contribution and participation in economic activities. Unfortunately, current inequalities prevailing in Muslim societies are largely responsible for the existence of poverty, market imperfection, unequal opportunity, exploitation, injustices and corruption. The institutional structure presently practiced in Muslim countries is based on secular principles driven by market mechanisms which exclude the poor, the financially weak, unskilled workers, and minorities. Institutions provide incentives as well as legal protection of economic development by curbing corruption and ensuring equity in society. "Equity in laws and fairness in their implementation involve striking a balance between strengthening the independence of justice systems and increasing accountability – especially to counter the risk that the powerful and wealthy might corrupt, influence or ignore the law" (World Bank 2005, 13).

Long-term strategies for development must involve the creation of institutions and research centres to encourage people develop new ideas and inventing better techniques for use in production processes. In adapting such policies, a careful selection of choices must be made by taking into consideration society's long-term sustainability and growth. Planners and policymakers must not compromise the social interest by giving access to foreign firms over management and exploitation of national resources. In an Islamic economy, the goal of implementing such policies must ensure that the Islamic principles to establish justice and equality be realised. As stated in the Qur'ān (4:141), "And never will Allāh grant to the unbelievers a way [to triumph] over the believers". This implies that Allāh wanted Islamic society to be completely independent in its economic, social and political features and not to rely on non-Muslims for their livelihoods or basic needs. To cultivate such divine guidance, development should be oriented towards the building of an infrastructure capable of harnessing the potentialities of indigenous inputs. Internally, the Islamic economy allocates certain portion of existing resources to promote development of educational, technical, managerial, and administrative institutions as well as to ensure reduced dependency on non-Muslims. As for the external organisation of society, it must be of a nature that reflects and suits its internal reality. Therefore, the principles on which the political, economic, social, educational, and legal aspects of its life are organised must help to create a humane social system, a system which ensures the appropriate organisation of society and its environment vis-à-vis its growth and development. In this age of globalisation, proper links between the internal and external forces need to be established to diminish shocks and maintain economic stability. This implies that even though the ingredients for change must come from within, via utilisation of the local resources, society can still seek foreign assistance to acquire knowledge, technology and scientific methods needed for improving the economic structure. The external organisation is to supplement the internal mechanisms for facilitating and accelerating development in order to reduce dependency as well as to help society achieving self-sufficiency.

The Islamic concept of development strategy for self-reliance comprises such fundamental principles as satisfaction of essential goods, preservation of cultural identity, Islamic cooperation, adoption of suitable scientific and technological methods and adequate managerial and supervision of utilisation of resources. In other words, the strategy of development must be balanced to include *all* sectors of the economy and must not be limited to the production of specialised products. As explained by the Malaysian scholar Professor Wan Mohd. Nor Wan Daud, for development to be balanced there are four major objectives that need to be met: (1) the principle of growth with equity in the distribution of national wealth, (2) a balanced societal development as an instrument of social and political stability, (3) moral and ethical development for the creation of a responsible, resilient, progressive and caring society, and (4) a criteria for prudent management of natural resources and ecology (Wan Mohd. Nor Wan Daud 1994).

The process of development must be indigenous if long-term socio-economic sustainability is to be maintained. In other words, society must not exceed its limits for being ambitious by excessively importing or borrowing from outside. Such processes may not necessarily contribute positively to the advancement of the society; rather they may cause bottlenecks, higher prices, uncertainties, inequalities, balance of payments disequilibrium and rising national debt. To minimise environmental risks, Muslim economies must employ indigenous technology in conjunction with the mobilisation of new ideas suitable for the existing production conditions in the country.

Development in Islam is thus 'responsible development', exhibiting comprehensive objectives that go beyond income maximisation. Development not only provides the basic needs and enhances economic efficiency but also promotes human security through creation of jobs and social safety nets for all people without discrimination. Economic justice also requires fair and equitable distribution of income and wealth to reduce poverty and improve living standards. Excessive consumption and repaid exploitation of resources are not acceptable from the Islamic perspective which mandates a balance between present and future consumption. Development must ensure sustainability through research and development, invention and innovation, good management and environmental protection. Future generations have equal rights to existing resources and, therefore, it is incumbent upon the present generation to take good care of the resource base. Materialistic culture usually produces undesirable environmental, economic and social consequences causing rapid exploitation of resources. Development in Islam does not allow resources to be used for production of prohibited goods and services. Thus destruction of forests, pollution of the environment, depletion of non-renewable resources and degradation of the soil are against the teaching of the *sharī'ah*. Self-interest in Islam is not confined to the interest of the individual alone but to the interest of the society as well. Greed represents and characterises human behaviour in relation to consumption of material products. As a consequence, development driven by individual self-interest may not contribute to the happiness of man.

Speeding up the process of development in Muslim countries requires sound planning and efficient policies that reflect Islamic fundamentals. Until now, most development models and theories employed in Muslim countries are secular, featuring mainly Western view of development. Although, Muslims could learn a great deal from Western experiences with development by reflecting on the contribution of these theories to the socioeconomic transformation, Western models exhibit cultural values and materialistic approaches which may not necessarily be suitable for development in non-Western societies. As John Brohman argues, European theoretical models arrest

> [...] indigenous development processes and pre-empt possibilities for alternative, more self-reliant and broadly based development policies. Indigenous social structures that have traditionally supported majority interests and have served as sources of identity and popular participation are under-

mined without being replaced by viable alternatives. Alien Western values, relationships, and institutions fuel rising tensions, uncertainties, and feelings of anomie – thereby subverting efforts to bring about needed socio-economic change (Brohman 1996, 326).

Most Muslim countries are still heavily dependent on production and exports of primary products and have, therefore, not been able to create dynamic sectors capable of producing goods and services for global markets. The advantage the Europeans have over Muslim countries is the growth in Total Factor Productivity (TFP) which results from investment in human capital and innovation. For example, during the period between 1960 and 2000 total factor productivity declined in the region of the Middle East and North Africa compared to the rest of world regions. As concluded by a recent World Bank study, "[t]he higher level of investment in education during the last four decades was not associated with higher economic growth or with appreciable gains in TFP growth compared to East Asia and Latin America" (World Bank 2007, 47).

Economic development on Islamic lines has to create a balance among sectors by focusing on the production of essentials, including food production. Self-sufficiency in food production is mandatory in an Islamic state to ensure life sustainability and reduce rural poverty. Development should equally provide the necessary inputs to encourage linkages within the economy and to provide incentives for local production. Broad-based economic development is important for balancing growth and promoting human security. Investment not only in human capital, but also in research and development is essential in Islam to generate indigenous technology which helps to close the knowledge and income gaps within sectors and among nations. This, however, requires the building of institutional arrangements to provide the necessary incentives for inventions and innovation in all economic activities. Islam does not prohibit the use of technology and science developed by others as long as it contributes to the economic well-being of Muslim societies.

The importance of knowledge

Knowledge occupies an important place in the overall development of Muslim society. The knowledge of the world is important but transcended by the knowledge of God as stated in the teachings of the *sharī'ah*. Knowledge advances the productivity of the economy through innovation and invention of new products, development of new methods in production, improvement in technological applications and advancement in scientific techniques. Islam encourages knowledge by advising its adherents to make efforts for knowledge acquisition and application. Historically, the rise of Muslim civilisation was identified with growth in scientific advancement and development of educational institutions which led to rapid economic growth and improvement in standards of living. Early Muslim scholars made substantial contributions to human civilisation by developing sci-

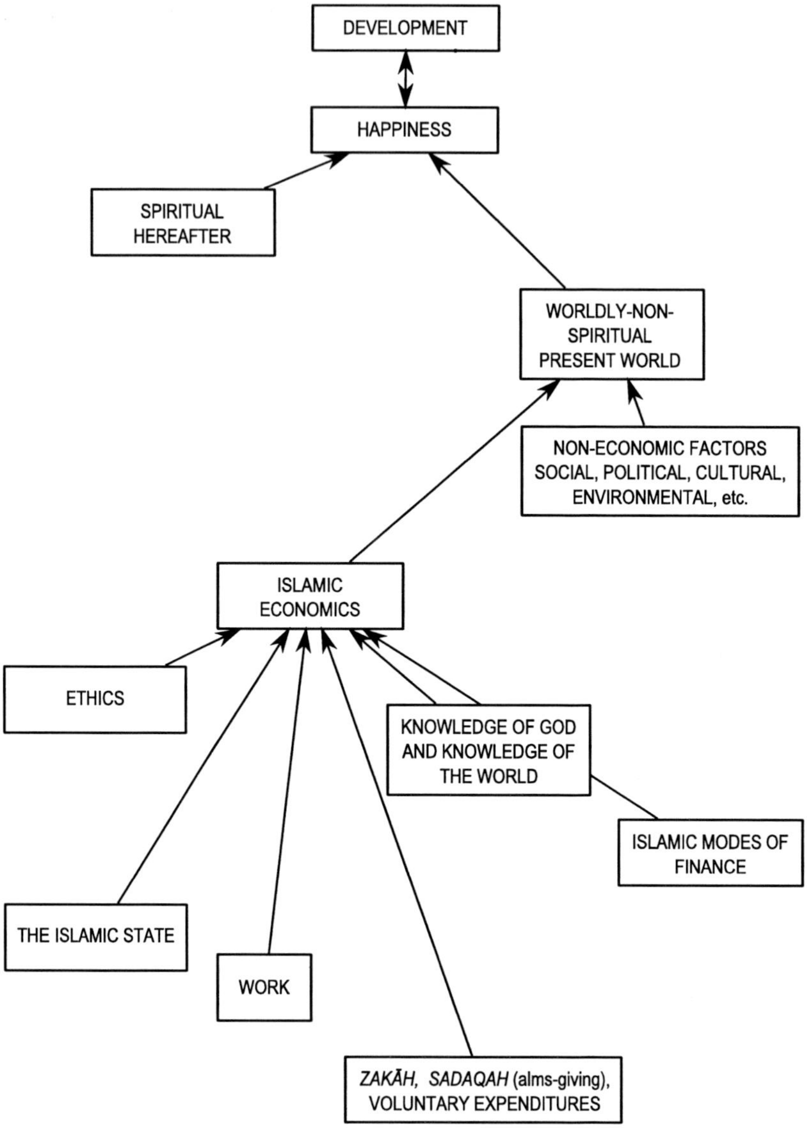

Development Alternatives: An Islamic View

entific methods and increasing the role of knowledge in the overall development of Muslim societies. Knowledge is the core of al-Ghazālī's teachings. In his view, knowledge is the product of human intellect without which morality and good conduct are not possible. For its part, Islam has inspired many of its followers to venture into the creation of new areas of knowledge. What inspired them? The answer is obvious. The divine guidance, revealed in the holy book of Islam, the Qur'ān, lays great emphasis on the contemplation and investigation of nature (Ishfaq Ahmad 2000).

Knowledge in Islam is made up by two branches: one that enhances man's capability to achieve material progress and improve his socioeconomic wellbeing, and another that promotes his spiritual needs to ensure the fulfilment of religious duties. On the material side, knowledge increases the country's capacity to produce human capital, encourage technical progress, develop managerial and organisational skills and enlarge research and development. These features are important for economic globalisation which endorses a knowledge-based economy in which knowledge becomes not only an important source for wealth-creation but also as a factor of production. The existing knowledge gap between rich and poor nations undermines the ability of the latter to promote rapid growth and catch up with the former. Modern production requires highly-trained workforces and the invention of new products and investment in research and development in order to boost the country's ability to compete in global markets. Unfortunately, many developing countries, including those of the Muslims, are not in a position to take advantage of the knowledge-based economy driven by globalisation due to their deficiency to apply, absorb and produce knowledge.

Building knowledge-capacity requires strategic planning capable of fulfilling a society's potential to overcome transitional difficulties impending on a knowledge-based economy. Public policies must address barriers to enlarge a country's capacity to build higher levels of skills and expand opportunities to facilitate rapid economic development. Human capital has become a necessary condition for endorsing rapid growth and strengthening the foundation for a knowledge-based economy. Educational institutions must develop life-long learning programs in order to process information and increase linkages with global markets. Practical skills, including computer literacy, become necessary for increasing productivity and meeting the demand requirements for skills. The Prophet says "To seek knowledge is a duty for every Muslim (male) and Muslimah (female)". He also said "Seek knowledge even as far as China". This makes education in Islam compulsory as well as universal to include all members of the community without discrimination against people because of their gender, religion, colour and race.

Despite his ability to make judgments, man is not rational to the extent of making accurate decisions concerning allocation and use of resources. The risk of future circumstances makes information and knowledge difficult to verify for making precise decisions about future events. The Qur'ān clearly states that man cannot predict what may happen tomorrow. Thus without the knowledge of God, the Muslim cannot achieve his ultimate objective to increase happiness in this life and gain the pleasure of God in the Hereafter. The rational behaviour of the Muslim is guided by the *sharī'ah* teachings and not exclusively driven by worldly motivation to maximise profits or utility. Adam Smith, the founder of modern economics, argues that man is rational by acting to maximise material gain. Under the capitalistic system, it is the private interest that motivates man to work hard and not necessarily the public welfare of the society at large. Such behaviour is in contrast to the principle of the Islamic economy where the interest of the individual is a derivative of the interest of the Muslim *ummah*. By nature, man is selfish and, therefore, without moral and ethical guidance individual interest may not necessarily serve the interest of the community. As one scholar put it, "[r]eligious edicts act as the ultimate defence against the domination of the material and economic sphere over the religious sphere" (Nomani, Rahnema 1995, 23).

Islam gives human capital and skill development high priority in total investment. Development in Islam is people-centred aiming at enhancing people's capabilities to ensure that man participates in the process as well as benefits from it. From an Islamic point of view, education is a religious duty; without it man remains incapable of sustaining his worldly life and increasing his spiritual requirements. Education induces society to produce knowledge and facilitate access to information. In turn, this provides equal opportunity for all to compete in society. At present, most Muslim countries lack equal educational opportunities to enhance equity and promote economic justice in which resources are fairly shared among all members of the society. Unlike capitalism, ownership in Islam is relative to prevent wealth-concentration in a few hands as well as to protect resources from being controlled by monopolies. The tendency toward absolute ownership springs from the material attainment of capitalism in which all efforts are directed at accumulating material wealth. The Islamic economic system, in turn, creates a balance between the material and spiritual aspects of life to ensure equity in production and consumption of resources.

The challenges of globalisation

The new economy driven by globalisation is a double edged-sword comprising both benefits and losses to those practicing globalisation. However, most developing countries, including those inhabited by Muslims, are in a disadvantage position due to their inability to compete with industrialised countries in the global markets. In the new economy, trade comprises manufactured goods and services mainly produced in industrialised countries. As a consequence, those with adequate technological capacity could benefit from globalisation whereas producers of primary products will experience difficulties in promoting their products. With the exception of a few Muslim countries, the majority falls in the later category where most exports are made of raw materials with little manufactured content. For example, in 2005 the share of high-technology exports of Arab countries in total manufactured exports accounted for 2 percent, reflecting the weak economic structure of these countries. To meet the challenges of globalisation, Muslims must increase the productive capacity of their economies by building a knowledge-based infrastructure capable of promoting economic growth and increasing global competitiveness.

Economic globalisation underscores the importance of liberalisation of trade and privatisation of the domestic economy. In countries where production for export remains low, it is likely that economic development suffers from low capacity to import, especially manufactured goods and services. Thus building sound infrastructures to strengthen the economic structure and to ensure the production of knowledge-based products has become a necessary condition for global integration. In the early stages of development, financial liberalisation and economic privatisation could create imbalances within the economic structure due to increased production for export at the expense of local markets. The 1997 financial crisis in Asia proved to be fatal to the economies of some Asian countries because of increasing dependency on foreign markets and inability of the local economies to manage globalisation. For example, in the case of Indonesia foreign capital flight in the aftermath of the crisis caused considerable economic, financial, social, and political fallout. In addition to the devaluation of the Indonesian Rupiah by about 80 percent, unemployment jumped to about 35 percent, creating severe social, economic and political problems. To benefit from the new economy, Muslims must integrate globalisation into national economic policies to ensure that the economy gains from linkage effects, ensuring development in Muslim societies strives to fulfil human needs through equitable distribution of wealth and efficient use of society's resources. Globalisation could be biased in favour of production of manufactured goods for export instead of production of agricultural products for local markets. The bulk of the Muslims worldwide still lives in rural areas which seem to be ignored by multinational business and foreign direct investment. Agricultural production is not only vital for achieving self-reliance, but is needed to support industrial production. Access to resources is a fundamental right in Islam, reflecting moral and ethical considerations that are deeply rooted in the teachings of the *sharī'ah*.

In the new economy, Muslim countries must endorse policies to restructure the economic system to ensure competitiveness in the global markets as well as to create knowledge-based products. The economy, driven by globalisation, is a knowledge-based economy which exhibits knowledge absorption and knowledge creation. However, deepening globalisation by encouraging production for exports may violate the objectives of development in Islam. In the Islamic economic system, priorities are given to production of essentials to meet people's basic needs and not necessarily to produce for exports. Distributive justice underscores the importance of fairness and equity in production and distribution of wealth and income. In other words, the objective of development to alleviate poverty, which remains one of the biggest challenges facing Muslim countries in the age of globalisation, could be jeopardised. As pointed out by Michel Chossudovsky (2003: 7), "this global economic restructuring promotes stagnation in the supply of necessary goods and services, while redirecting resources towards lucrative investments in the luxury goods economy". In other words, "the New World Order is based on the false consensus of Washington and Wall Street, which ordains the free market system as the only possible choice on the fated road to a global prosperity" (Chossudovsky 2003, 7). In contrast, the Islamic economic system ensures equity by sharing resources among individuals and regions which serves the interest and the welfare of all. Employing discriminatory measures that deny access to resources is prohibited in Islam, and therefore, it is in violation of the Islamic fundamentals to practice methods that lead to exclusion. Economic development is a comprehensive process involving all human endeavours. The allocation of resources must ultimately enhance people's capabilities to become more productive and more innovative for ensuring economic growth and improving material well-being. Achieving such objectives implies that development must be indigenously designed to develop both human capital and natural resources to strengthen the productive capacity of the economy and sustain growth. Globalisation could have a positive influence on the process of development by inducing indigenous growth through technology transfer, knowledge acquisition and information dissemination. Muslim countries must seize these opportunities offered by globalisation to reengineer their economic structures and build viable productive system capable of balancing development and increasing global competitiveness. However, a recent study by the International Monetary Fund (IMF) has shown that the main factor driving increases in inequality across nations has been technological progress (International Monetary Fund 2007, 153).

Because of their colonial history, the present institutional, organisational and administrative structures in most Muslim countries are closely linked to the secular institutions in Western countries. Exploitation of natural resources by multinational corporations has created economic duality which weakened the spill-over effects among sectors of the economy. Muslim countries need to take the initiative to strengthen local institutions to enhance market flexibility and accommodate globalisation. High dependency on multinational business could help the economy in the early stages of development but it may affect future growth by imposing constraints on sustainability. Indigenous development requires investment in locally-produced technology to free the economy from external influence. For example, the collapse of the Indonesian economy following the Asian financial crisis in 1997 was due to the halt of production activities by foreign corporations working in the country. Consequently, millions of workers were left unemployed causing severe economic and social problems. Muslims must encourage production of small-scale business to deepen the economic structure and induce local entrepreneurs to take part in the process of development. On the other hand, the dominance of public investment in Muslim countries could undermine growth by discouraging private enterprises from taking part in the economy. Islam provides little support for monopolistic control including state monopolies. The state plays the role of facilitator to provide protection against exploitation as well as to prevent violators including multinationals from mismanaging resources. The objective of big businesses driven by the forces of globalisation is to make high profit with little attention paid to the local economy. Poor countries, including those of the Muslim world, are lacking adequate infrastructure and advanced technology needed for building productive capacity and alleviate poverty. The non-existence of such infrastructures could cause 'brain-drain' by forcing skilled workers and qualified people to emigrate in search for better opportunities elsewhere, as is the case with millions of Muslims presently working outside their countries. Globalisation is encouraging factor mobility, especially in terms of labour, where cross-border employment is widely practiced in different regions. Responding to skilled-workers leaving native countries, Muslims need to adopt policies to discourage brain drain and encourage brain gain instead.

Wealth concentration retards a society's ability to foster the quality of life, human resource management, training and research and development to generate strong linkage effects and to stimulate the economy. In addition, the lack of research facilities, educational institutions, statistical information and government sponsored scientific programs has discouraged students who have finished their studies abroad from coming home due to the lack of investment and job opportunities. In doing so, the competitiveness-position of most countries continues to suffer because of trade disadvantages, technological weakness and hardening rules of globalisation.

The modernisation of the economy, which strengthened the economic links with the global financial and capital markets, has greatly increased the dependency of Muslim countries on the rest of the world. The adoption of the Western capitalist methods has created new patterns of economic activities in Muslim societies in violation of the fundamentals of Islamic economics. To a major extent this has been done with the assistance and approval of indigenous Muslim elite whose collaboration forged the existing socioeconomic conditions in Muslim societies during the past two centuries. Economic development was looked upon as a process for transferring technology to exploit resources for the world market. The political establishments were directly involved in the management, exploitation, control, and planning of national resources in favour of exports. For example, the extraction of petroleum and gas resources in the Middle East, North Africa, and the rest of the Muslim world was achieved through direct negotiations between government officials and foreign firms with little or no participation by the public. Individuals and private enterprises have to go through bureaucratic channels that are tightly controlled mechanisms to obtain contracts and licenses to participate in economic activities. In turn, this has given nationals very limited access to the indigenous resources by discouraging their involvement in the productive activities of the economy.

Human development in Muslim countries

Human development highlights the importance of education and health along with per capita income in measuring economic development. The complex nature of developmental process implies that economics alone is not sufficient to promote change. In most Muslim countries, the socioeconomic structure is influenced by a number of social, religious, ethical, political, cultural and economic factors which need to be taken into consideration for development to function. In Islam, development is directed at improving man's welfare by orienting all developmental activities, including allocation of resources, towards enhancing the quality of life. Such emphasis implies that development is people-centred aimed at enriching man both materially and spiritually. However, despite its orientation towards improving the socio-economic structure and man's wellbeing, development in Muslim countries lags still far behind what is required to meet people's basic needs and sustaining growth.

Development of human resources in Islam holds priority over all other factors of production due to the role that man plays in decision makings. While worldly knowledge is important, knowledge of God, which provides ethical and moral guidance aimed at implanting justice in production, consumption and distribution of resources takes precedence. In other words, development goes far beyond creating material goods alone but includes spiritual elements that induce cooperation, sharing, assisting and helping others. In Islam, it is a religious duty to participate in alleviating poverty among members of the society and, therefore, it is incumbent upon Muslims to assist in poverty reduction in order to free society from the illness of poverty. Human development underscores the importance of education and training in public participation as well as contribution to the advancement of society. Without education and knowledge, man remains incapable of fulfilling his duties for the betterment of other fellow human beings. Poverty hinders development by weakening the managerial, institutional, organisational and administrative factors in making and implementing decisions. In the new economy, access to knowledge and information requires human resources mobilisation to enhance managerial and organisational methods and conduct research for the application of the *sharī'ah* in such fields as economics, finance, environment and scientific studies. The Islamic economic system offers substantial incentives for action and knowledge, aiming at accelerating socioeconomic advancement. In Islam, it is the *human* factor that counts in the overall development and, therefore, investment in human capital stimulates growth by enabling the economy to create knowledge, conduct research and development, make efficient decisions and invent new products. In order to compete in global markets, countries need to increase the technological content of their exports as well as to create new products. Without technological input and political commitment, Muslim countries will continue to suffer from underdevelopment, which hinders their competitiveness positions in global markets. If the present global trends continue and nothing shows that Muslims are *actively* making efforts to induce change, the development gap is likely to widen, weakening in the process their position to compete with the rest of the world. Economic globalisation highlights knowledge-based products and information-dissemination to ensure productivity growth and knowledge creation. In this regard, the Islamic state has an important role to play as a facilitator for development by providing the institutional support and formulating policies to increase capital stock. Ultimately, Muslim countries must construct policies to become self-sufficient, especially in the production of essentials. Thus, cooperation and joint-ventures could help these countries to bypass some development stages and accelerate economic growth. As stated by the United Nations:

> There are many reasons why economic development continues to bypass many of the world's poorest people and places. One common reason is poor governance. When governments are corrupt, incompetent or unaccountable to their citizens, national economies falter. When income inequality is very high, rich people often control the political system and simply neglect poor people, forestalling broadly based development. Similarly, if governments fail to invest adequately in the health and education of their people, economic growth will eventually peter out because of insufficient number of healthy, skilled-workers. Without sound governance – in terms of economic policies, human rights, well-functioning institutions and democratic political participation – no country with low human development can expect long term success in its development efforts or expanded support from donor countries (United Nations 2003, 16).

In Islam, development is comprehensive and comprises all aspects of human life. The ultimate objective of development is increase man's happiness by meeting his material, social, cultural and spiritual requirements. Developmental processes are driven by moral and ethical considerations which underscore the importance of justice and fairness in the production, consumption and distribution. In other words, the Islamic concept of development is not limited to economics alone but also includes other aspects of human live. In this regard, development is man-centred, aiming at enhancing man's capabilities to develop in a meaningful way. In this way, not only production is important but also the distribution of wealth created by development.

Conclusion

In this paper, the concept of development in Islam has been discussed. During the last few decades, the experiences of Muslim countries with development have been inadequate to induce modernisation and enhance the quality of life. Income and knowledge gaps between the world's Muslims and non-Muslims have widened, keeping the former far behind the latter. The prospects for rapid transformation have also been deflated in recent decades by the negative aspects of globalisation which has kept Muslims at a disadvantageous position when competing in global markets.

There are both external and internal forces which influence development performance in Muslim countries. Heavy dependency of Muslim countries on world trade has weakened their economic structure by preventing diversification. In other words, production for manufacturing products and services remained inadequate to generate linkages and stimulate economic growth. In addition, changes in world prices and demand for primary products caused economic development

Table 2: Human Development Indicators, Muslim Countries, 2005

Human Development Index (HDI)	countries
low human development (less than 0.500)	Senegal, Eritrea, Nigeria, Chad, Mali, Niger, Burkina Faso, Sierra Leone, total population: 212.2 million (14 percent of total Muslims)
medium low human development (0.501–0.700)	Kyrgyzstan, Tajikistan, Morocco, Pakistan, Bangladesh, Madagascar, Sudan, Djibouti, Yemen, Gambia, total population: 432.7 million (29 percent of total Muslims)
medium high human development (0.701–0.800)	Kazakhstan, Turkey, Jordan, Lebanon, Tunisia, Iran (Islamic Republic of), Azerbaijan, Maldives, Algeria, Indonesia, Syrian Arab Republic, Turkmenistan, Egypt, Uzbekistan, total population: 568 million (38 percent of total Muslims)
high human development (above 0.800)	Brunei Darussalam, Kuwait, Qatar, United Arab Emirates, Bahrain, Libyan Arab Jamahiriya, Oman, Saudi Arabia, Malaysia, total population: 66.4 million (4.4 percent of total Muslims)
0.743	World (average)

(Source: United Nations, Human Development Report 2008)

in these countries to fluctuate affecting the levels of employment, income and government revenues and expenditures.

Internally, development has faced several challenges including inadequate financing, lack of skills, market imperfections, inefficient institutions and low technological capacity. Instead of adopting indigenous solutions to economic problems, Muslims implemented alien theoretical models – mainly of Western origin – to design their development planning and accelerate economic growth. The complex nature of development in terms of cultural, social and environmental factors has caused economic transformation in these countries to suffer from institutional deficiencies and low productivity.

Islamic economics has been discussed as an alternative to hitherto approaches to development in Muslim countries. The Islamic economic system highlights the importance of such Islamic fundamentals as justice, equity and freedom to the development of the economy. The principle of sharing resources and the concept of meeting society's basic needs increase the prospects to reduce unemployment, alleviate poverty, improve productivity and promote economic growth. Not only the material, but also the ethical, moral, and spiritual elements are important.

References

Afzal-ur-Rahman 1990: Economic Doctrines of Islam, vol. I. Lahore: Islamic Publications Ltd.

Ahmad, Ausaf 2000: Economic Development in Islamic Perspective Revisited. In: Review of Islamic Economics 9, 83–102.

Ahmad, Ishfaq 2000: Research and Development in the Islamic World: Past and Present Problems and Future Directions. In: Journal of Islamic Science 16, no. 1–2, 127–135.

Ahmad, Khurshid 1994: Islamic Approach to Development. Islamabad: Institute of Policy Study.

Brohman, John 1996: Popular Development. Oxford: Blackwell Publishers.

Chapra, M. Umer 1993: Islam and Economic Development. Islamabad: International Institute of Islamic Thought.

Chossudovsky, Michel 2003: The Globalization of Poverty and the New Order. Batu Caves, Selangor [Malaysia]: Thinker's Library.

Faris, Nabih Amin 2002: The Book of Knowledge. New Delhi: Islamic Book Service.

Griesgraber, Jo Marie; Bunter, Bernhard (eds.) 1966: Development. London: Pluto Press.

Hedley, Alan 2002: Running Out of Control: Dilemmas of Globalization. Bloomfield CT: Kumarian Press.

International Monetary Fund 2007: World Economic Outlook. Washington DC: International Monetary Fund.

Kholi, Syed F. 2000: International Cooperation for Sustainable Environment: Facing the Major Global Environmental Challenges. In: Journal of Islamic Science 16, no. 1–2.

Lapidus, Ira [2]2002: A History of Islamic Societies. Cambridge: Cambridge University Press.

Nomani, Farhad; Rahnema, Ali 1995: Islamic Economic Systems. Kuala Lumpur: Business Information Press.

Ozay, Mehmet 1990: Islamic Identity and Development. Kuala Lumpur: Forum.

Pfeifer, Karen 1997: Is There an Islamic Economics? In: Joel Beinin, Joe Stork (eds.), Political Islam. Essays from "Middle East Report" (MERIP Reader). Berkeley, Los Angeles: University of California Press, 154–165.

Preston, P. W. 1987: Rethinking Development. London: Routledge & Kegan Paul.

Rahman, Fazlur 1969: Economic Principles of Islam. In: Islamic Studies 8, 1–8.

Al-Roubaie, Amer; Vicas, Alex 1998: The Concept of Water Rights in Islam and Water Resource Stress in the Middle East: Economic Implications for International Security. In: Al-Shajarah 3, no. 1.

Al-Roubaie, Amer 1998: Economic Development Management: An Islamic Approach. Unpublished paper presented at the "International Conference on Islamic Development Management", University Sains Malaysia, Penang, Malaysia, December, 1998.

Al-Roubaie, Amer: Islamic Economics: A Reflection on Al-Ghazali's Contribution. Unpublished paper.

Sachs, Jeffery 2005: The End of the Poverty. London: Penguin Books.

Sardar, Ziauddin 1996: Beyond Development: An Islamic Perspective. In: European Journal of Development Research 8, no. 2, 36–55.

United Nations 2003: United Nations Development Programme, Human Development Report 2003. New York: United Nations.

Wan Mohd. Nor Wan Daud 1994: Some Basic Issues of Development in Malaysia. In: National Institute of Public Administration (ed.), Malaysian Development Experience. Kuala Lumpur: INTAN, 855–885.

Wilson, Rodney 1995: Economic Development in the Middle East. London: Routledge.

World Bank 2005: World Development Report 2006. Washington DC: Oxford University Press.

World Bank 2007: MENA Development Report, The Road Not Travelled: Education Reform in the Middle East and Africa. Washington DC: World Bank.

11

Building a Knowledge Society in the Arab World*

Amer Al-Roubaie and Rasha Shaker Abdul-Wahab

Abstract

Knowledge is at the heart of development policies in most countries in the Middle East. Not only is knowledge a strategic priority in sustaining economic growth, but it is also a determining factor in wealth creation and global competitiveness. Thus meeting the challenges facing the Arab World in the new global society underscores the importance of investment in human capital, science and technology, as well as and research and development. Modern technologies – including information and telecommunication technologies (ICTs), e-learning, data mining, satellite broadcasting, and electronic computers – have given rise to knowledge access and information dissemination. Building capacities which exhibit the use of technologies will facilitate access to technology transfer and knowledge absorption. The Arab world, given its financial capabilities and human resource endowments, is in a comfortable position to benefit from modern technologies by investing in education. The success of future development will depend on capacity building to support knowledge creation and managing globalisation. Applying data mining and e-learning techniques enhances the capacity of these countries to access to global knowledge and information which are extremely important for building a knowledge society. Most Arab countries are still behind in terms of knowledge production due to shortages of skills, lack of scientific facilities, weak incentives and inadequate educational institutions. This paper sheds some light on the current challenges facing Arab countries to promote a knowledge society and the potential prospects for overcoming these challenges. Arab countries

---

* This contribution is a revised version of a paper presented at the "International Conference on Technology Communication and Education" (Kuwait, 7–9 April 2008), which was organised by the Gulf University for Science and Technology (GUST), the Regional Center for Development of Educational Software (ReDSOFT), and Kuwait University's Computer Engineering Department, under the patronage of HE Sheikh Nasser Mohamed Al-Sabah, the Prime Minister of the State of Kuwait.

are financially sound but technologically not prepared to take advantage of the new economy driven by globalization.

Introduction

The Arab world represents highly diversified cultural, social, educational, religious and environmental characteristics which reflect some of the political and economic ideologies currently practiced in the region. Historically, not only the region of the Middle East was the birth place of all Semitic religions, but also a hub for the rise of great civilisations. Knowledge, crafts, agricultural innovation, and ideas were all products of the region which later gave rise to Western civilisation. However, knowledge and learning remain among the most distinguished contributions of the Middle East. Unfortunately, the region has lost its position not only by falling behind in knowledge production, but also by becoming heavily dependent on the rest of the world for meeting its scientific and technological requirements. The World Bank reflects on the deterioration of education in the Middle East and North Africa (MENA) by stating that the region has not "capitalized fully on past investments in education, let alone developed education systems capable of meeting new challenges. The education systems did not produce what the markets needed, and the markets were not sufficiently developed to absorb the educated labour force into the most efficient uses" (World Bank 2008, 2).

In recent years, globalisation has increased human contacts to the extent of placing information and knowledge within reach of everybody everywhere. Modern information and communication technologies (ICTs) have facilitated information dissemination, technology transfer, knowledge creation, socio-cultural exchanges, and human understanding. In building a knowledge society, education becomes vital due to its contribution to the stock of human capital, knowledge absorption, invention and innovation, as well as research and development (R&D). In other words, educational institutions, including schools, colleges and universities, play a vital role for speeding up the process of leapfrogging and sustaining economic growth. From an economic point of view, there has been a general understanding that economic change depends on organisational and individual learning. E-learning advances the process of knowledge at individual, organisational, managerial, national and international levels.

Arab countries are making substantial efforts to increase knowledge absorption through technology transfer, building ICT capacity, attracting foreign direct investment (FDI), and financing research and development. Ultimately, however, the potential gain from globalisation will depend on a nation's capabilities to create indigenous knowledge, invent new technologies, produce new products and increase labour market flexibility. Despite its financial and human potential, the Arab world is still suffering from market constraints and inadequate infrastructure to enhance global linkages and create indigenous knowledge.

E-learning strengthens the fundamentals for promoting a knowledge society. In most Arab countries, 'e-readiness' is inadequate to increase knowledge acquisition and to enhance technological innovations. However, building knowledge capacity requires the contribution of both public institutions *and* private enterprises. In this regard, the role played by governments becomes indispensable due to their financial, legal, managerial, organisational and institutional influence over the main determinants of a knowledge society. This paper highlights the role e-learning plays in the process of transforming Arab countries into knowledge-based societies. Knowledge becomes not only an important factor in production, but also a major determinant in wealth creation and sustainable development.

The knowledge society

Socio-economic transformation has been linked to a country's ability to absorb global knowledge and disseminate information. Nations with limited financial, scientific, technological, and educational capabilities could benefit from the new global trends by strengthening connectivity and increasing access to global knowledge and information. Promoting knowledge-based activities underscores the importance of organisational and institutional changes to facilitate the use of the new skills for the promotion of development. Gaining benefits from e-learning requires the building of technological and educational capacity in order to enable a country to produce as well as market and deliver knowledge and information content.

In recent years, terms such as 'knowledge organisation', 'knowledge economy', 'knowledge management', 'knowledge industry', 'knowledge workers' and 'knowledge leadership' have been widely used to identify the role played by knowledge in human advancement. However, not only is greater advancement in technological and scientific activities required for achieving the status of knowledge society but it is also creating a culture suitable for rapid modernisation. The concept of 'knowledge society', as explained by the United Nations, is thought to

> denote a more advanced developmental stage or to refer to a second-generation information society. Whereas an information society aims to make information available and provide the necessary technology, a knowledge society aims to generate knowledge, create a culture of sharing and develop applications that operate mainly via the Internet. The goal of the knowledge society is to fill societal needs, create wealth and enhance quality of life in a sustainable manner (United Nations Economic and Social Commission for Western Asia (UNESCWA) 2005, 3).

This implies that in a knowledge society the attitude toward learning also has to change, i. e. a new culture needs to develop that exhibits learning as a priority for human advancement. Knowledge is not a commodity that can be manufactured but has to be acquired through lifelong learning, training, and schooling. Achieving such objectives implies that institutions including universities must modify their existing programs and design new ones to strengthen learning and to enhance knowledge creation. The potential of e-learning in Arab countries is expected to have a positive impact on all aspects of human life – including the spheres of social, economic, political, environmental, scientific and technological development. Thus closing the 'digital gap' must be given top policy priority in all governments of the region.

A distinction is being made here between an 'information society' and a 'knowledge society'. The former is a prerequisite for the latter in the sense that information represents the building block for the knowledge society. The concept of knowledge society has a much broader meaning than just processing information and technological innovation. It includes all aspects of a nation's development, spanning economic, social, scientific, technological, industrial, cultural and political aspects. To carry out a task of such magnitude will require institutional structures comprising research centres, universities, workshops, and training facilities. For example, universities in particular play an important role in building capacity capable of promoting a knowledge society through production of skills, invention of new technology and development of new production methods (Menou 2001). The existing knowledge gap between Arab countries and the industrialised nations represents a barrier for achieving rapid modernisation. Recent literature on development studies closely links economic growth to absorption and creation of knowledge, and, therefore, knowledge acquisition will remain one of the greatest challenges facing Arab countries in the coming decades (World Bank 1999).

In the knowledge society, the Internet serves as a powerful instrument for knowledge acquisition and data dissemination. Sustainable development requires scientific knowledge and technological support which can be acquired through the Internet to meet knowledge deficiencies in economies where there are limitations on the production of knowledge as in the case of the Gulf Cooperation Council (GCC) member countries, i. e. Bahrain, Kuwait, Oman, Qatar, Saudi Arabia and the United Arab Emirates. As a consequence, speeding up development involves rapid knowledge acquisition and application to ensure that the processes of development are sustainable (Al-Roubaie, Al-Zayer 2007). So far, the experience of Arab countries with development has not been satisfactory due largely to the inadequacy of theoretical models and policies that are based on the Western approach to development. However, future development in Arab countries needs not be in isolation from the experiences of other countries including these of Western nations.

E-learning

As a tool for building capacity to absorb and create knowledge, e-learning should be adopted in Arab countries. E-learning facilitates leapfrogging by allowing countries to bypass several developmental stages (Choucri 1998). Access to knowledge has become within the reach of all nations, provided certain measures and effective policies are implemented to enhance technological development and increase global knowledge absorption. Building capacity for knowledge creation, characterised by the importance of investment in science and technology, increases human capital requirements, maintains high degree of labour flexibility, builds efficient institutions, and spurs research and development. Countries with limited resources could employ modern technologies, including e-learning, to deepen global integration and increase access to global knowledge.

In addition to the diversified learning resources and programs offered by e-learning, students are given greater access to knowledge and information via linkages to global sources. E-learning provides more flexible and mobile learning features which are suitable for different locations with little or no extra efforts. This makes e-learning suitable for isolated places as well as for those who cannot afford to take time off for training and acquiring new skills needed for improving their knowledge understanding. E-learning requires the use of network technology to facilitate access to information and knowledge which can be operated from home. For example, women with children along with family commitment would have access to new skills without the need for leaving their homes. In the Middle East, where the participation of women in the workplace and the economy is constrained by socio-cultural and religious values, e-learning increases labour market flexibility through greater participation of women. The region suffers from high unemployment rates – particularly women whose employment opportunities are limited. Modern offices rely on computer networks and Internet connections which can be set up in homes. E-learning is technology-based learning driven by an electronic fusion of computer and communication technologies. The new technologies empower people with skills, knowledge, information and ideas, which increase choices and enhance productivity.

As a process for enhancing educational standards, e-learning is defined as a "means of becoming literate, involving new mechanisms for communication: computer networks, multimedia, content portals, search engines, electronic libraries, distance learning, and web-enabled classrooms" (Stocks 2000, 2). Moreover, "e-learning is the use of network technology to design, deliver, select, administer, and extend learning" (Learnframe 2000, 6). In e-learning, the *'e'* stands for (1) *exploration* aiming at finding information and knowledge-related issues; (2) *experience* where the web can be used to enhance learning experience; (3) *engagement* which enables individuals to develop new method in learning that give them greater participation in societal affairs; (4) *ease* of use which gives access to all knowledge seekers and learners; and (5) *empowerment* by giving people the means to strengthen their capabilities and improve their participation. In sum, "e-learning is placing a wealth of educational material and resources online, making knowledge accessible to virtually every citizen on the planet" (Vlavianos-Arvanitis 2004, 2).

The following are some of the benefits of e-learning:

1. technology has revolutionised business, now it must revolutionise learning;

2. anywhere, anytime, anyone;
3. substantial costs savings due to elimination of travel expenses;
4. just-in-time access to timely information;
5. higher retention of content through personalised learning;
6. improved collaboration and interactivity among students;
7. online training is less intimidating than instructor led courses (Learnframe 2000, 10–12).

Perhaps the greatest challenge for the governments in the Middle East is to increase investment in e-learning by broadening the capability of getting connected to global networking and distance learning resource webs. At the global economic level, the competitiveness of a nation depends on the productivity of the economy which is characterised by highly skilled workforces, access to information, production of knowledge, use of ICTs and free mobility of capital and labour. Economic development is no longer a product of local decisions alone, but also depends on global linkages which increase knowledge absorption and skills acquisition (Mowlana 2001).

The Arab world

In most Arab countries, adequate capacity for knowledge absorption and creation is still limited despite their financial and human potential. Recent reports by the United Nations on the status of human development in the Arab World have attributed the current state of stagnation in these countries to low investment levels in education, particularly science and technology.[1] Educational institutions are poorly equipped to support knowledge creation strategy that meets the scientific and technological requirements of development. Similarly, low investment in human capital and inadequate expenditure on research and development is hindering rapid socioeconomic change. In other words, benefits from globalisation will be constrained by the lack of knowledge absorption and global linkages. As it can be seen from Table 1 below, the Middle East and Africa rank the lowest among other regions in the world in terms of the percentage of the population with access to the Internet. For example by 2005, only 2.4 percent of the population in the Middle East and Africa had been connected compared to 71.5 percent in North America and 11.1 percent on world average.

At the national level, e-learning could enhance development by increasing the participation of the community members in decision-making. It helps people to understand the complex and diverse national objectives of development by supporting or designing programs and policies which contribute to sustaining growth. Transforming the economy into a knowledge-based economy will require a diversified learning process that includes most of the population. E-learning speeds up

---

1 See *United Nations, Arab Human Development Reports* (several years).

a nation's capability to absorb knowledge and accelerate the process of technology transfer. In this age of global competitiveness, low levels of technology adoption and inadequacy of knowledge absorption hinder global integration. E-learning facilitates economic transformation by increasing a nation's capabilities to disseminate information and create knowledge. Similarly, e-learning enhances the R&D activities via access to research institutions and information from the rest of the world. For example, environmental, economic, demographic, and social challenges as well as climate change and poverty which are facing Arab countries could be eased through R&D. To this end, e-learning increases the productivity of the economy by facilitating transfer of technology, knowledge creation and information dissemination.

Table 1: Percentage of population connected to the internet

Region	*1995*	*1998*	*2000*	*2005*
North America	8.9%	27.6%	47.9%	71.5%
Western Europe	2.2%	8.8%	21.7%	50.1%
Eastern Europe	0.1%	1.0%	3.3%	15.2%
Asia-Pacific	0.1%	0.7%	1.7%	4.6%
South/Central America	0.1%	0.5%	2.1%	7.9%
Middle East/Africa	0.0%	0.3%	0.7%	2.4%
users worldwide	0.7%	2.5%	5.2%	11.1%

(Source: Learnframe 2000)

Another important outcome that has emerged out of the process of globalisation is the internationalisation of education, particularly at the university level. The Arab world should take advantage of new global opportunities by increasing connection to knowledge centres and make use of information available through the global networks and other electronic means. In other words, investment in e-learning technologies accelerates the educational processes by providing more choices and greater time flexibility suitable for different groups or ages in society, i. e. e-learning creates a 'literate environment' in which opportunities to continuing education is provided through electronic means. Access to such environment will include all ages making education available to all those who are willing to acquire it.

E-learning uses modern technologies to enhance communication and education. For example, computers provide an alternative means to becoming literate through multimedia, distance learning, electronic libraries and web-classrooms. E-learning could provide alternative for traditional learning, especially in countries where financial resources are limited. Governments can pursue such a policy by providing incentives and by building infrastructure to increase connectivity globalisation has broadened access to knowledge and information by linking nations through a wide range of electronic networking capable of transmitting information and knowledge globally. E-learning requires the development of new educational strategies about the purpose and value of education. In the Arab world, adapting e-learning methods could have a positive impact on national identity and narrow the existing generation gap driven by cultural globalisation. E-learning could be more effective in presenting a true picture of the cultural, social, linguistic and religious characteristics of the national identity than either television or radio. In other words, the use of e-learning could reverse the current state of cultural fragmentation and create a suitable environment for rapid modernisation deeply rooted in the heritage of the people. Today, the 'global village' requires people to communicate and to exchange ideas about business, information, knowledge, trade, social and cultural relations. Nations cannot cultivate the fruits of the knowledge society unless they gain access to modern technology. E-learning allows nations to leapfrog by increasing the knowledge capability which is needed to sustain development and enhance human understanding. Becoming an integral part of the global society, the Arab world must try to strike a balance between traditional values encapsulated by the Islamic fundamentals on one hand and the new culture driven by globalisation on the other. In this regard, e-learning should not only teach modern knowledge but should serve to protect the indigenous culture from being eroded by the influx of Western cultural products spread through modern information technologies. Similarly, in conservative societies where women's participation remains limited due to traditional and religious values, e-learning serves to erode the gender gap by allowing women to acquire knowledge, work, exchange views, and participate in the political process without contact with the other gender. The Arab World faces severe challenges not only in the sphere of education and knowledge deficiencies but also in areas related to the environment, agriculture, industry, water, health, pollution, population and poverty. If used effectively, e-learning provides opportunities for meeting such challenges by increasing public awareness, enhancing knowledge acquisition, developing new skills and empowering women. In most developing countries, education receives a large proportion of government expenditures. E-learning provides low cost education through the use of electronic technologies. Universities can play the role of intermediaries between industry and sources of knowledge and information by conducting research using both local and global knowledge.

E-learning should be used as a national tool to enhance human development and increase wealth creation. Education is not determined by schooling alone but by a number of technological, social, cultural, economic and political factors. In other words, e-learning should be designed to include organisation and top management of both public and private sectors to ensure that skills, knowledge and information are acquired and used in the national interest. An effective national policy must integrate all theses forces to ensure that e-learning serves the national objectives. Under such circumstances, government incentives for building e-learning capacity may not be sufficient without the cooperation of private agencies, international organisations and universities. The advantage of e-learning goes beyond literacy by contributing to industrial, environmental, economic and political development. There has been said much about democracy in the Middle East which can be enhanced through e-learning teaching. In general, however, decision making at all levels is subject to improvement through e-learning. In addition, environmental challenges such as population growth, urbanisation, water conservation, pollution, and waste management can be met through the introduction of effective e-learning programs. Similarly, the delivery of state services becomes much easier with the use of e-learning through an electronically enabled citizenry to whom the government is able to deliver faster and at lower cost. A just society should be open and accessible to all individuals despite divergences in social, religious, racial and economic backgrounds. Education serves as a balancing tool to establish equity and justice capable of narrowing ethnic and sectarian differences and promoting national unity. To meet these challenges, education needs to be reengineered to become a creative means for sustaining development. Globalisation is introducing a new society which requires greater interconnections, effective communication, creative ideas, more knowledge and better information.

In countries where illiteracy rate is high, e-learning offers an alternative and effective means for enhancing public knowledge and helping people to participate in development. As globalisation penetrates deeper, local knowledge becomes inadequate to make decision and formulate policies. Development is a complex process of structural changes which require scientific and technological knowledge may not be produced locally. E-learning accelerates structural changes through economic diversification, information dissemination, skills production and knowledge acquisition. Not only helps e-learning workers becoming familiar with modern production methods, but it also empowers top managers and company executives with skills and knowledge needed for making decisions. In the new economy, literacy is not sufficient for taking advantage of globalisation; instead connectivity and e-readiness is paramount. Building ICTs capacity provides new opportunities in terms not only of production and exports of new products but also in terms of stimulation of economic growth. Table 2 highlights the stages of development in Arab countries. As illustrated in the table, most Arab countries lag in their developmental stages, reflecting the failure to enhance efficiency and to mobilise innovation to strengthen the process of development.

Conclusion

Modern technologies have opened new avenues for developing countries to absorb knowledge and disseminate information. The knowledge feature of the new economy underscores the importance of building capacity to increase connectivity and access to global knowledge. The Arab countries, despite their huge financial endowments, remain behind in knowledge application and production. Attempts for building a knowledge society require substantial investment in human capital in order to facilitate the use of modern technologies in knowledge absorption and knowledge creation.

Table 2: Classification of Arab world countries in terms of stages of development

stage of development	*Arab world countries*	*other countries in this stage*	*important areas for competitiveness*
stage 1 (factor- driven)	Egypt, Mauritania, Syria, Morocco	India, China	basic requirements (critical) and efficiency enhancers (very important)
transition from 1 to 2	Algeria, Libya, Oman, Tunisia, Jordan	Colombia, Thailand, Venezuela	basic requirements (critical) and efficiency enhancers (increasingly important)
stage 2 (efficiency-driven)		Turkey, Russian Federation	basic requirements (very important) and efficiency enhancers (critical)
transition from 2 to 3	Bahrain	Barbados, Czech Republic, Korea	same as above, but innovation factors become increasingly important
stage 3 (innovation-driven)	Qatar, United Arab Emirates, Kuwait	United States, United Kingdom, Japan	all three areas important: basic requirements, efficiency enhancers and innovation factors

(Source: World Economic Form 2007)

In this paper, a brief assessment has been made about the impact of e-learning on building a knowledge society in the Arab world. As a means for acquiring knowledge and disseminating information, e-learning is a useful tool for promoting societal changes and for increasing human understanding. The Arab world lacks an adequate technological capacity which is necessary for acquiring knowledge and increasing human welfare. In recent years, globalisation has offered new opportunities, particularly for developing countries, to build capacity that serves to increase knowledge and to promote development. E-learning underscores the importance of giving access to education and information needed for inducing societal changes and promoting awareness about some of the important challenges facing many countries in this age of globalisation. Adopting e-learning could broaden public understanding and improve communications to enable decision makers and policy strategists to construct effective plans and sustain development.

In the Arab world, e-learning could endorse globalisation by increasing labour market flexibility via acquiring skills and absorbing knowledge. E-learning provides new opportunities for these countries to overcome some of the challenges including the gender, environmental, water and democratisation.

References

Printed sources

Al-Roubaie, Amer; Al-Zayer, Jamal 2006a: Knowledge Readiness and Sustainable Development in the GCC Countries. In: Allam Ahmed (ed.), World Sustainable Development Outlook 2006. Geneva: Inderscience Ltd., 2117–226.

Al-Roubaie, Amer; Al-Zayer, Jamal 2006b: Sustaining Development in the GCC Countries: the Impact of Technology Transfer. In: World Review of Entrepreneurship, Management and Sustainable Development 2, no. 3, 175–188.

Al-Roubaie, Amer; Al-Zayer, Jamal 2007: Knowledge Creation and Global Readiness in GCC Countries. In: Allan Ahmad (ed.), Science, Technology and Sustainability in the Middle East and North Africa. London: Inderscience Enterprises Ltd., 48–64.

Drucker, Peter 1994: Post-Capitalist Society. Oxford: Butterworth-Heinemann.

Hislop, Donald 2005: Knowledge Management in Organizations: A Critical Introduction. Oxford: Oxford University Press.

Steinmueller, W. Edward 2006: Learning in the Knowledge-Based Economy: The Future as Viewed from the Past. In: Cristiano Antonelli et al. (eds.), New Frontiers in the Economics of Innovation and New Technology. Essays in Honour of Paul A. David. Cheltenham, UK: Edward Elgar, 207–238.

United Nations Economic and Social Commission for Western Asia (UNESCWA) 2001a: Globalization and Labour Markets. New York York: United Nations.

United Nations Economic and Social Commission for Western Asia (UNESCWA) 2001b: Potential of Manufacturing SMEs for Innovation in Selected ESCWA Countries. New York: United Nations.

Internet resources

Choucri, Nazli 1998: Knowledge Networking: Leapfrogging for Technology. In: Cooperation South 2. URL: http://tcdc.undp.org/CoopSouth/1998_2/cop9827.pdf (accessed on 22 May 2008).

Learnframe 2000: Facts, Figures & Forces Behind e-Learning, learnframe.com. URL: http://www.learnframe.com/aboutelearning/elearningfacts.pdf (accessed on 22 May 2008).

Menou, Michel 2001: Educating Citizens of the Global Society. In: Cooperation South 1. URL: http://tcdc1.undp.org/CoopSouth/2001_oct/082-091.pdf (accessed on 22 May 2008).

Mowlana, Hamid 2001: From Medieval to Modern Times: Information in the Arab World. In: Cooperation South 1. URL: http://tcdc.undp.org/coopsouth/2001_oct/139-151.pdf (accessed on 22 May 2008).

Organization for Economic Cooperation and Development (OECD) 1996: The Knowledge-Based Economy. URL: http://www.oecd.org/dataoecd/51/8/1913021.pdf (accessed on 2 June 2008).

Schacter, Mark 2000: Capacity Building: A New Way of Doing Business for Development Assistance Organization. In: Policy Brief 6 [Ottawa, Institute of Governance]. URL: http://www.iog.ca/Publications/policybrief6.pdf (accessed on 22 May 2008).

Stokes, Peter 2000: E-Learning: Education Businesses Transform Schooling, Eduventures.com. URL: http://www.e-learningforkids.org/Documents/Ed_business_transform_learning.pdf (accessed on 22 May 2008).

United Nations Environment Programme (UNEP), Division of Technology, Industry and Economics 2002: Capacity Building on Environment, Trade and Development: Trends, Needs and Future Directions. URL: http://www.unep.ch/etu/etp/events/Capacity_Building/CB_discussion.pdf (accessed on 2 June 2008).

United Nations Development Programme (UNDP) 2002: Arab Human Development Report 2002. URL: http://www.pogar.org/publications/other/ahdr/ahdr2002e.pdf (accessed on 2 June 2008).

United Nations Conference on Trade and Development (UNCTAD) 2003: E-Commerce and Development Report 2003. URL: http://www.unctad.org/en/docs/ecdr2003_en.pdf (accessed on 2 June 2008).

United Nations Economic and Social Commission for Western Asia (UNESCWA) 2003: Knowledge Management Methodology: An Empirical Approach in Core Sectors in ESCWA Member Countries. URL: http://www.landray.com.cn/Uploads/Knowledge/20071023917289761l.pdf (accessed on 2 June 2008).

United Nations Economic and Social Commission for Western Asia (UNESCWA) 2005: Towards an Integrated Knowledge Society in Arab Countries: Strategies and Implementation Modalities. URL: http://www.escwa.un.org/information/publications/edit/upload/ictd-05-3.pdf (accessed on 2 June 2008).

Vlavianos-Arvanitis, Agni 2004: Bio-Education for Global Environmental Leadership. URL: http://www.envirosecurity.org/conference/presentations/roundtableD/ESSD-Roundtable_D_Education-I_Agni_Vlavianos-Arvanitis.pdf (accessed on 22May 2008).

World Bank 1999: World Development Report 1998/1999: Knowledge for Development. URL: http://www.worldbank.org/wdr/wdr98/contents.htm (accessed on 2 June 2008).

World Bank 2008: MENA Development Report. The Road not Traveled: Education Reform in the Middle East and North Africa. URL: http://siteresources.worldbank.org/INTMENA/Resources/EDU_Flagship_Full_ENG.pdf (accessed on 22May 2008).

World Economic Form 2007: Arab World Competitiveness Report 2007. URL: http://www.weforum.org/en/initiatives/gcp/Arab%20World%20Competitiveness%20Report/index.htm (accessed on 2 June 2008).

12

Law, Commerce and Ethics: A Comparison Between *Sharīʻah* and Common Law

Mohammad Hashim Kamali

Abstract

Ethics constitutes the common denominator of the various elements that feature in the title before us. Whether we speak of law or of commerce, the common law or the sharīʻah, ethics underline the basic tenor of the discussion throughout this essay. Thus the author begins with a brief comparison of the two legal traditions and proceeds to identify their commonalities and differences. The two traditions concur in their concern for equity and fairness in business transactions and contracts. Whereas common law applies the doctrine of discharge by frustration to dissolve a contract that no longer represents a fair exchange of values, the sharīʻah applies the doctrine of istiḥsān for the same purpose. There are certain lines of distinction between law and morality that both traditions seek to maintain, yet they are equally concerned not to isolate the one from the other to the extent that law no longer represents the society's vision of fairness. Whereas common law resonates the individualist philosophy by its advocacy of rights more than obligations, the sharīʻah gives greater prominence to obligation. Then again, common law upholds the doctrine of judicial precedent as a means of keeping the law abreast with social reality, the sharīʻah does not subscribe to the binding character of judicial precedent. Another point of difference between the sharīʻah and common law is that the latter applies the doctrine of caveat emptor (buyers beware) in its law of sale and purchase, whereas the sharīʻah reverses this order through its application of khiyar al-ʻayb (which effectively means 'sellers beware') both evidently out of their shared concern for fairness and smooth flow of market transactions. Other instances of comparison that are discussed between the two traditions refer to the means of proof, some procedural aspects of adjudication and possibilities that encourage cross-fertilization of ideas between them.

Introduction

This survey of themes of common interest to the *sharī'ah* (Islamic law as expounded in the Qur'ān and the *Sunnah*) and common law begins with a note on the relationship between law and ethics, then advances a brief comparison between the *sharī'ah* and common law, followed by a review of the Qur'ān and *Sunnah* on the ethical grounding of the *sharī'ah*. After addressing the ethical purpose of Islamic financial institutions in recent decades, I should like to proceed toward an exploration of corporate governance under common law and the *sharī'ah*. This is followed by three specialised themes: discharge by frustration, the theory of options, and the application of equity and good faith to contracts in the two legal traditions.

Law and ethics: an overview

Law and ethics are the two important components of social solidarity. The former regulates external actions and behaviours whereas the latter regulates the minds and souls of individuals. A legal ruling that incorporates the moral dimension of its subject matter is likely to inspire public confidence, whereas one that does not is likely to lead to disequilibrium, making enforcement difficult. For these reasons a theory of composite morality (one that integrates positive social values, public opinion and custom) may be needed to enable one to assess whether or not an act is ethically sound.

Advocates of a positivist theory of morality emphasise the importance of pragmatism. The ethical value of conduct is to be determined by juxtaposing it to the living conscience of contemporary man surrounded by a particular set of socio-economic and geographic conditions (Masoodi, Dhar 1995–1996, 7). Social values have a role to play in the ethical evaluation of conduct. For this reason, it would be unwise to apply medieval social values to contemporary realities. Moreover, it would be a mistake to turn a blind eye on the lines that divide law and morality and to extend the law to matters of moral concern.

Islamic law, which is rooted in the ethical code contained in the Qur'ān and *Sunnah*, acknowledges the role and value of social custom in the determination of rules governing human relationships *(mu'āmalāt)*. The *sharī'ah* tends to forge a near-total unity of law and morality in the areas of commands and prohibitions, while at the same time recognising levels of distinction which provide space for personal choice. On the scale of what is known as the 'Five Values' *(al-aḥkām al-khamsah)* – the five values that provide a basic yardstick in *sharī'ah* for the evaluation of human conduct: obligatory, praiseworthy, permissible, reprehensible, and forbidden – only the two ends of the scale, namely *wājib* (obligatory) and *ḥarām* (prohibited), are premised in the intrinsic unity of law and morality: whatever is *wājib* is morally sound and whatever is *ḥarām* is morally reprehensible. The other three value points on this scale, namely, praiseworthy *(mandūb)*, reprehensible *(makrūh)* and permissible *(mubāḥ)*, fall within the sphere of moral teachings that are not justiceable and that leave the individual with freedom of choice – yet they are still included in the *ḥukm shar'ī* (law or value of *sharī'ah*). Morality may thus be said to be an integral part of *sharī'ah* values, even if these values are not enforceable in the courts (for details on *ḥukm shar'ī* see Kamali 2003, 413 ff.).

The word *'sharī'ah'* is often used in reference to the entire corpus of Islamic law. However, Muslim jurists make a distinction between *sharī'ah* and *fiqh*. The former refers to that part of Islamic law which is contained in the clear texts of the Qur'ān and *Sunnah*, whereas the latter refers to that part of the law which is based on juristic interpretation and *ijtihād*. In this essay, we use 'Islamic law' in reference to both unless the context specifies otherwise.

It has rightly been observed that in the *sharī'ah*, law and morality meet and penetrate each other, and it is the moral rectitude of an action or behaviour that often provides the basis of its legality. In commercial transactions and contracts, morality and law tend to be either united or stand in close proximity to one another (al-Zarqā' 1418/1998, 1: 46). The *sharī'ah* allows basic freedom of contract and contractual stipulations so long as they do not violate public order and morality. According to a saying of the Prophet *(ḥadīth)*, "Muslims are bound by their stipulations, except for that which renders permissible what is unlawful or prohibits what is permissible" (al-Sijistānī 1416/1995, *Kitāb al-'aqdiyyah*, *ḥadīth* no. 3,594 – also quoted by al-Zarqā' 1418/1998, 57; al-Tirmidhī, *Kitāb al-aḥkām*, *ḥadīth* no. 1,352).

The *sharī'ah* requires all contracts to be based on good intention (*ḥusn al-niyyah*), i. e., free from fraud, cheating and deception by either party, failing which the law accords the aggrieved party the option of whether or not to ratify the contract. This is the purport of the renowned *ḥadīth:* "In Islam, harm may neither be inflicted nor reciprocated" *(la darar wa-la dirar fi'l-Islām)* (Ibn Mājah 1407/1987, *ḥadīth* no. 234). In another *ḥadīth* it is stated: "Acts are judged by their underlying intentions" *(innamā 'l-a'mālu bi 'l-niyyāt)*. If the non-disclosure of material facts leads to the imposition of exorbitant harm *(darar fahish)* in a contract, the contract is revocable. Also contracts are to be interpreted, especially with regard to what is not specified in the text, in the light of prevailing custom. A contract of hire for example, may specify the wages but not the mode of payment, with respect to which the prevailing custom will apply. Thus it may be concluded that Islamic law and ethics governing contracts are tempered by positivist considerations and the common mores and customs of society.

Islamic law and common law compared

The *sharī'ah* is an intrinsically duty-oriented legal system in which the notion of obligation, or concern for the rights of others, plays a more prominent role than that of right. The textual sources of Islam emphasise duty, which has a deeper grounding in morality than right does. Thus rulings on *ḥalāl* and *ḥarām* (permissible and forbidden), the perception of public good *(maṣlaḥah)*, and the understanding of corruption and harm *(mafsadah)* are strongly influenced by ethical considerations. In one statement, the Prophet declared: "I am sent in order to accomplish the virtues of morality" *(bu'ithtu li-utammima ḥusn al-akhlāq)* (al-Khaṭīb al-Tabrīzī, ed. al-Albānī, 1399/1979, 3: *ḥadīth* no. 5,096). It is noteworthy that the Prophet saw his mission as perfecting the moral legacy of his time and not, as it were, as the beginning of a clean slate. This, in turn, is reminiscent of the recurrent references in the Qur'ān to the validity of previous scriptures and affirmation of the ethical norms of Christianity (5:44; 6:90; 42:13) (see for details Kamali 2003, 306 ff., esp. n. 3). This qur'ānic affirmation also supports the conclusion that Islam endorses the ethical values of Christianity and Judaism and to a large extent, therefore, the essence of morality in common law. If there are differences in the details of the two religious traditions, one may assume that these are a reflection of differences in the cultural values, geographical settings and customs of their respective societies. In other words, the basic code of ethics is shared by the two traditions, even if positivist morality has dictated a different course in each one. We find additional similarities between the principles of *sharī'ah* and common law in the sphere of substantive law relating to the formation, types, termination and dissolution of contracts, rules pertaining to profit and loss, negligence and trust, legal personality and partnership etc.

Common law in England refers to "the ancient customary law of the land" (The Chambers 20th Century Dictionary 2008); it is the body of laws based on court decisions and customs in contrast with statute, law which is made by legislatures. Common law grew out of English custom and became established mainly by the adherence of judges to precedents or previous decisions – principle known as *stare decisis* (stand on things as decided). The decisions of earlier judges became the law of later ones. Thus experience rather than theorizing furnished the basis for the development of common law. No organised body of law existed in England prior to the Norman Conquest in 1066, but the Normans brought many new principles and greatly expanded legal institutions. The term common law itself came into general use during the reign of King Edward I (r. 1272–1307) who was responsible for a great deal of new legislation. Since by its very nature common law is relatively inflexible and not subject to change or adaptation to suit the needs of a particular case, the system of equity developed to permit the judges to resort to the general principle of justice when existing law was inadequate to resolve a case fairly. Eventually equity was merged with common law (The New Webster's International Encyclopedia 1996, 250). Despite its limited geographical origins, common law is used in all parts of the English-speaking world. Generally, contract law, property law, torts, and, to a lesser extent, criminal law are products of the common law tradition, except where this tradition has been changed by positive legislation.

Common law decision-making is similar to decision-making in Islamic law. In both systems legal specialists make the rules; in the former the legal specialists are sitting judges, in the latter, the legal specialists are usually legal scholars without a judicial office. In the common law system, *stare decisis* or binding judicial precedent, is the principal means of creating legal stability in Islamic law, the judge usually follows the established doctrine of a recognised 'school of law', or *madhhab*. In common law a jurisdictions, case law has served the purpose of keeping the law abreast social change; in the *sharī'ah* courts 'scholastic imitation' or *taqlīd* has restricted originality and innovative thought. Some modern Muslim commentators have recommended that the *sharī'ah* courts adopt a modified version of *stare decisis.*

Common law is currently applicable in Malaysia, Nigeria, the Sudan and Pakistan, although statutory legislation has brought many changes therein. This is a legacy of colonialism, which was actively engaged in a process of marginalising the *sharī'ah* in the former colonies. Many present-day Muslim countries have adopted commercial codes of European origin and, as a result, commercial law is regulated by codes that originated in continental Europe, although common law doctrines continue to apply in many of these jurisdictions.

A mixed pattern of legal development thus prevails: many Muslim countries can be placed under the category of common law jurisdictions, or in some respects, even under that of the civil law tradition. Thus, our attempt to compare the *sharī'ah* and common law has no clear geographical boundaries. Only in recent decades has Islamic commercial law seen a gradual revival through the emergence of Islamic financial institutions, and Islamic banking has also found a foothold in the West (see below). This is probably the first time in recent history that some Western countries have adopted parts of Islamic commercial law to govern the operations of Islamic banks in their respective jurisdictions. Another facet of this mixed pattern is that, for example, non-Muslims in Malaysia patronise Islamic banks, not for any religious reasons, but simply because they do not have to pay interest. They do not have to pay penalty interest that is imposed by a court decision either. So the longer they prolong the repayment the more they gain (Abdul Hamid bin Haji Mohamad 2003). Islamic financing, which does not follow fluctuating interest rates in the open market, offers greater stability in the available modes of transactions as compared to a loan/mortgage offered by conventional financing. The same logic, namely customer appeal, explains, *mutatis mutandis*, the adoption of Islamic banking by western financial institutions.

Common law rules are generally concerned with the interests of private persons and are therefore associated with the concept of 'private law'. In this respect too, they are similar to Islamic law. The legal tradition in both systems under review focus more on relations among individuals then on the relationship between the individual and the state. Thus, both the common law and *sharī'ah* tend to be concerned more with private ordering rather than a top-down system of regulations issued by a centralised government.

Law and ethics in the Qur'ān and the Sunnah

The Qur'ān requires honest fulfilment of all contracts (5:1) and enjoins the faithful to honour their promises (17:34). It is immoral to derive any income from cheating, dishonesty, misrepresentation, games of chance or breach of promise (4:29, 5:90, 61:2). Muslims are also enjoined to "avoid devouring your properties among yourselves wrongfully, but let there be among you traffic and trade by mutual consent" (4:29). The promotion of good and prevention of evil *(al-amr bi 'l-ma'rūf wa 'l-nahy 'an al-munkar)* is another qur'ānic principle (cf. 3:104; 9:71) of broad ethical import. Also known as *ḥisbah,* this principle not only teaches that objectionable behaviour must be checked, but also encourages the promotion of desired values and the creation of a proper enabling environment for them. The qur'ānic address, "God commands justice *('adl)* and fair dealing *(iḥsān)*" (16:90) opens the concept of justice to considerations of equity and fairness. Among the manifestations of this message are the Qur'ān's prohibition of usury *(ribā)*, monopoly, hoarding of wealth, and gambling (2:275, 5:90, 9:34). The Qur'ān also denounces any one who takes full measure from others when he buys but short changes others when he sells (83:1–3, 17:35).

Fulfilment of trust is the subject of the qur'ānic address: "God commands you to render the trusts *(amānāt)* to whom that they are due, and when you judge among people, you judge with justice" (4:58). The term *amānāt* in this verse has been interpreted as referring to a variety of trusts, both in government and in trade and in human relations. But since the reference to *amānāt* is immediately followed by the command to be just, the fulfilment of trusts must be carried out with a sense of justice. Elsewhere, the Qur'ān instructs the faithful not to "betray God and His Messenger, nor knowingly betray your trusts" (8:27), and then praises those who "faithfully observe their trusts and covenants" (23:8).

The Prophet of Islam is also reported to have said: "It is not permissible for a person to sell a thing if he knows that it has a defect, unless he informs the buyer about it" (Al-Bukhārī 1997, 3:165 *Kitāb al-buyū', ḥadīth* no. 292). It is reported in another *ḥadīth* that the Prophet "forbade *najash*" (Al-Bukhārī 1997, 3:198 *Kitāb al-buyū'*, *ḥadīth* no. 352), i. e., offering a high price for something without intending to buy it but merely to raise the price for someone else. In another *ḥadīth*, the Prophet declared that "one who cheats is not one of us" (al-Mundhirī 1979, ed. al-Albānī, *Kitāb al-imārah, ḥadīth* no. 1,335). The qur'ānic concept of vicegerency *(khilāfah)* (2:30, 6:165, 10:14) places Muslims under a moral duty to act with responsibility towards fellow humans, nature and the environment. Muslim entrepreneurs, workers and consumers are thus guided by the principle of economic trusteeship rather than by the pursuit of self-interest, the driving force of a market economy.

Islamic financial institutions

Islamic financial institutions (IFI), which emerged in the latter half of twentieth century, seek to ensure that investment goes to socially beneficial projects and that the parties involved in them share in both profit and loss. If the project succeeds, the Islamic financial institution shares in the profit. If it fails, the IFI shares the loss.

The Islamic financial sector is divided into Islamic banking, Islamic asset management companies, and Islamic insurance companies *(takāful)*. The first two, which involve risk against potential return, are interested in upside potential, whereas insurers actively aim to assume risk and offset it internally. Risk sharing is therefore the underlying philosophy of Islamic financing, which generally subscribes to the idea that rewards come with risk-sharing.

The Islamic financial system promotes greater reliance on profit and loss-sharing modes of financing (such as *muḍārabah* and *mushārakah*) and lesser reliance on debt. Debt must be tied to the purchase and sale of real goods and services within the framework of sales-based financing (such as *murābaḥah, ijārah, salām* and *istiṣnā'*), in which the financier bears some risk to justify the reward that he receives (Chapra, Ahmed 2002, 1 and 9). Since the giving or taking of interest is not permissible, the only permissible loan is interest free *(qarḍ ḥasan)*, which is a manifestation of cooperation and goodwill, aimed at helping the poor and the needy when they are in straitened conditions.

Of the three types of IFIs, Islamic banks have expanded at a rate of 10% – 15% a year ever since 1980, with their total assets currently exceeding US$ 250 billion. Their appeal has been strong enough for conventional banks like Citibank and HSBC to open Islamic 'windows' to attract the deposits of Muslim investors (Hassan, Chachi 2005).

Corporate governance

In recent decades the importance of business ethics in the Western world has changed dramatically. There is now greater awareness of 'ethical investment' among investors and a marked reluctance on their part to support unethical industrial and commercial practices. Numerous prominent institutions and civil society organisations have taken a fresh interest in promoting business ethics. One also hears of new terminology such as 'smart partnership' and 'stakeholder approach' to corporate governance (Nik Mustapha Nik Hassan 2002, 37–38).

The new approaches are generally based on the view that profit maximisation, traditionally the driving force of capitalist economies, must be constrained by ethical considerations and justice, and that regard for individual rights should be extended to all constituencies that have a stake in a business. The stakeholders of a firm thus include not only its owners but also customers, employees, suppliers, the government and society at large.

Although the stakeholder approach to corporate governance emerged in the writings of R. Edward Freeman (1984), but it was not until the 1990s that the idea gained prominence in the West. Wheeler and Sillanpa explain the approach as follows:

> The long-term value of a company rests primarily on the knowledge, abilities and commitments of its employees and its relationships with investors [...]. Loyal relationships are increasingly dependent upon how a company is perceived to create "added value" beyond the commercial transactions. Added value embraces issues like quality, service, care for people, the natural environment and integrity (Wheeler, Sillanpa 1997, 67).

The corporate responsibility agenda now encompasses considerations of fair pricing, ethical business practice and fair employment policies.

The stakeholder approach marked a departure from the liberal model that hitherto had underpinned the global trend towards privatisation and deregulation. The liberal model was advocated by the American economist, Milton Friedman, who rejected the idea of social responsibility in business management. To quote Friedman:

> If anything is certain to destroy our free society, to undermine its very foundation, it would be a widespread acceptance by management of social responsibilities in some sense other than to make as much money as possible. This is a fundamentally subversive doctrine (Friedman 1958, cited by Hassan 2002, 55, n. 13).

Many in the corporate world agree with Friedman, arguing that it is sufficient for business to obey the law and generate wealth, which, through taxation and private charitable choices, can be directed to social ends. The Anglo-American model of corporate governance "focused exclusively on the maximisation of shareholder value", and if this conflicts with the interests of other stakeholders, those other interests are to be ignored (Chapra, Ahmed 2002, 15, n. 12).

The Islamic teaching on business ethics shows greater affinity to the stakeholder model than to the liberal model. The principle of *ḥisbah*, that is, the promotion of what is right and prevention of what is wrong, permeates numerous *sharīʻah* institutions and principles. However, *ḥisbah* consists primarily of moral advice, and the person who applies it (i. e. the *muhtasib*) has no executive or judicial powers. His position lies between policeman and judge, and his main task is to uphold Islamic ethics through advice and guidance. The second Caliph ʻUmar b. al-Khaṭṭāb (d. 644) appointed a woman by the name of Shifā bt. ʻAbd Allāh as first *muḥtasib* of Medina (al-Zuhaylī 1417/1996, 6:764). Gradually the police and, in modern times, municipal authorities took over many of the functions of the *muḥtasib*, leaving to this office supervision of the market-place, so that the *muḥtasib* acquired the designation of 'market inspector'. His duties included supervision of weights and measurements, investigating immoral activities, insuring the purity of food supplies and the conformity of contracts and transactions concluded among traders to *sharī'ah*. The *muḥtasib* also ensured that cartels, monopolies, hoarding and profiteering were kept in check and that employers and employees did not engage in oppressive practices.

Umer Chapra and Habib Ahmed (2002, 14, n. 13) have addressed the issue whether Islamic law protects the rights of all stakeholders?. In answering this question they wrote: "In a value system which gives maximum priority to the realisation of justice and fairness, there can be no question about protecting the interests of all in an equitable manner."

This is the theory. However, when the same authors carried out a survey of Islamic banking practices in thirty countries (2002), they wrote: "The results of our survey do not, however, indicate that Islamic banks have been able to do this so far" (Chapra, Ahmed 2002, 14, n. 13). Since Islamic law emphasises justice and equitable distribution of income and wealth, one would prefer to see a dispersed ownership of shares in corporations as well as banks. The authors conceded that the early caliphs succeeded in ensuring honesty and efficiency in the market place "due to the prevalence of market discipline along with moral values, social setup and an efficient and impartial judicial system" (Chapra, Ahmed 2002, 8). To develop an efficient market that inspires public confidence requires joint efforts by many actors, both within and outside the market. Accountability in government and a conducive socio-political environment are just as important as an impartial judiciary.

The sharī'ah doctrine of options (al-khiyarāt)

An ethical dimension of the *sharī'ah* law of contract is found in the doctrine of options, especially the option of defect *(kiyar al-'ayb)* which entitles the purchaser in a sale contract to revoke the contract in the event of non-disclosure by the vendor of a material defect in the object of sale. When a buyer discovers a defect that existed in the merchandise at the time of the sale, he can reject the merchandise even after he has taken possession of them. If he was aware of the defect at the time of the sale or when he takes possession, and he knowingly completes the sale, he loses this option. The buyer's position in common law is less favourable in this respect: once he has accepted the goods he has no option to reject whether he knows of the defect or not (Hill, Abbas 1968, 103).

In common law, as in the *sharī'ah*, the buyer is entitled to inspect the goods before any agreement is reached, but if he discovers a defect in the object after the conclusion of the contract, he has no right of option, nor any right to compensation. Islamic law, on the other hand, envisages both these possibilities in favour of the buyer.

Khiyar al-'ayb stands in contrast with the common law concept of *caveat emptor,* which entitles the vendor to non-disclosure of defects in the subject matter of sale. *Caveat emptor* does not apply to fiduciary contracts in which the parties are bound to act in good faith. Despite this and certain other exceptions, "*caveat emptor* is just as much the rule in contracts for the sale of land as it is in contracts concerning the sale of goods" (Anson 1975, 257).

In *Bell v Lever Bros* (1932), Lord Atkins gave several examples of legitimate non-disclosure of defects in goods on the part of the seller. He observed that "failure to disclose a material fact which might influence the mind of a prudent contractor does not give rise to an option to avoid the contract".

The system of options in Islamic law generally seeks to minimise elements of ignorance and risk-taking in transactions, and to attain certainty in rights and obligations arising from contracts. To stipulate an option delays the legal consequences of a contract until it is ratified and the option is removed. Of the wide range of options recognised in *sharī'ah*, six may be mentioned: option of the session of contract *(khiyar al-majlis)*, option by stipulation *(khiyar al-sharṭ)*, option of inspection *(khiyār al-ru'yah)*, option of description *(khiyar al-wasf)*, option concerning fraud *(khiyar al-tadlīs)* and option of defect *(khiyar al-'ayb)*. Although the common law of contract contains similar concepts, the Islamic system is more extensive. For example, option of the session *(khiyar al-majlis)* is not easily accepted in common law. The option means that the parties to a sale have the option so long as they have not separated, even if the contract is concluded by mutual consent. The existence of this option in Islamic law shows that a mutual agreement, although essential, is not all that is important in a contract. The equity of a contract is also important. Accordingly, confirmation, inspection, or investigation is required to signify ratification of the agreement in the event that the parties have disrupted the session of contract by leaving it or turning to a different activity.

The Islamic system of options is "remarkably in favour of the purchaser" (Shimizu 1989, 70). Goods or services must fulfil the proper expectations of the purchaser; otherwise, he has the right to rescind the contract. This idea of "protecting the weak against exploitation by the strong" (Anson 1975, 71), imbedded in the theory of options, aims at certainty and equivalence of the counter-values to be exchanged in a transaction. Otherwise the purchaser can use a due option to remedy the situation.

Common law enables the parties to contract subject to an option that permits them to complete or not to complete their contract. The common law option is, however, a separate contract with an independent consideration, totally different from its counterpart in Islamic Law. Whereas at common law, option is treated as a subsidiary contract to hold an offer open for a certain period of time in respect of which there is no limitation as to the period involved unless otherwise imbedded in the option, under Islamic law options are attached to the main contract and can be exercised only within a limited period of time. In Islamic law the option holder does not pay for the option he reserves for himself; in common law, whereas option is a separate contract, the option holder is required to pay for the privilege (Hill, Abbas 1968, 109, n. 22).

Discharge by frustration

Most legal systems make provision for the discharge of a contract in those cases in which, subsequent to its formation, a change of circumstances renders the contract legally or physically impossible of performance. In English law, such a discharge is provided for by the doctrine of frustration. Although originally confined to maritime contracts, the doctrine subsequently was extended to cover all cases in which an agreement is terminated by supervening events beyond the control of either party. In *Taylor vs. Caldwell* (1863) the defendant had agreed to lease to the plaintiff a music-hall, which however, was destroyed by fire the day before the planned event. The plaintiff sued the defendant for damages, which the court did not award. Blackburn J, who adjudicated the case, stated: "In contracts in which performance depends on the continued existence of a given person or thing, a condition is implied that the impossibility of performance arising from the perishing of the person or thing shall excuse the performance" (Anson 1975, 25 and 478). From this time, English courts have shown themselves prepared to hold that "the continuance of a contract is conditional upon the possibility of its performance".

Case law also indicates a tendency to extend the scope of frustration outside the sphere of literal impossibility to cases that are regarded as connected, rather than identical, with that raised by the cases of impossibility (Anson 1975, 479, n. 22).

It would take us far afield to trace the case law. It may be observed, however, that English law held a restrictive view of discharge by frustration whenever frustration presented a threat to the sanctity of contract. The doctrine of frustration is thus viewed in English law as only a special case of the discharge of contract by impossibility of performance arising after the contract was made (Viscount Manghan in *Joseph Constantin Steamship Line Ltd. V. Imperial Smelting Corporation Ltd* [1942] A.C. 168, quoted in Anson 1975, 47–80).

In the Islamic law manuals the subject is treated in the context of individual contracts, such as sale, lease and hire *(bay', ijārah)*, and discussed under such headings as *āfāt samāwiyyah* (misfortune from heaven) and calamities *(jawā'ih)*. Islamic law tends to extend the scope of discharge by frustration to situations in which performance may be very difficult, even if still possible. This may be due partly to the recognition in Islamic law of the option of cancellation *(khiyar al-faskh)* which entitles the contracting parties to an option to rescind the contract when it encounters insurmountable and unforeseen difficulties. Ibn Qudāmah (d. 1240) thus gave the example of a worker/contractor who digs a well but then strikes hard rock or mineral ore, in which case he is not bound to continue the dig, especially if the ground below proves to be of a nature different than what was apparent. The worker is entitled to the option to rescind, and if he does so, he is entitled to a part of the contracted sum in proportion to the work done. Should underground water be encountered and render normal digging impossible, the situation is analogous to the striking of hard rock (Ibn Qudāmah 1367/1947–48, 5:422).

In a contract of hire of premises, either party may revoke the contract because of a change in personal circumstances, e. g. an owner, who incurs a debt which he can pay only by the sale of the premises, or a renter who becomes bankrupt and leaves the market, or wishes to undertake a journey, or changes his profession or craft. A ground for decision similarly exists where the hiring was for a particular purpose that has ceased to exist, e. g. if a person rents a bathhouse in a village for a stipulated period of time, and a general exodus of people from the village takes place, the bathhouse may be returned to the owner and there is no obligation to pay the rental (Coulson 1984, 86). To quote Coulson:

> A brief summary, therefore, of the traditional Shari'ah doctrine of frustration is that virtually any supervening circumstances which were unforeseen by the contracting party at the time of agreement and which render performance more difficult and burdensome than contemplated allows that contracting party who establishes the fact of such damage to rescind the contract (Coulson 1984, 87).

It thus appears that in Islamic law the principle of equity and fairness takes priority over that of binding force of contract when the two principles stand in opposition.

Modern legislation in Muslim countries of the Middle East is modelled on the Egyptian Civil Code of 1949. In the subsequent civil codes of Iraq (1951), Algeria (1975), Jordan (1976) and Yemen (1979), for example, the doctrine of "unforeseen circumstances" is expressed in virtually the same terms.

Under Article 146 (2) of the Iraqi Civil Code which replicates the Egyptian Civil Code 1949, when unforeseen circumstances arise due to "exceptional events which have a widespread and general effect" and frustrate contractual obligations "even though performance is not intrinsically impossible" and the contracting party shows that performance will involve "enormous loss", the court may "adjust the obligation to reasonable limits if justice so requires" (Ādam 1969, 47; Coulson 1984, 88).

'Abd al-Razzāq al-Sanhūrī (d. 1971), who played a key role in the formulation of the civil codes of Egypt and Iraq, explained that the theory of unforeseen events is expressive of a strong moral imperative, which is to protect the prejudiced party when contractual balance has been disrupted at his manifest disadvantage. It is hardly surprising, al-Sanhūrī adds, that the theory has had a stronger historical presence in religious legal systems. It existed in the Middle Ages in canonical law and has had an unequivocal imprint on Islamic jurisprudence. However, with the rise of *autonomie de la volonté* and the 'will theory' conception according to which contract obligations are founded on mutual consent, the doctrine of unforeseen events was dealt a mortal blow at the hands of the *civilistes* of old French law and disappeared altogether under the pressure of *pacta sunt servanda* (Latin for "agreements must be kept", a basic principle of international law) (al-Sanhūrī 1952–1970, 1:633). Al-Sanhūrī (1952–1970, 1:639) added that the doctrine of unforeseen events thrives today only because of its public law rehabilitation by the French *Conseil d'état* in the wake of the First World War.

Equity and good faith

The introduction of the European Consumer Directive 1994 triggered a fresh debate in the common law world over the infusion of the doctrine of good faith into contract law. The precise definition of good faith and its criteria may change in the light of unforeseen circumstances, but the doctrine requires honesty and fair dealing in the performance of contracts and transactions. It places merchants under a duty to observe "reasonable commercial standards of fair dealing in their trades" (Hassan 2002).

Whereas continental civil codes contain affirmative provisions relating to good faith, English law has resisted the idea and considered it as unworkable in practice and also repugnant to the adversarial ethics on which English law is premised. Elsewhere it seems that the concept of good faith has gained grounds. It has been upheld by German law and many American jurisdictions and it has made significant impact on several common law countries, including Australia and Canada and to some extent Malaysia. Sir Anthony Mason, Chief Justice of Australia, observed that "the quality of commercial life could profit from the infusion of good faith" (Mason 1989). Recent developments in Scotland also suggest that good faith will play an important role in Scottish law. The Malaysian Court of Appeal judge, Datuk Gopal Sri Ram, said in a lecture (Hong Kong, 12 September 1998) that as a principle of equity, good faith is implied in the performance of obligations in every contract. It is a principle that at one time formed part of equity jurisprudence but which has been forgotten by English courts.

Whereas English judges are opposed to a generalised theory of good faith on the ground of uncertainty, American and German systems embrace the view that the recognition of such general principles leads to greater rationality in the law and to the development of criteria to guide future transactions. German courts have used the principle of good faith as a basis of adjustment in contractual liabilities following the disastrous inflation which followed the First World War. It has also been used in cases involving inconsiderate use of rights, and generally as an 'equity reserve' that enables the courts to meet changing conditions.

The Egyptian Civil Code 1949, which was modelled on the French Civil Code of 1804, and two Egyptian laws, the Mixed Courts Code 1875 and Ahli Civil Code 1883, upheld the sanctity of *pacta sunt servanda* and shunned the notions of conscionability and good faith. Al-Sanhūrī was critical of the individualist leanings of the French Civil Code and departed from that precedent because he thought it was premised on a philosophy of legislation totally different from that of Islamic law. He also maintained that the two legal systems provide two very different responses to the question of unconscionability in contracts (Bechor 2001, 192 f.).

The increased power of the Christian church in medieval Europe initially led to the fall of the individualist spirit and allowed ecclesiastical jurists to constrain the autonomy of the individual will and consider unconscionability as a ground to avoid the enforcement of contracts. However, in the wake of the French revolution, the individualist spirit grew strong again to the extent that the French Civil

Code authorised enforcement of unconscionable sale of property contracts. The French code had incorporated this spirit and the old Egyptian Civil Code followed suit (al-Sanhūrī 1952–1970, 1:356 ff.; for an interesting account of al-Sanhūrī's work on the Egyptian Civil Code see also Shalakany 2001, 219 ff.).

The Egyptian Civil Code 1949 upheld the doctrine of good faith and gave it normative importance by juxtaposing it with that of the sanctity of contractual freedom in the same Article (147). The Article thus declared that the contract is the law of the contracting parties *(al-'aqd sharī'at al-'āqidayn)* and it can be revoked and modified only by mutual consent of the parties or for reasons provided by the law. The text continues:

> When as a result of exceptional *(istithnā'iyyah)* and unforeseen circumstances of a general character, the performance of the contractual obligation, without becoming impossible, becomes excessively onerous in such a way as to threaten the debtor with exorbitant loss, the judge may, in accordance with circumstances, and after taking into consideration the interests of both parties, reduce the exorbitant obligation to a reasonable level (Art. 147 (2)).

On a wider note the 1949 Code manifests the same pro-equity posture when it provides at the outset that the exercise of a right, whether based on contract or otherwise, is considered unlawful in the following cases: a) if the sole aim thereof is to harm another person; b) if the desired benefit is out of proportion to the harm caused thereby, and c) if the desired benefit is unlawful (Art 5).

Al-Sanhūrī added that unconscionability constitutes a social problem. When the legal system is a product of a civilisation founded on individualist values, the system will pay less attention to the question of unconscionability, due to the overriding influence of *autonomie de la volonté*, which was a product of the economic conditions of the eighteenth and twentieth centuries. However, if civilisation departs from individualist values, the doctrine of *autonomie de la volonté* gradually loses ground, and the legal system intervenes to put an end to unconscionability. In al-Sanhūrī's view *autonomie de la volonté* is incapable of accounting for contemporary developments in contract law where in the enforcement of obligations is premised more on social solidarity than on the individual will (al-Sanhūrī 1952–1970, 1:356; see also Shakalany 2001, 222 f.).

Our review of the evidence found in the Qur'ān and *Sunnah* relating to honesty, fair dealing, trustworthiness and justice supports the conclusion that honesty and good faith are normative *sharī'ah* values and constitute basic guidelines that parties in contracts and transactions must observe. There is also support in the *sharī'ah* for equity-based decisions when conformity to normal rules fails to uphold these values (see below).

Istiḥsān (juristic preference) is the nearest equivalent in Islamic law to the notion of equity in common law. Both are grounded in fairness and conscience, and both validate departure from positive law when its enforcement leads to unfair results. The main difference between them, is to be sought in the overall reliance of equity on natural law and natural justice, and of *istiḥsān* on the principles and objectives of *sharī'ah*. This difference need not be over-emphasised if one bears in mind the convergence of values between the *sharī'ah* and natural law. Thus, when a ruling of the existing law fails to comply with considerations of equity and fairness, or when it causes rigidity and hardship in particular cases, *istiḥsān* may be invoked to find a preferable solution that is in harmony with the higher values of *sharī'ah*, at the expense of departure from its specific rules.

In a system of law that is closely guided by conformity to the text and in which reliance on personal opinion is not encouraged, *istiḥsān*, which was initially advocated by the Hanafī school of law in the eighth century, invoked stiff resistance from many quarters. Indeed, Imam al-Shāfi'ī (d. 821) rejected *istiḥsān* altogether due to its heavy reliance on personal opinion and juristic preference. He threw his full support behind analogical reasoning *(qiyās)* because of its close adherence to the text of Qur'ān and *ḥadīth*. Across the centuries, however, prominent jurists, including some Shāfi'īs, have defended the notion of introducing greater flexibility and discretion in the *sharī'ah*. This enables the judge and jurist to follow the basic goals of justice and good conscience when strict application of the law, of an established precedent, or of analogy *(qiyās)*, fails to deliver its desired goal and purpose. This may be illustrated as follows:

(1) According to the normal rules concerning liability for loss *(ḍamān)*, the trustee *(amīn)* is not liable for loss or destruction of property in his custody, unless it is due to his negligence *(taqsīr)*. A craftsman or a tailor, for example, is not liable for loss or destruction of the material that is entrusted to him by a client, unless he is negligent. This is the normal rule, or the ruling of *qiyās* which was, however, deemed unsatisfactory and less than conducive to the smooth flow of transactions in the market place. Initially the fourth Caliph 'Ali (d. 661) ruled that the trustee is responsible for the loss of what is placed in his custody unless he can show that the loss was totally beyond his control. This was essentially a ruling of *istiḥsān* that was justified on the ground of public interest and the concern that trustees and tradesmen may exercise greater care in safeguarding people's property (See the chapter "*Istiḥsān* or Equity in Islamic Law" in Kamali 2003: 245-267; fuller treatment in Kamali 2005).

(2) All schools of Islamic law require the specification of subject matter and other material aspects of transactions, and forbid uncertainty and risk-taking *(gharār)* as well as usury *(ribā)* in contracts. Yet a certain amount of *gharār* and even *ribā* are tolerated on grounds of *istiḥsān*. For instance, the owner of a bath house does not specify the exact amount of water that may be consumed in a public bath but charges a fixed fee on admission. Similarly, sales transactions in the market place are often concluded without any verbal exchange of offer and acceptance. Although the normal rules of contract are not followed in either cases, these sales have been validated by *istiḥsān*. If the rules of sale concerning specification of subject matter and exchange of offer and acceptance were strictly enforced, the smooth flow of market transactions would be adversely affected. Hence the recourse to *istiḥsān*. The basic norm of *sharī'ah*

in all of this is to prevent hardship to people even at the expense of the neglect of the normal rules of contract.

(3) The inheritance case known as *al-mushtarakah* which occurred during the caliphate of 'Umar b. al-Khaṭṭāb (r. 634–644), typifies equity-based *istiḥsān:* A woman died leaving two uterine and two germane brothers, her mother and her husband. The qur'ānic rules of inheritance award one-third of the estate to the two uterine brothers, one-half to the husband and one-sixth to the mother, leaving nothing for the germane brothers, who as residuaries *('asābah)*, take a share only after the qur'ānic sharers *(dhawū al-furūd)* have taken theirs. The germane brothers complained to the Caliph. Although there were differences of opinion, the Caliph eventually decided, apparently on grounds of equity, that the one-third share of the uterine brothers should be divided equally between all the brothers.

Conclusion

The *sharī'ah* and common law pursue similar goals and the ethical contents of their respective rules governing trade and commerce bear harmony despite their other differences. Notwithstanding the *sharī'ah* textualist orientation, which is not shared by common law, the Shari'ah is open to evolution and change in the sphere of commercial transactions *(mu'āmalāt).* However, the *sharī'ah* has been either isolated or much of it replaced by statutory legislation of Western origin. Only recently has it been revived, especially with the emergence of Islamic banking and finance. Common law, which has not experienced a wholesale disruption of this kind, has continued to grow and to expand its sphere of application in many Muslim countries. Time will tell whether the resources of the *sharī'ah* and its guidelines on commerce will attract sufficient interest to stimulate cross-fertilisation of ideas between the two legal traditions.

As noted, although the two legal traditions have alongside one another in many Muslim countries, there is little evidence of one penetrating and influencing the other. The usual pattern has been one of separation rather than receptivity and integration. The colonial policy in this regard basically aimed at isolating the *sharī'ah* and restricting its scope of application to the sphere of personal law. *Sharī'ah* courts continued to operate, but with drastically reduced jurisdictions. This pattern of development was not supportive of cross fertilisation of ideas between the *sharī'ah* and common law. *Sharī'ah* was no longer applicable in the sphere of public law, and commercial codes of European origin were introduced to replace the *sharī'ah* law of transactions *(mu'āmalāt).* The colonial policy of restriction and isolation of *sharī'ah* was naturally met with apprehension and resistance by Muslim judges, *'ulamā'*, and religious leaders almost everywhere in the Muslim world, and the result was an uneasy coexistence.

Only in the Indian subcontinent, which is basically a common law jurisdiction, can a modicum of receptivity between the *sharī'ah* and common law be said to have materialised in what is known as 'Anglo-Mohammadan law'. As the name implies, Anglo-Mohammadan law superimposes English common law on Islamic law, especially in the areas of marriage and divorce for the Muslims of India, and to the exclusion of public law. This was a one-dimensional process. The English judges of India questioned the legitimacy of *sharī'ah* and were not inclined to open the common law to the influence of *sharī'ah*. Anglo-Mohammadan law developed in India partly due to the *sharī'ah*'s openness to such a prospect. This is because marriage in *sharī'ah* law is basically a civil contract which need not be solemnised by an official or institution, although there is nothing in the *sharī'ah* to discourage religious influence on aspects of marriage. In practice too the prayer leader *(imām)* of the local mosque, especially in rural areas, usually was invited to solemnize the marriage contract. A typical *sharī'ah* marriage contract thus consists of the agreement of prospective spouses, in the presence of two witnesses, and a dower *(mahr)* which the husband is required to give to his bride. The majority of legal schools, excepting the Hanafīs, also require the presence of *wālī* (guardian) of the bride. Indeed the entire range of the *sharī'ah* law of civil transactions *(mu'āmalāt)* consists largely of civil contracts that do not depend on religious ceremonies for their conclusion. A contract of sale, lease and hire, agency, partnership and the like are all civil contracts, subject to certain restrictions that originate in morality and religion. Thus *sharī'ah* does not validate the sale of a prohibited object or a sale that involves usury *(ribā)*.

A basic principle of Islamic law that applies to civil transactions and contracts is that of permissibility *(ibāḥah)*, which means that all objects and transactions are presumed permissible, unless there is a clear text to the contrary. This principle is conveyed in the *fiqh* legal maxim which declares that "permissibility is the normative position [of *sharī'ah*]" *(al-aṣl fī 'l-ashyā' al-ibahah)*. Only devotional matters *('ibādāt)* and relations between the opposite sexes are excluded from the scope of *ibāḥah*. Since *'ibādāt* are all regulated by the text and *ibāḥah* is a presumption, a presumption does not apply to textually regulated matters. The basic norm with regard to *'ibādāt* is that of prohibition *(hazar)*, i. e., no one may invent, practice or permit a new form of worship on the basis of *ibāḥah*. One other exception of note is sexual relations between men and women, which are normally prohibited unless made permissible through marriage.

Unlike the *'ibādāt*, which are regulated by the text, a great deal of the *sharī'ah* law of civil transactions is governed by rational principles which remain open to further development, reconstruction and *ijtihād*. There is consequently no *a priori* restriction of the source of ideas and principles that may influence the *mu'āmalāt* transactions. Evidence suggests that the *sharī'ah* law of *mu'āmalāt* has, in fact, been influenced in varying degrees by social custom, both pre-Islamic and post-Islamic, Hellenistic thought, Persian and Roman legal traditions. Without going into details, I may say that in the sphere of civil transactions, the *sharī'ah* remained open to the influence of common law, provided that such influence did not contravene a clear text or principle of Islam (specific examples of pre-Islamic customary rules that influenced the *sharī'ah* can be found in Kamali 2003 [chapters on *Sunnah* and Custom *('urf)*, respectively]).

In Malaysia, which follows common law, the *sharī'ah* has been retained in the sphere of personal law, and there are *sharī'ah* courts, Islamic Religious Councils and *muftīs* (jurisconsults) in federal and provincial districts throughout the country. Malaysia also has retained a regime of separation between the *sharī'ah* courts and civil courts of general jurisdiction (which have traditionally been dominant). Although a constitutional amendment to a section of the Federal Constitution 1957 (Art. 121A) in 1988 granted the *sharī'ah* courts a degree of independence, in reality they have a long way to go to gain equal status.

In the last two decades or so, Malaysia has witnessed rapid development in Islamic banking, finance, and insurance, and certain aspects of Islamic commercial law have been revived through statutory legislation. This means that some of the hitherto applied common law provisions in the areas of contract, sale of goods, and partnership have been augmented or partially replaced by the *sharī'ah*. Yet there is no question of a wholesale takeover or replacement of common law by the *sharī'ah*; Malaysia has consistently applied a dual banking system and therefore retained its existing body of laws. One other area of interest that may be mentioned is the law of evidence, which is currently being examined, in committee, with a view to establishing uniformity in the otherwise dual legal system. The general impression so far is one of mutual reciprocity in this area. The principles of evidence in the two legal traditions are substantially concurrent and it is deemed to be desirable, even necessary, to have a unified system of evidence and proof in the *sharī'ah* courts and civil courts of Malaysia.

Lastly, a note may be added on the position of judges and jurists in the two legal traditions under review. Common law, which is basically judge-made law, has evolved through case law; this adds an element of formality which normally does not obtain in *sharī'ah* law. Since the latter does not subscribe to the doctrine of judicial precedent, the task of interpretation and reconstruction has been handled mainly by jurists and jurisconsults who acted outside the organised judiciary. This suggests, theoretically at least, that Muslim jurists were not bound by court formalities, and the development of legal rules did not depend on judicial sanction. Since the task of legal reconstruction was handled by private jurists outside the formalities of governments and courts, one would assume a certain degree of openness on the part of Muslim jurists, as well as the legal system, to cross fertilisation of ideas between the *sharī'ah* and common law.

References

Abdul Hamid bin Haji Mohamad 2003: Harmonisation of Sharia and Civil Law in Malaysia: Present Reality and Future Action. Unpublished paper presented at the International Conference on the Harmonisation of Sharia and Civil Law, Kuala Lumpur, 20 October 2003.

Ādam, ʿAbd al-Saṭṭār 1969: Al-Sharīʿah al-islāmiyyah wa ʾl-qānūn al-miṣriyyah. Cairo: n. p.

Anson, Sir William Reynell [24]1975: Anson's Law of Contract, ed. A. G. Guest. Oxford: Clarendon Press.

Al-Bukhārī, Muḥammad b. Ismāʿīl 1997: The Translation of the Meanings of Sahih Al-Bukhâri, tr. Muhammad Muhsin Khan, 9 vols. Riyadh: Darussalam [includes the Arabic text].

Bechor, Guy 2001: Contractual Justice in Egyptian Civil Law. In: Islamic Law and Society 8, 179–200.

Chapra, Umer; Ahmed, Habib 2002: Corporate Governance in Islamic Financial Institutions. Jeddah: Islamic Development Bank.

Coulson, Noel J. 1984: Commercial Law in the Gulf States: The Islamic Legal Tradition. London: Graham and Trotman.

Friedman, Milton 1958: Three Major Factors in Business Management: Leadership, Decision Making and Social Responsibility. Speech delivered at Eighth Social-Science Seminar, 19 March 1958 (cited by Hassan 2002).

Hassan, Abul; Chachi, Abdelkader 2005: The Role of Islamic Financial Institutions in Sustainable Development. In: Islamic Finance and Economic Development, ed. Munawar Iqbal and Ausaf Ahmad. Houndmills, Basingstoke UK: Palgrave Macmillan, 59–83.

Hassan, Syed Misbahul 2002: Good Faith and Fair Dealing in Commercial Transactions: Some Comparative Perspectives. Unpublished paper presented at the International Conference on Law and Commerce, Kuala Lumpur, International Islamic University Malaysia (IIUM), 25–26 June 2002.

Hill, D. J.; Abbas, Abu Bakar Sadiq 1968: Comparative Survey of the Islamic Law and the Common Law Relating to the Sale of Goods. In: Journal of Islamic and Comparative Law 2.

Ibn Mājah, Abū ʿAbd Allāh Muḥammad b. Yazīd 1407/1987: Sunan Ibn Mājah, ed. Fuʾād ʿAbd al-Bāqī. Beirut: Dār al-Kutub al-Islāmiyyah.

Ibn Qudāmah, Muwaffaq al-Dīn Abū Muḥammad ʿAbd Allāh b. Aḥmad [3]1367/1947–48. Al-Mughnī. Cairo: Dār al-Manār.

Kamali, Mohammad Hashim [3]2003: Principles of Islamic Jurisprudence. Cambridge: The Islamic Texts Society.

Kamali, Mohammad Hashim 2005: Equity and Fairness in Islamic Law. Cambridge: Islamic Texts Society.

Al-Khaṭīb al-Tabrīzī, Muḥammad b. ʿAbd Allāh [2]1399/1979: Mishkāt al-maṣābiḥ, ed. Muḥammad Nāṣir al-Dīn al-Albānī. Beirut: Al-Maktab al-Islāmī.

Mason, Sir Anthony 1989: Foreword to "Contract: Death or Transfiguration". In: University of New South Wales Law Journal 12, no. 1, 2–3.

Masoodi, Ghulamus Saqlain; Dhar, Lalita 1995–1996: Euthanasia in Western and Islamic Legal Systems: Trends and Developments. In: Islamic and Comparative Law Review 15–16.

Al-Mundhirī, Zakī al-Dīn Abū Muḥammad ʻAbd al-ʻAẓīm b. ʻAbd al-Qawī 1979: Mukhtaṣar Saḥīḥ Muslim, ed. Muḥammad Nāṣir al-Dīn al-Albānī. Kuwait: Wizārat al-Awqāf wa ʼl-Shuʻūn al-Islāmiyyah.

Nik Mustapha Nik Hassan 2002: Business Social Responsibility from the Islamic Perspective. In: Nik Mustapha Nik Hassan, Shaikh Mohd Saifuddeen Shaikh Mohd Salleh (eds.), Corporate Governance from the Islamic Perspective. Kuala Lumpur: Institute of Islamic Understanding (IKIM).

Al-Sanhūrī, ʻAbd al-Razzāq 1952–1970: Al-Wāṣiṭ fī sharḥ al-qānūn al-madanī al-jadīd, 10 parts in 12 vols. Cairo: Dār al-Nahḍah al-ʻArabiyyah.

Shalakany, Amr 2001: Between Identity and Redistribution: Sanhuri, Genealogy and the Will to Islamise. In: Islamic Law and Society 8, no. 2, 201–244.

Shimizu, Hedeyuki 1989: Philosophy of the Islamic Law of Contract: A Comparative Study of Contractual Justice. Tokyo: Institute for Monetary and Economic Studies, Bank of Japan (IMES Working Paper Series 15).

Al-Sijistānī, Abū Dawūd Sulaymān b. al-Ashʻath 1416/1995: Mukhtaṣar Sunan Abī Dawūd, ed. Muṣṭafā Dīb al-Bughā. Damascus: Dār al-ʻUlūm.

The Chambers 20th Century Dictionary 10 2008. Edinburgh: Chambers Harrap Publishers Ltd.

The New Webster's International Encyclopedia 1996. Naples FL: Trident Press International.

Al-Tirmidhī, Abū ʻĪsā Muḥammad 1400/1980. Sunan al-Tirmidhī. Beirut: Dār al-Fikr.

Wheeler, David; Sillanpa, Maria 1997: The Stakeholder Corporation: A Blueprint for Maximising Shareholder Value. London: Pitman Publishing Company.

Al-Zarqā', Muṣṭafā Aḥmad 1418/1998: Al-fiqh al-islāmī fī thawbihi al-jadīd. Damascus: Dār al-Qur'ān.

Al-Zuhaylī, Wahbah 1417/1996. Al-fiqh al-islāmī wa adillatuhu, 9 vols. Damascus: Dār al-Fikr.

13

Modern Approaches to Islamic Law

Sayyed Ahmad Kazemi-Moussavi

Abstract

With the increased attention placed on Islamic law in the recent years, there is a need for a deeper understanding of the current debates on the modern Muslim approaches toward the rules of the sharī'ah. Being a complex amalgam of legal, ethical and ritual rules, the sharī'ah often appears as the major source of inspiration, identity and social solution for numerous Muslims. The sharī'ah is not, however, a static entity, as it was often reshaped and represented in form of fiqh (lit. 'jurisprudence'), echoing the requirement, in fact, the pertinent mindset of time. The principle method Muslim scholars have thus far used for reshaping Islamic law is uṣūl al-fiqh, a specific legal methodology to deduce rules from the sources (mainly from the Qur'ān and the Sunnah, the recorded 'way of life' of the Prophet). Nowadays, the approach of Muslims toward the sharī'ah has entered a new phase, in light of their acquaintance with modern scholarship. This scholarship recognises a critical role for the human rationale in legal corroboration that is unparalleled in Muslim traditional thought. Some contemporary Muslim scholars seek to reform both Islamic law and its legal methodology not only by using principles recognised in the sharī'ah, but by borrowing methods, such as empiricism and hermeneutics, beyond the conventional scope of Islamic law. A glance at what is currently going on in Muslim reformist legal thought might thus be helpful in understanding how Muslim thinkers try to face the contemporary world.

Introduction

In the past, Muslim scholarship had already experienced novel approaches to the *sharī'ah* and its legal methodology that were proposed by the Mu'tazilite (or Islamic rationalist) thinkers, but none of them assigned to the human rationale centrality in both perception and analysis as the modern approaches do. The modern Muslim discourse on the *sharī'ah* and its methodology can be identified with two series of scholars: 1) those who sought to reform Islamic law and ethics from *within* the *sharī'ah*, that is to say by aligning the method of understanding the *sharī'ah* with the contemporary requirements, and 2) those who tried to introduce an approach from *outside* the revealed law, i. e. by applying modern skills of epistemology or hermeneutics to the *sharī'ah*. Indeed, the traditional discourse on the law and its methodology, too, continued its course in the modern era, regardless of the new developments.

Among the scholars who proposed reform from *within* the *sharī'ah*, Abū Sulaymān al-ʿAlwānī and Hashim Kamali (Hāshim Kamālī) are noteworthy. Moreover, from among those who allow hermeneutical readings of the *sharī'ah*, we have chosen Naṣr Ḥāmid Abū Zayd and Abdolkarim Soroush (ʿAbd al-Karīm Surūsh) who incorporated the achievements of the human mind 'beyond the text' and obviously beyond the conventional legal methodology. Both groups of scholars allow the use of modern sciences and methods in religious learning, but with different scopes and perspectives. Moreover, both groups blame *uṣūl al-fiqh* – a specific legal methodology to deduce rules from the sources (mainly from the Qur'ān and the Sunnah, the recorded 'way of life' of the Prophet) – for loosing touch with social realities, and hold the limitation of independent scholarly judgment *(ijtihād)* responsible for the stagnation of Islamic law. A glance at the history of independent reasoning in Islam, therefore, seems necessary for a better understanding of the current debates on modern approaches to Islamic law. Muslim scholarship had already experienced new approaches to the *sharī'ah* by assigning a considerable weight to the role of reason in elaborating and explaining Revelation. As we will see below, these experiences begin manifestly with a Mu'tazilite mould of thought and continue to the modern era.

Historical currents

Since the eighth century, there emerged some Muslim scholars who approached the divine guidance as a corroboration of the human rationale. In a bold undertaking, Qāḍī 'Abd al-Jabbār (d. 1024) attempted to build the principle of centrality of the texts of the *sharī'ah* and their literal interpretation upon human reasoning. He dedicated several headings in order to make out the particular conditions for the divine address *(khiṭāb)* and in accordance to what the human mind might consider as proper (al-Asadābādī 1960, 17, 39–70). In his account, the divine 'commands and prohibitions' appear as indicators of innate good and evil, relating them to the 'nature of things' (al-Asadābādī 1960, 17, 107–152). He considered the notion of 'justice' behind the *uṣūlī* maxims of 'generals and particulars' *('āmm* and *khāṣṣ)* (al-Asadābādī 1960, 17, 30–38). Moreover, he added to it legal methodological topics, such as 'permissible action' *(ibāḥah)*, in accordance to which an act is to be regarded 'permissible on principle', unless it is specifically 'forbidden'. This view indicates a highly developed position in which the human rationale has an innate quality of appraising things *before* the arrival of Revelation.

The orthodox Ash'arite reaction to the above Mu'tazilite approach rationalisation did not by itself introduce a new approach to the *sharī'ah* other than returning to the original and often strict interpretation of divine guidance. Nevertheless, exceptionally talented characters such as al-Ghazālī (d. 1111) attempted new approaches under the umbrella of the same Ash'arite orthodoxy. Besides his innovative insight, a key to al-Ghazālī's success seems to be his incorporation of Aristotelian logic that contributed to both his language and to his method of organising the topics of his works, in particular in his writings on *uṣūl al-fiqh*. Prior to al-Ghazālī, Ibn Ḥazm (d. 1064), al-Juwaynī (d. 1085), and (to a lesser extent) al-Bāqillānī (d. 1012) had made use of Aristotelian logic in *uṣūl al-fiqh*. Nevertheless, it was al-Ghazālī who set an example for the succeeding jurists in terms of how to juxtapose logic with legal methodology. In fact, each historical approach to the *sharī'ah* involved introducing new elements into or juxtaposing new components with the *sharī'ah*.

A new dimension was given to legal methodology by the fourteenth century which aimed at merging the social notion public welfare *(maṣlaḥah)* into legal methodology. The important figure in this trend was Abū Isḥāq al-Shāṭibī (d. 1388), who combined the *exterior* factor of public welfare with an *interior* consideration, that is to say, the end-goals and objectives of the law *(maqāṣid al- sharī'ah)*. In the chapter six we saw how he legitimized common practices *(al-taṣarrafāt al-'ādiyah)* in a wider scope and in the light of their main socio-philosophical end goals for human good. In his *al-Muwāfaqāt*, he elaborated on methods and theories of harmonizing the legal norms *(aḥkām)* with the philosophy of the law what he identified with the notion of *maṣlaḥah*. This way of approaching the law led him to either propose or maintain several additional postulates as the key methodological premises for understanding the law according to its objective. These postulates particularly propounded throughout theoretical premises, which al-Shāṭibī laid down as an introduction to his work (al-Shāṭibī n. d., vols. 1 and 2). Furthermore, al-Shāṭibī treated the category of 'permissible acts' and 'common practices' in a wider scope and in the light of their main socio-philosophical end-goals for the human good. Al-Shāṭibī's theory of public welfare provides a wider scope of *uṣūl al-fiqh* which was never employed (or even noticed) by the traditional jurists until the contemporary era (al-Shāṭibī n. d. 1, 68–85).

During the pre-modern period of Islamic history, the most significant approach toward the *sharī'ah* belongs to the Indian Muslim thinker Shāh Walī-Allāh of Delhi (d. 1762). In his magnum opus, *Ḥujjat Allāh al-Bālighah*, Shāh Walī-Allāh deliberated on the history of the rise and development of a number of socio-juridical notions and their social objectives. He offered a chapter on 'human development' *(irtifāq)*, in accordance with the divine inspiration. In the view of Shāh Walī-Allāh, language, management of the household, the art and manner of economic transactions, and the necessity of assigning a leader to govern the Muslim community are among the *irtifāqāt* (Dihlawī 1990, 1: 119–152; Engl. tr. in Hermansen 1995, 113–144). His conception of human development, therefore, turns into the evolution of human society. The scope and function of this *irtifāq,* however, still remain incomparable with modern proposals of the sorts. Shāh Walī-Allāh extends the scope of *ijtihād* in order to allow a *mujtahid* (a Muslim scholar who exercises *ijtihād* or 'independent legal reasoning') to adopt a new esoteric or spiritual approach to the *sharī'ah*. He considers *ijtihād* as "the only instrument left with us for solving the problems emerging out of the swiftly changing conditions of modern times" (Jalbani 1988, 59; quoting Shāh Walī-Allāh's Persian work *Muṣaffā*). In one of his Persian writings entitled the *Muṣaffā*, Shāh Walī-Allāh – a Muslim scholar ascribing to the Hanafite school of jurisprudence, unequivocally states that *ijtihād* should be independent, like that of al-Shāfi'ī, the founder of another major Sunnite legal school, because the existing texts of the Traditions of the Prophet *(ḥadīth, plur. aḥādīth)* cannot adequately cover numerous *newly* arising cases.

Turning now to Shi'ite school of Islam, one can see a new wave of *uṣūlī* rationalism among the Shi'ite scholars of the nineteenth century which eventually combined the literal discourses of *uṣūl al-fiqh* with a series of rational argumentations, giving a new orientation to Shi'ite law. The towering figure in this regard was Shaykh Murtaḍā Anṣārī (d. 1864) who matured this trend of 'Usulism' in the theological seminaries of the Iraqi shrine city of Najaf. Anṣārī's point of departure in his works on *uṣūl* is epistemological and begins with the question of *how* legal knowledge should be attained. He proposes that the position which a *mukallaf* (a capacitated person) usually takes in the understanding of the legal norms is either: 1) of a 'certain character' *(qaṭ')*, or 2) of 'valid conjecture' *(ẓann)*, or 3) of 'doubt' *(shakk)* (Anṣārī 1987, 1: 2). The first category applies essentially to certain knowledge of things which are subjects of the legal norms. The second category, i. e. 'valid conjecture' is, according to Anṣārī, an avenue to reach the *inner* reality, and it includes contextual signs *(al-amārāt al-ma'mūlah)* which attach validity to the *outward* meanings of the revealed texts. These signs either have rational bases or entail a rational argument (Anṣārī 1987, 1: 41, 54, 290). The third category of the understanding of the proper legal norm is embedded with *shakk* (doubt).

Anṣārī's frequent use of rational principles gives the impression that he might not consider the *existing* sources of the law adequately elaborated in order to respond to newly arising questions. The negative 'presumption of continuity' *(istiṣḥāb al-'adam) per se* implies the lack of any applicable rule and a return to existing practices which are mainly based on customs. The frequent application of this kind of *istiṣḥāb* seems to aim at equipping the *sharī'ah* with customary laws rather than at sticking to remotely applicable *aḥkām* or 'legal norms'. However, Anṣārī's theoretical elaboration on the *rational* avenues for arriving at a plausible solution impressed the Shi'ite milieu of time, and the practical principles found a distinct place in succeeding Shi'ite law and legal methodology.[1]

One of the most celebrated *literal* approaches to legal methodology is *Kifāyat al-uṣūl*, the work of Ayatollah Muḥammad Kāẓim Khurāsānī (d. 1911), the Grand Mufti of Najaf, whose favourable *fatwā*s, or legal rulings, too, were crucial for the triumph of the Iranian Constitutional Movement of 1906–1909. His approach to

---

1 Ja'farī-Langrūdī (1991, 48–49) maintains that since the nineteenth century, Shi'ite law was overshadowed by *al-uṣūl al-'amaliyyah* which were employed by *mujtahids* in place of legal fictions *(furū'-i qānūnī)*.

the law is heavily imbued with semantics of the legal texts, to the extent that the authority of the sources of the law and rational reasoning appear only in the light of *literal* interpretations. Khurāsānī, in his introduction, expressively states that the objective of *uṣūl al-fiqh* is to draw generalization out of various subject matters instead of merely elaborating on the four sources of the law. He explains that if one focuses on the sources, his argument would ultimately turn into focusing on how to establish the authority and applicability of the 'four legal indicants' *(al-adillah al-arba'ah)*. Moreover, the scope of *literal* interpretation is much wider than discoursing on *adillah*, or the fixed texts (Khurāsānī 1988, 7–9).

One of the most innovative aspects of Khurāsānī's approach is the employment of his knowledge of theology for the sake of a weighty analysis on linguistics. He refers to Ibn Sīnā's (known as Avicenna to the medieval Latin West) and Kwājah Naṣīr al-Dīn al-Ṭūsī's conceptions of *al-dalālah al-taṣdīqiyyah* (lit. 'confirmative devotion') in order to highlight the importance of 'intention' *(irādah)* in understanding the implications of a word which can go beyond its verbal meanings (Khurāsānī 1988, 16–17).[2] As such, Khurāsānī presents a well-elaborated account on various ways of reading the real, intended, implied, or sometimes intricate meanings of the legal texts. This part of Khurāsānī's work attracted various later authors, some of whom considered this kind of approach as the beginning of Shi'ite hermeneutics if its logical and theological backgrounds were well-understood.[3] Discussing the problem of conflict of laws, Khurāsānī also points to the 'second designation' *(al-'unwān al-thānawiyyah)* of an action that may exceptionally overrule or postpone the first and direct application of the law in cases of difficulty, as constraint, exigency, or compulsion can (Shabistarī 2002, 437–460). This argument provided an *uṣūlī* pretext for some Shi'ite governments to excuse themselves to carry out the law whenever their expediency requires (for a detailed study on the history of Islamic legal methodology also see Kazemi-Moussavi, forthcoming).

Against this background, we now turn to *modern* developments in the approaches of the contemporary Muslim thinkers to the *sharī'ah* and its legal methodology. As stated above, the degree of interaction between reason and divine guidance sets the criterion for assessing the novelty of their achievements.

Modern approaches: 'Abd al-Ḥamīd Abū Sulaymān (b. 1936)

'Abd al-Ḥamīd Abū Sulaymān is among those authors who sought to reform Islamic legal methodology from *within* the *sharī'ah*, that is to say, to align the

---

2 Khurāsānī had for two years studied theology and philosophy with the theosopher of Tehran, Mīrzā Abū 'l-Ḥasan Jilwah, before his departure to Najaf in 1861.

3 The notion of *al-dalālah al-taṣdīqiyyah* (lit. 'confirmative implication') became part of literal interpretation in *uṣūl al-fiqh* and practically helped the development of contemporary Shi'ite hermeneutics; see Shabistarī 2002, 115, n. 2.

method of understanding the *sharī'ah* with the contemporary requirements. His approach toward the *sharī'ah* is imbued with an assumed crisis in the mind of the Muslims that prevented them from appreciating Islamic values in the light of time-space factors. He did not write a work on Islamic legal or theoretical methodology, rather he presented a broad criticism of the traditional methodology in which he re-evaluated the sources of the law and the method of juridical interpretation with reference to the problem faced by Muslim governments in their international relations. Here, we shall content ourselves with the new proposals that Abū Sulaymān offered to Islamic jurisprudence.

Abū Sulaymān refers to his approach toward the *sharī'ah* as *aṣālah* or 'innovative', in contrast to some traditional approaches which he labels as 'imitative' (Abū Sulaymān 1997, 4 and 18). This approach unveils itself in his treatment of the authority of the sources of Islamic law, although Abū Sulaymān adds many qualifications to bring his approach into line with the orthodox perception of the *sharī'ah*. He divides the sources into two types: *primary sources*, including the Qur'ān, S*unnah*, 'consensus' *(ijmā')*, and 'analogy' *(qiyās)* and *secondary sources*, such as 'juridical preference' *(istiḥsān)*, 'consideration of public interest' and 'obstruction of ostensibly legitimate means' *(sadd al-dharāyi')* (Abū Sulaymān 1997, 37–38; 1994, 65; it should be noted that Abū Sulaymān includes *'urf* ('custom') and *'aql* ('reason') among the sources as well). Concerning the authority and application of the primary sources, Abū Sulaymān makes the following rather new observations:

1) According to Abū Sulaymān, the Qur'ān, the revealed source of Islamic law, should not be considered a subject for abrogation, nor be divided into Meccan or Medinese verses. Rather, it should be regarded as part of the same whole whose application must be aligned with certain space-time considerations that are to be applied "in the light of changing circumstances in the overall flow of human life and experience" (Abū Sulaymān 1994, 117; 1997, 53). This suggests a rather broad context which ultimately might run contrary to the most basic principles of religion. Abū Sulaymān, aware of the problem, reluctantly, tries to filter the idea through the channel of *uṣūl al-fiqh*, which ultimately resolves the problem of space-time consideration through the principles of *ḍarūrah* (lit. 'necessity') and *talfīq* (lit. 'piecing together'), as some Muslim muftis, such as Rashīd Riḍā (d. 1935), accordingly determined the problem of charging interest in today's banking system (Abū Sulaymān 1994, 66–69). Here, Abū Sulaymān speaks about the necessity of methodological reform, but does not elaborate on the suggested change save for abrogation.

The problem of conflicting laws was a *raison d'être* for the formation of *uṣūl al-fiqh*. Muslim scholars attempted to solve the problem firstly by hierarchical consideration for the sources of the law, and secondly by setting rules for cases of 'abrogation' *(naskh)* and 'particularisation' *(takhṣīṣ)* followed by a semantic interpretation. The philosophy of abrogation was not enough elaborated by Muslim scholars, to the extent of justifying the flexibility of the law embedded in the Islamic legal system. Abū Sulaymān writes:

> The concept of *naskh*, as traditionally elaborated, reflects a static understanding of the methodology of Islamic thought, for it acts without taking notice of the difference between the general and universalistic nature of the qur'ānic teachings as opposed to the specific and particularised treatment of subjects found in the Sunnah. The traditional concept of *naskh* also reflects a total lack of appreciation for the elements of time and place in the process of interpreting and applying texts, as well as in comparing and analysing them (Abū Sulaymān 1997, 49).

By 'static understanding of methodology', Abū Sulaymān means the prevalent juristic legal methodology that upholds the late Medinese verses and Traditions as 'standard Islam', leaving in disuse plenty of Meccan and the early Medinese verses and experiences. For instance, the universal verse of the early Medinese period, "Let there be no compulsion in religion, truth stands out clear from error" (II: 259) has fallen into disuse in preference to the late Medinese verse: "When the forbidden months are past, fight and slay the pagans wherever you find them." (IX: 5) According to the eleventh-century author Ibn Salāmah (d. 1019), this verse alone abrogated 124 earlier verses (al-Muqirrī 1984, 98). In the view of Abū Sulaymān, however, such a rather selective approach suited well the Umayyads and early Abbasids under whose rule Muslim jurisconsults standardised legal methodology. According to him, "[c]ontemporary Muslim jurists, though they have attempted to reinterpret many cases of *naskh*, seem to accept the same concept of permanent *naskh*". Abū Sulaymān's suggestion to solve the problem is "to reconcile verses that seemed to contradict one another in the light of space-time factors" (Abū Sulaymān 1994, 83–84). In reality, this suggestion was already practiced by Muslim societies of the past and present in the context of 'necessity' *(ḍarūrah)* and 'public interest' *(maṣlaḥah)*. By adding space-time considerations, Abū Sulaymān, nevertheless, tends to concretise the problem in a formula adaptable to the changing situations of today's societies.

2) More than the Qur'ān, the Traditions of the Prophet, in Abū Sulaymān's view, involve space-time element, i. e. they should be read in the context of their *own* space-time dimensions. While appreciating al-Shāfi'ī's effort to establish the authority of the Sunnah, Abū Sulaymān refutes his analogy to the Prophet's time on attacking the *mushrikūn* (the pagan Arabs) 'at least once a year' (Abū Sulaymān 1994, 78–79). He finds the patterns set by the prophetic Traditions on campaigning not applicable to today's circumstances of warfare (Abū Sulaymān 1994, 77). Abū Sulaymān criticises the present arrangement of the Traditions and finds it amazing that despite the highly technical terminology used in their categorisation, the Traditions appear neither well-arranged nor authentic. In his words, "[a]s a result, whenever an author cites a Tradition, he is automatically subjected to criticism that serves little more than to distract readers from the point the author was trying to make" (Abū Sulaymān 1997, 57).

3) *Ijmā'* or the principles underlying Muslim 'consensus' is useless to Abū Sulaymān, unless an *effective* methodology is produced by new intellectual at-

titudes from the part of the Muslims. Basing *ijmāʻ* purely on the agreement of *mujtahids* who eventually boil down to the authoritative *ʻulamāʼ* or scholars of the past serves only to add to the present state of confusion. With today's complex techniques, different subjects require the consensus of *all* expert segments of the society. This way of looking at the problem eventually diverts Abū Sulaymān's attention to employing formulas such as empiricism and systematisation in jurisprudence (Abū Sulaymān 1994, 85–87). It is evident here that Abū Sulaymān is not concerned with *functional* aspects of the Muslim 'ijmāʿic' consensus that has built commonly and traditionally accepted knowledge of Muslim societies.

4) Abū Sulaymān considers *qiyās* or 'juristic analogy' as a product of the historical development in the eighth century which aimed to maintain the basic models and patterns set by the period of the four Rightly-Guided Caliphs. As a supplement to *qiyās*, the principles of *maṣlaḥah* and *siyāsah sharʻiyyah* ('Islamic public policy') were worked out by the later jurisconsults in response to the political conditions of the time (Abū Sulaymān 1994, 74–75). Abū Sulaymān does not assign any religious or rational value to *qiyās* and the above-mentioned principles, rather under the impression of his space-time theory. Instead, he contents himself with the historical analysis of the cases.

As such, Abū Sulaymān, in his chapter on the 'Reform of Legal Methodology', disapproves of the suitability of sources of Islamic law for today's requirements, save for a new reading of Qur'ān and Sunnah. In his critical reading of Islamic history, he makes a number of interesting observations that may be helpful to our understanding of the present stagnation of Muslim thought. A particularly remarkable one is a series of unduly rifts that Abū Sulaymān finds between religious and political leadership and between religious and empirical sciences (Abū Sulaymān 1994, 25, 87). He considers the replacement of the Rightly-Guided Caliphate with hereditary kingship as the main cause of the rift between the government and the Muslim course of scholarship and legal interpretation. This rift, in his view, not only led up to the isolationist growth of both of them, but it also is to be considered "the underlying cause of all the maladies that would later beset the *ummah* [i. e. the Muslim community]" (Abū Sulaymān 1997, 26).The lack of empiricism in the genre of religious sciences resulted in an disorientation of the latter from the time-space dimension necessary for the updating of legal norms.

Ṭāhā Jābir al-ʻAlwānī (b. 1935)

Born in 1935 in Iraq, al-ʻAlwānī graduated from the College of *Sharīʻah* and Law at al-Azhar University in Cairo, Egypt, in 1959. He continued at the college and earned a Master's Degree in 1968 and a doctorate in *uṣūl al-fiqh* in 1973. Dr. al-ʻAlwānī then taught for ten years at the Imām Muḥammad Ibn Saʿūd University in Riyadh, Saudi Arabia. He emigrated to the United States in 1983. In 1985, he became a founding member and is currently the president of International Institute of Islamic Thought (IIIT), which is headquartered in Hendon, Virginia, United

States. He is renowned for his time-honoured ideas, out of his command of the *sharī'ah* and legal methodology. He edited and published *al-Maḥṣūl*, the great work of Imām Fakhr al-Dīn al-Rāzī (d. 1209) on *uṣūl al-fiqh*. This work had a deep impact on his own legal outlook as depicted in several treatises and articles written later by al-'Alwānī on legal methodology and the history and principles of Islamic jurisprudence. He has also written at length on the ethics of disagreement in Islam, the appraisal of *ijtihād* as the practice and knowledge of source-based methodology, and on the Islamisation of knowledge. Within the contexts of legal methodology and particularly *ijtihād*, as we will see, al-'Alwānī offers new proposals for the social problems facing today's Muslim societies.

Al-'Alwānī considers the decline of *ijtihād* as the main cause of the present crisis of Islamic law. In several treatises, he surveys the history of *ijtihād* and the rise of *taqlīd* (following the opinion and practice of others unquestionably) and concludes that the present crisis of Islamic jurisprudence *(fiqh)* started with the prevalence of the idea of a 'closure of the door of *ijtihād*' in the tenth century (al-'Alwānī 1991b, 317). He even marks the year 922, the date of the demise of the historian-cum-jurisprudent al-Ṭabarī – supposedly the last *mujtahid* – as the beginning of the presently prevailing crisis experienced by Islamic law. The 'closure of the door of *ijtihād*' came practically to mean an official banning of public recognition for the existence or appearance of any new *mujtahid*. As a result, al-'Alwānī argues, Islamic law was confined to following the opinions of one of the four early *imāms*, i. e. Abū Ḥanīfah, Mālik, al-Shāfi'ī and Ibn Ḥanbal):

> It was for this reason that Imām al-Ḥaramayn [d. 1086] claimed that there was *ijmā'* [consensus] among the scholars of his day that *taqlīd* of one of the *Ṣaḥābah* [the Companions of the Prophet] was not acceptable. Rather, people were to adhere to the *fiqh* of the four *imāms* who had probed and examined the *sharī'ah*, who had classified and given form to questions of *fiqh*, and who had digested the teaching and opinions of the Companions and the Successors (al-'Alwānī 1991b, 321, based on al-Juwaynī 1985, 2: 1146 [al-'Alwānī does not take into consideration that the very idea of 'closure of the door of *ijtihād*' was challenged by some contemporary authors such as Hallaq (1984)]).

The circulation of such supposed consensus on banning the *ijtihād* in the juristic circle of the thirteenth century led Ibn al-Salah al-Sharazūrī (d. 1246) to claim that "following one of the four *imāms* was 'obligatory' *(wājib)*, as only their teaching had been systematised, clarified and preserved" (al-'Alwānī 1991b, 321). *Ijtihād* as an intellectual exercise could not come to a complete halt, but, as a result of the above tacit consensus, it acquired an oblique path on which several temporary rather miscellaneous formulas such as *al-ḥiyal wa 'l-makhārij* or 'legal stratagems and dodges', were proposed by traditional scholars to make an outlet for day-to-day problems facing Muslim societies. Al-'Alwānī refutes this kind of marginal and superfluous solutions which often skirt the issue without setting a norm to deal with the core problem (al-'Alwānī 1991b, 321). His own proposals have so far presented been in two categories:

1) In his earlier works, al-'Alwānī focuses on a critical presentation of the history of Islamic jurisprudence and the methodology of *ijtihād*, most of which may be considered as traditionally-oriented proposals. In 1990, al-'Alwānī published a treatise on the nature and history of the development of Islamic legal methodology, characterising it as "the most important method of research ever devised by Islamic thought" (al-'Alwānī 2003, xi). His evaluation of the nature and place of legal methodology centres on the history of the development and the role *uṣūl al-fiqh* played in conforming Revelation to reason. He laid emphasis on the period of the Companions of the Prophet who are the source on the Prophetic instructions, after the Qur'ān. His main topic, however, is related to the issue of *ijtihād*. To restore the practice of *ijtihād* to its proper place, he proposes that a) special attention should be paid to the methods of exercising *ijtihād* by traditional scholars who developed theories for *qiyās* ('legal analogy'), *istiḥsān* ('juristic preference') and *maṣlaḥah* (consideration of 'public interest'); b) since it is impossible to have an absolutely all-inclusive *mujtahid*, a scholarly council is necessary to be formed. This council should include experts specialising in *all* aspect of life; 3) it is necessary to take an interest in knowing the purpose and end-goals of the *sharī'ah* and setting guidelines for organising the study of problems (al-'Alwānī 2003, 68–70).

2) More up-to-date ideas of al-'Alwānī appear in his works on *ijtihād* and *maqāṣid*. In an article published in 1991, al-'Alwānī proposes that the dynamism of *ijtihād* should be used in restructuring an Islamic methodology *(al-minhaj)* suitable for the Islamisation of contemporary knowledge. To erect such a methodology, he alarms, it can be next to impossible to free oneself from the categorisation and concepts upheld by Western scholarship or from their influence. For this reason, he does not sketch a structure for such methodology other than notifying the need for definition, perspective, and proper point of departure (al-'Alwānī 1991a, 130–32). In a panoramic assessment of the progression of *ijtihād*, al-'Alwānī divides methodological *(uṣūl al-fiqh)* studies into the two general categories of 'specialised' and 'non-specialised' studies.

'Specialised studies' match up more or less with the above-mentioned traditional approach of al-'Alwānī. 'Non-specialised studies', in turn, may be subdivided further into two categories: secular and non-secular. Those who follow secular approaches tend, according to al-'Alwānī, to stretch the meaning of *ijtihād* to the breaking point in order to justify their dream of modernisation and Westernisation' (al-'Alwānī 1991a, 134). Addressing this group, he offers the following remarks that should be attended before approaching any methodology: i) knowledge of the historical background to *ijtihād* and *taqlīd* is necessary to understand the issues related to matters such as the division between *intellectual* (mainly juridical) and *political* authority in Islam; ii) the connection between *ijtihād* and the 'higher objectives' (*maqāṣid*) of the *sharī'ah* is important to illustrate the affinity between *ijtihād*, or the antipathy between *taqlīd* and the *maqāṣid*; iii) minute attention is required to the realisation of multiplicity in *ijtihād* and to clarify the truth behind 'differences of opinion' (*ikhtilāf*); and finally iv) the element of continuous self-renewal should be preserved through the meeting of and adjusting to changing circumstances. *Ijtihād* should thus not be considered a purely legalistic and legislative function (al-'Alwānī 1991a, 138–40).

The above outline points only to the positive side of al-'Alwānī's proposals. He does not fail, however, to equip his arguments with numerous mistakes and shortcomings performed by Muslims in exhorting *ijtihād*, especially during their recent history. Aiming to make Islamic legal methodology relevant to today's problems, he does not find any avenue better than *ijtihād* in such broad sense to bring the higher objectives *(maqasid)* of the *sharī'ah* into account to conform to timely requirements. No need to emphasize that al-'Alwānī wishes to see all changes *within* the limits of the *sharī'ah* rules and Islamic spirit.

Al-'Alwānī's continuous search for adjusting the new questions facing today's Muslims to appropriate Islamic contexts led him to another juridical formula, i. e. 'knowledge of priorities' *('ilm al-awlawiyyāt)*. In a work published under the rubric of *maqāṣid al-sharī'ah*, al-'Alwānī signifies the important role that knowledge of 'rational priorities' can play in balancing and stabilising Islamic jurisprudence. He justifies this fact with examples taken from topics from the fields of 'conflict of laws' *(ta'arruḍ)* and 'preferences' *(tarājih)* which originally stem from reason rather than Revelation. However, what he means by *awlawiyyāt* in this context is much broader that merely literal preferences. Identifying properly those 'priorities' requires a comprehensive knowledge of and deep insight into all aspects of the *sharī'ah*, including theology and jurisprudence (al-'Alwānī 2001, 63–66).

The negative effects resulting from disregarding the 'priorities' constitute a topic on which al-'Alwānī has elaborated in terms of twenty-four 'unwanted outcomes' and within the context of his own proposals on the issue. The first result of ignoring the 'priorities' is that Muslims tend to plunge into *detailed* aspects of the *sharī'ah* to the extent that they were not able to systematise them and link them up with the subtle relation between 'cases' and 'principles'. The second result is the fact that they preferred to stick to *taqlīd* and blind following rather than applying the tools offered by *ijtihād* and intellectual initiatives. The third result consists in the circumstance that they tend to put 'supererogatory' before 'obligatory' actions by attaching too much significance to *optional* undertakings rather than to *necessary* ones. The forth negative outcome is their reliance on supposed 'postulates' by refraining from seeking the relationship between 'cause' and 'effects'. Subsequently, they often fail or even decline to identify the causality of things. The fifth result is their reliance on 'big names' of iconic scholars from whom Muslims expect to hear the truth, instead of verifying those icons by authenticity of what they actually said. In the view of al-'Alwānī, this in fact could even be considered a new form of a kind of 'idolatry' *(ṣanamiyyah)* that keeps away Muslims from a thorough contemplation of the facts. Throughout the rest of his elaboration al-'Alwānī signifies how trivial trends of thought and superfluous spiritual displays have occupied the Muslim mind without any real contribution to religion and society (al-'Alwānī 2001, 78–82).

The above outline points to remarkable focuses and explanations that al-'Alwānī has made on the principles of *awlawiyyāt,* although their origins can be traced back to al-Ghazālī's formula of *munāṣabah* (lit. 'relevancy') and al-Shāṭibī's theory of *maqāṣid.* Later in his book, al-'Alwānī even acknowledges al-Ghazālī, and especially al-Shāṭibī, as precursors of the idea of 'priorities' which was not followed up by Muslims since trivial notions have kept them away from a proper course of dealing with substantial problems (al-'Alwānī 2001, 123–129). Al-'Alwānī does not hesitate to point out the fact that his concept of 'priorities' should indeed be understood alongside the 'higher purpose' *(maqāṣid)* and commands of the *sharī'ah,* as the title of his book suggests.

Al-'Alwānī is one of only a few Muslim authors who in their writings present scholarly opinions of Islamic thinkers regardless of their sectarian or devotional attachments. He even refers to, and sometimes incorporates, the somehow Shi'ite-oriented works of thinkers, among them Sayyid Jamāl al-Dīn Afghānī (d. 1897) and Muḥammad Ḥusayn Nā'īnī (d. 1936), as much as he refers to their Sunnite counterparts such as Shaykh Muḥammad 'Abduh (d. 1906) and 'Abd al-Raḥmān al-Kawākibī (d. 1902) (al-'Alwānī 2001, 67–69). It is evident from his pioneering work *The Ethics of Disagreement in Islam*, al-'Alwānī is well aware that he should not expect all Muslims, regardless of their circumstances and background, to realise the ideal vision of Islam (al-'Alwānī 1997, 131). In this book, al-'Alwānī finds examples of tolerant and open-minded attitudes towards disagreements from the Islamic history particularly from the precedents set by the Companions of the Prophet.

Mohammad Hashim Kamali (b. 1944)

Mohammad Hashim Kamali (Muḥammad Hāshim Kamālī), who was born in Afghanistan, served since 1985 as Professor of Islamic law and jurisprudence at the International Islamic University Malaysia and also as Dean of the International Institute of Islamic Thought and Civilisation (ISTAC), Kuala Lumpur, between 1985 and 2007. He is currently the CEO and Chairman of the International Institute of Advanced Islamic Studies (IAIS) of Malaysia. In his work, he combines an elaboration of traditional Islamic legal methodology with proposals for an adaptation of legal issues to new changes that have taken place in Muslim societies. A glance at Kamali's numerous works on legal methodology, *ḥadīth* studies, and human liberties in Islam, would be sufficient for gauging his innovative and multifaceted contributions to the field. In the 2003-edition of his *Principles of Islamic Jurisprudence* Kamali first recapitulates most topics of legal methodology, before attempting to present a new scheme for *uṣūl al-fiqh* in order to reorient some of its disciplines to the newly arising issues.

In his introductory remarks, Kamali defines *uṣūl al-fiqh* as both 'methodology' and 'principles.' 'Methodology', in his view, concerns mainly methods of 'reasoning', such as 'analogy *(qiyās)* and 'presumption of continuity' *(istiṣḥāb)*, whereas 'principles' include also general directives which occupy the larger part of the sources and can be used as raw material in the development of law. The components of the 'methodology' or 'principles' are, however, the same and include primarily knowledge of the sources of the law and their order of priority, then legal rules which may be deduced from the sources, and finally the exercise of *ijtihād*. Kamali separates *ijtihād* from the 'deduction of rules' in order to give it an independent identity aimed at further adaptation and refinement in order to respond to the changing needs of Muslim society (Kamali 2003, 1–2). In the second part of his introduction, Kamali distinguishes between two main approaches toward the study of *uṣūl al-fiqh*, i. e. 'theoretical' and 'deductive'. According to him, "[w]hereas the former is primarily concerned with the exposition of theoretical doctrines, the latter is pragmatic in the sense that theory is formulated in light of its application to relevant issues" (Kamali 2003, 9). The arrangement of the contents in his work on *uṣūl al-fiqh* indicates that Kamali stands closer to the latter approach as we will see below.

Kamali commences his account with a discussion on the authority of the sources of Islamic law i. e. Qur'ān and *Sunnah*. He subsequently turns to literal and then textual implications *(al-dalālāt)* of the source texts. The former deal mainly with the proposition of words – such as 'allegorical' *(mu'awwal)*, 'metaphorical' *(majāz)*, 'clear' *(wāḍiḥ)*, or 'unclear' – whereas the latter centre on textual implications, such as alluded, inferred, or required meanings. Kamali discusses the above-mentioned issues under the rubric of "Rules of Interpretation I" and "Rules of Interpretation II", which lack specific characterisation, but separate the two above-mentioned sets of implications (Kamali 2003, 117–186).

The next topic in his book deals with the 'commands and prohibitions' of the revealed texts. Kamali perceives this issue as a matter of the qur'ānic (and prophetic) language that follows up the discussion on the sources (Kamali 2003, 187). Nevertheless, from a different perspective, 'commands and prohibitions' could be considered as constituent parts of Islamic 'legal norms' *(aḥkām)* and could trigger a discussion of *alfāẓ* ('literal interpretations') and their transformation into *aḥkām*. In line with the elaboration on the revealed text is the discussion of the problem of abrogation *(naskh)* that Kamali then sets forth. He does not content himself with depicting the opinions of the traditional authors, like Ibn Salāmah, but rather reflects contemporary the views of al-Zuḥaylī and Abū Sulaymān, and eventually concludes that "*Naskh* is basically factual and has little juridical substance of its own, nor does it seem to have a direct bearing on the substance of legal theory" (Kamali 2003, 225). For the same reason, one can transfer the topic of *naskh* from the *adillah* ('indicants') to 'conflicts of evidences', a secondary issue discussed toward the end of Kamali's work.

Kamali then turns to two other sources of Islamic law, *ijmā'* and *qiyās*, on which he elaborates at length, including the traditional and contemporary viewpoints. Subsequently, he brings up two rather methodologically trivial topics, namely "Revealed Laws Preceding the *sharī'ah* of Islam" and "The *Fatwā* of a Companion". Concerning the former, Kamali, on the authority of Abū Zahrā', concludes that "[d]isagreement among jurists on the authority or otherwise of the previous revelations is of little practical consequence, as the *sharī'ah* of Islam is generally self-contained and its laws are clearly identified" (Kamali 2003, 312). The latter, the *fatwā* of a Companion, either fits into the category of *ijtihād* or provided "to be a persuasive source of guidance" and, having "priority over *ijtihād* of other *mujtahids*", may be squeezed into the context of legal norms.

After having dealt with revealed indicants, there remain a number of supplementary indicants which can simply be arranged under the rubric of 'rational indicants' *(al-adillah al-'aqliyyah)*, as done by some Muslim writers on legal methodology. They include *istiḥsān* ('equity in Islamic law'), *masāliḥ mursalah* ('considerations of public interest'), *istiṣḥāb* ('presumption of continuity') and *sadd al-dharā'i'* (lit. 'blocking the means'). Kamali, however, follows the general pattern set by the early Muslim authors and deals with each of the aforesaid topics as an independent subject matter. In Islamic jurisprudence, the main object of analysis of the sources and legal indicants is to arrive at a 'legal norm' *(ḥukm shar'ī)*, as propounded by Kamali. He first submits the five *sharī'ah* values *(ḥalāl, mandūb, mubāḥ, makrūh* and *ḥarām)*, then the three legal sanctions *(ṣaḥīḥ, fāsid* and *bāṭil)*, and lastly the three pillars of legal norm or *ḥukm shar'ī*. By this, he is also defining what is in the range of the authority of the jurist *(ḥākim)*, that is to to say, the subject matter which is referred to *(maḥkūm fīhi)* by him. He must be capable of understanding the *ḥukm (maḥkūm 'alayh)*. This pattern of *ḥukm* analysis which was proposed by al-Ghazālī and elaborated by Shawkānī and Abū Zahrā' reiterates the status of 'legal norm' from an individual perspective.

Kamali completes his arrangement of contents of legal methodology with three essential topics of 'custom' *('urf)*, 'conflict of evidences' and *ijtihād*, each of them deserving an independent category, as characterised by Kamali. *'Urf* is an important social concept and practise that can well supplement the legal sources theoretically and practically. The theoretical role of *'urf* can be seen in the principle of 'presumption of continuity' *(istiṣḥāb)*, which origins from the natural practice of the people. The next subject, 'conflict of evidence', encompasses several juridical issues to which Islamic legal methodology owes its origin partly. In the early stages, the argument on the conflicting authority of the legal sources, especially problems of 'abrogation' and 'particularisation' *(takhṣīṣ)* gave birth to *uṣūl al-fiqh*. In dealing with his last topic in this part, Kamali not only elaborates on the procedure, variety, and qualification of *ijtihād*, but also presents an interesting account on how statutory legislation leaves a discouraging effect on the practice of *ijtihād* in the present time. He concludes his remarks by referring to Muḥammad Iqbāl's proposal for revitalising *ijtihād* through instituting an assembly scholars practising 'consensus' or *ijmā'* into the fabric of modern Muslim governments. He also quotes the Egyptian scholar Sulaymān Muḥammad al-Tamāwī who proposed that modern Muslim governments should provide the necessary education to train up-to-date *mujtahids* (Kamali 2003, 494–497).

In the last chapter of his work, Kamali presents a new scheme for *uṣūl al-fiqh*, exploring novel avenues of the utility and relevance of the discipline to today's statutory legislation. Similar to al-'Alwānī and Abū Sulaymān, Kamali's point of departure here is historical, blaming the isolation of Islamic legal scholarship, in general, legal methodology, in particular, from the state authority of respective governments. This approach, although it ignores the phenomenological aspects of the position of government vis-á-vis the governed in Muslim states, signals the beginning of a Muslim struggle to reduce the existing tension between theory and practice in Islamic thought. We will see below how Kamali entertains ideas to bridge the gap between government and legal scholarship. The second point of view is related to the time-space considerations with which the traditional scholars often dispensed. We have already seen how Abū Sulaymān suggested empiricism to equip Muslim jurisprudence with time-space considerations. In his "A New Scheme for *Uṣūl al-Fiqh*", Kamali blames on *taqlīd*, literal approach and rigid interpretation for ignoring the role of time-space in the understanding of the Qur'ān and the *Sunnah*, but in his paper "Toward a *Maqāṣid*-Oriented Legal Theory", he reintroduces al-Shaṭibī's idea on consideration of end goals *(maqāṣid)* of the *sharī'ah* in connection with public interest as a possible method to canalize the time-space elements into the jurisprudence (Kamali 2002, 12–25).

At last, Kamali presents his evaluation of the mid-points suggested by another contemporary author, Jamāl al-Dīn 'Aṭiyyah, to balance between the need for continuity and preservation of Islamic values and purposeful move to change the existing impasse regarding Islamic legal methodology. The Islamic neglected values, in this regard, include the two important qur'ānic notions of 'consultation' *(shūrā)* and obedience to 'those who are in charge of community affairs' *(ūlū al-amr)*, none of which have been integrated into *uṣūl al-fiqh*. The expected move is to share governing authorities in theoretical consensus, even to put their decisions on a par with, or next to, transmitted proofs (Kamali 2003, 500–512). Relying on the above premises, Kamali supports the first three out of the following five of 'Aṭiyyah's suggestions for a new division of the sources of the *sharī'ah:*

> (1) The transmitted proofs, which include the Qur'ān, *Sunnah* and revealed laws preceding the *sharī'ah* of Islam; (2) ordinances of the *ūlū al-amr* [lit. 'those in authority'] which includes *ijmā'* and *ijtihād*; (3) the existing conditions or status quo, insofar as it is harmonious with the preceding two categories, and this includes custom *('urf)* and the presumption of continuity *(istiṣḥāb)*; (4) rationality *('aql)* in areas where full juridical *ijtihād* may not be necessary (the day-to-day rulings of government departments, for example, that seek to ensure good management of affairs may be based on rationality alone); (5) original absence of liability *(al-barā'ah al-aṣliyyah)*, which presumes permissibility and freedom from liability as the basic norm of the *sharī'ah* in respect of things, acts and transactions that have not been expressly prohibited (Kamali 2003, 509, quoting from 'Aṭiyyah's *Naẓariyyah*).

The significance of the above-mentioned suggestions essentially lies in their contribution to the legitimacy of government of which Muslim states have recently been in pressing need. *Uṣūl al-fiqh* developed on the assumption that its principles should have universal and everlasting character. To infuse government ordinances into legal structure seems to require another context, whether annexed to legal methodology or balanced to its principles. Muslim scholars have already proposed the context of *siyāsah shar'iyyah* (lit. 'religious policy') that can overrule the source-based rules of the *sharī'ah*, but this appears to lack the universal and durable value needed for the preservation of a tradition.

Kamali's effort toward the harmonisation of *sharī'ah* and civil law is a commendable attempt, as it narrows down the existing gap between the Muslims' ideal conception of the *sharī'ah* and their statutory laws. The problem, nevertheless, appears in the method of legitimising statutory law, leave alone the ordinances of government. The core problem lies in the idea of 'representative government', which is lost or misunderstood in most Muslim political systems. When a Muslim government does not act as believing in its representative and restrained nature of the authority, how can *uṣūl al-fiqh* legitimise or perpetuate its self-serving ordinances within the context of *ijtihād* or *ijmā'*? In order to offer a wider and more flexible framework for Islamic law, Muslim scholars in the past provided additional contexts, such as *maqāṣid, masāliḥ, siyāsah shar'iyyah*, and *al-'anāwīn al-thānawiyyah* (lit. 'secondary titles') without touching upon the conventional sources of the *sharī'ah*. Some of these pretexts were historically used by respective governments to legitimise their ordinances, but the core problem remained the same.

In his final conclusion, Kamali once more attempts to bring the existing instruments of legal methodology in service of today's social realities, that is to say to merge ordinances of government with *ijtihād* and 'statutory laws', leading toward *ijmā'*, consensus (Kamali 2003, 518). In this respect, the government and the Muslim legislative assembly are entrusted with the role of being the main repository of *ijtihād* and *ijmā',* and this move *per se* is considered to be in line with *maqāṣid.* The conventional scope of *maqāṣid*, subdivided into five or six headings, is evidently not enough and should be revised and supplemented "in conformity with new developments and demands of the contemporary age" (Kamali 2003, 517). As such, one can see that most of the proposed pretexts aim at bestowing more legality to ordinances of government, without aligning them with 'theories of government' as understood today. On balance, one may expect to see that the 'supremacy of the *sharī'ah*', one of the first principles of Islamic legal methodology, be interpreted in such manner to guarantee the restrained nature of governmental authority. Moreover, and in a more specific sense, the principle of *amānah* (lit. 'trust', e.g. Qur'ān IV, 58) can be construed for securing the right of the Muslim community, the *ummah*, to put (or to withdraw) their trust in an elected government.

Naṣr Ḥāmid Abū Zayd (b. 1943)

The contemporary Egyptian author Naṣr Ḥāmid Abū Zayd is among the first Islamicists who approached the *sharī'ah* by applying hermeneutics as a method of inquiry into the interpretation of legal texts. In its modern sense, hermeneutics was formulated in nineteenth-century Europe as an intellectual discipline concerned with the nature and presuppositions of the interpretation of literal texts (Harver 1987, 6: 279–287). The Muslim legal discourse had already developed interpretive disciplines, such as *tafsīr* ('exegesis'), *ta'wīl* ('allegorical interpretation'), and even *ijtihād* in the sense of 'independent legal judgment'. None of these devises, however, was used to extend the meaning of a text beyond the intention of Lawgiver, nor beyond the religious context in which the text evolved, whereas modern hermeneutics argues that a literary text has its own afterlife, independent of the author. To understand it has little or no relationship to understanding of the author's intent (Harver 1987, 6: 281).

The early works of Abū Zayd centred on evaluating the Muslim methodological approaches toward semantics, legal implications, and the interpretation of the legal texts, by often referring to the theories of the European founders of hermeneutics, such as Friedrich Schleiermacher (d. 1834) and Wilhelm Dilthey (d. 1911) (Harver 1987, 6: 13–49). He examined the writings of Mu'tazilite and Ash'arite scholars, such as al-Jāḥiẓ (d. 869), Qāḍī 'Abd al-Jabbār (d. 1024) and Abū Bakr al-Bāqillānī (d. 1012), in addition to the works of literary critics and grammarians, like 'Abd al-Qāhir al-Jurjānī (d. 1078) and 'Amr b. 'Uthmān Sībawayh (d. 796) (see Abū Zayd n.d., a collection of seven articles published in Egyptian journals between 1981 and 1988). In the light of theories of hermeneutics, Abū Zayd attempted to present a new reading – often critical – of the writings of the above-mentioned Muslim authors.

The most controversial work of Abū Zayd is *Mafhūm al-naṣṣ* (The Concept of Text), a version of his discourses on the qur'ānic sciences. In this book, he advocates a new way of reading the religious texts in the light of modern hermeneutics. To signify the importance of 'the text,' Abū Zayd calls refers to classical Arab-Islamic civilisation as 'Civilisation of the Text' *(ḥaḍārat al-naṣṣ)*, in contrast to Greek civilisation, which he dubs 'Civilisation of Reason' *(ḥaḍārat al-'aql)*. His emphasis, however, is laid on the understanding of texts that require interpretative skills to discern the cultural context surrounding the presentation of a text. The Qur'ān, indeed, is the prime source-text of Islam. In subdividing the qur'ānic verses, Abū Zayd prefers to categorise them into those revealed *before* the *hijrah* as 'faith-building', in contrast to the post-*hijrah* verses (622–632) which are more 'society-building' in nature (Abū Zayd n. d.: 15). Nevertheless, the textual output of the Qur'ān was, in Abū Zayd's view, overshadowed by the immense sanctity later attached to it as the Holy Book of Islam (Abū Zayd 1987, 9–13).

In one of his later works, *Naqd al-khiṭāb al-dīnī* (A Critique of Religious Discourse), Abū Zayd notes the abuse of the Holy Book by Mu'āwiyah (d. 680), the founder of the Umayyad Dynasty, who flagged qur'ānic papers on lances in an attempt to divert the Muslims' attention from their own *ijtihād* to an expected direct judgment of the Qur'ān. "The Qur'ān is just pieces of writings", Abū Zayd quotes the fourth Rightly-Guided caliph, 'Alī b. Abī Ṭālib (d. 661), who is believed to have said in the War of Ṣiffīn, "it [i. e., the Qur'ān] does not speak; only men speak for it". Abū Zayd concludes that texts require a certain scope of rational interpretation that only the human mind can afford (Abū Zayd 1992, 74).

Abū Zayd claims that the understanding of a text revolves around the data and perceptions of the time of the reader, and he quotes from *Literary Identity* written by the contemporary author Peter W. Nesselroth, to the effect that the process of understanding a text does not begin with reading the text, but rather it starts prior to that with the dialogue between the culture shaping the reader's perception and the text. In the case of the Qur'ān, knowledge of 'occasions of revelation' is necessary for eliciting a legal norm *(ḥukm)* or for inferring a meaning of it. But Muslim interpreters often separated the text from the legal norm, and some of them even claimed that the *ḥukm* or the command of God existed before the coming the text (Abū Zayd 1987, 89). Abū Zayd draws out three factors that may cause this misunderstanding:

1) The literal implication *(al-dalālah al-lughawiyyah)* was confused by some of interpreters with the legal implication *(al-dalālah al-shar'iyyah)*, as in Qur'ān LXXX: 14, "He will prosper he who purifies himself". 'Purification' in this Meccan verse does not imply *zakāt* (canonically prescribed alms, the 'poor-tax') which, according to the famous qur'ānic scholar al-Suyūṭī (d. 1505), was historically established after the *hijrah*, the Prophet's emigration from Mecca to Medina.

2) Some interpretations were attributed to the Companions of the Prophet whose explanations are associated with the Medinese period, whereas the content of the verse belonged to Meccan era. To solve the problem, the later Muslim scholars had to assume that the *ḥukm* existed before the text. Qur'ān XL1: 33, a Meccan verse, reads: "Who is better in speech than who calls [people] to Allāh, performs righteous deed and says 'I am of those who bow in Islam'". It is related from 'Ā'ishah (the renowned wife of the Prophet, d. 678), that this verse was revealed referring to the muezzin (the caller to prayer), whereas history tells us that the *adhān* (the Muslim call for prayer) was only established in the early Medinese period (Abū Zayd 1987, 93–94).

3) Confusing the sequence of verses with the particular occasion of a revealed text resulted in different readings of a verse and in gainsay assumptions: firstly, that the text was revealed *before* the occasion arose, and secondly that the text preceded its suitability and necessity to be a legal norm. An example is the Qur'ān LIV: 45: "Soon will their multitude be put to flight, and they will show their backs." Al-Suyūṭī quoted the second Rightly-Guided Caliph 'Umar, that he had heard the Prophet reciting this verse during the Battle of Badr, when the army of the Meccan pagans was defeated. Yet the sequence of verses suggests a similarity between the ancient Egyptian Pharaohs and the likewise pagan Meccans. Another 'between-the-lines' meaning can be understood in conformity with future tense that had been used in the verse in that it applies to the Day of Resurrection. Abū

Zayd concludes that different readings of a text result from the expanse of the reader's standpoint, and that the evolution of one's knowledge opens the way for a new understanding of the text (Abū Zayd 1987, 89–95).

In the quest for finding a new meaning or function for legal principles, Abū Zayd, in *Mafhūm al-naṣṣ*, draws on a number of methodological topics from Islamic legal methodology, such as 'the general and its particularisation', 'occasions of revelation', 'abrogation', 'implication and divergent meaning' and 'absolute and qualified'. For instance, he evaluates 'abrogation' as the main proof that there exists a dialectical relationship between Revelation and external realities, and says that its function is to adapt to changes and to advance law-giving (Abū Zayd 1987, 117, 120). He considers both the generalisation and particularisation of the qur'ānic verses as a means to maintain the unity of the law and to fully understand both the verbal expressions and the occasions in which the law was given (Abū Zayd 1987, 195). The relationship between the 'real' and the 'metaphor", too, is a relationship of change and open to transformation, an argument with which AbūZayd finally concludes his arguments in *Mafhūm al-naṣṣ* in a somewhat Sufi-like fashion (Abū Zayd 1987, 245–297).

To pave the way for exploring alternative concepts for the religious texts, Abū Zayd tries to refute some Islamic legal maxims such as "there is no room for *ijtihād* wherever a text is available." He claims that the statement *(manṭūq)* of the Qur'ān is fixed and permanent, but its conception *(mafhūm)* is changeable and open to variable approaches. To establish this claim, Abū Zayd refers to the history of Muslim rational approaches (especially by the Mu'tazilites) in addition to practical principles of legal methodology, such as the priority of consideration of 'public interest' *(maṣlaḥah)* over the text, the 'preservation of objectives' *(maqāṣid)* of the law, and 'suitability' *(munāsabah)* of *ratio leges* in analogous applications. These principles were mainly proposed by the fourteenth-century jurist al-Shāṭibī and endorsed partly by Ibn Taymiyyah (d. 1328) and others. Pursuing different objectives or grounding themselves on variable information, Muslim jurists historically presented varying conceptions out of certain texts (Abū Zayd 1992, 82–86, see also 59).

A legal case in point is a daughter's share of inheritance which principally should screen *(ḥajaba)* the right of all second-degree relatives in the absence of other first-degree heirs, such as brothers. According to most Sunnite schools of law, a daughter is not entitled to inherit more than her 'determined share' *(farḍ)*, which is *half* from her parents' bequest. The rest should be returned to either the *'aṣabah* (paternal male residuary) or to the public treasury *(bayt al-māl)* in the absence of other first-degree heirs. Only the Shi'ite school of law (especially the Ja'farite school) clearly gives the right to the daughter to appropriate the second half of the bequest by returning *(radd)* it to her, regardless of the presence of the *'aṣabah*. The above problem was strongly debated in the Egyptian media in the 1980s. Abū Zayd supported those writers who had advised the government to enhance women's rights by adopting the Shi'ite position in the law of inheritance. He argues that the different understanding of the same qur'ānic verses by Shi'ites (and some Ḥanafites, thus Sunnites) point to the fact that there is room for *ijtihād* and a new understanding of the qur'ānic verses. He refers to two spheres for understanding the verses: i) to find out the meaning *(ma'nā)*, and ii) to delineate the 'end goal' *(maghzā)* of the law. It was the focus of the seventh century Muslims, Abū Zayd opines, to adjust the meaning of the verses according to the existing Arab customs. They sometimes sacrificed the spirit and overall objectives of the Qur'ān for its verbal consistency, but this was not the case for some Sufi-minded authors, as it should not be the case for our contemporary understanding of the text (Abū Zayd 1992, 85–86, 105 and 219–20).

Abū Zayd claims that contemporary Muslim juridical understanding of the religious discourse *(al-khiṭāb al-dīnī)* is often more strict than that of their predecessors. He quotes al-Suyūṭī's account on verbal categorisation of the qur'ānic verses as an example of the historical approach to the text of the Qur'ān. In his *al-Itqān*, al-Suyūṭī plainly claims that all general-legal verses of the Qur'ān are particularised, except Qur'ān IV: 23: "Forbidden to you [for marriage] are your mothers". According to Abū Zayd, al-Suyūṭī divides the levels of clarity of the qur'ānic verses as follows: i) a clear verse is one which does not bear two meanings, and this is a *naṣṣ* (or the text); ii) the verse bears two meanings but one of them is preferable, and that one is *ẓāhir* ('apparent'); iii) should both meanings bear equal weight, then the verse is *mujmal* ('generalised'); iv) if both meanings are not equal, but the stronger *(aqwā)* does not fit into the overall apparent meaning closely, rather a remote meaning is preferable, and that is called *mu'awwal* ('allegorically interpreted') (al-Suyūṭī 1951, 2: 16; Abū Zayd 1992, 92). Abū Zayd concludes that the concept of *naṣṣ*, according to al-Suyūṭī and most traditional authors, meant nothing but 'clear verse', whereas *naṣṣ* appears often as a 'fixed and sacred verse' in the writings of the later, and especially present, juridical authors. Moreover, this leaves practically no room for a *rational* reflection of the human mind (Abū Zayd 1992, 91–94).

As such, we see that Abū Zayd's employment of hermeneutics in reading Islamic texts has produced a plausible criticism of some Muslim traditional methods in approaching the *sharī'ah*. This criticism proposes a drastic change in both the application and functions of traditional methods, so as to be able to keep up with timely and contemporary considerations. In comparison with the rational approaches of the past, such as the *maqāṣid*-theory of al-Shāṭibī, Abū Zayd's theory does not, however, provide enough religious basis to legitimise or compromise the application of the new approach within the well-founded structure of the *sharī'ah*. Abū Zayd's writings, nevertheless, influenced some Muslim milieus in North Africa and Indonesia. One may draw parallels between his writings and some new legal proposals for reform in the civil law of the Maghreb (Morocco, Algeria, and Tunisia), where some protagonists have stated that "[t]he idea of an immutable and sacred 'Muslim law' is the fruit of a doctrinal development and a dominant version of history that presents it as a compact and definitive whole" (Collectif 95 Maghreb Egalité 2003, 14).

Abdolkarim Soroush (b. 1945)

An epistemological approach to the *sharī'ah* is proposed by the contemporary Iranian professor of philosophy Abdolkarim Soroush ('Abd al-Karīm Surūsh). Born in Tehran in 1945 and trained in a religious school, Soroush graduated from the Faculty of Pharmacology of Tehran University, but continued his studies in Philosophy of Science at the University of London from 1974 onward. He retuned to Iran after the revolution of 1979 and took office as a member of the Council on the Cultural Revolution to 'purge' and reopen Iranian universities. Four years later, he broke with revolutionary ideas, and began to develop his epistemological approach towards man, nature and religion. His first, and probably most controversial, proposal was the idea of 'theoretical contraction and expansion of the *sharī'ah*', primarily published by him in form of a series of articles in 1987 and later as a book.

Soroush's point of departure in this book is 'scientific', in the sense that the way how we derive knowledge from sciences reshapes our views of the world and affects our understanding of religion. He gives an example of how the discovery of the theory of the earth's orbit around the sun has shaken the existing worldviews not only from the cosmological standpoint but also philosophically and epistemologically. Mankind never completes the knowledge of science or religion (Soroush 1992a, 83–88 and 92). By such commensuration of religion with science, it is obvious that Soroush wants to introduce scientific theories into religion.

Muslim jurisprudence, Soroush concludes, was impressed by its surrounding knowledge in the past, and should be more contingent on knowledge of the time today. He quotes an old Sufi expression that 'there are ways to approach God at the number of whole people.' Later on, he relates the famous saying often ascribed to 'Alī b. Abī Ṭālib that "The Qur'ān does not talk to you. I tell you what knowledge is in it concerning the past and future and the remedy of your pains and to put in order your affairs" (Soroush 1992a, 178). We have seen above that the Egyptian author Abū Zayd, too, made use of a similar saying of 'Alī in the War of Ṣiffīn.[4] It seems that the figure of 'Alī as the 'Speaker of the Qur'ān' served as legitimation for not only Twelver Shi'ite and Ismā'īlī interpretations of the Qur'ān, but also for today's hermeneutical readings.

Unlike Abū Zayd, however, Soroush does not present a specific interpretation of the qur'ānic text, but he strongly prescribes what he calls a 'dynamic jurisprudence' to take the place of the presently inflexible dormant one. The scope of this reform which is proposed by him under the headline "The Contraction and Expansion of the *sharī'ah*" is summarised by him as follows:

> Reconciling eternity and temporality, the sacred and the profane, separating constant and variant, form and substance, reviving innovative adjudica-

---

4 Abū Zayd bases his quotation on al-Ṭabarī's report, whereas Soroush's source of reference is *Nahj al-balāhah,* edited by Fayḍ al-Islām.

> tion in religion; finding courageous jurisconsults; reinvigorating religious jurisprudence, changing the appearance while preserving the spirit of religion; acquainting Islam with the contemporary age; establishing the new Islamic theology (Soroush 2000, 30).

The above outline points to an ambitious reform that recounts no less than the revivalist attempts of al-Ghazālī and Shāh Walī-Allāh to whose works Soroush frequently refers. He characterises his theory of 'contraction and expansion' of religious understanding as primarily a theological theory (Soroush 2000, 38) and thus does not feel much need for its juridical elaboration, save for some sporadic critical observations, as we will see below. He criticises the present Islamic legal methodology from an epistemological point of view. Quoting Ayatollah Khomeini's saying that "*Ijtihād* as understood and practiced by the *ḥawzah* (Islamic seminaries) is insufficient", Soroush concludes that "[t]his pronouncement revealed that *ijtihād* itself is in need of another *ijtihād*. And if *ijtihād* continues to be what it heretofore has been, not much hope could be pinned on it" (Soroush 2000, 29). Soroush aspires for a courageous jurist *(faqīh)* to pronounce reason-based religious *fatwā*s, but he does not define the method how reason should religiously expand or contract revealed ordinances.

Soroush's major contribution lies in his multiplied elaboration of the cohabitation of reason and Revelation, as he finds the former's fervour to unravel the latter's mystery an equally beautiful sight (Soroush 2000, 36). Like the Mu'atazilite thinkers, Soroush acknowledges God's dictums via the human rationale. He says: "It is up to God to reveal a religion, but up to us to understand and realise it" (Soroush 2000, 31). This realisation may have variable presentations of the same Revelation. To realise the meaning of a revealed text, we can get help from friends and foes alike. For the sake of purity of religion we should not reject modern sciences (Soroush 2000, 35). It is evident that by expansion of the role of human conception, Soroush aims at juxtaposing reason with Revelation within a new scope that is much broader than that of the historical Mu'tazilites. Unlike Abū Zayd and Shabistarī, Soroush, does not reduce religion to a 'spiritual experience', neither does he indicate what is left from prophecy out of human conception. The way he admires the beauty of spirituality discloses the mysterious effects of religious rituals and experiences on his mind. This he combines with allegorical expressions from classical Persian mystical literature. In no way, however, he considers that temporal culture can be a substitute for religion (Soroush 2000, 36; 1992b, 63–103).

Soroush's emphasis on the epistemological dimensions of knowledge is considered by another contemporary author as detour around the direct metaphysical discussion of subjectivity. According to Vahdat (2002, 200), "[i]n doing so, he [Soroush] added a hermeneutic element, likening the external world to a text in need of interpretation". Subjectivity as a pillar of modernity is defined here as "the property characterizing the autonomous, self-willing, self-defining and self-conscious individual agent" (Vahdat 2002, 1). Soroush's distinction between 'religion in itself' and our 'knowledge of religion' seems to this author somewhat parallel to "Kant's distinction between noumena and phenomena", as Soroush writes "religion is sacred and heavenly, but knowledge of religion is mundane and human" (Vahdat 2002, 201). Another observation on Soroush's theory of utilising science to comprehend religion reveals that he has overlooked the main difference between *religion as a worldview* and *science as an approach*, because "[a] s a worldview, religion comes to know the world *a priori*. The world it wants to comprehend is an invention of religion itself. [...] Its interest, however, lies not so much in a praxis based on these bigger truths, but rather in accepting and cultivating in them. The scientific outlook on the other hand sees the world *a posterior*. The world it wants to understand is not a creation of itself, since it regards nature as an independent entity" (Boroujerdi 1994, 257–58; quoting partly from Dūstdār 1980, 5–15).

In his recent writings, Soroush puts emphasis on extra-religious values which, in his view, are independent of religion, without being incompatible with it. He blames a supposed epistemological inflexibility on the prevalence of Ash'arite theological tradition, stating that "[o]ne of the main principle of Ash'arite Islam is that there are no objective, external values; all values must come through religion" (Soroush 2002, 2–3). In contrast, in his view, the defeated Mu'tazilite school of thought attempted to show that rationality *per se* was acceptable in Islam, even when not based on religion. In spite of this rather harsh, unqualified, and 'off-the mark' criticism of the orthodox Ash'arite theological approach, however, Soroush admires reformist thinkers of Sunnite Islam who strove to revive rational thought. He is said to plan to publish a new book under the title *Reinventing the Mu'tazilite Experiment* (Soroush 2002, 3). By emphasising extra-religious values and appropriating them in religious contexts, Soroush signals the non-applicability of a dichotomous distinction of all values between secular and religious ones. In fact he also speaks about obviating such a distinction in terms of political rule (Soroush 2002, 3).

Due to his epistemological approach, Soroush's ideas on government cannot be based on the prefixed texts. He dismisses the idea that forming government was a necessarily part of Revelation. "The Prophet", Soroush claims, "has left no rulings on governance. It is up to people to decide their government" (Soroush 2002, 3). The relationship between man and God is direct, and no mediating position in spirituality or faith is conceivable. Soroush does not find any support in the Traditions for the claim of Muslim clerics to governance. He even refutes the use of the term of *wilāyah* (lit. 'amity', 'closeness') for political leadership as it conveys several profoundly esoteric meanings none of them appropriate for political authority (Soroush, November 1998 – January 1999, 20; instead of *wilāyat*, Soroush proposes that *za'āmat* to be used for 'political leadership'.).

Concluding remarks

Contemporary reformist Muslim legal thinkers – among them most prominently Soroush – aimed to change the common understanding of a fixed Islam and *sharī'ah* through hermeneutical distinction between religion and religious knowledge. It is a truism that knowledge of religion requires human interpretation based on man's rational ability. As it is said, *God* is the One who reveals religion and His people are the ones to *understand* God's work. This seems to be another way of cohabitation of Revelation and reason that has precedents in Islamic thought. Via reason, nevertheless, Soroush allows the intrusion of sciences, which can offer various new facets for an already established belief system. Here, we find that Soroush is able to criticise traditional approaches towards religious knowledge without touching upon the very essence of the religion of Islam. The views of the contemporary Muslims reformist thinkers presented in this contribution run often contrary to *traditional* Islamic scholarship, which has been harshly criticised by them. Although is goes beyond saying that this criticism went often 'beyond the mark' the reformist thinkers are nevertheless to the fact that contemporary Islamic thought (especially legal thought) is by no means static and is trying to face the realities of our times without necessarily ascribing to entirely secular worldviews which are part of a different cultural and social context.

References

Books

Abū Sulaymān, 'Abd al-Ḥamīd 1994: Towards an Islamic Theory of International Relations: New Directions for Methodology and Thought. Herndon VA: International Institute of Islamic Thought (IIIT).
Abū Sulaymān, 'Abd al-Ḥamīd 1997: Crisis in the Muslim Mind, tr. Yusuf Talal Delorenzo. Herndon VA: International Institute of Islamic Thought (IIIT).
Abū Zayd, Naṣr Ḥāmid 1987: Mafhūm al-naṣṣ. Cairo: al-Markaz al-Thaqāfī al-'Arabī.
Abū Zayd, Naṣr Ḥāmid 1992: Naqd al-khiṭāb al-dīnī. Cairo: Sīnā' li 'l-Nashr.
Abū Zayd, Naṣr Ḥāmid n. d.: Ishkālāt al-qirā'ah wa 'l-āliyyāt al-ta'wīl. Cairo: al-Markaz al-Thaqāfī al-'Arabī.
al-'Alwānī, Ṭāhā Jābir 1997: The Ethics of Disagreement in Islam. Herndon VA: International Institute of Islamic Thought (IIIT).
al-'Alwānī, Ṭāhā Jābir 2001: Maqāṣid al-sharī'ah. Beirut: Dār al-Hādī.
al-'Alwānī, Ṭāhā Jābir 2003: Source Methodology in Islamic Jurisprudence. London, Washington DC: International Institute of Islamic Thought (IIIT).
Anṣārī, Murtaḍā 1987: Farā'id al-uṣūl. 2 vols, ed. 'Abd-Allāh Nūrānī. Qum: Mu'assasat al-Nashr al-Islāmī.
al-Asadābādī, ʿAbd al-Jabbār 1960: Al-Mughnī fī abwāb al-tawḥīd wa 'l-'adl. 20 vols. Cairo: al-Shirkah al-ʿArabiyyah li 'l-Ṭabʿ wa 'l-Nashr.

Collectif 95 Maghreb Egalité 2003: Dalil pour l'égalité dans la famille au Maghreb. Rabat: Collectif 95 Maghreb Egalité.
Dihlawī, Shāh Walī-Allāh 1990: Ḥujjat Allāh al-bālighah. 2 vols. Beirut: Dār IIḥyā' al-'Ulūm.
Dūstdār, Ārāmish 1980: Mulāḥiẓātī falsafī dar dīn, 'ilm, wa tafakkur. Tehran: Āgāh.
Hermansen, Marcia K. (tr.) 1995: The Conclusive Argument from God. Leiden: E. J. Brill.
Ja'farī-Langrūdī, Muḥammad Ja'far 1991: Maktabhā-yi ḥuqūqī dar Islām. Tehran: Ganj-i Dānish.
Jalbani, G. N. 1988: Teaching of Shāh Waliyullāh of Delhi. New Delhi: Kitab Bhavan.
al-Juwaynī, ʿAbd al-Malik 1985: Al-Burhān. Qatar: Maṭbaʿah al-Dawḥah al-Ḥadīthah
Kamali, Mohammad Hashim 2002: Issues in the Legal Theory of Uṣūl and Prospect for Reform. Kuala Lumpur: International Islamic University Malaysia (IIUM).
Kamali, Mohammad Hashim 2003: Principles of Islamic Jurisprudence. Cambridge: Islamic Texts Society.
Khurāsānī, Muḥammad Kāẓim 1988: Kifāyat al-uṣūl. Qum: Mu'assasah Āl al-Bayt.
al-Muqirrī, Hibāt-Allāh b. Salāmah b. Naṣr 1984: Al-Nāsikh wa 'l-mansūkh min Kitāb Allāh. Beirut: al-Maktabah al-Islāmī.
Shabistarī, Muḥammad Mujtahid 2002: Hermeneutics, Kitāb wa Sunnah. Tehran: Intishārāt-i Ṭarḥ-i Now.
al-Shāṭibī, Abū Isḥāq Ibrāhīm n. d.: Al-Muwāfaqāt fī uṣūl al-aḥkām. 4 vols. in 2 books. Cairo: Dār al-Fikr.
Soroush, Abdolkarim [ʿAbd al-Karīm Surūsh] 1992a: Qabḍ wa basṭ-e thiyurī-yi sharīʿat. Tehran: Ṣirāt.
Soroush, Abdolkarim 1992b: Rāzdānī wa rawshanfikrī wa dīndārī. Tehran: Ṣirāt.
Soroush, Abdolkarim 2000: Reason, Freedom and Democracy in Islam, tr. Mahmoud Sadri and Ahmad Sadri. Oxford, New York: Oxford University Press.
al-Suyūṭī, Jalāl al-Dīn 1951: Al-Itqān fī 'ulūm al-Qur'ān. Cairo: Muṣṭafā Albānī al-Ḥalabī.
Vahdat, Farzin 2002: God and Juggernaut: Iran's Intellectual Encounter with Modernity. Syracuse NY: Syracuse University Press.

Articles
al-'Alwānī, Ṭāhā Jābir 1991a: Ijtihad and Taqlid. In: American Journal of Islamic Social Sciences 8, no. 1, 129–142.
al-'Alwānī, Ṭāhā Jābir 1991b: The Crisis in Fiqh and the Methodology of Ijtihād. In: The American Journal of Islamic Social Sciences 8, no 2, 317–337.

Boroujerdi, Mehrzad 1994: The Encounter of Post-Revolutionary Thought in Iran with Hegel, Heidegger, and Popper. In: Şerif Mardin (ed.), Cultural Transitions in the Middle East. Leiden: E. J. Brill, 236–259.

Hallaq, Wael 1984: Was the Gate of ijtihad Closed? In: International Journal of Middle East Studies 16, 3–41.

Harver, A. 1987: Hermeneutics. In: The Encyclopedia of Religion, 16 vols. New York: Macmillan, 6: 279–287.

Kazemi-Moussawi, Ahmad (forthcoming): The Role of Legal Methodology In Changing Approaches to the Sharīʿah".

Soroush, Abdolkarim [ʿAbd al-Karīm Surūsh] November 1998 – January 1999: Wilāyat-i bāṭinī wa wilāyat-i siyāsī. In: Kiyān-e farhangī 44, 20.

Soroush, Abdolkarim 2002: Reason and Freedom in Islamic Thought. Lecture delivered by Soroush at the CSID Second Annual Conference, Islam Democrat 4, no. 1 (January 2002), 2–5.

14

Muslims and Resources for Peace in Islam

Karim Douglas Crow

Abstract

Islam is an Asian Tradition offering definite resources for peace and understanding, yet it also be understood in the context of its Southwest Asian prophetic roots. After first clarifying in what manner Islam functioned historically as an intermediate force and mediator between Western and Eastern civilisations, the author turns to examine Islam's approach to peace and neutralising violence in human societies. The basic dilemma is seen to be how Muslims themselves today comprehend the guidance mediated by Islamic values and teachings regarding peacemaking and peacebuilding, and the several barriers blocking Muslim societies from refreshing and creatively re-appropriating the values inherent within their own tradition. He argues that examples for Islam's vital emphasis on various levels of active struggle, the commitment in Islam to social equity and political justice, and Islam's specific ideals and practices for active reconciliation between individuals and groups, were set by the Prophet himself as the primary precedents for using peaceful action during his mission. Finally, a possible alternative to 'Islamic Action' (jihād) is sketched as one avenue of approach.

Just as human beings could not fly until they had understood the law of gravity and a host of other necessities, they cannot exist peaceably in ignorance of the causes of tension in a multi-cultural world united by one dominant culture.

Theodore H. von Laue (1987, 315)

Introduction

Recent remarks by Pope Benedict XVI renewed debates over a clash-of-civilisations by focusing attention on the crucial question whether the Islamic religion undervalues rationality (in contrast to Christianity) and is thereby more inclined to privilege or sanction violence. Violence as the enemy of reason, he argued, has no role in eliciting consent in religion; and to act against reason is to act against God's very nature. Given Pope Benedict's implicit role as spokesman for Western civilisation, his remarks evoked widespread if muted support from many quarters in Europe and the United States (e. g. *Time* magazine, 20 November 2006). The association of Islam with unreason and violence in the minds of Europeans is nothing new. Until the mid-twentieth century, a widespread occidental view prevailed that Muslims, like other Orientals and 'Asiatics', were inferior and irrational in civilisational terms, compared to European societies – an attitude that sprang from assumptions inherent in positivist rationalism put to service in the European colonialist enterprise. More than a few are questioning (like R. J. Neuhaus, a prominent American Catholic who has the ear of President George W. Bush) whether Muslims are capable of "signing on to the modernity project" since their mentality and motives are perceived to spring out of an inherent rejection of rationality that is the benchmark of post-Enlightenment ideals forming the backbone of modernity in the West.[1] Indeed, the old idea is still going strong that the West represents humanity in its rational self-conscious mode.[2]

Islam is one of the great Asian traditions of universal reach shaping the lives of numerous peoples and societies for well over a millennium. Originating in Southwest Asia, it quickly spread its polity and culture from the Iberian Penin-

---

1 A central project of the eighteenth-century Enlightenment was to separate morality from religion, to ground morality in a universal reason not in any special revelation. Ultimately this has led in contemporary science & philosophy to the disconnection of 'fact' from 'value' across all realms of thought, leaving values in a shadowy realm.

2 Reason and rationality are the birthright of all humans, which is not to deny that Western peoples elaborated a particular application and expansion of rationality that is currently accepted as the 'default' mode by the world, due to Westernisation. For the more inclusive and integral understanding of reason in Islam that stresses both cognition and conation, see Crow 2003.

sula to Central Asia and the borders of China. Spain was conquered from 712 onward by the military leader and conqueror of North Africa, Mūsā b. Nuṣayr (640–716), on behalf of the Umayyad caliph in Damascus, al-Walīd I b. ʻAbd al-Malik (r. 705–715). The Muslim penetration of the Iberian Peninsula was part of a strategic deployment of Islamic forces far to the west, originally intended to encircle the Byzantines from the rear. Simultaneously, Umayyad power confronted imperial Chinese troops in Central Asia and established a permanent Muslim presence on the Indian subcontinent in Sind. In the following era, Muslim powers spread Islam through South Asia, while from the tenth century onward networks of merchant-scholars diffused their faith in the lands of Southeast Asia. This historical experience of immediate advance and political dominance accompanying the success of the Islamic polity was taken as confirmation of its universal providential mission and divine support. The burden of such a triumphalist worldview in the post-colonial global era is obvious and still echoes loudly in the perceptions of many Muslims.

The Islamic presence in Central, East, South, and Southeast Asia experienced vicissitudes under the Western imperial powers, while the post-colonial period has left Muslim societies searching for renewed sense of authenticity and identity in the face of wrenching changes: experiencing communal life as a disadvantaged minority for Han Chinese, Indian,[3] Philippine or Thai Muslims; emerging from Soviet suffocation for the newly independent states; stridently asserting new national entities for Pakistan and Bangladesh; and inheriting states from Britain and the Netherlands for Malaysia and Indonesia. It is frequently forgotten that after the Arab peoples, the second largest ethno-linguistic group among Muslims today consists of the more than 250 million speakers of Malay and Indonesian, splintered among six nation-states now growing further apart by linguistic drift and nationalist identity. Given the dynamism and cultural assertion marking this region, the Muslims of Southeast Asia may expect to play a more pronounced role within the global Muslim community as the twenty-first century unfolds.[4]

Neither eastern nor western

Compared to its two brother faiths rooted in the same prophetic monotheist tradition – Judaism and Christianity – Islam has historically occupied an intermediate and mediating position between Europe and Asia. We should recall that the West

3 India's 138 million Muslims (more than the total population of Pakistan) were recently the subject of the Indian government's Sacchar Committee Report underlining their depressed social and economic conditions, deemed worse than that of the lowest-caste Hindus.

4 Recently, the media organisation *Al-Jazeera* launched a worldwide English language cable TV news service whose four offices are located in Doha, Washington DC, London, and Kuala Lumpur.

and Islam share similar roots, putting into question whether there really is an irrevocable difference of ultimate values between the two. Thus, both admit the primacy of the 'Biblicist' (Judaic-Christian) Prophetic Tradition[5] for their worldview. Naturally, Islam insists upon the finality of the 'Mohammedan' revelation, while acknowledging and validating the salvific status of its brother faiths. The Hellenic ('Graeco-Roman') civilisation of late antiquity with its cultural and intellectual products, too, had a strong impact on Islamic civilisation and Islam also drew upon selected aspects of Hellenic thought and experience, especially the intellectual and scientific components admitted into Muslim rationalist scientific disciplines. Islam may be said to a large extent to have shared the West's legacy of Greek thought, even though this legacy was received through a 'cultural filter' that excluded aspects perceived to be incompatible with Prophetic revealed knowledge. Europe's reception of the intellectual legacy of Antiquity, prompting the Renaissance that led to the Enlightenment, was facilitated by the Islamic Hellenic legacy being translated in the thirteenth and fourteenth centuries from Arabic into Latin and Hebrew.

Yet Islam integrated further sources into the confluence of its civilisational synthesis that became central to its political and cultural experience: the civilisations of the East including Sassanid Persian (for statecraft and administration), Indian Sanskrit (for mathematics and linguistics), and various Central Asian, South Asian and Southeast Asian components relative to specific regional developments over its historical unfolding. It was Islamic rulers and commercial contacts that did the most to propagate and diffuse the values and norms of Southwest Asian Prophetic monotheistic tradition over wide areas of sub-Saharan Africa, South Asia, and Southeast Asia.[6] This was the case well before the era of European colonial penetration accompanied by missionaries preaching their faith to the 'natives' – not a unitary Christian teaching, but one packaged in competing brands depending on the colonials' country of origin. Historically speaking, in civilisational terms,

---

5 By 'Prophetic Tradition' we understand the historical manifestation of providentially revealed norms and values on which are based the five or more faith communities rooted in the teachings of the Biblicist-Islamic line of prophets: the Mosaic-Samaritan, Judaic-Rabbinic, 'Baptist', Christian, Manichaean, and Islamic dispensations. (The prophetic line of John the Baptist has an historical claim as an independent line – e. g. the Mandaeans of Iraq [Judaic-Baptist Gnostics] who recognise his role, while the Qur'ān treats John the Baptist (Yaḥyā b. Zakariyyā' as an independent prophet in his own right. Baptist teachings played some role in the formation of Islamic ideas, particularly among early Shiʿites)

6 It is true that before Islam, Judaism was present in Iraq, the Iranian lands, and South Arabia, and that Nestorian Christianity had reached Central Asia, India and China; but their presence and impact remained confined to a minority foreign cult with few exceptions. Furthermore, Manichaean teachings may have helped prepare the ground for Islam particularly in Central Asia. In the history of Middle Eastern religions, Mani may be viewed as a type of forerunner to the Prophet of Islam.

Islam cast a wider net and Islamic civilisation integrated a greater diversity of cultural and intellectual achievements than did Europe.

Therefore, from the point of view of its civilisational roots and socio-spiritual values, should one perceive Islam as belonging within the construct of 'the West'? Arnold Toynbee, for instance, advocated such a view in his *Study of History.* This may remind one of the confusions created by speaking of Christianity as a 'Western' tradition while ignoring the fact of its West Asian roots, not to mention the historical reality of the Eastern Christian communities, such as the medieval Nestorians whose activities stretched from Persia to China and who had converted the Seljuk Turkish and Mongol nobility to the Christian faith before their eventual Islamisation. It may be more accurate to identify Islam as a middle realm, geographically bridging East and West – a 'mid-most community' *(ummat*^{un} *wasaṭ*^{un}*)* – partaking in varying degree of the same roots as the West, while simultaneously open to the East, being in ideological and spiritual terms 'neither eastern nor western' *(lā sharqiyy*^{an} *wa lā gharbiyy*^{an}*)*. Both these, it should be noted, are qur'ānic terms.

It is significant that today many people are now defining themselves and others in terms of overarching monolithic compartments, such as 'Jews and Crusaders' and 'secular materialists', or 'irrational fanatics' and 'trans-national terrorists'. It has also been argued that for much of the millennium spanning from the seventh until the eighteenth century, world history consisted largely of the interaction between Christian Europe and the Islamic polities of Spain, North Africa, and Asia. This interaction was characterised by dramatic moments of conflict and rivalry, of ideological confrontation and cultural barriers. However, confrontation across barriers was not the most significant feature of this process of interaction. Islamic polities established what may be deemed the first major world system of trade and commerce, marked by far-flung mercantile exchanges, uniting regions separated until then by insurmountable barriers of geography, ethnicity, and culture. The synthesis achieved by classical Islamic civilisation depended upon the confluence of a number of streams feeding into it, operating through the medium of 'cultural filters' that permitted some components to pass through while excluding other elements. The reverse is the case today for Muslim societies in our era of Westernisation and global confluence.

Global confluence / cultural anarchy

The overwhelming consequences of Westernisation on all cultures and societies are often taken for granted like a continuous background hum. It is important to refresh our awareness and to highlight several crucial results that have great bearing for any discussion about Islam's possible contribution to regional and global peacemaking – or any religious tradition for that matter. Before the Western impact, traditional societies, such as those of the Islamic lands, existed in reasonable harmony within the intellectual, spiritual and material resources at their disposal.

It was the process of Westernisation (transformed in the internal revolution of re-culturation termed 'modernisation' and 'development') that forced them into a complex world beyond their comprehension and resources, destroying their former bonds of collective community, individual moral socialisation and value formation. Most non-Western peoples have been re-cultured to comply with the requirements of the global state system (in some cases superficially and reluctantly), and statehood is now the universal framework for human existence. The nation-state system has universalised Western institutions, including government bureaucracy, armed forces, diplomatic service, literacy and mass education, communications, industrialism and large-scale organisation, while enforcing a continuous mobilisation of competition for wealth and power (the literature on this is vast; for a succinct and prescient overview see von Laue 1987, 315–16). In their global interdependence the intensely competitive self-consciousness among all peoples is accompanied by judgemental and moralising cross-cultural comparisons (witness Pope Benedict XVI, or the 'Jihadists' slogan of 'Jews and Crusaders'). Global confluence promotes a more uniform global community while simultaneously aggravating global anarchy and violence. Cultural confusion and incomprehension attending global interdependence has hardened diversity and multiplied insecurity, encouraging relapse into divisive and self-righteous fundamentalisms, whether in religion or politics (see in particular Marty and Appleby 1991–1995).

Commodities, weapons, machines, even written constitutions, may cross easily over cultural boundaries, but not those complex cultural constructions deeply imbedded in the internal dynamics of specific cultures, elaborated during the span of continuous historical experiences, such as gender equity, 'democracy', 'freedom', and alike. Such achievements represent elaborated cultural phenomena that are not so readily transplanted, since they take for granted and require a set of aptitudes, social habits and skills, and organisational and cognitive patterns that must first be instilled through re-culturation. As an example, secularism arose from the peculiar experience of eighteenth and nineteenth-century Europeans breaking free from the intellectual, social and spiritual domination of organised religion, hand in hand with the consolidation of science and material advancement shaping economic and political realities. To assume that all other cultures or societies must inevitably undergo the identical process is fallacious. The pattern of evolution experienced by Western European and North American societies may not easily serve as guide or blueprint for the cultural development of other societies who function individually and collectively in different modes constrained by their own specific historical and social dynamics. In the words of von Laue, "societies or politics culturally conditioned over long stretches of time cannot readily transform themselves according to a different cultural pattern: non-Western cultures cannot follow the Western upward-bound route" (von Laue 1987, 314). Thus the issue is "[w]ho understands whom on whose terms? In the last analysis, cross-cultural understanding is a matter of raw power: who has the power to make his own understanding prevail?" (von Laue 1987, 376). To fail to anticipate and act on this reality when attempting cross-cultural understanding only invites cognitive imperialism (whereby one's effort to comprehend others remains trapped within prevailing power relations) and results in the abdication of responsible intellectual insight whether in historical research or policy studies.

Culture and religion

Nor may one neglect the intimate connection that great religious traditions and related ethico-spiritual practices and teachings possess with culture, above all the potential for promoting the coming transition from the nation-state and specific ethno-religious collectivity to the global community at large – the inescapable logic of our global interdependence. This 'change of mind' imposes the transcendent perspective of a more inclusive awareness beyond the constraints of particular national boundaries. It imposes as well new obligations and restrictions on both individuals and governments in adjusting to a greatly expanded community of common interests. The change occurs first within individuals, percolates through influential circles and organisations, before tincturing the worldview and goals of ruling groups and governments. Yet such a transformation is not a certainty, but merely *one* possibility among others, and one should not view it as inevitable or necessary however urgently hoped for. The resources religion may provide for advancing toward closer global cooperation beyond the nation-state, for outgrowing parochial mentalities by instilling universal values nourished from the unconscious depths of human experience, demands both individual and collective discipline, creativity, and a live moral sense. In the past, this order of change was often accomplished by war and conquest combined with widespread recognition of common interests transforming a collectivity into a greater community with an enhanced level of organisation and cognitive and artistic skills. Our age of global confluence and the events of the twentieth century show that force and threat of force shall not achieve the needed transformation – that persuasion and shared conviction hold out greater promise and hope.

Culture embraces the inter-human social dimension, the arena of human interaction with nature and environment and material artefacts and an internal structuring of the individual's inward-universe – the consciousness (mind and soul) – by cognitive and conative disciplines releasing creative activity supporting effective collective organisation. Religion enters into all three arenas, being especially relevant for the psycho-spiritual mechanism enabling the harnessing of individual will and psychic energies for projection of communal goals. Culture requires either a firm power-base to exist and operate meaningfully, or a firm ethnic and spiritual bond animating a people (as a potential polity) beyond state boundaries. Therefore, religion retains precious resources for the hoped-for transformation of mind, with its techniques of socialisation, disciplining, and creative imagination elaborated and explored over many generations – one of the most precious legacies of humanity. Yet when tied to the narrow identity of parochial in-group awareness, or the downward transcendence of large-group regression in mass movements, religion devolves into an opposite force buttressing cross-cultural ignorance and inviting violence. The phenomenon of ethico-religious nationalism over the past several centuries is instructive in displaying the ambivalent power that religion may exercise in human affairs (e.g., Orthodoxy and Greeks, Serbs, Russians; Zionism; several Islamist movements).[7]

Furthermore, we need to remind ourselves of the inherent limitations when we think and speak in generalities such as 'Islam' – whereas the reality always remains specific to particular Muslim societies differing widely in their political, economic, social-cultural and technological aspects, even while they share many concrete as well as intangible features. Moreover, we must remember that 'civilisation' does not in itself necessarily imply or require technological advancement. Levi-Strauss pointed out years ago that the chief difference between the war-painted American Indian and the nuclear bomber pilot is a technological one, since the purpose of their activity is the same. From the viewpoint of essential human values, some among us may even wish to characterise contemporary modernity as a highly sophisticated technologically advanced form of barbarism.

Perhaps what has to be done before pronouncing on the broad and variegated reality of Islam regarding peace is to first reach some consensus *within* the Muslim faith community about what should be the real positions on key issues. The assumption that *every* civilisational block, or *every* faith community, is in agreement among themselves over which of their own values are uppermost in the search for harmonious relations with other groups, and what questions are most relevant to pose to others and how to properly discourse with others is an assumption contradicted by reality. At least that is the reality of the situation with Muslims. Nor should one be quick to portray 'the West' as a monolithic entity, despite current US military dominance and mercantile hegemony. In the Islamic case, we find that there is no authoritative centralised leadership nor any complete agreement over who may act as *legitimate* spokespersons for the Muslims, but rather several and conflicting voices. Authority in Islam was always diffused or shared between the power holders, the scholars *('ulamā')*, and spiritual exponents. Currently, there is a distinctly ubiquitous trend toward authoritarian abuse by leaders of all three stripes.

Islam: traditions for peace?

There is a widespread perception that contemporary Muslims have lagged behind in pondering the nature and causes of violence, blood-shed and war, while the religion of Islam is commonly seen by many non-Muslims to possess an inherent disposition or bias facilitating violence. Yet recently it was a Muslim, Pro-

---

7 Among many other works, see Nelson-Pallmeyer 2005; Juergensmeyer 2003; de Vries 2002; Schwartz 1998. The thought of Freud, Jung, and Adler, as well as the works of Jacques Lacan and René Girard, runs like a thread through many of these works.

fessor Muhammad Yunus, who was awarded the 2006 Nobel Prize for Peace in recognition of his prolonged efforts to help the poor through micro-credits. Ethical concerns often overlap and are congruent with religious teachings and ideals, but not necessarily nor in all cases. In our secular global era we often hear of 'ethical culture' and pursuit of a 'global ethics' – but specifically divorced from any particular religious claim or dogma upheld by organised religions. Furthermore, a close study and intimacy with the Islamic religious, intellectual and spiritual traditions may convince one that peace and Islam are joined at the hip conceptually, despite historical and contemporary indications of Muslim amnesia. *Peace Studies* as a genuine field of interest yielding practical efforts among Muslims remains in its childhood when compared to other faith traditions. Therefore, we begin where we are, embracing hope and energy to move along a path that only now shows a way forward as to be defeated by the terror of our situation is not an option for thinking Muslims.

We are firmly convinced that Muslims should gladly accept and benefit from the wisdom of our fellows, whether Jewish, Christian, Buddhist, or Hindu, who offer Muslims the fruit of their own insights and experience. The same is true of the disciplines of political science, conflict studies, or non-traditional security studies. It is more than likely that Muslim thinkers and activists in search of a realistic effective peacemaking ethic for this age may look beyond the boundaries of the Qur'ān and the *Sunnah*, reflected in the Traditions, i.e. the prophets recorded 'way of live' *(aḥādīth)* – the two 'canonical' sources of revealed authority in Islam – and avail themselves of modern disciplines developed and taught in Western societies.[8] What stops Muslims from accomplishing this, and would this be seen as a legitimate endeavour? Creative efforts do not shrink from taking this path, although a significant mass of Muslims recoil from explicitly adopting principles or models borrowed from Western disciplines deemed unredeemingly secular, materialist or simply profane. There exists a spectrum of responses, but almost everyone feels the need to provide a degree of religious authenticity by forging links to scripture and tradition. In this manner, tradition has always adapted and grown to encompass fresh challenges and new situations.

The influence of organised religion in fomenting violence is nothing new. Religious identity clearly gives an effective basis for recruiting people, motivating them for direct action, and nurturing a strong common bond and discipline. Yet religious faith may also restrain or even neutralise violence, may encourage people to transcend national or religious boundaries and express solidarity with people of differing races and traditions, and guide people in their struggle for justice and peace. Faith may empower people to engage in effective social and political action promoting meaningful change. Muslims rooted in traditional cultures may be inspired by their religious tradition to act boldly and peaceably for justice and peace.

---

8 See e.g., on the efforts of a group of American Christians of various denominations Stassen (ed.) 2004. Consult also: Carnegie Commission on Preventing Deadly Conflict 1997. For an overview of Muslim practices see Abu-Nimer 2003).

Islam in its best *modus operandi* may be understood as internally equipped with sufficient resources to accomplish such transformative growth – even while Muslims generally insist that 'Islam' in its essentialist mode is permanent and unchanging. What can change and adapt and grow – indeed what must grow to survive and flourish – is the mentality and understanding that Muslims display regarding permanent timeless truths: how Muslims comprehend and appropriate and exemplify in their own conduct and activities the guidance and values mediated within teachings revealed by God through the intermediary of prophets. All the traditions derived from the Southwest Asian line of prophetic guidance share this burden and perpetual challenge.

Values are essential for revitalising the universal rather than the nationalist or particularist side of religious identity, as well as for emphasising a religious commitment that affirms the unity and sacredness of all human life. Islamic values have the potential to shape a more compassionate and tolerant future. By 'Islamic Values' we mean those moral-ethical attitudes and spiritual ideals that sincere faith implants into humans through their family and community upbringing, and which grow into interior motivating impulses. Values operate by the inner willing of conscience and are expressed in praiseworthy character traits and admirable models for behaviour. Islamic values, when sensitively understood and practiced, make a more powerful contribution to peace and reconciliation than to war and bloodshed – by providing the social and psychic foundation for service to others, implementing social, economic and political reforms, and ultimately of transforming human society in harmony with God's providential plan.

However, this demands a *creative* use of traditional precepts and teachings to communicate the need for change in thinking and in action through a language that motivates people for the highest purpose by employing the most worthy and just means.

A very well known practice that is on everyone's lips today is that of *jihād*, 'Peaceable Striving' – a practice that may be understood conceptually not merely as defensive in repelling hostile aggression, but *pro-active* in terms of intervention and making initiatives, demonstrating good intentions and willingness to advance common interests. It also encompasses aspects of individual and communal purification to solidify striving and induce discipline, education, and social engagement. Ultimately, at a deeper level, 'peaceful striving' is to be pursued purely for the sake of God's approbation and good-pleasure, and it demands purity of motive and immaculate inner activity, being the 'Major Combat' requiring the individual to struggle against the weaknesses and imperfections of one's soul *(jihād al-nafs)*.

The 'struggle against one's own base-self' was a highly developed practical discipline in Islamic experience, stressing the function of *jihād* as a means for penance and expiation of sin *(kaffārah)*, based on utter sincerity of intention, while warning against base motives, such as greed for plunder, revenge, self-glory or naked power. At its deepest level, *jihād* requires willingness to sacrifice and experience active conscious suffering, even martyrdom (certainly not suicide, which is forbidden by Islam and considered as the ultimate act of ungratefulness toward

God). In this highest meaning, *jihād* embraces suffering undertaken consciously, not mechanically or passively like most of our everyday suffering, but voluntary suffering rendered as an offering or payment to accomplish a higher purpose which makes one truly human. This order of suffering is deemed a sacred activity.

Peaceful change: Islamic applications

Concrete elements connected to timeless Islamic principles and contemporary concerns strongly support the validity of an understanding of *authentic* Islamic Peaceful Action (more detailed discussion with references to Islamic and contemporary sources may be found in Crow 2000, 2001, 2005a, and 2005b):

- Islam's *vital emphasis on active struggle* and the high value placed on readiness to engage in moral, spiritual, and physical combat is one element. Historically, much Muslim political and spiritual practice is coloured by a martial spirit of selfless action and sacrifice in opposing injustice and defending freedom of faith and conscience. This reflects the valorisation of the ancient heroic 'warrior ideal' transposed onto a higher interiorised spiritual plane (*al-jihād al-akbar*, major peaceful-striving, being the interior precondition and corollary for the outward *al-jihād al-aṣghar*, minor combative-struggle).
- Another element is the overriding *commitment in Islam to social equity and political justice (qisṭ* and *'adl)* in promotion of humane values and in construction of an ethical social order through opposing injustice, corruption and repression. Combating evil or 'wicked tyranny' *(al-ṭāghūt)* is a prominent theme in the qur'ānic recounting of prophetic history: "For We assuredly sent amongst every people a messenger [with the command], 'Serve Allāh and eschew evil'" (Qur'ān 16:36). In Islamic religious teaching, this commitment is viewed as harmonising with the divine purpose for creation and the imperative to make sacred the profane or worldly. Coupled with this stress on equity is an equally emphatic concern to safeguard the stability of social order and temporal authority to preserve the interests of faith, life, and property. Thus *fitnah*, 'civil dissension' and 'communal strife', was always actively discouraged in the wider interests of community stability.
- Complementing this emphasis on justice and upon an equitable social and political order, Islam propounds *specific ideals and practices for active reconciliation between individuals and groups*. Islamic teachings thereby seek a balance between the dictates of justice and equity, and those of human clemency, harmony, and selfless love embraced by the notion of *al-iḥsān*, 'surpassing goodness': "Allāh commands justice, the doing of good and liberality to kith and kin *[al-'adl wa 'l-iḥsān]*, and He forbids all shameful deeds, and injustice and unjust oppression *[al-munkar]*" (16:90). The Qur'ān renounces the use of forceful coercion in favour of active goodwill and persuasion in order to elicit intentional assent or compliance. The verse "Let there be no compulsion I religion" (2:256) is a keynote of the qur'ānic appeal to human conscience, intelligence,

and motivation. The very name of the faith, *al-Islām*, 'peace', 'security', derives etymologically from the noun *al-silm*, 'peace-making', 'conciliation' between conflicting parties.

- Islamic scholars maintain that *the Prophet himself set the primary precedent for using peaceful action during his mission*, particularly during the years of the Meccan stage of his career (610–622) before his migration to Medina. Muslims were instructed to actively contend with their Arab pagan opponents by inviting to the truth of divine revelation brought by the Prophet through preaching with peaceful persuasion and firm admonition against the falsity of idol worship and evil social customs then prevalent among Arabs (25:52):

> Therefore listen not to the unbelievers, but strive against them with the utmost strenuousness [by peaceably inviting to the Truth through sincere persuasion] *(jahidhum bi-hi jihād^an kabīr^an)*!

The early Muslims in Mecca were exhorted not to abandon this 'great striving' *(jihād kabīr)* and to remain steadfast by enduring all provocations and hostility without employing coercive force (the important ideal of *ṣabr* or long-suffering patience), even while the pagan Quraysh severely abused and persecuted them, eventually leading them to migrate to other lands in order to practice their faith freely – first to Abyssinia, then north to the oasis town of Yathrib – renamed *al-Madīnah*, Medina, literally 'the City' (of the Prophet).

The Prophet maintained the conduct of this primary peaceable *jihād* until he and his associates achieved the most appropriate atmosphere and conditions for the second form of *jihād*, the 'Combative Struggle' whose defensive nature was a necessary means for self-preservation in the face of concerted aggression and belligerency. Thus, during the first fifteen years out of the nearly twenty-three years of his prophetic mission, the Prophet and his associates (*al-Ṣaḥābah* or Companions) operated entirely by conducting their Peaceful *Jihād*. The original Islamic 'state' of the Medinese community *(ummah)* established by the Prophet after his Migration *(hijrah)* from Mecca was realised and established solely by peaceable means. Only *after* this polity had been successfully achieved and consolidated was the combative or martial struggle deemed valid for defending its security and very existence – an entity that itself was created and set in place only by means of the Peaceful *jihād*.

- Many Muslim thinkers assert that sacred history demonstrates that many of the prophets – Ibrāhīm (Abraham), Yaḥyā (John the Baptist), 'Īsā (Jesus Christ), to name only a few – were dispatched to guide humanity adopted forms of Peaceful Action in their historical missions, and this paradigm stands as the ideal human pattern for emulation. From the first homicide when Cain slew Abel, the first son of Adam set the model for Peaceful Action by refusing to employ violence against his brother: "If you do stretch your hand against me to slay me, it is not for me to stretch my hand against you to slay you: for I do fear Allāh, the Cherisher of the Worlds" (see 5:27–32 and accompanying exegesis of these verses in classical qur'ānic exegesis).[9]

- The Prophet of Islam strongly and unequivocally forbade Muslims taking the life of other Muslims, while also specifying certain legitimate exceptions (capital punishment for adultery, murder, and apostasy). Key teachings of *ṣulḥ* ('conciliation'), *'afw* ('forgiveness'), and *al-ḥusnā* ('the surpassing good') – all related to the higher Islamic ideal of convincing and eliciting consent – are based on the reverence for human life, the inherent self-worth of the individual, and the possibility for individual and communal change; or in traditional religious discourse, for God to 'guide them aright'. Self-correction and personal uprightness are basic to inducing a change in others, thereby regenerating society and transforming human relationships from within outwards. The communal social context of human affairs is paramount in traditional Muslim experience – and still operates strongly today.
- The Islamic ideal of freedom of conscience and the promotion of pluralism and tolerance are closely related elements. The qur'ānic imperative addressed to the differing religious communities – "then strive together towards all that is good" *(fa-'stabiqū 'l-khayrāt)* (2:148, 5:48) – requires humans of *all* faiths and teachings to compete in 'hastening to the good'. This forms the basis for harmonious inter-religious relations, while implicitly rejecting all attitudes of religious exclusivity and exceptionalism, supersessionist privilege, and of ethnic or racial election. Islam perceives a wisdom and divine purpose in differences or dissimilarities among people, without denying each their own distinctiveness and specificity. The One behind multiplicity, the Unity beyond difference, taught by Islam is best expressed by its inimitable artistic creations that speak directly to the heart.

Concluding remarks

Thinking Muslims must search for fresh ways to realise and make Islamic values real and effective in our world. This search requires them to regain a critical attitude to the legacy of their past as well as a creative response to present needs and conditions, and to nourish hope and trust for realising a better future. Muslims must actively seek to extract the spiritual paradigm of purpose and meaning at the core of Islam – the *permanent essential values* – and implement them in authentic action guided by intelligence, wisdom, and loving-mercy.

---

9 The Syrian thinker Jawdat Sa'īd, in his prescient study (1966 and 1993), was perhaps the first thinker to employ the phrase *al-'amal al-silmī* / Peaceful·Action (1993, 151). Jawdat Sa'īd has expanded and amplified his original understanding of this essential Islamic teaching in a number of works and public discussions since 1966.

References

Abu-Nimer, M. 2003: Nonviolence and Peace Building in Islam: Theory and Practice. Gainesville FL: University Press of Florida.

Carnegie Commission on Preventing Deadly Conflict 1997: Preventing Deadly Conflict: Final Report. Washington DC: Carnegie Commission on Preventing Deadly Conflict.

Crow, K. D. 2000: Nurturing an Islamic Peace Discourse. In: The American Journal of Islamic Social Sciences 17, 54–69.

Crow, K. D. 2001: Nonviolence, Ethics, and Character Development in Islam. In: Abdul Aziz Said et al. (eds.), Peace and Conflict Resolution in Islam: Precept and Practice. Lanham MD, New York, Oxford: University Press of America, 213–226.

Crow, K. D. 2003: Islam and Reason. In: Al-Shajarah [Kuala Lumpur: International Institute of Islamic Thought and Civilization (ISTAC)] 8, no. 1, 109–137.

Crow, K. D. 2005a: Jihad: Peaceful · Striving & Combative · Struggle. Kuala Lumpur: Centre for Civilisational Dialogue, University of Malaya.

Crow, K. D. 2005b: "Kalashnikov Islam" and the Deformist Mentality. Paper read at the International Conference on Dialogue of Civilizations and the Construction of Peace, jointly organised by the Centre for Civilisational Dialogue and the Oxford Centre for Islamic Studies, 26–27 March 2005. Kuala Lumpur: Pusat Dialog Peradaban, University of Malaya (forthcoming).

Juergensmeyer, M. [3]2003: Terror in the Mind of God: The Global Rise of Religious Violence. Berkeley: University of California Press.

von Laue, T. H. 1987: The World Revolution of Westernization: The Twentieth Century in Global Perspective. Oxford: Oxford University Press.

Marty, M. E.; Appleby, R. S. (eds.) 1991–1995: The Fundamentalism Project. Chicago: University of Chicago Press.

Nelson-Pallmeyer, J. 2005: Is Religion Killing Us? Violence in the Bible and the Quran. London, New York: Continuum International Publishing Group.

Sa'id, Jawdat [5]1993 [1966]: Madhhab Ibn Ādam al-Awwal: mushkilāt al-'unf fī 'l-'amal al-islāmī [The doctrine of Adam's first son: the problem of violence in Islamic action]. Damascus: Maṭba'at Zayd b. Thābit al-Anṣārī. Beirut: Dār al-Fikr a-Mu'āṣir.

Schwartz, R. M. 1998: The Curse of Cain: The Violent Legacy of Monotheism. Chicago, London: University of Chicago Press.

Stassen, G. (ed.) 2004: Just Peacemaking: Ten Practices for Abolishing War. Cleveland OH: Pilgrim Press.

de Vries, H. 2002: Religion and Violence: Philosophical Perspectives from Kant to Derrida. Baltimore MD: The Johns Hopkins University Press.

Contributors

Christoph Marcinkowski

Dr. Christoph Marcinkowski is a German scholar working interdisciplinary in Islamic and Middle Eastern, as well as Southeast Asian and Security Studies. Since September 2008, he is Principal Research Fellow and Head of the Publications Committee at the International Institute of Advanced Islamic Studies (IAIS), a Malaysian think-tank, and concurrently Visiting Senior Research Fellow at the Asia-Europe Institute (AEI) in the University of Malaya at Kuala Lumpur. He had been with AEI as Senior Research Fellow since May 2007. At AEI, he is also teaching in its Masters and Ph.D. programmes courses related to multiculturalism and regional integration. His research interest is currently focussing on future strategies for multicultural and multireligious societies in Asia and Europe, as well as on Pope Benedict XVI's views on European identity *vis-à-vis* a resurging Muslim world.

Professor Marcinkowski has published 8 books and about 100 articles on Islamic history and culture, as well as on contemporary and strategic issues related to Islam in the Middle East, Europe, and Southeast Asia. Among his publications are several seminal books and monographs, such as *Religion and Politics in Iraq* (Singapore: PN, 2004), *From Isfahan to Ayutthaya: Contacts between Iran and Siam in the Seventeenth Century* (Singapore: PN, 2005), and *A New Middle East? Looking Behind the Iran-Iraq Issue* (in progress). His award-winning *Mīrzā Rafī'ā's Dastūr al-Mulūk: A Manual of Later Safavid Administration. Annotated English Translation, Commentary on the Offices and Services, and Facsimile of the Unique Persian Manuscript* (Kuala Lumpur: ISTAC, 2002), continues to be an often-cited reference work in the fields of Iranian and Islamic Studies. Aside from being a peer-reviewer for several international academic journals, he is also the Managing Editor of AEI's new journal, *The Asia-Europe Forum*, as well as General Editor of the new *AEI Monograph Series*. Moreover, at IAIS, he is the Managing Editor of its new *IAIS Journal of Civilisation Studies*. Professor Marcinkowski's academic achievements are annually referred to in *Marquis' Who is Who in the World* (New Providence NJ, United States).

Previously, he had also been Associate Professor of Islamic History at the renowned International Institute of Islamic Thought and Civilization (ISTAC) at Kuala Lumpur. Currently, he is also involved in facilitating the newly established academic contacts between AEI and Switzerland's University of Fribourg. Professor Marcinkowski, who holds a Ph.D. in Islamic Civilisation from ISTAC (1998) and a M.A. in Iranian Studies, Islamic Studies, and Political Science from the Free University of Berlin, Germany (1993), has also spent several years of research in the Middle East. Several distinguished Visiting Fellowships had been awarded to him, such as by the Institute for Iranian Studies at Columbia University, New York City, United States (2004–2005), where he had also been a member of the editorial team of *Encyclopedia Iranica*. The encyclopaedia is one of the key tools in the academic discipline of Iranian Studies and sponsored by the National Endowment for the Humanities (NEH), an eminent independent grant-making agency in the United States dedicated to supporting research, education, preservation, and public programs in the humanities. Moreover, from 2006 to 2007 he had been Visiting Research Fellow in Singapore at the S. Rajaratnam School of International Studies (RSIS, formerly known as Institute of Defence and Strategic Studies, IDSS) at Nanyang Technological University, NTU, and a Visiting Affiliate at the Asia Research Institute, ARI, at the National University of Singapore, NUS. Aside from his Fellowships abroad, he has been at home in Kuala Lumpur since 1995.

Christian Giordano

Professor Dr. Dr. h. c. Christian Giordano was born in 1945 as an Italian citizen in Lugano, Switzerland, and is since 1989 Full Professor and Permanent Director of the Department of Social Anthropology in the University of Fribourg, Switzerland. He studied Sociology/Ethnology, History of Art, languages, and History, with a special interest in the history of South Asia, before becoming involved himself in teaching and research at several leading European universities, such as Bern (Switzerland), Heidelberg (Germany), Basle (Switzerland), Frankfurt am Main, and Munich (Germany), after receiving his Ph.D. in Sociology/Ethnology from Heidelberg with a thesis on patronage structures in the Sicilian workers and artisans associations between 1750 and 1890. Finally, he was appointed Full Professor of Social Anthropology in 1989 at Fribourg.

His main fields of interdisciplinary research are: interethnic relations, multiculturalism and legal pluralism; nationalism and territoriality; antagonistic social memories and histories; transnational migration; personal networks, social capital and systemic trust; patronage relations, corruption strategies and mafia-structures; legality, legitimacy and failed statehood; honour, shame and feud (particularly working as forensic expert in criminal trials in Switzerland and Germany). He was doing anthropological field work in many parts of Europe, South America, Mauritius, and Malaysia. His seminal book *Die Betrogenen der Geschichte* (The Betrayed of History, 1992) was included and reviewed in the *Lexikon der soziologischen Werke,* a selection of the 750 most important publications in the Sociology. He published books and articles in French, Italian, English, Spanish, Russian, Polish, Croatian, Bulgarian, Romanian, Lithuanian, Serbian, and Macedonian. Moreover he cooperated with the *International Encyclopaedia of the Social and Behavioural Sciences (IESBS)*, with the *Wörterbuch der Soziologie*, with the *Metzler Lexikon Religion. Gegenwart-Alltag-Medien,* and with the *Brill Dictionary of Religion*. He is also General Editor of the collection *Freiburger Sozialanthropolo-*

gische Studien and member of several editorial boards of international journals, such as *Focaal, International Journal of Anthropology, Etudes Rurales, Ethnologia Balcanica, Journal for South East European Anthropology,* and *Eastern European Countryside.* Together with Ina-Maria Greverus he founded in the early 1990s the journal *Anthropological Journal on European Cultures* (today: *Anthropological Yearbook of European Culture*).

Professor Giordano was Guest Professor or Visiting Fellow at over 20 renowned European and Latin American universities and wrote and/or edited 45 books and published more than 190 peer-reviewed articles and book chapters. In 1999, he received an honorary doctorate from the West-University of Timisoara, Romania. Also since 1999, he is Honorary Member of the Association of the Bulgarian Scientists, section Sociology. Professor Giordano's role had been crucial in concluding the recent *Memorandum of Understanding* between the University of Fribourg and the University of Malaya and its Asia-Europe Institute (AEI).

Hans Daiber

Professor Dr. Hans Daiber is since 1995 holder of the Chair of Oriental Languages at the Johann-Wolfgang-Goethe-University at Frankfurt am Main, Germany. He has published widely on Islamic philosophy, theology and science, the Greek heritage in Islam, as well as the history of Arabic literature and its transmission in Arabic manuscripts. He has taught at the Free University of Amsterdam (1977–1995), at the University of Tokyo (1992) and at the International Institute of Islamic Thought and Civilization, ISTAC) in Kuala Lumpur, Malaysia. His main academic fields of interest are Arabic language and Islam, including Islamic philosophy, theology, history, and sciences, with a special focus on Greek-Syriac-Arabic-Latin translations. He is an expert in analyzing and describing Arabic manuscripts and has a special interest in the history of the transmission of Ancient Greek knowledge, via medieval Islam, to Europe. Since 1981 he is an Ordinary Member of the Royal Dutch Academy of Arts and Sciences. His doctoral dissertation (1967) was evaluated as Best Thesis of the Year at the University of Saarbrücken, Germany, and appeared in print in 1980 under the title *Aetius Arabus*. In 1973 he received his qualification for teaching Arabic and Islam with his monograph *Das theologisch-philosophische System des Mu'ammar Ibn 'Abbad as-Sulami (gest. 830 n. Chr.)*, which appeared in print in 1975. From 1973 to 1975 he was Research Fellow of the German Oriental Institute in Beirut, Lebanon. He wrote 15 monographs and 85 articles and is the editor of the two scientific series *Islamic Philosophy, Theology, and Sciences* of which so far 71 volumes have been published, and *Aristoteles Latinus*, which consists so far of 19 volumes. His latest publication is *Bibliography of Islamic Philosophy. Supplement* (Leiden: Brill, 2007), a continuation of his seminal work *Bibliography of Islamic Philosophy* (Leiden: Brill, 1999).

Ataullah Bogdan Kopanski

Professor Dr. Ataullah Bogdan Kopanski, a US-citizen and convert to Islam, was born in the historical region of Silesia, in what is now Poland. He is a Full Professor of History in the Kulliyyah (Faculty) of Islamic Revealed Knowledge and Human Sciences in the International Islamic University Malaysia (IIUM). Previously, he had been teaching in universities of the United States, Pakistan, Turkey, Syria, and the Republic of South Africa. Professor Kopanski holds a Ph.D. in Philosophy of History and a M.A. in History, both from the University of Silesia, Poland, as well as a Diploma of Conservation Skills from the North American School of Conservation in Scranton, Pennsylvania, United States. He specialises in the history and civilisations of the Islamic communities of Eurasia and its ancient heritage. His fields of academic interest include also historical and cultural aspects of the Christianisation and Islamisation processes of Europe, the Middle Ages and Early Modernity in general, war crimes and atrocities against Muslims, military history, Native American history, and the culture and history of Muslim Eurasia, in particular the Caucasus and Russia. Being a prolific writer, he is the author of several books, among them *The Sabres of the Two Easts: An Untold History of Muslims, their Allies and Foes in Eastern Europe* (Islamabad: Institute of Policy Studies, 1995). He has also worked extensively on the issue of the borderlands between Islam and Christian Europe from the early Ottoman period until the late seventeenth century. He also did research on European pessimistic historical-philosophical thought from Hobbes to Ortega y Gasset, in terms of the 'Traditional Cultures / Technological Progress' dichotomy. Of special significance to Professor's Kopanski's contribution to this volume is also previous research carried out by him on the issue of the extent of knowledge on Islam and the Ottomans in Polish public opinion between the fourteenth and sixteenth centuries. This period coincided with the apex of power of both the Polish-Lithuanian Commonwealth (in Polish referred to as *Rzeczpospolita Obojga Narodów*, the 'Commonwealth of Both Nations') and the Ottoman Empire (Ottoman-Turk. *Devlet-i Âliyye-i Osmaniyye*, the 'August Ottoman State').

Muhidin Mulalić

Dr. Muhidin Mulalić, a scholar from Bosnia-Herzegovina, is currently teaching multiculturalism and comparative religion at the International University of Sarajevo (IUS). He holds a Ph.D. (2007) from the International Islamic University Malaysia (IIUM). His doctoral dissertation was entitled "The Origin and Development of Early Muslim Historiography and its Climax in al-Ṭabarī". He also holds a M.A. (2001) from the International Institute of Islamic Thought and Civilization (ISTAC) in Kuala Lumpur, Malaysia. His master's thesis, written under the supervision of Professor M. Ismail Marcinkowski, was entitled "A Contemporary Study of the Conception of History, based on the Works of Eusebius and al-Ṭabarī". His

B.A (Hons), too, was granted by IIUM. Prior to his return to Sarajevo, he had been a Lecturer at the Institute of Liberal Studies at Universiti Tenaga Nasional (UNITEN) in Kajang, Selangor, Malaysia (2002–2007). His fields of expertise include comparative history of civilisations, philosophy, comparative religion, historiography, multicultural education, teaching and learning, holistic education, and philosophy of education. Dr. Mulalić received the Best Research Award for the academic year 2004/2005 from the Institute of Liberal Studies at UNITEN. He was also awarded the Postgraduate Scholarship (2000–2002) by the Islamic Charitable Society (IQRA), which is based in the United Kingdom. Presently, Dr. Mulalić, who is a prolific writer, is currently working on a new book, *A Handbook for the Study of Major World Religions*, forthcoming in 2008, which is meant to present expressively the world's faiths to a wider reading audience. Dr. Mulalić is also the author of *A Survey of Early Muslim Historiography* and *A Guide to Writing Research Papers in the Humanities and Social Sciences*, two books which are also forthcoming in 2008.

Mesut Idriz

Dr Mesut Idriz, who is based in Kuala Lumpur, is a scholar in Islamic cultural history from the Republic of Macedonia. He has a strong interest and research background in the study of the Muslim communities in the Balkans, from the Ottoman period up to the present. He obtained both his MA (1998) and his PhD (2002) from the International Institute of Islamic Thought and Civilization (ISTAC), Kuala Lumpur, Malaysia, in the field of Islamic Civilisation. His doctoral dissertation, a study which focuses on interfaith relations in an Ottoman town in what is now Macedonia, is entitled *Manastir in the Second Half of 18th Century: A History of a Balkan City with Special Reference to the Ottoman Judicial Records*. He was lecturer in Islamic Civilisation at ISTAC and at the Faculty of Human Sciences in the International Islamic University Malaysia (IIUM), from 2002 to 2007. Currently, he is Chief Coordinator and Academic Editor at MPH Publishing Group, one of Malaysia's leading publishing houses. He is a frequent presenter of papers at international conferences. His academic research interests focus on the comparative study of the history of education in the Muslim lands and the West, the relations between the Muslim world and medieval Europe, and the study of Ottoman-Turkish manuscripts and archival materials related to and preserved in the Balkans. Together with Dr Syed Ali Tawfik Al-Attas, the Director General of the Institute of Islamic Understanding (IKIM), a Kuala Lumpur-based think tank, he is the author of the book *The Ijâzah of 'Abdullah Fâhim: A Unique Document from Islamic Education* (Kuala Lumpur: MPH, 2007).

Osman Bakar

Professor Dato' Dr. Osman Bakar,a scholar from Malaysia, is the Deputy CEO of the International Institute of Advanced Islamic Studies (IAIS) in Kuala Lumpur. He is also Professor Emeritus of Philosophy at the University of Malaya, as well as Professor of Islamic Thought and Civilisation at the International Institute of Islamic Thought and Civilization (ISTAC) in the International Islamic University Malaysia (IIUM). In addition, he is a Senior Fellow at the Prince Al-Waleed Center for Muslim-Christian Understanding, Georgetown University, Washington DC, Senior Research Fellow at the Center for Civilisational Dialogue (founded by him in 1995), University of Malaya, and Visiting Research Fellow at Doshisha University, Kyoto, Japan. He was also the holder of the Malaysia Chair of Islam in Southeast Asia at Georgetown University.

Osman Bakar was born in Temerloh in the Malaysian State of Pahang. He completed his undergraduate studies with Honours and received his MSc in Mathematics (specializing in Algebra) from London University. In 1981, he joined Temple University, Philadelphia, United States, from where he obtained an M.A. in Comparative Religion. Also from Temple University, he obtained his Ph.D. in Philosophy of Science/Islamic Philosophy. During later stages of his distinguished academic career, he served as the Deputy Vice Chancellor/Vice President of Academics and was the first holder of the Chair of the Philosophy of Science at the University of Malaya in Kuala Lumpur, a post he held until 2001. He is one of the founding members of the Islamic Academy of Science of Malaysia and has also served as its President. His research interests include Southeast Asian Islam – in particular Malay-Indonesian Islam – contemporary Islamic thought, as well as religion and science in the Islamic context, both classical and modern.

Professor Osman Bakar is a scholar, teacher and author whose writings are well-known throughout today's world of scholarship – in the West as well as in the Muslim world – and many of his essays have appeared as articles in distinguished journals, as chapters in books, and in encyclopaedias. Several of his books, such as *Classification of Knowledge in Islam: A Study in Islamic Philosophies of Science* (Cambridge: Islamic Texts Society, 1998), *Tawhid and Science: Essays on the History and Philosophy of Islamic Science* (Kuala Lumpur: Nurin Enterprise, 1991), and *Islam and Civilizational Dialogue: The Quest for a Truly Universal Civilization* (Kuala Lumpur: University of Malaya Press, 1997), among others, have also been translated into other languages, such as Albanian, Arabic, Chinese, French, Indonesian, Persian, Spanish, Turkish, and Urdu.

Professor Osman Bakar has received additional recognition for his work, including the Fulbright Visiting Scholarship at Harvard University's Department of the History of Science (1992). He has also served as a consultant to various agencies, such as the United Nations and UNESCO. He is also a member of C-100 (Council of 100 Leaders) of The West-Islamic World Initiative for Dialogue established by the World Economic Forum, based in Switzerland. Moreover, he was also the holder of the Malaysia Chair of Islam in Southeast Asia at the Center for

Muslim-Christian Understanding, Edmund A. Walsh School of Foreign Service, Georgetown University, United States, and was a member of the Center's Academic Council. At Georgetown University, he taught courses on Contemporary Islam in Southeast Asia, Religion and Science in Islam, Islamic Philosophy, and Dialogue of Civilisations, subjects also dealt with by him in his 15 books and more than 250 articles. Professor Osman Bakar was also formally President of the Malaysian Islamic Academy of Science of which he was a co-founder. He was awarded twice the title of *Dato'* (the Malaysian equivalent to a knighthood), by His Royal Highness the Sultan of Pahang (1994) as well as by His Majesty the King of Malaysia (2000).

Nilüfer Narlı

Professor Dr. Nilüfer Narlı, a leading Turkish sociologist, holds a degree in Education with a major in Philosophy and a minor in Sociology, and a MSc in the Humanities with a major in Logic, Philosophy of Science, and Philosophy from the Middle Eastern Technical University, Ankara. She also holds a Ph.D. in Social Sciences with a major in Political Sociology from the School of Comparative Social Sciences, University Sains Malaysia (USM), Penang. She is currently a Full Professor of Political Sociology at the Faculty of Arts and Sciences at Bahçeşehir University, Istanbul. Previously, she had been Vice Rector of that university until September 2006. Currently, she is also chairing the university's Sociology Department of which she is the founder. Before being appointed as Vice Rector in September 2005, she had been the founding Dean to the Faculty of Communication at Kadir Has University, Istanbul (October 2003 – August 2005). Prior to that, she had been the founding chair of the Sociology Department at Marmara University, Istanbul, where she also chaired the Sociology and Anthropology Department of the Middle East Studies Institute. She is currently acting as Advisory Board Member for *Perceptions*, a journal of international affairs, published by the Centre for Strategic Research, Ankara, and of the Middle East and Balkan Studies Foundation (OBIV), an Istanbul-based think tank. She was granted an Eisenhower Fellowship in 1993.

Her specialisation and current research interests involve Islamist movements, migration, illegal human mobility in the Balkans, civil-military relations and good governance in Turkey, conflict and development in the Middle East, as well as media and conflict. She was a trainer in conflict resolution at seminars of the Southeast Europe Leadership Initiatives for Women NGOs in the Balkan countries in 2000 and 2001 and has taken a leading role in the organization of international conferences on regional cooperation in the Middle East as well. Narlı has published widely in her field of expertise. She is the author of *Unveiling the Fundamentalist Woman: A Case Study of Malay Undergraduates* (Istanbul: ISIS Press, 1991) and has edited *Trafficking in Persons in South East Europe – A Threat to*

Human Security (Istanbul: Bahçeşehir University / Vienna: PfP Consortium of Defence Academies and Security Studies in Austria, 2006).

Wazir Jahan Karim

Professor Dato' Dr. Wazir Jahan Karim, a Malaysian economic anthropologist, is the Executive Director of the Academy for Socio-Economic Research and Analysis (ASERA), a non-profit research foundation dedicated to economic justice (George Town, Penang, Malaysia). From February 2007 to February 2008 she had been Senior Research Fellow at the Asia-Europe Institute (AEI) in the University of Malaya at Kuala Lumpur, where she had been convening the AEI Research Hub on 'Capacity-Building and Human Capital'. Professor Wazir holds a B.Soc. Sc. (1972) from the University of Singapore (now National University of Singapore, NUS), a Master's degree in Economic Anthropology (1974), and a PhD in Anthropology (1977), both from the London School of Economics and Political Sciences, LSE, University of London. She is the Founder Director of the Women's Development Research Centre at Universiti Sains Malaysia, USM, and held the post from 2001 to 2004. She pioneered Gender Studies in Malaysia and, in 1978-1985 and 1989-2001, directed the first field-based development research programme on women and children (KANITA). She is also the first women to have lived with the indigenous Ma' Betise' people to conduct anthropological research in the mangrove rainforests on the West Coast of Peninsular Malaysia. Wazir has authored and edited several books on minorities and on Islam and women, including *Ma' Betise'. Concepts of Living Things* (London: Athlone Press, 1981), *Emotions of Culture. A Malay Perspective* (Singapore: Oxford University Press, 1990), *Women and Culture. Between Malay 'Adat' and Islam* (Boulder CO: Westview Press, 1992), *'Male' and 'Female' in Developing Southeast Asia* (Oxford: Berg Publishers, 1995), and (with D. Bell and P. Caplan) *Gendered Fields. Women, Men, Ethnography* (London: Routledge, 1994). She has co-authored and co-edited (with Mohd Razha Rashid) *Cultural Minorities of Peninsular Malaysia. Survivals of Indigenous Heritage* (AKASS and Toyota Foundation). Her contributions to chapters in books and referred articles in journals number more than 70.

Professor Wazir has received several awards, fellowships and citations for outstanding scholarship and academic excellence including the Raymond Firth Prize (1977) from LSE, the Rotary Golden Medal for Most Outstanding Scholar in the Social Sciences (1999), the Anugerah Sanjung for Best International Scholar, USM (2004, Outstanding Woman Academician, State of Penang (2005). She is frequently cited in *Malaysia's Who's Who on Women Leaders*. She has been a Ford Foundation Fellow (1974–1975), Commonwealth Fellow (1975–1977), Fulbright Fellow (1984), and British Academy Fellow (1990). Several Visiting Professorships led her to the Institute of Anthropology, University of Oslo (1991), the Centre for the Study of Cultures and Languages of Asia and Africa at the Tokyo University of Foreign Studies (1995–1996), Tokyo's Sophia University (1996), the

United Nation's University (2003), the Department of Malay Studies and Centre for Women Studies, University of Victoria, Wellington, New Zealand (1998), and the University of Kent at Canterbury (2001). In 2003, she held the Andrew's Chair in Asian Studies at the University of Hawaii, Manoa. In 2005, she was appointed Distinguished Fellow of Malaysia's Social Institute. She is also a member of Malaysia's National Women's Advisory Council. In 2006, she was a Visiting Fellow at the School of Advanced Study, Clare Hall, University of Cambridge. She is now a life member/fellow of Clare Hall. In 2007, in recognition of her achievements as a scholar and social activist, the Malaysian State of Penang awarded her the *Darjah Setia Pangkuan Negeri* (D.S.P.N.), which carries the title *Dato'*.

Amer Al-Roubaie

Professor Dr. Amer Al-Roubaie, a Canadian scholar who was born in Iraq, is a Professor of Economics and currently the Dean of the College of Business and Finance at Ahlia University in the Kingdom of Bahrain. In 1967, he received his B.A. from the University of Baghdad (1967), and in 1974 his M.A. from the University of New Brunswick, Canada. He holds a Ph.D. in Economics from McGill University, Montreal, Canada (1986). His main area of research is sustainable development in general and economic development in the Middle East with emphasis on oil resources, the environment, and labour migration. Recently, Professor Al-Roubaie has written a book entitled *Globalization and the Muslim World* (Kuala Lumpur: Malita Jaya Publishing, 2002), underlining some of the important challenges facing Muslims in the age of globalisation. In addition, he has published numerous other articles on the same subject. Prior to his present position, Professor Al-Roubaie taught economics in both Canada and the United States. Since the early 1990s, for more than ten years, he had also been an Associate Professor, and subsequently Full Professor of Economics, at the International Institute of Islamic Thought and Civilization (ISTAC) at Kuala Lumpur, Malaysia, where taught course related to economics, banking and finance. In 2004, he received the Best Researcher Award from the Malaysia's International Islamic University (IIUM). He is also a much sought-after speaker at international conferences, such as at the 2003 Kuala Lumpur meeting of the Organisation of the Islamic Conference (OIC).

Rasha Shaker Abdul-Wahab

Dr. Rasha Shaker Abdul-Wahab is an Associate Professor of Computer Science in the Department of Information Technology, College of Mathematics, at Ahlia University, Manama, in the Kingdom of Bahrain. She obtained her Ph.D. from the University of Technology in Baghdad, Iraq. Dr. Abdul-Wahab has published extensively in the fields of Evolutionary Algorithm, Data Mining, and E-Learning.

In artificial intelligence, Evolutionary Algorithms (EAs) are search methods that take their inspiration from natural selection and survival of the fittest in the biological world. EAs differ from more traditional optimisation techniques in that they involve a search from a 'population' of solutions and not from a single point. Data Mining is the principle of sorting through large amounts of data and picking out relevant information. It is usually used by business intelligence organisations and financial analysts, but it is increasingly used in the sciences as well to extract information from the enormous data sets generated by modern experimental and observational methods. Her research interests include also Knowledge Discovery in Databases (KDD) – a field that is evolving to provide automated analysis solutions – and Evolutionary Techniques. In computer science, evolution strategy (ES) refers to an optimisation technique based on ideas of adaptation and evolution. At Ahlia University, Dr. Abdul-Wahab is currently supervising several Ph.D. projects in those areas.

Mohammad Hashim Kamali

Professor Dr. Mohammad Hashim Kamali, a Canadian citizen born in Afghanistan, served as Professor of Islamic law and jurisprudence at the International Islamic University Malaysia, and also as Dean of the International Institute of Islamic Thought and Civilisation (ISTAC), Kuala Lumpur between 1985 and 2007. He is currently the CEO and Chairman of the International Institute of Advanced Islamic Studies (IAIS) of Malaysia. He studied law at Kabul University and then served as Assistant Professor. Subsequently, he served as Public Prosecutor with the Ministry of Justice, Afghanistan (1965–1968). He completed his LL.M in comparative law and received his PhD in Islamic and Middle Eastern law from the University of London (1976). He was subsequently employed by BBC as a broadcasting support staff in Reading, United Kingdom (1976-1979).

Professor Kamali served as Assistant Professor at the Institute of Islamic Studies, McGill University, Montreal, and was subsequently appointed as a Research Associate with the Canada Council for Social Science and Humanities (1979–1985). In 1991, he was a Visiting Professor at Capital University, Ohio, United States. Later he served as Visiting Professor at the Institute for Advanced Studies *(Wissenschaftskolleg)*, Berlin, Germany (2000–2001). He is currently a Fellow of that Institute and also a member of the Royal Academy of Jordan. He served as a member and Chairman of the Constitutional Review Commission of Afghanistan (May – September 2003). He is currently on the International Advisory Board of eleven academic journals published in Malaysia, the United States, Canada, Kuwait, India, Australia and Pakistan. Between May and June 2004, and subsequently, in October 2007, he served as United Nations consultant on constitutional reforms in the Maldives and also as a UN constitutional law expert on the constitution of Iraq (2005–2006).

He is currently a *Sharīᶜah* Advisor with the Securities Commission of Malaysia, Chairman of the CIMB *Sharīᶜah* Committee, and Chairman of the Shariah Board, Stanlib Corporation of South Africa. Professor Kamali has addressed over 120 national and international conferences, published 16 books and over 110 academic articles. He delivered the Prominent Scholars Lecture Series *(Silsilah Muḥāḍarat ᶜUlamā' al-Bārizīn)* No. 20 at the Islamic Research and Training Institute of Jeddah, Saudi Arabia (1996), and the Multaqa Sultan Ahmad Shah Lecture in Kuantan, Malaysia (2002). His books – *Law in Afghanistan* (Leiden, 1985), *Principles of Islamic Jurisprudence* (Cambridge, 1991 and 2003), *Freedom of Expression in Islam* (Cambridge, 1997), *Freedom, Equality and Justice in Islam* (Cambridge, 2002), and *A Textbook of Ḥadīth Studies* (Leicester, United Kingdom, 2005) – are used as textbooks in leading English-speaking universities worldwide. A revised edition of his book, *An Introduction to Sharīᶜah* (Kuala Lumpur, 2006) was published by Oneworld Publications, Oxford, in February 2008. He received the Ismāᶜīl al-Fārūqī Award for Academic Excellence twice, in 1995 and 1997, and he is listed in a number of leading *Who's Who*s in the World.

Sayyed Ahmad Kazemi Moussavi

Professor Dr. Sayyed Ahmad Kazemi Moussavi, a Canadian-Iranian scholar, is currently professor of Islamic law and Persian language in the University of Maryland, United States, where is teaching courses related to 'Islam in Iran' and 'Modern Iran'. Prior to this, he had been a Full Professor at the International Institute of Islamic Thought and Civilization (ISTAC) at Kuala Lumpur, Malaysia (1992–2005), and at Istanbul's Fatih University (Summer 2000). Born and educated in Iran, he received his bachelor degree in law from Tehran University. Subsequently, he served as a judge for five years before transferring to the Imperial Iranian Ministry of Foreign Affairs in 1968. Before retiring from diplomatic service in 1980, in the aftermath of the events that had led to the change of regime in his native country, he had served at the Imperial Iranian embassy in Canada. In Canada, Kazemi Moussavi joined Montreal's McGill University, from where he received his Ph.D. in Islamic Studies in 1991 with a dissertation on 'Islamic Institutions'. Subsequently, he taught at McGill University and Tehran University before joining ISTAC's faculty in 1992, first as an Associate Professor and subsequently Full Professor.

Professor Kazemi Moussavi is the author of several books, including *Religious Authority in Shi'ite Islam* (Kuala Lumpur: ISTAC, 1996), *Shi'ite Ulama and Political Power* (Bethesda MD: Ibex Publishers, 2004, in Persian) and (with Karim Douglas Crow) *Facing One Qiblah* (Singapore: PN, 2005). He has also published more than 50 articles in distinguished academic and cultural journals. Since early 2008, Professor Kazemi Moussavi is a Visiting Professor at Tehran University.

Karim Douglas Crow

Dr Karim Douglas S. Crow is an American Muslim scholar of Lebanese-American parentage who was born and raised in Beirut. In October 2008, he joined Kuala Lumpur's International Institute of Advanced Islamic Studies (IAIS) as a Principal Research Fellow. From September 2006 to October 2008, he had been Associate Professor in Contemporary Islam at the S. Rajaratnam School of International Studies, Nanyang Technological University, Singapore. In October 2008, he joined Kuala Lumpur's International Institute of Advanced Islamic Studies (IAIS) as a Principal Research Fellow.

Professor Crow took his university education in Beirut and Cairo, and his Doctorate from The Institute of Islamic Studies at McGill University (Montreal, Canada). During 1980–1992 he taught Islamic Studies and Arabic Language and Literature at Columbia University, New York University, Fordham University, the University of Virginia, and the University of Maryland. In 1999 and 2000–2005 he served as Professor of Islamic Thought, teaching philosophy, theology and intellectual traditions, at the International Institute of Islamic Thought and Civilisation (ISTAC) in Kuala Lumpur. Dr. Crow has published articles and book chapters on Islamic metaphysics, contemporary Islamic intellectual and spiritual currents, Islamic peace studies, and values and ethics, and an edited volume (with Sayyed Ahmad Kazemi), *Facing One Qiblah: Legal and Doctrinal Aspects of Sunni and Shi'a Muslims* (Singapore: Pustaka Nasional, 2005). He has been conducting research for many years on Islamic understandings of intelligence-reason, and his textual study of tradition history *'When God Created Wisdom': Islamic 'Aql Creation Narratives*, is under consideration by Brill Publishers in Leiden, The Netherlands.

Currently, he is working on an historical survey of Islam and rationality, a book on the wisdom of the Prophet Muḥammad, and a monograph on the life and thought of Imām Ja'far al-Ṣādiq (d. 765). Dr Crow is an Advisor for several non-governmental programs and institutions treating Islamic peace issues in the Arab world and Southeast Asia. Between 1996 and 2000 he directed the project 'Islam and Peace' for the international NGO Nonviolence International (Washington DC), travelling to numerous countries in the Muslim world. Since 2000 he serves as curriculum advisor for an NGO program in Aceh, Indonesia, on peace education for high school youth, and as consultant for an internationally-funded peace training program with the *'ulamā'* of Aceh. Combining scholarship in a wide range of interests with community engagement in peace education, Dr Crow's life and work bridges the Muslim world and the West.